MANUFACTURING CONSENT

NOAM CHOMSKY AND THE MEDIA

MANUFACTURING CONSENT

NOAM CHOMSKY AND THE MEDIA

The companion book to the award-winning film
by Peter Wintonick and Mark Achbar

BLACK
ROSE
BOOKS

Montréal\New York
London

Film transcript and editor's notes
copyright 1994 © Necessary Illusions

Reprinted 1995

Black Rose Books No. X207
ISBN 1-551640-02-3 (paperback)
ISBN 1-551640-03-1 (hardcover)

cover photo: Renzo
video-wall: courtesy Erin Mills Town Centre, Erin Mills, Ontario
image of Chomsky: courtesy Ed Robinson
book design & production: ASSOCIÉS LIBRES, Montréal

BLACK ROSE BOOKS   BLACK ROSE BOOKS
C.P.1258   340 Nagel Drive
Succ. Place du Parc   Cheektowaga, New York
Montréal, Québec   USA 14225
Canada H2W 2R3

Printed in Canada

A publication of the Insitute of Policy Alternatives of Montreal (IPAM)

CANADIAN CATALOGUING IN PUBLICATION DATA

Main entry under title:

Manufacturing Consent: Noam Chomsky and the Media

Includes bibliographical references and index.
ISBN 1-551640-02-3 (paperback)
ISBN 1-551640-03-1 (hardcover)

1. Manufacturing Consent: Noam Chomsky and the Media (Motion
Picture). 2. Chomsky, Noam--political and social views. 3. Mass
media--Political aspects. 4. United States--Foreign relations
5. Chomsky, Noam 6.Linguistics. I. Achbar, Mark

P85.C47M36 1994   302.23   C94-900195-3

For Marjorie, Ben and Francine Achbar

ACKNOWLEDGMENTS

Many people were involved in the process of putting this book in your hands. My sincere thanks to:

Peter Wintonick and Francis Miquet, my friends and partners, for allowing this project to usurp some of Necessary Illusions' meager resources;

Linda Barton and Dimitrios Roussopoulos of Black Rose Books, for their encouragement and confidence;

Rodolfo Borello and Andrew Forster, for their design sensitivity and their professionalism in working to an impossible deadline;

Jane Broderick, for copy editing the book and creating the index, to the same impossible deadline;

Merrily Weisbord and Robert Del Tredici, my mentors in the medium of print;

Caroline Voight, Stacy Chappel, and Robert Kwak for their command of the keyboard, and Susan Grey, for her additional research;

Blake Gulband and Nat Klym, for their practical advice;

The National Film Board of Canada, especially Steven Morris, Trevor Gregg, Maurice Paradis and David Verrall, for their cooperation and technical support;

David Pollack, of Inframe Productions, and Colin Pearson, for their generous contribution of image grabbing technology, and Jason Levy for his time;

Martine Côté and Kate McDonell, for their help in processing the images;

Tom Tomorrow, for his illustrated attitude;

James McGillivray, for finally delivering the cards;

Cha Cha Da Vinci and Leah Léger for keeping their zapper on the pulse of Springfield;

Christine Burt, for her tactful assessments;

Elaine Shatenstein and Cleo Paskal, whose editorial comments substantially improved the quality of this effort;

John Schoeffel, for his useful suggestions throughout;

David Barsamian, whose interviews added so much to the film and this book;

Carlos Otero, for his example and help with setting priorities;

Sabrina Mathews, whose curiosity guided much of the substance of the additonal material and whose stamina kept the machine running;

Edward S. Herman, whose chapters in *Manufacturing Consent: The Political Economy of the Mass Media* provided the unifying concepts behind much of our film;

Carol Chomsky, for her generosity in providing and reproducing family photos for the film and for her support and corrections on the rough cuts.

And to Noam Chomsky, whose work has been the focus of mine for over six years, for his encouragement, his inexhaustible energy, his willingness to respond to all our questions and requests, and for his bemused tolerance of our cameras, which made possible the film on which this book is based.

TABLE OF CONTENTS

INTRODUCTION

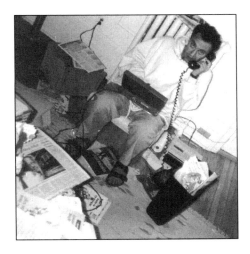

Having been active in the peace and anti-nuclear movements in the early 1980s, I was drawn, in 1985, to a talk entitled "The Drift Toward Global War," by Noam Chomsky. The speaker's name was familiar to me but the ideas it represented were not.

The long, oak-paneled hall at the University of Toronto was filled well beyond capacity. I set up my tape recorder near the podium just in time for the superlative-strewn introduction. Applause, then Chomsky, and down to business. Every 45 minutes I quickly flipped my cassette, or inserted a new one, anxious not to miss a word.

That night, a soft-spoken man with a dark, ironic sense of humor, and a command of facts I had never before encountered, irrevocably shifted my political paradigm. After what seemed like minutes of sustained applause, I apprehensively approached the mild-mannered speaker with others for whom two and a half hours was not enough. For a moment, no one spoke. There was an awe-struck lull, which I shattered, intruding on his personal space with my microphone for the first of many times. I found a tolerant, empathetic man prepared to patiently rearrange the oxide on my cassette—and my understanding of the abuse of power in the world.

Regardless of the ineloquence of the question, Chomsky immediately grasped the intent, and answered, I later came to realize, at the same level at which he would answer a historian interviewing him for the BBC. I was struck by his utter lack of condescension. That moment, and many others I've since witnessed and filmed, are, I believe, deep reflections of Chomsky's faith in the ability of so-called ordinary people to understand and act on the issues he raises. He actually tries to live the egalitarian philosophy he espouses.

I listened to the cassettes I recorded that night many times over the next two years. And I kept an eye and an ear out for Mr. Chomsky, regularly scanning the mass media. But he was nowhere to be found. You could dig up his books if you hunted in the right stores, but he wasn't "out there" in any appreciable way.

Fortunately, in 1987, at the invitation of Dimitri Roussopoulos, the publisher of this book, Chomsky came to speak at Concordia University in Montréal, the city I then called home. Again, the hall was filled to overflowing. I sat with Terri Nash, whose Oscar-winning film, *If You Love This Planet*, based on a a lecture by anti-nuclear activist Helen Caldicott, was reaching substantial audiences in schools and on television. I remember thinking, "Maybe I can do for Noam what Terri did for Helen."

This book, like the film on which it is based, is designed as a stepping-stone to related texts by Chomsky, Edward S. Herman, and others and to organizations active in a range of issues. I have presented a complete transcript of the film, and, as topics arise, have sought out relevant passages from different sources, though mainly from Chomsky's writings, talks and interviews, which offer further insight, with the hope of enticing the reader back to the source. The Resource Guide, beginning on page 239, lists several non-mainstream organizations and sources of information in print, audio, film, video, and on computer networks. I consider this Resource Guide as a work-in-progress and welcome suggestions for additions and improvements in future printings.

In reviewing an early draft of this book, Chomsky expressed reservations about the utility of the format. Although several collections of his talks and interviews have been published, to my surprise he questioned the ability of the spoken word transcribed, as compared to the written word in articles and books, to clarify issues: "The more considered and careful versions that reach print in the normal course of affairs," he wrote, "are far preferable." He voiced this concern along with eight single-spaced pages of much-appreciated notes aimed at improving this book. Several are included verbatim.

While they are more precise and detailed than extemporaneous talks can be, Chomsky's writings are also more complex, dense with references, grammatically sophisticated, and often assume substantial prior knowledge. Chomsky is an impressive yet plain-spoken verbal communicator and many find those words transcribed to be an accessible route to his thinking. The popularity of his talks and interviews published in various forms attests to this. Both have value, I think, and are mutually reinforcing.

As in the interview excerpt which follows, Chomsky also expressed concern about the "personalization" of issues. This posed a dilemma for Peter Wintonick and me as filmmakers and has again to some degree with this book. In making the film, we felt it was impossible, indeed undesirable, to divorce the man and his ideas from the personal history that helped shape those ideas. Our basic criterion for inclusion of biographical information was: does it bear on Chomsky's political formation?

The self-referential style of the film was part of our solution—including Chomsky's proviso on the irrelevance of the personal. In 1970, on Dutch television, he stated that he was "rather against the whole notion of developing public personalities who are treated as stars of one kind or another, where aspects of their personal life are supposed to have some significance." Yet, in the film, one can see that exclusion of the personal while speaking with a mass audience is not a hard and fast rule. One's actions are a measure of the sincerity of one's stated values, and many of Chomsky's are exemplary and instructive, and merited inclusion in the film and hence in this book. His stories are important not because they are his, but because they are moral metaphors we can map onto our own experience.

In the film, we examined not only Chomsky's ideas *about* the media, but also his relationship *with* the media, which is substantially different inside and outside the U.S. Chomsky's experience can be seen as a case study of sorts, illustrating the media's treatment of dissident voices in society. Though not elected to the position, he speaks for many of us who feel that if his voice cannot heard neither can ours.

The film communicates on several levels simultaneously, using all manner of visual, sonic and musical devices to call attention to its own manipulative techniques—including personalization, often mocking the conventions of commerical media and traditional documentaries. As Chomsky in his writings sometimes appropriates the voice of his opponents, by adopting a sarcastic or ironic tone, so too did we, by using the multi-level language of film. I can only encourage readers who have already seen the film to bear this in mind, and those who have not seen it to turn to page 238 and find a way to do so.—MA

Eleanor Levine

You haven't seen the documentary about you, *Manufacturing Consent*. Why haven't you seen it and do you plan on seeing it?

Chomsky

I haven't seen it and I don't intend to. There are several reasons, some of them are merely personal. I mean I just don't like to hear or see myself because I think about how I should have done it differently. There's also a more general reason. I'm very uneasy about the whole project. For one thing, no matter how much they try, and I'm sure they did try, the impression it gives, and I can tell that from the reviews, is the personalization of the issues. That's the wrong question for a number of reasons.

I can begin with the very title of the film. The title of the film is *Manufacturing Consent*. The title is taken from a book, a book written by Edward Herman and me. And if you look at the book, you'll find that his name comes first. Well, his name came first at my insistence. Usually, when we write a book, we give the names alphabetically, like mine comes first, C before H. But on this book I insisted that his name come first for the simple reason that he did most of the book. And in fact, most of the things people write about in the reviews of the film are his work. Here we already begin to see what's wrong. These are all cooperative activities and they shouldn't be personalized and associated with one individual.

I think the reason the film—I haven't seen it, I presume—I was giving talks to various audiences, that sort of thing, but why am I giving talks to various audiences? Because all over the country, in fact all over the world, there are lots of people dedicated to working hard every day, educating, getting involved in various forms of activism, building up the popular grass-roots organizations. They really get things done. Now those people need a speaker and so I'm glad to oblige—you know, it's good for me, it's good for them—but they're the ones who are the leaders, they're the ones who do the work, not me, and if the film gives the impression that somehow—I mean, I get letters from people. People say, "How can I join your movement?" I know the filmmakers don't want to give that impression, but it's somehow implicit in the medium....

And if the impression is given that there's some leader or spokesman or something like that organizing, galvanizing things, that's absolutely the wrong lesson. The lesson there is follow your leader. The lesson ought to be: take your life into your own hands.

Movie Guide, April 16, 1993. See also page 88.

Paul Cienfuegos

In watching your reactions to the film about you, you've shown a lot of discomfort. Today when you talked to our group, again you said something critical about it. I'm sure you realize the political potency the film is having. I'd love to hear you say something *positive* about the film.

Chomsky

The positive impact of it has been astonishing to me. Outside the United States it's shown all over the place. Even inside the United States, it's shown to some extent but everywhere else it's shown on national television. I didn't realize this myself until I was travelling around Europe last year and you go to Finland and everybody saw it on television. That sort of thing. And I'm invited to film festivals all over the world. Literally. The result of that is there's a ton of reviewing. The reviewing is extremely interesting. Quite fascinating. The reviews are often written by guys who write TV criticism for the newspapers, you know, completely apolitical people. The reaction is extremely positive. I'd say like 98% of it is *very* positive. In fact, about the only thing that got a lot of people pissed off, including Phil Donahue, are some remarks I made about sports. People got kind of angry.... And furthermore, I get a ton of letters. Like I get a letter from some steel worker in Canada saying, "Yeah, I took my friends three times and we think it's great," and so on and so forth.... I think it's double edged. It certainly energized a lot of people. I think it did a tremendous amount of good just for East Timor alone and it's had a good impact in other respects, but it also has this negative aspect, which seems to me to be unavoidable....

Mark Achbar

I'm sure you're aware that [in the film] we have you saying almost verbatim what you just said here about when you give a talk it's because there's all these people organizing.

Chomsky

Yeah, but there's something about the medium which prevents it from getting across.

Recorded at the Z Media Institute, Woods Hole, Massachusetts, Summer, 1994, by Alternative Radio. A complete set of reviews is available from Necessary Illusions. See Resource Guide, page 256.

NOTES ON PROCESS

In the opening minutes of the film, Chomsky speculates that we must have shot "500 hours worth of tape" in the process of making *Manufacturing Consent*. While it may have felt to him like 500 hours of lights, cameras and microphones, we actually gathered roughly 120 hours of mostly 16mm film, but, in keeping with our meta-media-shoot-with-whatever-you-can-get-your-hands-on aesthetic, we also shot Betacam, 3/4", 1/2" and 8mm videotape. On one occasion we even took a video feed from a surveillance camera. About a third of the total 120 hours comprises archival images and sounds culled from some 185 sources.

The first images shot with the film *Manufacturing Consent* in mind were exposed on September 25, 1987, outside Convocation Hall at the University of Toronto where Chomsky was about to give a lecture. Vietnamese protesters were burning a copy of his and Edward Herman's book *The Political Economy of Human Rights, Volume I*, a fiery testament to the power and importance of their work, and the lengths to which some will go to suppress it.

Our cameras observed Chomsky's lectures, discussions, and media encounters over a period of four years. I distinguish our cameras from ourselves because on a couple of occasions they traveled without us. We were not in Japan, for instance, when Chomsky was awarded the prestigious Kyoto Prize, though we'd certainly like to have been. We simply couldn't afford the trip and ended up directing a local crew by fax. In another instance, video-equipped friends living in Washington, DC, were given free rein to capture, first-hand, the essence of George Bush's inauguration and send us the footage when they were finished. But we did finally manage to do a fair bit of traveling just keeping up with Chomsky's relentless schedule: a total of 23 cities in seven countries. It reached the point that if we weren't there to greet him at the airport with our cameras rolling, he thought he'd arrived in the wrong place. In all, the film took five years to complete. The credits acknowledge the efforts and support of over 300 people and organizations.

We made an early decision not to hand-hold viewers with an "official" narrator. Chomsky, we felt, was fully capable of speaking for himself, and by allowing him to present his arguments in his own words we would be reinforcing the subjectivity of the film.

A distillation of interviews, lectures and media encounters form the theoretical and informational backbone of the film and often serve as auditory springboards for visual explorations of the media and its mechanisms. Questions posed by interviewers and audience members at Chomsky's talks helped direct the film into different subject areas. As well, other activists, critics and commentators contributed to sub-narratives.

During the preparation and filming of *Manufacturing Consent*, we strove to democratize the production process and make it inclusive of others. Extensive consultative screenings with audiences were organized throughout the editing process. Over 600 individuals helped guide the film to its present form. They were engaged by the idea that their opinions on the work would actually make a difference.

Chomsky's consistency of thought and presentation relieved us of a chronological imperative in editing material spanning 25 years. We were guided less by a commitment to visual unity than by thoughtlines, themes, transitions, and emotional and narrative coherence in linking scenes.

People absorb information most effectively through a variety of channels: visual, aural, textual; through narrative, metaphor, etc. By synthesizing many cinematic styles, we tried to make the film work on all these levels while trying to retain a sense of humor.

Manufacturing Consent is a self-reflexive film about media, and it employs a variety of audiovisual strategies to heighten mediation-consciousness. In addition to simply showing the crew or the film and video technologies in the frame, we used such techniques as animation, pixillation, dramatization and re-contextualization. Several scenes were re-framed in an improbable dystopian mediascape where films of radical philosophers play on huge video walls in ultra-modern shopping centers. The central framing device, "the world's largest permanent point-of-purchase video-wall installation," functions as an electronic brain out of which the film unravels. (Shoppers, however, seem barely distracted from their mission.) Explicit in Chomsky's discourse, and implicit in re-contextualizing footage of him in unlikely locations, are questions of access and problems of marginalization for people with unconventional views. By using a media-within-media perspective, we tried to reveal processes of media construction (including our own), in an attempt to create in the viewer a sense of critical engagement.

PART ONE

THOUGHT CONTROL IN A DEMOCRATIC SOCIETY

They who have put out
the peoples eyes
reproach them
of their blindnesse

JOHN MILTON—1642.

ERIN MILLS TOWN CENTRE, ERIN MILLS, ONTARIO

Kelvin Flook

Three, two, one, take two. Good morning. Welcome to Erin Mills Town Centre, the home of the world's largest permanent point-of-purchase video wall installation. My name is Kelvin Flook and I'm your video host all day here at EMTV. I want to take this opportunity to extend a very special and warm welcome to the film crew from Necessary Illusions. We've got an excellent line-up of television programming for you today, so let's get on with it.

Between acting jobs, Kelvin Flook works as a video host on Erin Mills Television (EMTV), a closed-circuit, non-stop video wall installation containing 264 television monitors. The four-sided installation is the centerpiece of Erin Mills Town Centre, a shopping mall just west of Toronto. When Mr. Flook is not playing clips from *Manufacturing Consent*, the usual fare is advertisements for stores in the mall, sports programming, fashion shows produced in the mall, and, on Saturday mornings, cartoons to occupy children while their parents shop.

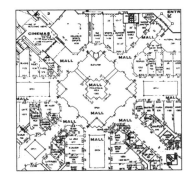

NECESSARY ILLUSIONS
After a combined total of over 30 years in media production, Mark Achbar and Peter Wintonick met in 1985 through shared concerns about militarism, the destruction of the environment and the role of the mainstream media in perpetuating myths related to these issues. Recognizing the potential for alternative media to improve the situation, they created an organization whose mandate and objectives have evolved from these concerns. Francis Miquet joined Necessary Illusions in 1989.

OBJECTIVES
- To develop a critical public awareness of the power and role of mainstream media and the potential of alternative media to counteract these forces.
- To encourage and protect free and creative expression through all manner of media.
- To assist individuals and groups to produce and use media to organize for positive social change.
- To develop and execute strategies for increased independent production.
- To develop audiences through creative and alternative means of distribution and exhibition.
- To develop a working process which is democratic, cooperative, egalitarian and non-hierarchical.

SHOPPING MALL VIDEO WALL

Marci Randall Miller interviews Noam Chomsky on KUWR (Public Radio), Laramie, Wyoming

Marci Randall Miller
So how long have they been working on this documentary?

Chomsky
Gosh, they've been working on it— I don't know how long, but every country I show up they're always there.

Marci Randall Miller
They're there, huh?

Chomsky
They were in England, they were in Japan—all over the place. They must have five hundred hours worth of tape by now.

Marci Randall Miller
Wow. I bet they put together a real doozie when they're done, huh?

Chomsky
I can't imagine who's going to want to hear somebody talk for an hour, but I guess they know what they're doin'.

THE WHITE HOUSE

Peter Wintonick, carrying a large "shotgun" microphone, approaches a group of students

Peter Wintonick

So, where are you all from?

Students

Florida.

Peter Wintonick

Florida?

Students

Yeah, Gulf Coast.

Peter Wintonick

You all talk like a chorus.

Students

(Giggle)

Peter Wintonick

We're making a film about Noam Chomsky. Does anyone know who Noam Chomsky is?

Students

NO...

Many are the authors who may wonder if anyone is paying attention to what they write.

Professor Noam Chomsky, MIT's preeminent linguistics authority, doesn't have that problem.

Recent research on citations in three different citation indices show that Professor Chomsky is one of the most cited individuals in works published in the past 20 years.

In fact, his 3,874 citations in the Arts and Humanities Citation Index between 1980 and 1992 make him the most cited living person in that period and the eighth most cited source overall—just behind famed psychiatrist Sigmund Freud and just ahead of philosopher Georg Hegel.

Indeed, Professor Chomsky is in illustrious company. The top ten sources during the period were: Marx, Lenin, Shakespeare, Aristotle, the Bible, Plato, Freud, Chomsky, Hegel and Cicero.

But that isn't all. From 1972 to 1992, Professor Chomsky was cited 7,449 times in the Social Science Citation Index—likely the greatest number of times for a living person there as well, although the research into those numbers isn't complete. [Theresa Tobin checked statistics for 40 top authors in the Social Sciences but admits she may have overlooked someone. To date, no one has corrected her research.] In addition, from 1974 to 1992 he was cited 1,619 times in the Science Citation Index.

"What it means is that he is very widely read across disciplines and that his work is used by researchers across disciplines," said Theresa A. Tobin, the Humanities Librarian who checked the numbers. "In fact," she added, "it seems that you can't write a paper without citing Noam Chomsky."

From MIT's Tech Talk, *Volume 36, Number 27, April 15, 1992*

In his office hallway, Chomsky has a poster of Bertrand Russell. A quote at the bottom of it says: "Three passions, simple but overwhelmingly strong, have governed my life: the longing for love, the search for knowledge and unbearable pity for the suffering of mankind."

According to his secretary, as of 1993 Chomsky had written 72 books. The current bibliography of his writings (the third published so far in hard cover) contains over 700 entries. Just over half relate to political subjects. *Noam Chomsky: A Personal Bibliography, 1951-1986* was compiled by E.F. Konrad Koerner and Matsuji Tajima with the collaboration of Carlos P. Otero (John Benjamins, 1986)

For more on Bertrand Russell, see Philosopher All-Stars Trading Cards at the back of the book.

I doubt that these [citation indices] can even be close to true. If they were, they would be meaningless (consider what it means that Marx, Lenin, Mao and Castro are listed high on citation indices in Western literature). Even if they were true and meaningful, they would be utterly irrelevant to any topic addressed here. Take a really important 20th–century figure: Bertrand Russell, who should be among the most cited, surely, if the rankings meant anything. Did his high ranking make his views on nuclear disarmament important? That's stressing exactly the wrong lessons. —NC

KUWR (PUBLIC RADIO), LARAMIE, WYOMING

KUWR is based on the campus of the University of Wyoming in Laramie, population 24,410

Marci Randall Miller (student)

Good afternoon and welcome to "Wyoming Talks." My guest today is well-known intellectual Noam Chomsky. Thank you for being on our program today.

Chomsky

Very glad to be here.

Marci Randall Miller

Well, I know probably the main purpose for your trip to Wyoming is to discuss "thought control in a democratic society." Now, all right, say I'm just Jane USA and I say, "Well, gee, this is a democratic society and what do you mean 'thought control'? I make up my own mind. I create my own destiny." What would you say to her?

Chomsky

Well I would suggest that Jane take a close look at the way the media operate, the way the public relations industry operates; the extensive thinking that's been going on for a long, long period about the necessity for finding ways to marginalize and control the public in democratic societies. But particularly to look at the evidence that's been accumulated about the way the major media, the sort of agenda-setting media—I mean the national press and the television and so on—the way they shape and control the kinds of opinions that appear, the kinds of information that comes through, the sources to which they go, and so on, and I think that Jane will find some very surprising things out about the democratic system.

The public relations industry expends vast resources "educating the American people about the economic facts of life" to ensure a favorable climate for business. Its task is to control "the public mind," which is "the only serious danger confronting the company," an AT&T executive observed 80 years ago.

Necessary Illusions, page 16. Also see "The Clinton Vision" on page 162 of this book

A 1975 study on "governability of democracies" by the Trilateral Commission concluded that the media have become a "notable new source of national power," one aspect of an "excess of democracy" that contributes to "the reduction of governmental authority" at home and a consequent "decline in the influence of democracy abroad." This general "crisis of democracy," the commission held, resulted from the efforts of previously marginalized sectors of the population to organize and press their demands, thereby creating an overload that prevents the democratic process from functioning properly. The study therefore urged more "moderation in democracy" to mitigate the excess of democracy and overcome the crisis.

Quotes within the above paragraph are from *The Crisis of Democracy: Report on the Governability of Democracies to the Trilateral Commission*, by M.P. Crozier, S.J. Huntington, and J. Watanuki, (New York University, 1975); *Necessary Illusions* pages 2-3

NOTE: To reduce repetition, bibliographic information on books by Noam Chomsky and Edward S. Herman referred to in this book is listed the Resource Guide.

The Trilateral Commission was set up in 1973 with three main objectives:
1) To foster cooperation among North America, Western Europe and Japan (the so-called advanced regions) via leading private citizens;
2) To develop external and internal policies for its members;
3) To effect a "renovation of the international system" so that the global power structure set up after World War II could become more equitable.

The impulse for the Commission came from David Rockefeller, who had hoped it would bring "the best brains in the world to bear on the problems of the future." Initially, there were 180 Commissioners, but by 1980 the number had already grown to about 300.

Source: *Trilateralism: The Trilateral Commission and Elite Planning for World Management*, edited by Holly Sklar (Black Rose Books, 1980)

Gary Bauslaugh *(Dean of Studies, Malaspina Colllege)*
I'd like to welcome all of you to this lecture today. Several years ago, Professor Chomsky was described in *The New York Times Book Review* as follows: "Judged in terms of the power, range, novelty and influence of his thought, Noam Chomsky is arguably the most important intellectual alive." Professor Noam Chomsky.

Chomsky
I gather there are some people out behind that blackness there but if I don't look you in the eye it's 'cause I don't see you, all I see is the blackness. Perhaps I ought to begin by reporting something that's never read—the line about the "arguably the most important intellectual" in the world and so on comes from a publisher's blurb. And you always got to watch those things (audience laughs) because if you go back to the original you'll find that that sentence is actually there— this is in *The New York Times*—but the next sentence is: "Since that's the case, how can he write such terrible things about American foreign policy?" And they never quote that part. But in fact if it wasn't for that second sentence I would begin to think that I'm doing something wrong. And I'm not joking about that. It's true that the emperor doesn't have any clothes, but the emperor doesn't like to be told it, and the emperor's lapdogs like *The New York Times* are not going to enjoy the experience if you do.

"Judged in terms of the power, range, novelty and influence of his thought, Noam Chomsky is arguably the most important intellectual alive today. He is also a disturbingly divided intellectual. On the one hand there is a large body of revolutionary and highly technical linguistic scholarship, much of it too difficult for anyone but the professional linguist or philosopher; on the other, an equally substantial body of political writings, accessible to any literate person but often maddeningly simple-minded. The 'Chomsky problem' is to explain how these two fit together."

The New York Times Book Review, February 25, 1979

Bill Moyers

Good evening, I'm Bill Moyers. What's more dangerous, the big stick or the big lie? Governments have used both against their own people. Tonight I'll be talking with a man who has been thinking about how we can see the developing lie. He says that propaganda is to democracy what violence is to a dictatorship. But he hasn't lost faith in the power of common people to speak up for the truth.

You have said that we live entangled in webs of endless deceit, that we live in a highly indoctrinated society where elementary truths are easily buried. Elementary truths such as...?

Chomsky

Such as the fact that we invaded South Vietnam. Or the fact that we're standing in the way of significant—and have for years—of significant moves towards arms negotiations—or the fact that the military system is to a substantial extent—not totally—but to a substantial extent, a mechanism by which the general population is compelled to provide a subsidy to high-technology industry. Since they're not going to do it if you ask them to, you have to deceive them into doing it. There are many truths like that, and we don't face them.

Bill Moyers

Do you believe in common sense? I mean you're a—

Chomsky

Absolutely, I believe in Cartesian common sense. I think people have the capacities to see through the deceit in which they are ensnared, but they've got to make the effort.

The question of the legitimacy of the American intervention is in part a question of principle, and in part turns on the character of the American war. As to the question of principle, it seems to me quite clear that we have neither the authority nor the competence to intervene with military force in the internal affairs of Indochina. In fact, this principle is even written into law. The "supreme law of the land" (as expressed, in this case, by the United Nations Charter, a valid treaty) is quite unequivocal in this respect. It states that forceful intervention is legitimate only if authorized by the Security Council or in "collective self-defense" against armed attack.

Efforts to argue that the American intervention is not, technically, criminal, therefore seek to establish that we are engaged in collective self-defense of South Vietnam against an armed attack from the North. However, as the record clearly shows, the American intervention long preceded any direct North Vietnamese involvement, and has always been far greater in scale, a fact conceded even by the Pentagon....

There is a great deal of unchallenged documentary evidence that demonstrates, conclusively I believe, that the U.S. is not engaged in collective self-defense against an armed attack but rather, that it extended its long-term forceful intervention in Vietnam to a full-scale invasion of South Vietnam in early 1965, because the N.L.F. [National Liberation Front] had won the internal civil struggle, despite the extensive (and illegal) direct American intervention.

Defenders of American actions frequently argue that questions of law are too complex for the layman and should be left to experts. However, in this case, a careful reading of the arguments, pro and con, reveals little divergence over questions of law. The issues debated are factual and historical: specifically, is the U.S. engaged in collective self-defense against armed attack from North Vietnam? This is an issue concerning which the layman is in a position to make a judgment, and the responsible citizen will not be frightened away from doing so by the claim that the matter is too esoteric for him to comprehend. Extensive documentation is available, and, I believe, it shows clearly that the American war is criminal, even in the narrowest technical sense.

From Chomsky's essay, "On The Limits Of Civil Disobedience" in a collection of essays —The Berrigans, edited by William Van Etten Casey, S.J., and Philip Nobile, pages 39-41 (Avon Books, 1971)

See also page 152 of this book

The military system in the United States is basically a government-guaranteed market for high-technology production.... It is not a conservative program; in fact, quite the contrary. Reagan's program was to increase the state's component of the state capitalistic system by the classic means.... In effect, this means the government will intervene by increasing demand for arms and high technology production to get things moving again....This is a very harmful system economically; it does spur production but in a very wasteful manner. Therefore, we have to make sure that our commercial rivals also harm their economy, roughly to the extent that we harm ours; otherwise we're in trouble.... Japan is a rival. Europe is a rival, too. We can no longer tolerate the wastefulness of this type of economic pump priming and still expect to be competitive in world trade.... We're putting resources into military production and those resources are not going into things that can be sold, that meet consumer needs in the market.... If our engineers are working on the latest technique for making a missile hit 3 mm closer than it did before, and the Japanese engineers are working on better home computers or something, you know what's going to happen.... [T]he Japanese system is geared for the commercial market.... Our system, on the other hand, works quite differently, since our system is the Pentagon system. It is only by accident that it has any commercial utility.... a crucial point is that none of this has anything to do with military threats. Nothing.

From an interview with Stephen W. White and Elaine Smoot, in National Forum, reprinted in Language and Politics, pages 350-353

See also Deterring Democracy, page 93

Bill Moyers

Seems a little incongruous to hear a man from the ivory tower of the Massachusetts Institute of Technology, a scholar, a distinguished linguistics scholar, talk about common people with such appreciation.

Chomsky

I think that scholarship, at least the field that I work in, has the opposite consequences. My own studies in language and human cognition demonstrate to me at least what remarkable creativity ordinary people have. The very fact that people talk to one another is a reflection— just in a normal way, I don't mean anything particularly fancy—reflects deep-seated features of human creativity which in fact separate human beings from any other biological system we know.

On the one occasion when U.S. TV allowed me a bit of time to talk (the Bill Moyers show), there was a huge response, about 1000 letters they told me, more than they'd received for almost anything else. Other friends who do a lot of public speaking tell me the same thing (Alex Cockburn and Howard Zinn, particularly). Apparently, many people are hungry for something, anything, that departs from the increasingly doctrinaire and narrow ideological framework and that deals with problems that concern them, but that are largely excluded from public discourse.

Unfortunately, there are very few people to meet the demand. The few of us who do are deluged with invitations. I can't accept a fraction of them, and am generally scheduled several years in advance. The "left intellectuals" (or whatever the right word is) are either involved in unintelligible varieties of postmodernism (mostly nonsense, in my opinion), or otherwise talking to one another. Most of the "intellectual community" is, as usual, serving power in one or another way. It leaves a huge gap, a matter of great importance these days, I think. —NC

December 9, 1992 (letter to John Schoeffel)

According to its producer, Gail Pellett, when first aired, this interview generated more requests for transcripts than any of the other 50 programs in the "World of Ideas" series.

This interview and others in the series are published in *A World of Ideas: Conversations with Thoughtful Men and Women about American Life Today and the Ideas Shaping Our Future*, by Bill D. Moyers, edited by Betty Sue Flowers (Doubleday, 1989). Transcripts of individual programs can also be ordered (see Resource Guide)

Announcer

Tonight. Scientists talk to the animals, but are they talking back? The Journal. With Barbara Frum and Mary Lou Findlay.

Barbara Frum (anchorperson)

Communicating with animals is a serious scientific pursuit.

Reporter

This is Nim Chimpsky. Nim, jokingly named after the great linguist Noam Chomsky, was the great hope of animal communication in the 1970s. For four years Petitto and others coached him in sign language, but in the end they decided it was a lost cause. Nim could ask for things, but not much more.

Laura Ann Petitto

I would have loved to have a conversation with Nim and understand how he looked at the universe. He failed to communicate that information to me. And we gave him every opportunity.

Laura Ann Petitto is an associate professor at McGill University in Montréal. She was 18 when she moved in with Nim and lived with him for three and a half years. Project Nim was a federally-funded multi-million-dollar study.

Nim presented researchers with the following intriguing challenge: On the one hand, chimpanzees (Nim included) *do* demonstrate impressive cognitive and communicative abilities. Yet, on the other, all chimpanzees fail to master key aspects of human language structure, even when you give them a means to bypass their inability to produce speech sounds—for example, by exposing them to natural signed languages. This dichotomy led Petitto to hypothesize that perhaps *something* existed at birth in our species *in addition* to the mechanisms for producing and perceiving speech sounds, per se, and *in addition* to our general cognitive capacities to symbolize. Indeed, Petitto's findings with Nim caused her to question popular hypotheses about human language acquisition, especially those that asserted that the human brain had no endowment for language.

Petitto discovered that deaf infants exposed to signed languages produce manual "babbling" just as hearing infants in the process of acquiring speech produce vocal babbling—a finding that was surprising because the motor control of the hands (in sign) and the tongue (in speech) are distinctly represented in different parts of the brain. She further discovered that hearing infants between the ages of six and 24 months exposed to sign and spoken language show no preference for speech but learn signed and spoken languages as if they were learning—for example, Spanish and Portuguese. "Why did those children, who were exposed to sign and speech, not prefer speech? It implies that they are not looking for speech, they're looking for the structure encoded in speech: that's the key point," Petitto told *McGill News*, an alumni publication.

In Petitto's subsequent research she has focused on identifying the core mechanisms in the brain and the environmental factors that trigger language acquisition. She has recently articulated a theory in which she proposes that the human brain is biologically endowed with a "structure recognition mechanism" at birth—a mechanism that predisposes infants to be sensitive to particular aspects of natural language structure, rather than to the speech mode, per se.

When Project Nim ended, Nim Chimpsky was sent, with three of his brothers, to the Norman, Oklahoma, Primate Colony, where he was to live out his natural life.

However, contrary to the arranged agreement, the Primate Colony sent the four chimpanzees to the New York Cancer Research Institute where they were used as subjects in experimental research. Petitto and her colleagues were unaware of the situation until a Norman, Oklahoma, journalist leaked them the information. They immediately got a court injunction to stop the research. It was too late for Nim's brothers, who were too sick to survive.

Fortunately, Cleveland Amory, a wealthy animal rights activist, came forward and offered Nim a home on his animal reserve in Texas.

For more on Laura Ann Petitto's work, see the March 1991 issue of *Science* magazine

Jonathan Steinberg (historian, Cambridge University)
Noam Chomsky, theorist of language and
political activist, has had an extraordinary career.
I can think of none like it in recent American
history and few anywhere at any time. He has
literally transformed the subject of linguistics.
At the same time he has become one of the
most consistent critics of power politics in all its
protean guises. Scholar and propagandist, his
two careers apparently reinforce each other. In
1957 he published his *Syntactic Structures*, which
began what has frequently been called the
Chomskyan Revolution in linguistics. Like a
latter-day Copernicus, Chomsky proposed a
radically new way of looking at the theory of
grammar. Chomsky worked out the formal rules
of a universal grammar which generated the
specific rules of actual or natural languages.
Later he came to argue that such systems are
innate features of human beings; they belong to
the characteristics of the species, and have
been, in effect, programmed into the genetic
equipment of the mind like the machine
language in a computer.

What is language, how do we acquire it and how do we use it?

For three centuries, the conventional
explanation for language—indeed for all
human knowledge—has been that put forward by the empiricists. Knowledge, they
have said, comes from experience. The
position was articulated in the 17th and 18th
centuries by such philosophers as John
Locke, who described the mind as an
"empty cabinet," and by David Hume, who
argued forcefully that "all the laws of nature
and all the operations of bodies without
exception are known only by experience."
By experience, he meant that everything we
know comes through our senses—that is,
primarily, from what we hear and touch and
see.

An empiricist would say that a child
learns language as a habit. Words are
repeated by his parents, and repeated
again, and eventually the child begins to
imitate. His parents smile when he correctly
imitates, but frown and repeat the phrase
when he makes a mistake. Thus, say the
empiricists, the child begins to speak.

Chomsky rejects this view with such
vehemence that he once declared: "The
empiricist view is so deep-seated in our way
of looking at the human mind that it almost
has the character of a superstition."

...Chomsky goes so far as to theorize that
the 4,000 or so known languages all rest on
the same basic principles, genetically determined, which he describes as "invariant
properties," or "linguistic universals," or
"universal grammar." They are true of languages past and present, no matter how
the speaker, no matter what the circumstances.

A child, in Chomsky's view, "knows" the
principles of language before he says his
first words; he uses these structures to learn
the grammar of his own language. Of
course, the child is not born with the mas-
tery of any particular tongue. He must learn
a great deal first, and he must grow, physically and emotionally, before he can grasp
all of language's subtleties. "Knowledge of
language," Chomsky is careful to point out,
"results from the interplay of initially given
structures of the mind, maturational

processes and interaction with the environment."

Chomsky's theories rest upon two obser-
vations about language. The first is that a
grammar describes a basic knowledge
shared by all speakers of the language. The
second in that our use of language is fundamentally creative.

Although we may make many mistakes in
our speech at any given time—perhaps
because we are tired or confused or in a
hurry—all normal speakers do possess this
common knowledge, which Chomsky calls
"language competence." That is, we can
hear a sentence that we have never heard
before, and yet grasp immediately its meaning and judge whether it is grammatically
correct.

Relatively little in the way of language
"data" is supplied to the child, in terms of
things said and shown to him by those who
"teach" him to speak. Yet very soon the
child comes to show great linguistic abilities.

This suggests a second aspect of creativity—that we can, theoretically at least, say
an unbounded number of sentences that
have never been said before. When we do
speak, moreover, it is usually coherent and
appropriate to the situation. "This creativity
is apparent," said Chomsky, "in the richness
and complexity and enormous range of
what you can produce. It comes down to
this: You are free to say what you want, you
can say what you think, and you can think
what you want."

From "The Chomskyan Revolution," by Daniel Yergin, in *The New York Times Magazine*, December 3, 1972

From a discussion between Chomsky and Jean Piaget, with other psychologists and philosophers observing and participating over several days

Chomsky

The general approach I'm taking seems to me rather simple-minded and unsophisticated—but nevertheless correct. Maybe I will use the blackboard.

One needn't be interested in this question, of course. I am interested in it. And the interesting question from this point of view would be: What is the nature of the initial state? That is, what is human nature in this respect?

If I understand him correctly, Piaget assumes that cognitive development passes through a series of stages, and that at each stage it is essentially uniform; thus the principles operating in one domain (say, language) are the same as those operating in every other domain (say, problem solving), at any given stage. Two questions arise: (1) is this true?; (2) how does the child pass from one stage to the next? As for (1), the evidence indicates that the assumptions are probably false. There is no known analog to, say, the principles of language in other cognitive domains; it is simply dogmatic to insist, in the face of everything that is known, that linguistic development mirrors the development of sensorimotor skills, etc.... As for (2), it seems to me that even if we accept the belief that there is a series of "cognitive stages," the Geneva school faces a self-imposed dilemma as to how transition takes place. The transition either results from new information (which they deny) or from some intrinsic process of maturation (which they also deny). No one has proposed any other possibility....

It seems to me that what is now known indicates that language develops along an intrinsically determined path, involving specific mechanisms of the language system, which is, in this respect, rather analogous to a physical organ. As in the case of the visual system and others, the course of development is influenced by an interaction with the environment. The task is to fill in the details and find the operative principles, and, of course, to relate all of this to physical mechanisms of the brain.

From a written response to questions submitted by Dr. Celia Jakubowicz, reprinted in *Language and Politics*, pages 384-385

The Piaget "debate" is not relevant. First, it was not filmed. Second, it was not a "debate." Harvard University Press concocted that framework, much to the annoyance (and over the strenuous objections) of the people who took part in the conference, me included, in order to sell the book. —NC

The book in question is *Language and Learning: The Debate Between Jean Piaget and Noam Chomsky*, edited by Massimo Piatelli-Palmarini (Harvard University Press, 1979)

Jean Piaget (1896-1980) was a Swiss psychologist, known for his contributions to child psychology, especially for his theory of cognitive and intellectual development, according to which development proceeds in genetically determined stages that always follow the same sequential order. Piaget showed that young children reason differently from adults and are often incapable of understanding logical reasoning. He wrote on the applications of dialectics and structuralism in the behavioral sciences and attempted a synthesis of physics, biology, psychology and epistemology. His writings include *The Child's Conception of the World* (translated 1929) and *Genetic Epistemology* (translated 1970) .

Source: *The Concise Columbia Encyclopedia*, 1983

The discussion with Piaget and others was not filmed, but fortunately it was videotaped, through the organizational efforts of Rhonda Hammer who teaches communications studies at the University of Windsor. The 24 hours of tape are stored at Laval University in Québec.

SCHOOLYARD, MONTRÉAL, QUÉBEC

Mira Burt-Wintonick, six-year-old daughter of Christine Burt and Peter Wintonick, reads to her father

Mira Burt-Wintonick
That in turn explains—the—

Peter Wintonick
astonishing—you try the next one—

Mira Burt-Wintonick
f..a..c..i..l..ee..tee

Peter Wintonick
Facility.

Mira Burt-Wintonick
Facility.

"THIRD EAR," BBC-3 (PUBLIC RADIO), LONDON, ENGLAND

Jonathan Steinberg *(voice-over)*
That in turn explains the astonishing facility that children have in learning the rules of natural language, no matter how complicated, incredibly quickly, from what are imperfect and often degenerate samples.

Mira Burt-Wintonick
Complain—

Peter Wintonick
Complicated

Mira Burt-Wintonick
Complicated—

Peter Wintonick
It's a complicated word. You know what complicated means? It means it's complicated.

What does the mind know when it knows a language, and how does it know it? To penetrate this question, Chomsky began devising a system of rules that could generate grammatical sentences. Other linguists, including [Chomsky's mentor, Zelig] Harris, had devised such systems, but Chomsky borrowed from mathematics and logic to create a so-called generative grammar more rigorous and comprehensive than any predecessor.

Working with this tool, Chomsky showed that language is far more complex than anyone had suspected—too complex to be entirely learned, he contended. For example to turn the sentence "The man is here" into a yes or no question, one merely puts the verb before the subject: "Is the man here?" But how does one turn the slightly more complex sentence "The man who is tall is here" into a question? One might expect a child who has just mastered the simpler example to place the first "is" in front of the sentence and say, "Is the man who tall is here?" But children never make this mistake, according to Chomsky. They always move the *main* verb, not the first verb, to the front of the sentence.

Chomsky points out that this rule is quite subtle, and in fact it is difficult to express either in formal linguistic terms or in a computer program. Yet children apply it without ever being explicitly taught to do so.

"Free Radical: A Word (or Two) about Linguist Noam Chomsky," by John Horgan, in *Scientific American*, May 1990

Chomsky's current model...conceives of universal grammar as a set of simple principles that interact with one another, and with the properties of words, to give rise to all the complexities of language. There is also a more powerful lexicon, or dictionary of words, that underlies the theory. Chomsky now holds that a word's entry in the dictionary specifies not only its sound and its role in syntax (verb, noun, preposition) but also the fundamentals of its meaning. For example, the word hit requires a recipient of the action and a subject. Chomsky goes further, arguing that the essentials of most words predate experience. "The concept 'climb,'" Chomsky has written, "is just part of the way in which we are able to interpret experience available to us before we even have the experience."

Such principles make up the universal grammar that underlies all languages, Chomsky says. He likens language to an elaborately wired box of switches—root concepts and grammatical principles—set in one position or another by experience. Chinese sets the switches in one pattern, English in another. But the fundamental conceptual framework of how concepts and syntax interlock is the same.

From David Berreby's review of *The Linguistics Wars* by Randy Allen Harris (Oxford University Press, 1994) in *The Sciences* January/February, 1994

For recommended introductory readings in Chomsky's linguistics, see Resource Guide

Chomsky

If in fact our minds were a blank slate and experience wrote on them we would be very impoverished creatures indeed. So the obvious hypothesis is that our language is the result of the unfolding of a genetically determined program. Well, plainly there are different languages; in fact the apparent variation of languages is quite superficial.

It's certain—as certain as anything is—that humans are not genetically programmed to learn one or another language. So you bring up a Japanese baby in Boston, it will speak Boston English. If you bring up my child in Japan, it'll speak Japanese. From that it simply follows by logic that the basic structure of the languages must be essentially the same.

The critique that first exposed the weaknesses of behaviorist psychology is in Chomsky's review of Skinner's *Verbal Behavior*, an extended review which appeared in 1959 in *Language* (volume 35, pages 26-58—often reprinted, in particular in *The Structure of Language: Readings in the Philosophy of Language*, edited by J. A. Fodor & J. J. Katz: Prentice-Hall, 1964), and with a preliminary note by Chomsky of great interest, in *Readings in the Psychology of Language*, edited by L. A. Jakobovits and M. S. Miron.: (Prentice-Hall, 1967). This review was to prove extremely influential (for some it sounded the death-knell of behaviorism).

Carlos P. Otero, in *Noam Chomsky: Critical Assessments* (Routledge, 1993)

Our task as scientists is to try to determine exactly what those fundamental principles are that cause the knowledge of language to unfold in the manner in which it does under particular circumstances, and, incidentally, I think there is no doubt the same must be true of other aspects of human intelligence and systems of understanding and interpretation and moral and aesthetic judgment, and so on.

If in fact humans are indefinitely malleable, completely plastic beings, with no innate structures of mind and no intrinsic needs of a cultural or social character, then they are fit subjects for the "shaping of behavior" by the state authority, the corporate manager, the technocrat, or the central committee. Those with some confidence in the human species will hope this is not so and will try to determine the intrinsic human characteristics that provide the framework for intellectual development, the growth of moral consciousness, cultural achievement, and participation in a free community.... It seems to me that we must break away, sharply and radically, from much of modern social and behavioral science if we are to move toward a deeper understanding of these matters...

The principles of Skinner's "science" tell us nothing about designing a culture (since they tell us virtually nothing), but that is not to say that Skinner leaves us completely in the dark as to what he has in mind. He believes that "the control of the population as a whole must be delegated to specialists—to police, priests, owners, teachers, therapists, and so on, with their specialized reinforcers and their codified contingencies."(*Beyond Freedom and Dignity*, p.155)

...[C]onsider freedom of speech. Skinner's approach suggests that control of speech by direct punishment should be avoided, but that it is quite appropriate for speech to be controlled, say, by restricting good jobs to people who say what is approved by the designer of the culture... In fact, by giving people strict rules to follow, so that they know just what to say to be "reinforced" by promotion, we will be "making the world safer" and thus achieving the ends of behavioral technology. (*Beyond Freedom and Dignity*, pages 74, 81)

From "Psychology and Ideology," in the *Chomsky Reader*, page 154, an expanded version of Chomsky's review of B.F. Skinner's *Beyond Freedom and Dignity* (Alfred A. Knopf, 1971), which originally appeared in *The New York Review of Books*, December 30, 1971

Let's think again of a human child, who has in his mind some schematism that determines the kind of language he can learn. And then, given experience, he very quickly knows the language, of which this experience is a part, or in which it is included. Now this is a normal act; that is, it's an act of normal intelligence, but it's a highly creative act.

If a Martian were to look at this process of acquiring this vast and complicated and intricate system of knowledge on the basis of this ridiculous small quantity of data, he would think of it as an immense act of invention and creation. In fact a Martian would, I think, consider it as much of an achievement as the invention of, let's say, any aspect of a physical theory on the basis of the data that was presented to the physicist. However, if this hypothetical Martian were then to observe that every normal human child immediately carries out this creative act and they all do it in the same way and without any difficulty, whereas it takes centuries of genius to slowly carry out the creative act of going from evidence to scientific theory, then this Martian would, if he were rational, conclude that the structure of the knowledge that is acquired in the case of language is basically internal to the human mind; whereas the structure of physics is not, in so direct a way, internal to the human mind. Our minds are not constructed so that when we look at the phenomena of the world, theoretical physics comes forth, and we write it down and produce it; that's not the way our minds are constructed.

From *Reflexive Water: The Basic Concerns of Mankind*, edited by Fons Elders (Souvenir Press, 1974), page 155

Colorless green ideas sleep furiously

Jonathan Steinberg
The implications of these views have washed over the fields of psychology, education, sociology, philosophy, literary criticism and logic.

Chomsky
Well, a small industry has been spawned by one linguistic example, namely, Colorless green ideas sleep furiously, which has been the source of poems and arguments and music and so on.

Howard Lasnik
This is a very interesting sentence because it shows that syntax can be separated from semantics, that form can be separated from meaning. Colorless green ideas sleep furiously. Doesn't seem to mean anything coherent but sounds like an English sentence. If you read it back to front—furiously sleep ideas green colorless—that wouldn't sound like English at all.

Chomsky
Well that tells us that there's more to what determines the structure of a sentence than whether it has meaning or not...

Howard Lasnik
For a sentence to be a sentence of English in terms of its structure, it doesn't seem to matter much what the words mean or whether they go together in a meaningful way, [what matters is] just that they're together in a way that obeys the rules of syntax.

From *The Human Language*, a series of one-hour films on "The Human Language, What It Is and How It Works" (see Resource Guide)

There's more to what determines the structure of a sentence than whether it has meaning or not...

SERPENT'S TAIL PUBLISHING, ENGLAND

Chomsky is interviewed by contributors to Radical Philosophy *magazine*

Jonathan Rée

In the fifties and sixties, the bridge between your theoretical work and your political work seems to have been the attack on behaviorism. But now behaviorism is no longer an issue—or so it seems—so how does this leave the link between your linguistics and your politics?

Chomsky

Well, I've always regarded the link— I've never really perceived much of a link to tell you the truth.

EXCERPT: NOS (PUBLIC TV), HOLLAND (1971)

Chomsky

Again I would be very pleased to be able to discover intellectually convincing connections between my own anarchist convictions on the one hand and what I think I can demonstrate, or at least begin to see about the nature of human intelligence on the other. But I simply can't find intellectually satisfying connections between those two domains. I can discover some tenuous points of contact.

David Barsamian

You are invariably asked in lectures and interviews to draw connections between your linguistics and your politics. I'm not going to ask you that question. What's really interesting is why the question is asked.

Chomsky

That is an interesting question. I think there are two reasons. One reason is that there's an assumption that you can't just be a human being. You can't be interested in genocide because you don't like genocide. It must be coming out of something else. There's also an assumption that unless you're a professional expert on something, you can't be talking about it. So there are any number of reviews, including favorable reviews, I should say, reviews from activists on the left will review a book of mine and say, oh, my God, this propaganda analysis is fantastic, because he can use linguistics to deconstruct ideology or something like that. I don't even know what the word "deconstruct" means, let alone how to use it.

Chronicles of Dissent, page 269

Student

Professor Chomsky, would you address your critics who say that you are suspect as a social critic because you are a linguist?

Chomsky

You shouldn't pay any attention to what I say as a linguist or as anything else. You should ask whether it makes any sense. You could just as well say I'm suspect as a linguist because I have no training in linguistics, which is in fact true. I don't have any professional background in linguistics. I didn't take the standard courses. That's why I'm teaching at MIT. I couldn't have gotten a job at a bona fide university. (*laughter*) That's no joke, actually. You know, I didn't have professional qualifications in the field. At MIT they didn't care. They just cared whether it was right or wrong. It's a scientific university. They don't care what's written on your degree. My own personal career happens to be very odd. I have no professional qualifications in anything. And my work has spread all over the place.

It's a very strange question. It's as if there's some sort of profession, "Social Critic," and only if you sort of pass the prerequisites in that profession then somehow you're allowed to be a social critic.

From an audience Q & A following a panel discussion at the University of Wyoming

Audiotapes and transcripts of David Barsamian's interviews with Noam Chomsky are available from Alternative Radio (see Resource Guide); this exchange is from "Pearl Harbor," November 16, 1991

Michel Foucault

Il n'y a de créativité possible qu'a partir d'un système de règles. Le problème alors la que je me pose—et je ne suis pas tout à fait d'accord avec Monsieur Chomsky—c'est lorsqu'il place ces régularités à l'intérieur en quelques sort de l'esprit ou de la nature humaine. Je me demande si le système de régularités de contraintes qui rend possible une science on ne peut pas les trouver ailleurs en dehors de l'esprit humain, dans des formes sociales dans des rapports de productions, dans des luttes de classes, etc.

(Creativity is only possible within a system of rules. The problem that I have—and I do not agree completely with Mr. Chomsky—is when he places these constraints within the mind or within human nature. I wonder if the system of regulation of constraints which makes a science possible cannot be found outside the human mind, in social structures, in relations of production, in class struggles, etc.)

Chomsky

If it is correct, as I believe it is, that a fundamental element of human nature is the need for creative work or creative inquiry, for free creation without the arbitrary limiting effects of coercive institutions, then of course it will follow that a decent society should maximize the possibilities for this fundamental human characteristic to be realized. Now, a federated, decentralized system of free associations incorporating economic as well as social institutions would be what I refer to as anarcho-syndicalism. And it seems to me that it is the appropriate form of social organization for an advanced technological society, in which human beings do not have to be forced into the position of tools, of cogs in a machine.

Just looking at the epoch that we are in now, it seems to me that our present level of technology permits enormous possibilities for eliminating repressive institutions.... It is often said that advanced technology makes it imperative to vest control of institutions in the hands of a small managerial group. That is perfect nonsense. What automation can do first of all is to relieve people of an enormous amount of stupid labor, thus freeing them for other things. Computers also make possible a very rapid information flow. Everybody could be put in possession of vastly more information and more relevant information than they have now. Democratic decisions could be made immediately by everybody concerned.... Of course, that is not how this technology is actually used. It is used for destructive purposes.

From an interview with *New Left Review*, reprinted in *Language and Politics*, page 147. See also *Reflexive Water: The Basic Concerns of Mankind*, edited by Fons Elders (Souvenir Press, 1974), pages 193-194

French philosopher Michel Foucault (1926-1984) "genealogically" and "archaeologically" investigated the history of sexuality, and the institutions of the penitentiary, the insane asylum and the hospital. He viewed the new sciences and institutions born out of the "Enlightenment", as affects of power as knowledge. Foucault viewed the "panopticon", the method of surveillance in the modern prison, as the technique through which the modern State executes and regulates its control throughout society. Unlike the monarchical State, which could use brute force to control its population, he believed the relatively recent advent of the "democratic" State requires internal and sublime coercion to perform this function.

James McGillivray, researcher, Philosopher All-Stars Trading Cards

Chomsky
... There is no longer any social necessity for human beings to be treated as mechanical elements in the productive process; that can be overcome, and we must overcome it, by a society of freedom and free association, in which the creative urge that I consider intrinsic to human nature will in fact be able to realize itself in whatever way it will....

Fons Elders (moderator)
Do you believe, Mr. Foucault, that we can call our societies in any way democratic, after listening to this statement from Mr. Chomsky?

Michel Foucault
No, I don't have the least belief that one could consider our society democratic. (*laughs*) If one understands by democracy the effective exercise of power by a population which is neither divided nor hierarchically ordered in classes, it is quite clear that we are very far from democracy. It is only too clear that we are living under a regime of a dictatorship of class, of a power of class which imposes itself by violence, even when the instruments of this violence are institutional and constitutional; and to that degree there isn't any question of democracy for us.... I admit to not being able to define, nor for even stronger reasons to propose, an ideal social model for the functioning of our scientific or technological society.... It seems to me that the real political task in a society such as ours is to criticize the workings of institutions, which appear to be both neutral and independent; to criticize and attack them in such a manner that the political violence which has always exercised itself obscurely through them will be unmasked, so that one can fight against them.

This critique and this fight seem essential to me for different reasons: firstly, because politi-

cal power goes much deeper than one suspects; there are centers and invisible little-known points of support; its true resistance, its true solidity is perhaps where one doesn't expect it. Probably it's insufficient to say that behind the governments, behind the apparatus of the State, there is a dominant class; one must locate the point of activity, the places and forms in which its domination is exercised. And because this domination is not simply the expression in political terms of economic exploitation, it is its instrument and, to a large extent, the condition which makes it possible; the suppression of the one is achieved through the exhaustive discernment of the other. Well, if one fails to recognize these points of support of class power, one risks allowing them to continue to exist and to see this class power reconstitute itself even after an apparent revolutionary process.

Chomsky
Yes, I would certainly agree with that, not only in theory but also in action. That is, there are two intellectual tasks: one, and the one that I was discussing, is to try to create the vision of a future just society; that is to create, if you like, a humanistic social theory that is based, if possible, on some firm and humane concept of the human essence or human nature. That's one task.

Another task is to understand very clearly the nature of power and oppression and terror and destruction in our own society. And that certainly includes the institutions you mentioned, as well as the central institutions of any industrial society, namely the economic, commercial and financial institutions and in particular, in the coming period, the great multi-national corporations, which are not very far from us physically tonight [i.e., the Phillips Corporation at Eindhoven, Holland].

Those are the basic institutions of oppression and coercion and autocratic rule that do not appear to be neutral despite everything they say: well, we're subject to the democracy of the market place, and that must be understood precisely in terms of their autocratic power, including the particular form of autocratic control that comes from the domination of market forces in an egalitarian society.

Surely we must understand these facts, and not only understand them but combat them. And in fact, as far as one's own political involvements are concerned, in which one spends the majority of one's energy and effort, it seems to me that this must certainly be in that area. I don't want to get personal about it, but my own certainly are in that area, and I assume everyone's are.

Still, I think it would be a great shame to put aside entirely the somewhat more abstract and philosophical task of trying to draw the connections between a concept of human nature that gives full scope to freedom and dignity and creativity and other fundamental human characteristics, and to relate that to some notion of social structure in which those properties could be realized and in which meaningful human life could take place.

And in fact, if we are thinking of a social transformation or social revolution, though it would be absurd, of course, to try to sketch out in detail the goal that we are hoping to reach, still we should know something about where we think we are going, and such a theory may tell it to us.

Foucault
Yes, but then isn't there a danger here? If you say that a certain human nature exists, that this human nature has not been given in actual society the rights and the possibilities which allow it to realize itself...that's really what you have said, I believe.

Chomsky
Yes.

Foucault
And if one admits that, doesn't one risk defining this human nature—which is at the same time ideal and real, and has been hidden and repressed until now—in terms borrowed from

our society, from our civilization, from our culture? ...[I]t is difficult to say what human nature is. Isn't there a risk that we will be led into error?...

Chomsky
... Our concept of human nature is certainly limited, it's partially socially conditioned, constrained by our own character defects and the limitations of the intellectual culture in which we exist. Yet at the same time it is of critical importance that we know what impossible goals we're trying to achieve, if we hope to achieve some of the possible goals. And that means that we have to be bold enough to speculate and create social theories on the basis of partial knowledge, while remaining very open to the strong possibility, and in fact overwhelming probability, that at least in some respects we're very far off the mark....

Foucault
... I will be a little bit Nietzchean about this; in other words, it seems to me that the idea of justice in itself is an idea which in effect has been invented and put to work in different types of societies as an instrument of a certain political and economic power or as a weapon against that power. But it seems to me that, in any case, the notion of justice itself functions within a society of classes as a claim made by the oppressed class and as a justification for it.

Chomsky
I don't agree with that.

Foucault
And in a classless society, I am not sure that we would still use this notion of justice.

Chomsky
Well, here I really disagree. I think there is some

sort of an absolute basis—if you press me too hard I'll be in trouble, because I can't sketch it out—ultimately residing in fundamental human qualities, in terms of which a "real" notion of justice is grounded. I think it's too hasty to characterize our existing systems of justice as merely systems of class oppression; I don't think they are that. I think that they embody systems of class oppression and elements of other kinds of oppression, but they also embody a kind of groping towards the true humanly, valuable concepts of justice and decency and love and kindness and sympathy, which I think are real....

Foucault
Well, do I have time to answer?

Elders
Yes.

Foucault
How much? Because...

Elders
Two minutes. [*Foucault laughs*]

Foucault
But I would say that that is unjust. [*everybody laughs*]

Chomsky
Absolutely, yes.

Foucault
No, but I don't want to answer in so little time. I would simply say this, that finally this problem of human nature, when put simply in theoretical terms, hasn't led to an argument between us; ultimately we understand each other very well on these theoretical problems.
On the other hand, when we discussed the

problem of human nature and political problems, then differences arose between us. And contrary to what you think, you can't prevent me from believing that these notions of human nature, of justice, of the realization of the essence of human beings, are all notions and concepts which have been formed within our civilization, within our type of knowledge and our form of philosophy, and that as a result form part of our class system; and one can't, however regrettable it may be, put forward these notions to describe or justify a fight which should—and shall in principle—overthrow the very fundaments of our society. This is an extrapolation for which I can't find the historical justification. That's the point.

Chomsky
It's clear.

Reflexive Water: The Basic Concerns of Mankind, edited by Fons Elders (Souvenir Press, 1974), pages 170-187

Jonathan Steinberg

Since the 1960s, Noam Chomsky has been the voice of a very characteristic brand of rationalist, libertarian socialism. He has attacked the abuses of power wherever he saw them. He has made himself deeply unpopular by his criticism of American policy, the subservience of the intelligentsia, the degradation of Zionism, the distortions of media and self-delusions of prevailing ideologies.

EXCERPT: "MIT PROGRESSIONS" (1969)

On the steps of the Massachusetts Institute of Technology (MIT) in Cambridge, Chomsky addresses a group of students, including Z Magazine *editor Michael Albert*

Chomsky

Under the liberal administrations of the 1960s, the club of academic intellectuals designed and implemented the Vietnam war and other similar, though smaller actions. This particular community is a very relevant one to consider at a place like MIT because of course you're all free to enter this community and in fact you're invited and encouraged to enter it. The community of technical intelligentsia and weapons designers and counter-insurgency experts and pragmatic planners of an American empire is one that you have a great deal of inducement to become associated with. The inducements in fact are very real.

I remember a book by Norman Podhoretz, some right-wing columnist, in which he accused academics in the peace movement of being ingrates because we were working against the government but we were getting grants from the government. That reflects an extremely interesting conception of the state, in fact a fascist conception of the state. It says the state is your master, and if the state does something for you, you have to be nice to them. That's the underlying principle. So the state runs you, you're its slave, and if they happen to do something nice for you, like giving you a grant, you have to be nice to them, otherwise it's ungrateful. Notice how exactly opposite that is to democratic theory. According to democratic theory you're the master, the state is your servant. The state doesn't give you a grant, the population is giving you a grant. The state's just an instrument. But the concept of democracy is so remote from our conception, that we very often tend to fall into straight fascist ideas like that...

From an interview with David Barsamian,
Language and Politics, page 747

As to how I tolerate MIT, that raises another question. There are people who argue, and I have never understood the logic of this, that a radical ought to dissociate himself from oppressive institutions. The logic of that argument is that Karl Marx shouldn't have studied in the British Museum which, if anything, was the symbol of the most vicious imperialism in the world, the place where all the treasures an empire had gathered from the rape of the colonies were brought together. But I think Karl Marx was quite right in studying in the British Museum. He was right in using the resources and in fact the liberal values of the civilization that he was trying to overcome, against it. And I think the same applies in this case.

Reflexive Water: The Basic Concerns of Mankind, page 195

MIT OFFICE, CAMBRIDGE, MASSACHUSETTS

Chomsky
Jamie, this came with the mail.

(Turns to student waiting)
Be with you in a second.

(Enters office, sees that lights, crew, etc., haven't moved)
Oh God, they've still got their cameras—

David Barsamian (Independent radio producer)
All right? Then we'll start. In your essay
"Language and Freedom" you write, "Social
action must be animated by a vision of a future
society." I was wondering what vision of a future
society animates you?

Chomsky
Well, I have my own ideas as to what a future
society should look like—I've written about
them. I think that, at the most general level, we
should be seeking out forms of authority and
domination, and challenging their legitimacy.
Now, sometimes they are legitimate, that is, let's
say, they're needed for survival. So, for example,
I wouldn't suggest that during the second world
war—the forms of authority—we had a
totalitarian society basically, and I thought
there was some justification for that under the
wartime conditions. And there are other forms
of [coercion]. Relations between parents and
children, for example, involve forms of
coercion, which are sometimes justifiable.

But any form of coercion and control requires
justification. And most of them are completely
unjustifiable. Now, at various stages of human
civilization, it's been possible to challenge some
of them, but not others. Others are too deep-
seated, or you don't see them or whatever. And
so, at any particular point, you try to detect
those forms of authority and domination which

are subject to change and which do not have any legitimacy, in fact which often strike at fundamental human rights, and your understanding of fundamental human nature and rights.

Well, what are the major things, say, today? There are some that are being addressed in a way. The feminist movement is addressing some. The civil rights movement is addressing others. The one major one that's not being seriously addressed is the one that's really at the core of the system of domination, and that's private control over resources. And that means an attack on the fundamental structure of State capitalism. I think that's in order. That's not something far off in the future.

See transcript at right for the continuation of this interview

I think if you look at the present scene, the future society that I'd like to see is one where you continually do this, and continually extend the range of freedom and justice and lack of external control and greater public participation.

The 18th-century revolutions have not been consummated. Even the texts of classical liberalism were talking about things like wage slavery, people being condemned to work under command instead of working out of their own inner need and not controlling the work process. That's at the core of classical liberalism. That's all been completely forgotten. But that ought to be revived. That's very real. That means an attack on the fundamental structure of State capitalism. I think that's in order. That's not something far off in the future. In fact, we don't have to have fancy ideas about it. A lot of the ideas were articulated in the 18th century, even in what are the classical liberal texts and then later in at least the libertarian parts of the socialist movement and the anarchist movement. I think that is a very live topic which ought to be faced. A vision of a future society from this point of view would be one in which production, decisions over investment, etc., are under control. That means control through communities, through workplaces, through works councils in factories or universities, whatever organization it happens to be, federal structures which integrate things over a broader range. These are all entirely feasible developments, particularly for an advanced industrial society. The cultural background for them exists only in a very limited way but could be made to exist. That's a picture of part of a future society, it's not the only one because there are a lot of other forms of hierarchy and authority which should be eliminated. The kinds of systems that have existed are state capitalist, of the kind we're familiar with, or state bureaucratic like the Soviet system with a managerial bureaucratic military elite that commands and controls the economy from the top in totalitarian fashion. That's fortunately collapsing. Our system is not subject to any internal challenge, but it ought to be. The picture of a future society that evolves is one that you can proceed to sketch out.

Audiotape and a transcript of this interview are available from Alternative Radio under the title "MIT, Cambridge, Mass.," recorded February 2, 1990

That means an attack on the fundamental structure of State capitalism. I think that's in order. That's not something far off in the future.

EXCERPT: "JOURNALISM" (1940)

Narrator

The alphabet has only twenty-six letters. With these twenty-six magic symbols, however, millions of words are written every day.

EXCERPT: "DEMOCRACY'S DIARY" (1948)

Narrator

Nowhere else are people so addicted to information and entertainment via the printed word. Every day the world comes thumping on the American doorstep and nothing that happens anywhere remains long a secret from the American newspaper reader. It comes to us pretty casually, the daily paper. But behind its arrival on your doorstep is one of journalism's major stories. How it got there.

It is basic to the health of a democracy that no phase of government activity escape the scrutiny of the press. Here reporters are assigned to stories fateful not only to our nation but to all nations. Congress, says the First Amendment, shall pass no law abridging the freedom of the press and the chief executive himself throws open the doors of the White House to journalists representing papers of all shades of political opinion.

"Journalism" was produced by Vocational Guidance Films Inc., as part of the "Your Life Work" series. Hundreds of films like this have been gathered by The American Archives of the Factual Film (see Resource Guide)

"Democracy's Diary" was commissioned by *The New York Times*. There have been very few films made inside *The New York Times* because, it seems, they are extremely selective about who they allow in to film. Cameras are barred from tours given to the public, but we managed to provide viewers with some rare glimpses inside Fortress NYT. On the filmmakers' access, see page 87.

Chomsky

But it is worth bearing in mind that there is a contrary view. And in fact the contrary view is widely held and deeply rooted in our own civilization. It goes back to the origins of modern democracy. To the seventeenth-century English Revolution, which was a complicated affair like most popular revolutions. There was a struggle between Parliament, representing largely elements of the gentry and the merchants, and the Royalists, representing other elite groups. And they fought it out. But like many popular revolutions there was also a lot of popular ferment going on that was opposed to all of them. There were popular movements that were questioning everything, the relation between master and servant, the right of authority altogether, all kinds of things were being questioned. There was a lot of radical publishing—the printing presses had just come into existence. This disturbed all the elites on both sides of the civil war. So as one historian pointed out at the time, in 1660, he criticized the radical democrats, the ones who were calling for what we would call democracy, because they are making the people so curious and so arrogant that they will never find humility enough to submit to a civil rule.

Condemning the radical democrats who had threatened to "turn the world upside down" during the English Revolution of the 17th century, historian Clement Walker, in 1661, complained:

> They have cast all the mysteries and secrets of government... before the vulgar (like pearls before swine), and have taught both the soldiery and people to look so far into them as to ravel back all governments to the first principles of nature. They have made the people thereby so curious and so arrogant that they will never find humility enough to submit to a civil rule.

Necessary Illusions, pages 131-132
See also: "The Bewildered Herd and its Shepherds," in *Deterring Democracy*, page 357

THE
Parliament of VVomen.

With the merrie Lawes by them newly
Enacted. To live in more Eafe, Pompe, Pride,
and wantonneffe : but efpecially that they might have fu-
periority and dominere over their husbands : with a new way
found out by them to cure any old or new Cockolds, and
how both parties may recover their credit
and honefty againe

London. Printed for W. Wilfon and are to be fold by him in
Wilt-yard in Little Saint Bartholmewes. 1545.

During the English Revolution [in the17th century] some of the central issues of politics were fought over and argued through in a way that brought to the fore those who had been held down by the feudal system...

Looking back three hundred years and more to the events of that period it is astonishing—and deeply satisfying—to note that many of the basic questions which we still debate today were raised and fought over by a group of men and women who called themselves the Levellers and who succeeded in formulating a structure of constitutional ideas that was to become the basis for the French and American revolutionaries....Even more remarkable were the Diggers, or True Levellers, who established the clear outlines of democratic socialism, including a demand for the common ownership of land, for equal rights for women, for an accountable Parliament and for the provision of public services in health and education.

From *Britain's First Socialists: The Levellers, Agitators and Diggers of the English Revolution*, by Fenner Brockway (Quartet Books, 1980), pages ix-x

The Levellers not only advocated democracy for society, they applied it to their own organization, again extraordinary in the far-away seventeenth century when authoritarianism and bureaucracy were the order of the day...

An astonishing feature was the speed with which each section of the party worked —petitions printed at an underground press, 10,000 signatures collected in two days, presented to Parliament the third day; pamphlets by their leaders continuously smuggled from prison, printed clandestinely, distributed widely...; the massive turn-out at marches organized on an immediate issue within a few hours....

The Diggers not only held socialist principles, but they put them into practice.... Wherever common lands were occupied, egalitarian communities were established, all working, all sharing. Bravely they withstood the raids of gangsters recruited by the landlords angry that the common land which they had arrogated for the grazing of their cattle should be used in common.... Finally, by the intervention of the state and the courts, they were defeated.

Britain's First Socialists, pages 145-151

The radical democrats of the seventeenth-century English revolution held that "it will never be a good world while knights and gentlemen make us laws, that are chosen for fear and do but oppress us, and do not know the people's sores. It will never be well with us till we have Parliaments of countrymen like ourselves, that know our wants." But Parliament and the preachers had a different vision: "[W]hen we mention the people, we do not mean the confused promiscuous body of the people," they held. With the resounding defeat of the democrats, the remaining question, in the words of a Leveler pamphlet, was "whose slaves the poor shall be," the King's or Parliament's.

Quotes above are from *The World Turned Upside Down*, by Christopher Hill (Penguin, 1984), pages 60, 71; *Necessary Illusions*, page 23

GEORGETOWN UNIVERSITY, WASHINGTON, DC

Chomsky

Now, underlying these doctrines, which were very widely held, is a certain conception of democracy. It's a game for elites, it's not for the ignorant masses, who have to be marginalized, diverted and controlled—of course for their own good.

The same principles were upheld in the American colonies: The dictum of the founding fathers of American democracy that "the people who own the country ought to govern it"— quoting John Jay.

Now, in modern times, for elites, this contrary view about the intellectual life and the media and so on, this contrary view in fact is the standard one, I think, apart from rhetorical flourishes.

"AMERICAN FOCUS," STUDENT RADIO, WASHINGTON, DC

Elizabeth Sikorovsky

From Washington, DC, he's intellectual, author and linguist Professor Noam Chomsky. *Manufacturing Consent.* What is that title meant to describe?

Chomsky

Well, the title is actually borrowed from a book by Walter Lippmann, written back around 1921, in which he described what he called "the manufacture of consent" as "a revolution" in "the practice of democracy," What it amounts to is a technique of control. And he said this was useful and necessary because "the common interests"— the general concerns of all people—"elude" the public. The public just isn't up to dealing with them. And they have to be the domain of what he called a "specialized class."

That the manufacture of consent is capable of great refinements no one, I think, denies. The process by which public opinions arise is certainly no less intricate than it has appeared in these pages and the opportunities for manipulation open to anyone who understands the process are plain enough.

The creation of consent is not a new art. It is a very old one which was supposed to have died out with the appearance of democracy. But it has not died out. It has, in fact, improved enormously in technic, because it is now based on analysis rather than on rule of thumb. And so, as a result of psychological research, coupled with the modern means of communication, the practice of democracy has turned a corner. A revolution is taking place, infinitely more significant than any shifting of economic power.

Within the life of the generation now in control of affairs, persuasion has become a self-conscious art and a regular organ of popular government. None of us begins to understand the consequences, but it is no daring prophecy to say that the knowledge of how to create consent will alter every political calculation and modify every political premise... It has been demonstrated that we cannot rely upon intuition, conscience, or the accidents of casual opinion if we are to deal with the world beyond our reach.

Public Opinion, by Walter Lippmann (Free Press, 1965; first published in 1922), page 158

The lesson is, I think, a fairly clear one. In the absence of institutions and education by which the environment is so successfully reported that the realities of public life stand out sharply against self-centered opinion, the common interests very largely elude public opinion entirely, and can be managed only by a specialized class whose personal interests reach beyond the locality. This class is irresponsible, for it acts upon information that is not common property, in situations that the public at large does not conceive, and it can be held to account only on the accomplished fact.

Public Opinion, page 195

John Jay [1745-1829] was the president of the Continental Congress and the first chief justice of the U.S. Supreme Court [a position he held from 1789 to 1795]. His biographer describes this as "one of his favorite maxims."

Necessary Illusions, page 14

Walter Lippmann (1889-1974) was a political philosopher and journalist whose writings constitute a sustained and close commentary on American public affairs for a period of nearly six decades. He brought to the discussion and analysis of current social and political problems a degree of learning unprecedented in American journalism. Thoughout his career he retained an independent, critical stance on foreign and domestic issues and combined a rigorous commitment to democratic principles with a deep sense of the pragmatic limitations of real political situations. He is certainly among the most thoughtful and cultured newspapermen of all times...

The main focus of Lippmann's thinking in the 1920's was on the relation of knowledge to public opinion in mass society. He was one of the first social thinkers to become aware of the growing distance between people's stereotyped impressions of their political environment and the complex realities of modern society. The news media increased this gap, according to Lippmann, by disseminating selected, simplified, and dramatized episodes of political life instead of explaining the facts and connections that lay behind these events. Lippmann became doubtful whether citizens could be adequately and objectively informed of the knowledge required for self-government, conceived along Jeffersonian lines. Lippmann proposed that there should be a system of collaboration between administrators, policymakers, and fact-finding experts. The role of the citizenry would be to maintain surveillance over the decision-making procedures of these knowledgeable rulers. *Liberty and the News, Public Opinion*, and *The Phantom Public* express Lippmann's pessimism concerning the compatibility of democracy with the social conditions of modern society. *An Enquiry into the Principles of the Good Society* advanced the principle of disinterestedness on the part of statesmen as a cure to the excesses of majority rule and as an antidote to the dangers of elitism.

Alan Waters in *Thinkers of the Twentieth Century* (St. James Press, 1987)

THE ENGINEERING APPROACH

This phrase quite simply means the use of an engineering approach—that is, action based only on thorough knowledge of the situation and on the application of scientific principles and tried practices to the task of getting people to support ideas and programs. Any person or organization depends ultimately on public approval, and is therefore faced with the problem of engineering the public's consent to a program or goal... The engineering of consent is the very essence of the democratic process, the freedom to persuade and suggest. The freedoms of speech, press, petition, and assembly, the freedoms which make the engineering of consent possible, are among the most cherished guarantees of the Constitution of the United States...

Today it is impossible to overestimate the importance of engineering consent; it affects almost every aspect of our daily lives. When used for social purposes, it is among our most valuable contributions to the efficient functioning of modern society... The responsible leader, to accomplish social objectives, must therefore be constantly aware of the possibilities of subversion. He must apply his energies to mastering the operational know-how of consent engineering, and to out-maneuvering his opponents in the public interest.

From "The Engineering of Consent,"
by Edward Bernays, in *The Annals of the American
Academy of Political and Social Science,*
March 1947, pages 114-115
See also: *Necessary Illusions*, pages 16-17

GEORGETOWN UNIVERSITY, WASHINGTON, DC

Chomsky

Notice that that's the opposite of the standard view about democracy. There's a version of this expressed by the highly respected moralist and theologian Reinhold Niebuhr, who was very influential on contemporary policy makers.

His view was that "rationality belongs to the cool observers" but because of "the stupidity of the average man" he follows not reason but faith, and this naive faith requires "necessary illusion" and "emotionally potent over-simplifi-cations" which are provided by the myth-maker to keep the ordinary person on course.

Contending factions in a social struggle require morale; and morale is created by the right dogmas, symbols and emotionally potent oversimplifications. These are at least as necessary as the scientific spirit of tentativity. No class of industrial workers will ever win freedom from the dominant classes if they give them-selves completely to the "experimental techniques" of the modern educators. They will have to believe rather more firmly in the justice and in the probable triumph of their cause, than any impartial science would give them the right to believe, if they are to have enough energy to contest the power of the strong.

Moral Man and Immoral Society: A Study in Ethics and Politics, by Reinhold Niebuhr
(Charles Scribner's Sons, 1960; first published in 1932), pages xv-xvi

Reinhold Niebuhr's vocation was teaching theological students. His major contribution to the health of the church in the world was preparing students of theology to be socially responsible. For four decades he taught Christian social philosophy at Union Theological Seminary in New York City.... [W]hile protecting the American tradition of the separation of church and state he expected his students to be actively engaged through their church or secular vocations in the continual process of applying Christian insight into the nature of humanity and history to social problems....

In international relations, particularly in the area of American foreign policy, his thought became influential among philosophers of foreign policy in the period after World War II. George Kennan has noted this contribution in commenting on the school of foreign policy thought known as realism: "He was the father of us all." He criticized illusions of U.S. omnipotence and innocence while urging the U.S. to exercise power responsibly in the post-war world.

Ronald Stone, *Thinkers of the Twentieth Century*
(St. James Press, 1987)

For more on Niebuhr's ideas, and their reception, see Chomsky's review of several books by and about him in *Grand Street*, Winter 1987 (see Resource Guide)

Chomsky

It's not the case, as the naive might think, that indoctrination is inconsistent with democracy. Rather, as this whole line of thinkers observes, it's the essence of democracy.

The point is that in a military State or a feudal State or what we would nowadays call a totalitarian State, it doesn't much matter what people think because you've got a bludgeon over their head and you can control what they do.

But when the State loses the bludgeon, when you can't control people by force and when the voice of the people can be heard, you have this problem. It may make people so curious and so arrogant that they don't have the humility to submit to a civil rule and therefore you have to control what people think.

And the standard way to do this is to resort to what in more honest days used to be called propaganda. Manufacture of consent. Creation of necessary illusions. Various ways of either marginalizing the general public or reducing them to apathy in some fashion.

KYOTO PRIZE, BASIC SCIENCES, JAPAN (1988)

In prestige and monetary value ($350,000), the Kyoto Prize has been likened to the Nobel prizes. Only three prizes are given by the Inamori Foundation. Chomsky was recognized for his work in basic sciences.

Japanese Translator *(narration of award slide show)*
The oldest of two boys, Avram Noam Chomsky was born in Philadelphia, Pennsylvania, in 1928.

As a Jewish child, the anti-Semitism of the time affected him.

Both parents taught Hebrew and he became fascinated by literature at an early age, reading American and English literature as well as translations of French and Russian classics.

He also took an interest in a grammar book written by his father on Hebrew of the middle ages.

He recalls a childhood absorbed in reading, curled up in a sofa, often borrowing up to twelve books at once from the library.

He is married to Carol, and they have three children.

EXCERPT: NOS (PUBLIC TV), HOLLAND (1971)

Chomsky
I don't like to impose on my wife and children a form of life that they certainly haven't selected for themselves, namely one of public exposure, exposure to the public media—that's their choice and I don't believe that they have themselves selected this, I don't impose it on them. And I would like to protect them from it, frankly. The second, and perhaps sort of principled point, is that I'm rather against the whole notion of developing public personalities who are treated as stars of one kind or another where aspects of their personal life are supposed to have some significance, and so on.

Anti-Semitism has changed, during my lifetime at least. Where I grew up we were virtually the only Jewish family...in a largely Irish-Catholic and German-Catholic community...in Philadelphia. And the anti-Semitism was very real. There were certain

paths I could take to walk to the store without getting beaten up. It was the late 1930s and the area was openly pro-Nazi. I remember beer parties when Paris fell and things like that. It was not like living under Hitler, but it was a very unpleasant thing. There was a really rabid anti-Semitism in that neighborhood where I grew up as a kid and it continued. By the time I got to Harvard in the early 1950's there was still very detectable anti-Semitism. There were very few Jewish professors on the faculty at that time. There was beginning to be a scattering of them, but still very few. This was the tail end of a long time of Waspish anti-Semitism at the elite institutions.

Over the last thirty years that's changed very radically. Anti-Semitism undoubtedly exists, but it's now on a par, in my view, with other kinds of prejudice of all sorts. I don't think it's more than anti-Italianism or anti-Irishism, and that's been a very significant change in the last generation, one that I've experienced myself in my own life, and it's very visible throughout the society.

From "Israel, the Holocaust, and Anti-Semitism,"
in Chronicles of Dissent, page 96

James Peck
You once said, "It is not unlikely that literature will forever give far deeper insight into what is sometimes called 'the full human person' than any modes of scientific inquiry may hope to do."

Chomsky
That's perfectly true and I believe that. I would go on to say it's not only unlikely, but it's almost certain. But still, if I want to understand, let's say, the nature of China and its revolution, I ought to be cautious about literary renditions. Look, there's no question that as a child, when I read about China, this influenced my attitudes—*Rickshaw Boy*, for example. That had a powerful effect when I read it. It was so long ago I don't remember a thing about it except the impact. And I don't doubt that, for me, personally, like anybody, lots of my perceptions were heightened and attitudes changed by literature over a broad range—Hebrew literature, Russian literature, and so on. But ultimately, you have to face the world as it is on the basis of other sources of evidence that you can evaluate. Literature can heighten your imagination and insight and understanding, but it surely doesn't provide the evidence that you need to draw conclusions and substantiate conclusions.

"Interview," The Chomsky Reader, pages 3-4. This interview contains
many insightful reflections on Chomsky's background

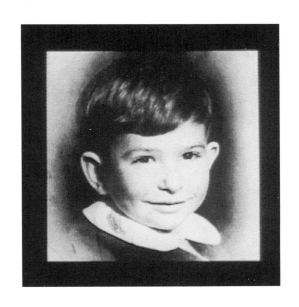

RECEPTION ROOM, LARAMIE, WYOMING

Sound Recordist

Take One in reception room.

Young Woman

You said that you were just like us. You went to school and got good grades and—what made you start being critical, you know, and seeing the different—What started the change?

Chomsky

Well, you know, there are all kinds of personal factors in anybody's life. I mean, first of all, don't forget I grew up in the Depression.

ROWE CONFERENCE CENTER, ROWE, MASSACHUSETTS

Chomsky

My parents actually happened to have jobs, which was kind of unusual—they were Hebrew school teachers, so sort of lower middle-class. For them, everything revolved around being Jewish. Hebrew, and Palestine, in those days and so on. And I grew up in that milieu. So, you know, I learned Hebrew and went to Hebrew school and became a Hebrew school teacher, went to Hebrew college, led youth groups, summer camps, Hebrew camps, the whole business. The branch of the Zionist movement that I was part of was all involved in socialist binationalism and Arab-Jewish co-operation— all sorts of nice stuff.

I remember people coming to our door selling rags. I saw how desperate these people were, how humiliated. As a boy I heard Hitler on the radio. He targeted the underdogs.

I remember, in Philadelphia, watching police brutally beating women strikers at a textile plant. I remember seeing these women tear off their clothes, hoping the police would be embarrassed and back off. The police beat them anyway.

I understood about underdogs early on.

"Conversations," by Marian Christy, *Boston Globe*, May 31, 1989

By the side of the road, men hold signs that read "Will Work For Food," a sight that recalls the darkest days of the Great Depression. But with a significant difference. Hope seems to have been lost to a far greater extent today, though the current recession is far less severe. For the first time in the modern history of industrial society, there is a widespread feeling that things will not be getting better, that there is no way out.

Year 501: The Conquest Continues, page 281

At the Rowe Conference Center, Chomsky informally addressed about 60 people over three days in a question and answer format. This wide-ranging discussion was recorded by Wintonick and Achbar and is available through Alternative Radio in a seven-tape set. For one person's reaction to a weekend with Chomsky, see page 223.

Barsamian

What did they think of your hopping on a train and going up to New York and hanging out at anarchist bookstores on Fourth Avenue, and talking to your working-class relatives there?

Chomsky

They didn't mind because, I mean, I don't want to totally trust my childhood memories, obviously, but—the family was split up. Like a lot of Jewish families, it went in all sorts of directions. There were sectors that were super-Orthodox. There were other sectors that were very radical and very assimilated and working-class intellectuals. And that's the sector that I naturally gravitated towards. It was a very lively intellectual culture. For one thing, it was a working-class culture, had working-class values. Values of solidarity, socialist values, and so on. There was a sense somehow that things were going to get better. I mean, an institutional structure was around, a method of fighting, of organizing, of doing things, which had some hope.

Chomsky

And I also had the advantage of having gone to an experimental progressive school, you know, I went to a Deweyite school which was quite good. Run by a university there. And you know, there was no such thing as competition, there was no such thing as being a good student. I mean, literally, the concept of being a good student didn't even arise until I got to high school—I went to the academic high school—and suddenly discovered I'm a good student. And I hated high school because I had to do all the things you have to do to get into college. But until then it was kind of a free, pretty open system. And I don't know, there were lots of other things—maybe I was just cantankerous.

If I think back about my experience, there's a dark spot there. That's what schooling generally is, I suppose. It's a period of regimentation and control, part of which involves direct indoctrination, providing a system of false beliefs. But more importantly, I think, is the manner and style of preventing and blocking independent and creative thinking and imposing hierarchies and competitiveness and the need to excel, not in the sense of doing as well as you can, but doing better than the next person. Schools vary, of course, but I think that those features are commonplace. I know that they're not necessary, because, for example, the school I went to as a child wasn't like that at all.

I think schools could be run quite differently. That would be very important, but I really don't think that any society based on authoritarian hierarchic institutions would tolerate such a school system for long.

From an interview with James Peck in *The Chomsky Reader*, page 6

[T]he purpose of education... cannot be to control the child's growth to a specific predetermined end, because any such end must be established by arbitrary authoritarian means; rather the purpose of education must be to permit the growing principle of life to take its own individual course, and to facilitate the process by sympathy, encouragement, and challenge, and by developing a rich and differentiated context and environment.

This humanistic conception of education clearly involves some factual assumptions about the intrinsic nature of man, and, in particular, about the centrality to that intrinsic nature of a creative impulse. If these assumptions, when spelled out properly, prove to be incorrect, then these particular conclusions with regard to educational theory and practice will not have been demonstrated. On the other hand, if these assumptions are indeed correct much of contemporary American educational practice is rationally as well as morally questionable.

From "Toward a Humanistic Conception of Education," in *Work Technology and Education: Dissenting Essays in the Intellectual Foundations of American Education*, edited by Walter Feinberg and Henry Rosemont, Jr. (University of Illinois Press, 1975)

John Dewey was a philosopher whose writings on education during the late 19th and early 20th century were groundbreaking. Founder of a philosophical school called Pragmatism, Dewey's thought affected educators throughout the world. It continues to have an impact on education today, notably at the elementary level. His theories are explained in *School and Society* (1899), *The Child and the Curriculum* (1902), and *Democracy and Education* (1916).

Source: *Encyclopedia Britannica*, 1990

Dewey was one of several philosophers and educators who advocated "progressive education" including W. Godwin, A.S. Neil, Paulo Friere, Francisco Ferrer and Ivan Illich.

A. NOAM CHOMSKY
The immortal 110th could not have produced a better scholar than "Chum." In all the various scholastic activities at our school, he was at the fore. Many are the lower classmen who can attest to his outstanding skills as a tutor. His fine organizational ability has proved itself during his term as Chairman of the tutors. Among his other numerous activities are memberships in many clubs. His pleasant disposition also makes him well liked by all who come in contact with him. We are not wrong in predicting a brilliant future in chemical research for "Chum."

"The Odyssey,"
Oak Lane Country Day School, 1945

Jonathan Steinberg

As a historian I have read with interest and amazement your long review article of Gabriel Jackson's *Spanish Civil War,* and that's a very respectable piece of history, and I can appreciate how much work goes into that. When do you find the—

Chomsky

You know when I did that work?

Jonathan Steinberg

When did you do that work?

Chomsky

I did that work in the early 1940s when I was about twelve years old. The first article I wrote was right after the fall of Barcelona in the school newspaper. It was a lament about the rise of fascism in 1939.

I think there may be some confusion about my early interest in the Spanish Civil War. You say that in a BBC interview I said that I did the basic work for that in the school newspaper. Are you sure that is what I said? If so, it would have been incorrect, though maybe things got confused in the context of an interview. The facts, as best I can recall them, are that after the fall of Barcelona I wrote an article in a class newspaper, which would certainly be unresurrectible except by the most extreme chance.* That would have been early 1939. By about 1941, I was beginning to go pretty regularly to New York (trains in those days), and was hanging around second-hand bookstores on Fourth Avenue, the Freie Arbeiter Stimme office [an anarchist publication], etc., picking up literature on all sorts of topics, including the anarchists in the Spanish Civil War. But nothing about that would have been in the 1939 school newspaper article, which was about the ominous expansion of fascism, with the fall of Barcelona being the most recent example. I was intrigued at the time by left libertarian ideas, but only learned more about Spanish anarchism, and obtained relevant documentation, from the early 40s. —NC

September 10, 1991 (letter to Mark Achbar)

*Our research efforts turned up only Hedy Margolies, from Chomsky's first grade class who remembered him as the one with the "squeaky knickers"—because of the sound the fabric of his pants made when he walked.—MA

The article under discussion is "Objectivity and Liberal Scholarship," in *The Chomsky Reader,* pages 83-120 (excerpted from *American Power and the New Mandarins*).

On the telling biases plaguing mainstream history of the Spanish Revolution, see "Objectivity and Liberal Scholarship," in *The Chomsky Reader,* pages 83-120 (excerpted from *American Power and the New Mandarins*).

In Chomsky's opinion: "Burnett Bolloten's *Grand Camouflage* was a major work, invaluable to students of the Spanish Civil War. His new work, *The Spanish Revolution,* is a work of still greater importance."

Cited in *Radical Priorities,* page 244

Chomsky

Actually, I guess one of the people who was the biggest influence in my life was an uncle who had never gone past fourth grade. He had a background in crime, then left-wing politics, and all sorts of things. But he was a hunchback, and as a result he could get a newsstand in New York; they had some program for people with physical disabilities. Some of you are from New York, I guess. You know the 72nd Street kiosk?

Woman

Yes!

Chomsky

You know that? That's where I got my political education. 72nd Street—it's a place where you come out of the subway. Everybody goes towards 72nd Street. And there were two news-stands on that side which were doing fine and there's two newsstands on the back. And nobody comes out the back. And that's where his newsstand was. (*laughter*) But it was a very lively place, he was a very bright guy, it was the thirties, there were a lot of émigrés and so on—a lot of people were hanging around there. And in the evenings, especially, it was sort of a liter-ary political salon. A lot guys hanging around, arguing and talking, and as a kid, like I was eleven, twelve years old, the biggest excitement was to work the newsstand.

KUOW (LISTENER-SUPPORTED RADIO), SEATTLE, WASHINGTON

Ross Reynolds
You write in *Manufacturing Consent* that it's the primary function of the mass media in the United States to mobilize public support for the special interests that dominate the government and the private sector. What are those interests?

Chomsky
Well, if you want to understand the way any society works, ours or any other, the first place to look is who is in a position to make the decisions that determine the way the society functions.

UNIVERSITY OF WYOMING, LARAMIE

Chomsky
Societies differ, but in ours, the major decisions over what happens in the society—decisions over investment and production and distribution and so on—are in the hands of a relatively concentrated network of major corporations and conglomerates and investment firms. They are also the ones who staff the major executive positions in the government. They're the ones who own the media and they're the ones who have to be in a position to make the decisions. They have an overwhelmingly dominant role in the way life happens. You know, what's done in the society. Within the economic system, by law and in principle, they dominate. The control over resources and the need to satisfy their interests imposes very sharp constraints on the political system and on the ideological system.

David Barsamian

When we talk about manufacturing of consent, whose consent is being manufactured?

Chomsky

To start with, there are two different groups, we can get into more detail, but at the first level of approximation, there's two targets for propaganda. One is what's sometimes called the political class. There's maybe twenty percent of the population which is relatively educated, more or less articulate, plays some kind of role in decision-making. They're supposed to sort of participate in social life—either as managers, or cultural managers like teachers and writers and so on. They're supposed to vote, they're supposed to play some role in the way economic and political and cultural life goes on. Now their consent is crucial. So that's one group that has to be deeply indoctrinated. Then there's maybe eighty percent of the population whose main function is to follow orders and not think, and not to pay attention to anything—and they're the ones who usually pay the costs.

As early as 1947 a State Department public relations officer remarked that "smart public relations [has] paid off as it has before and will again." Public opinion "is not moving to the right, it has been moved—cleverly —to the right." "While the rest of the world has moved to the left, has admitted labor into government, has passed liberalized legislation, the United States has become anti-social change, anti-economic change, anti-labor."

Necessary Illusions, page 31

Ron Linville

All right. Professor Chomsky—Noam. You outlined a model—filters that propaganda is sent through, on its way to the public. Can you briefly outline those?

Chomsky

It's basically an institutional analysis of the major media, what we call a propaganda model. We're talking primarily about the national media, those media that sort of set a general agenda that others more or less adhere to, to the extent that they even pay much attention to national or international affairs.

A Propaganda Model

The mass media serve as a system for communicating messages and symbols to the general populace. It is their function to amuse, entertain, and inform, and to inculcate individuals with the values, beliefs and codes of behavior that will integrate them into the institutional structures of the larger society. In a world of concentrated wealth and major conflicts of class interest, to fulfill this role requires systematic propaganda.

In countries where the levers of power are in the hands of a state bureaucracy, the monopolistic control over the media, often supplemented by official censorship, makes it clear that the media serve the ends of the dominant elite. It is much more difficult to see a propaganda system at work where the media are private and formal censorship is absent. This is especially true where the media actively compete, periodically attack and expose corporate and governmental malfeasance, and aggressively portray themselves as spokesmen for free speech and the general community interest. What is not evident (and remains undiscussed in the media) is the limited nature of such critiques, as well as the huge inequality in command of resources, and its effect both on access to a private media system and on its behavior and performance.

A propaganda model focuses on this inequality of wealth and power and its multilevel effects on mass-media interests and choices. It traces the routes by which money and power are able to filter out the news fit to print, marginalize dissent, and allow the government and dominant private interests to get their messages across to the public. The essential ingredients of our propaganda model, or set of news "filters," fall under the following headings:

(1) the size, concentrated ownership, owner wealth, and profit orientation of the dominant mass-media firms;

(2) advertising as the primary income source of the mass media;

(3) the reliance of the media on information provided by the government, business, and "experts" funded and approved by these primary sources and agents of power;

(4) "flak" as a means of disciplining the media; and

(5) "anticommunism" as a national religion and control mechanism.

These elements interact with and reinforce one another. The raw material of news must pass through successive filters, leaving only the cleansed residue fit to print. They fix the premises of discourse and interpretation, and the definition of what is newsworthy in the first place, and they explain the basis and operations of what amount to propaganda campaigns.

From "A Propaganda Model," *Manufacturing Consent*, pages 1-2

For detail describing and supporting the Propaganda Model far beyond what this book and the film could possibly present, read *Manufacturing Consent: The Political Economy of the Mass Media* and *Necessary Illusions: Thought Control in Democratic Societies*. All of Chomsky's and Herman's political writings support the model, but not with specific reference to it, as in these two books.

KUOW (LISTENER-SUPPORTED RADIO), SEATTLE, WASHINGTON

Chomsky
Now the elite media are sort of the agenda-setting media. That means *The New York Times, The Washington Post*, the major television channels, and so on. They set the general framework. Local media more or less adapt to their structure.

ABC TV NEWS, NEW YORK

Man (answers phone)
World News.

Director
It's a **sound bite** that says that there's a beach head—

Copy Editor
I think we may get out in time, we've got a minute for all the time so if that's 35—

News Director
This is the operative sound bite for us—he's ours.

Peter Jennings
I love this sound bite.

News Director
I think, I think, Peter—

Peter Jennings
I think 6:28 is a good one.

News Director
Yeah, but I think, I think, I think six is a good start.

This arcane exchange was constructed from out-takes of footage shot inside ABC News for *The World Is Watching*, an exceptional hour-long documentary that shows the propaganda model in action.

The filmmakers gained unprecedented access to film inside ABC TV News— following a news crew on the ground in Nicaragua, while simultaneously documenting the editorial process in the ABC newsroom in New York City. (See Resource Guide)

See also: *Visualizing Deviance: A Study of News Organization*, by Richard V. Ericson, Patricia M. Baranek and Janet B. L. Chan (University of Toronto Press, 1987)
    Based on extensive field research in print and broadcast news organizations, this study analyzes how journalists make decisions as to what is newsworthy, thereby playing a significant role in determining social values. The authors suggest that in Western societies, the essence of news is its emphasis on social deviance and control. The study shows that the media's definition of deviance includes such behavior as violations of common-sense knowledge and straying from bureaucratic procedures.

Floor Director
Two and a half minutes to air; forty-five
seconds now.

Chomsky (voice over)
And they do this in all sorts of ways: by selection of topics, by distribution of concerns, by
emphasis and framing of issues, by filtering of
information, by bounding of debate within
certain limits. They determine, they select, they
shape, they control, they restrict—in order to
serve the interests of dominant, elite groups in
the society.

Peter Jennings (on air)
There is an unusual amount of attention focused
today on the five nations of Central America.

EXCERPT: "DEMOCRACY'S DIARY" (1948)

Narrator
This is "Democracy's Diary". Here for our
instruction are triumphs and disasters, the
pattern of life's changing fabric. Here is great
journalism. A revelation of the past, a guide to
the present and a clue to the future.

EXCERPT: "PAPER TIGER TV"
(PUBLIC ACCESS TV), NEW YORK (1978)

Chomsky
The New York Times is certainly the most important newspaper in the United States, and one
could argue the most important newspaper in
the world. The New York Times plays an enormous role in shaping the perception of the
current world on the part of the politically
active, educated classes. Also The New York Times
has a special role, and I believe its editors
probably feel that they bear a heavy burden, in
the sense that The New York Times creates history.

**Whether or not you agree with Mr. Chomsky's con-
clusions, his reading of the American scene is persuasive:** that the government is most responsive to the
wishes expressed by the minority of citizens who vote,
which is also one of the principal points made by John
Kenneth Galbraith in his recent book "The Culture of
Contentment." As Mr. Chomsky sees it, his mission is
to wake up and activate the electorate.

From a review of Manufacturing Consent: Noam Chomsky and the Media,
by Vincent Canby, in The New York Times, March 17, 1993

**When the film opened in New York City at Film
Forum,** The New York Times published the review
quoted above, which, in its capsule description, including credits, running time, etc., managed to omit Noam
Chomsky's name from the title of the film so that it
read, in large bold type: "MANUFACTURING CON-
SENT AND THE MEDIA." At 3 a.m. the day of publication, Mark Achbar informed the paper of its Freudian
slip, and the night editor endeavored to correct the
problem in the editions not yet printed. The next day,
after several phone calls from the U.S. distributor,
Zeitgeist Films, the Times printed a correction.

Narrator

What happened years ago may have a bearing on what happens tomorrow. Millions of clippings are preserved in the *Times* library, all indexed for instant use. A priceless archive of events and the men who make them.

Chomsky

That is, history is what appears in *The New York Times* archives; the place where people will go to find out what happened is *The New York Times*. Therefore it's extremely important if history is going to be shaped in an appropriate way, that certain things appear, certain things not appear, certain questions be asked, other questions be ignored, and that issues be framed in a particular fashion. Now in whose interests is history being so shaped? Well, I think that's not very difficult to answer.

THE NEW YORK TIMES

Karl E. Meyer, (editorial writer)

The process by which people make up their minds on this is a much more mysterious process than you would ever guess from reading *Manufacturing Consent*. You know, there's a saying about legislation that legislation is like making sausage, that the less you know about how it's done, the better for your appetite. The same is true of this business. If you were in a conference in which decisions are being made on what to put on page one or whatnot, you would get, I think, the impression that important decisions were being made in a flippant and frivolous way. But in fact, given the pressures of time to try to get things out, you resort to a kind of a short hand. And you have to fill that paper up every day.

"A JOURNAL TO CORRECT THE RECORD"

Lies Of Our Times

Welcome to *Lies Of Our Times*, a monthly magazine of media criticism. "Our Times" are the times we live in; but they are also the words of *The New York Times*, the most cited news medium in the United States, our paper of record. Our "Lies" are more than literal falsehoods; they encompass subjects that have been ignored, hypocrisies, misleading emphases, and hidden premises—the biases which systematically shape reporting.

Our coverage is based on the research of more than one hundred correspondents—not only media critics, but also academics, journalists, literary figures, and activists. We have also solicited the help of a variety of public interest and human rights groups, to advise us of their dealings with the media. We will pay close attention to press releases, stories, proposed columns, and letters that fail to make it into the mass media. We urge you, our readers, to share your media experiences with us. And of course, do not limit yourselves to *The New York Times*.

We can, to be sure, only address a sampling of the universe of media lies and distortions. But, over time, we hope that *Lies Of Our Times* will go a long way toward correcting the record.

Lies Of Our Times, January 1990

A native of Wisconsin, Karl E. Meyer wrote his doctoral thesis at Princeton University on the politics of loyalty. Author of several books, he spent 15 years with *The Washington Post* before moving to *The New York Times*.

Mr. Meyer was asked if the editorial board of the *Times* would agree to an on-the-record discussion with Noam Chomsky but Mr. Meyer declined. The same proposition was put to a senior editor at *Newsweek*. She politely suggested we try *Time*.

In the late 60s chomsky met with *New York Times* editors through Harrison Salisbury and, according to Chomsky, "they just wanted to talk about linguistics, but I managed to sneak in some queries about why they were suppressing the bombing of Laos."

Legislation is like making sausage. The less you know about how it's done, the better for your appetite. The same is true of this business.

Karl E. Meyer

It's curious in kind of a mirror-image way that Professor Chomsky is in total accord with Reed Irvine who at the right-wing end of the spectrum says exactly what he, Chomsky, does, about the insinuating influence of the press, of the big media as quote "agenda-setters," to use one of the great buzz words of the time. And, of course, Reed Irvine sees this as a left-wing conspiracy foisting liberal ideas in both domestic and foreign affairs on the American people. But in both cases I think that the premise really is an insult to the intelligence of the people who consume news.

Flak refers to negative responses to a media statement or program. It may take the form of letters, telegrams, phone calls, petitions, lawsuits, speeches and bills before Congress, and other modes of complaint, threat and punitive action....

The ability to produce flak, and especially flak that is costly and threatening, is related to power....Flak from the powerful can be either direct or indirect. The direct would include letters or phone calls from the White House to Dan Rather or William Paley, or from the FCC to the television networks asking for documents used in putting together a program, or from irate officials of ad agencies or corporate sponsors to media officials asking for reply time or threatening retaliation. The powerful can also work on the media indirectly by complaining to their own constituencies (stockholders, employees) about the media, by generating institutional advertising that does the same and by funding right-wing monitoring or think-tank operations designed to attack the media. They may also fund political campaigns and help put in power conservative politicians who will more directly serve the interests of private power in curbing any deviationism in the media....

Although the flak machines steadily attack the mass media, the media treat them well. They receive respectful attention, and their propagandistic role and links to a larger corporate program are rarely mentioned or analyzed.

Manufacturing Consent, pages 26-28

Media critic Reed John Irvine (1922-) has been the chairman of the board of the conservative organization Accuracy in Media since 1971 and the editor of the AIM report since 1985. He is also a syndicated columnist and radio commentator, as well as the author of *Media Mischief and Misdeeds* (1984) and the co-author (with Cliff Kincaid) of *Profiles of Deception* (1990).

Irvine was an adviser on international finance from 1963 to 1977 and an economist on the board of governors of the Federal Reserve System in Washington from 1951 to 1963.

Source: *Who's Who in America,* 47th edition, 1992

Filter: Flak as a means of disciplining the media

AIM was formed in 1969, and it grew spectacularly in the 1970s. Its annual income rose from $5,000 in 1971 to $1.5 million in the early 1980s, with funding mainly from large corporations and the wealthy heirs and foundations of the corporate system. At least eight separate oil companies were contributors to AIM in the early 1980s, but the wide representation in sponsors from the corporate community is impressive. The function of AIM is to harass the media and put pressure on them to follow the corporate agenda and a hard-line, right-wing foreign policy. It presses the media to join enthusiastically in Red-scare band-wagons and attacks them for alleged deficiencies whenever they fail to toe the line on foreign policy. It conditions the media to expect trouble (and cost increases) for violating right-wing standards of bias....

Manufacturing Consent, pages 27-28

GEORGETOWN UNIVERSITY, WASHINGTON, DC

Chomsky

Now, to eliminate confusion, all of this has nothing to do with liberal or conservative bias. According to the propaganda model, both liberal and conservative wings of the media— whatever those terms are supposed to mean — fall within the same framework of assumptions.

AMERICAN UNIVERSITY, WASHINGTON, DC

Chomsky

In fact, if the system functions well, it ought to have a liberal bias, or at least appear to. Because if it appears to have a liberal bias, that will serve to bound thought even more effectively.

In other words, if the press is *indeed* adversarial and liberal and all these bad things, then how can I go beyond it? They're already so extreme in their opposition to power that to go beyond it would be to take off from the planet. So therefore it must be that the presuppositions that are accepted in the liberal media are sacrosanct—can't go beyond them. And a well-functioning system would in fact have a bias of that kind. The media would then serve to say in effect: Thus far and no further.

In both the 1980 and the 1984 elections, they (the Reagan administration) identified the Democrats as the "party of special interests," and that's supposed to be bad, because we're all against the special interests. But if you look closely and ask who were the special interests, they listed them: women, poor people, workers, young people, old people, ethnic minorities—in fact, the entire population. There was only one group that was not listed among the special interests: corporations. If you'll notice the campaign rhetoric, that was never a special interest, and that's right because in their terms that's the national interest. So if you think it through, the population are the special interests and the corporations are the national interests, and since everyone's in favor of the national interest and against the special interests, you vote for and support someone who's against the population and is working for the corporations.

This is typically the case of the way the framework of thought is consciously manipulated by an effective choice and reshaping of terminology so as to make it difficult to understand what's happening in the world.

Chronicles of Dissent, page 48

A useful rule of thumb is this: If you want to learn something about the propaganda system, have a close look at the critics and their *tacit assumptions*. These typically constitute the doctrines of the state religion.

From "The Manufacture of Consent," reprinted in *The Chomsky Reader*, page 126

The basic presuppositions of discourse [on foreign policy] include:
• U.S. foreign policy is guided by a "yearning for democracy" and general benevolent intent...
• the use of force can only be an exercise in self-defense and...those who try to resist must be aggressors, even in their own lands...
• no country has the right of self-defense against U.S. attack...
• the United States has the natural right to impose its will, by force if necessary and feasible.

These doctrines need not be expressed, apart from periodic odes to our awesome nobility of purpose. Rather, they are simply presupposed, setting the bounds of discourse, and among the properly educated, the bounds of thinkable thought.

Source: *Necessary Illusions*, page 59

The lecture at American University (recorded April 16, 1989) was also broadcast by C-Span, an all-information channel, known for its "gavel-to-gavel" coverage of political events.

Chomsky

We ask what would you expect of those media on just relatively uncontroversial, guided-free market assumptions? And when you look at them you find a number of major factors determining what their products are. These are what we call the filters, so one of them, for example, is ownership. Who owns them?

The major agenda-setting media—after all, what are they? As institutions in the society, what are they? Well, in the first place they are major corporations, in fact huge corporations. Furthermore, they are integrated with and sometimes owned by even larger corporations, conglomerates—so, for example, by Westinghouse and G.E. and so on.

Filter: the size, concentrated ownership, owner wealth, and profit orientation of the dominant mass-media firms

Student
What I wanted to know was how, specifically, the elites control the media— what I mean is—

Chomsky
It's like asking: How do the elites control General Motors? Well, why isn't that a question? I mean, General Motors is an institution of the elites. They don't have to control it. They own it.

Student
Except, I guess, at a certain level, I think, like, I guess, I work with student press. So I know like reporters and stuff.

Chomsky
Elites don't control the student press. But I'll tell you something. You try in the student press to do anything that breaks out of conventions and you're going to have the whole business community around here down your neck, and the university is going to get threatened. I mean, maybe nobody'll pay any attention to you, that's possible. But if you get to the point where they don't stop paying attention to you, the pressures will start coming. Because there are people with power. There are people who own the country, and they're not going to let the country get out of control.

There are people with power. There are people who own the country, and they're not going to let the country get out of control.

Bill Moyers

What do you think about that?

Tom Wolfe (author)

This is the—the old cabal theory that somewhere there's a room with a baize-covered desk and there are a bunch of capitalists sitting around and they're pulling strings. These rooms don't exist. I mean I hate to tell Noam Chomsky this.

Bill Moyers

You don't bel—you don't share that, do you?

Tom Wolfe

I think this is the most absolute rubbish I've ever heard. This is the current fashion in universities. You know, it's patent nonsense and I think it's nothing but a fashion. It's a way that intellectuals have of feeling like a clergy. I mean, there has to be something wrong.

On "Posner & Donahue," an interview/discussion program on CNBC, the preceding clip of Tom Wolfe speaking with Bill Moyers was played for Noam Chomsky, the only guest on the hour-long program on July 22 and 27, 1993:

Chomsky
Well, I actually agree with that comment. I mean, the idea that there would be a high cabal running things in a country like the United States is idiotic. That would say it is like the Soviet Union. It's totally different, which is precisely why I say the exact opposite... Now why does Wolfe or whoever it was, hear this as being a conspiracy? The point is that any analytic commentary on the institutional structure of the country is so threatening to the commissar class they can't even hear the words.

Posner
Is he part of the commissar class, Tom Wolfe?

Chomsky
Of course. Yeah. He can't even hear the words. So if I say there is no high cabal, what he hears is there *is* a high cabal.

Posner
But don't you think the reason he can't hear the words is because he believes profoundly in the things he's been taught? That this is democracy, that there is freedom. It's like a lot of people, like myself, who used to be members of the Communist Party and who profoundly believed in the ideas and very painfully let go...
Don't you think that there are a lot of honest people—Tom Wolfe being one of them —that profoundly believes—

Chomsky
No, I'm not questioning—

Posner
—he's not a member of the commissar class. He just has his ideals.

Chomsky
No, now wait a minute—yeah, but you see, what you are de—

Posner
And you're threatening—you threaten those ideals.

Chomsky
That's right. You see, what you're describing in the Soviet Union is what I would call the commissar class; that is, the people who profoundly believed... all the way up to the editors of *Pravda*. If you did an in-depth analysis with them, how many of them would be total cynics?

Posner
Not many.

Chomsky
Yeah. That's right. Because most of them completely believed. That's the way systems work. In fact, the way belief systems form, really, if you think about it, is—we even know this from our personal lives—you sort of decide to do something for whatever reason. And then you create a system of beliefs that justifies it and says "I was right." Well, the end effect of this is the people who function within a system of power and authority, whether it's an editor of *Pravda* or an op-ed writer for the *Times* or a concentration camp guard...they're usually quite sincere about it. And they have worked up a system of beliefs that says, "Yes, this is just and right and I am completely free and independent." If they couldn't have that system of beliefs, they couldn't continue.... I agree with you when you say it's a tight-closed system of beliefs. It's a kind of fundamentalism, which means you simply cannot hear critical analysis and it's interesting to see what in the United States can't be heard.

Posner & Donahue transcripts (See Resource Guide)
For further discussion of conspiracy theories, please turn to page 131

In North America
there are:

7 major movie studios

and more than:

1,800 daily newspapers
11,000 magazines
11,000 radio stations
2,000 TV stations
2,500 book publishers

23 corporations own and control
over 50% of the business in each medium;
in some cases they have a virtual monopoly

They are:

Bertelsmann
Buena Vista Films (Disney)
Capital Cities/ABC
CBS
Cox Communications
Dow Jones
Gannett
General Electric
Harcourt Brace Jovanovich
Hearst
Ingersoll
International Thomson
Knight Ridder
Media News Group (Singleton)
Newhouse
News Corporation Ltd. (Murdoch)
New York Times
Paramount Communications
Reader's Digest Association
Scripps-Howard
Times Mirror
Time Warner
Tribune Company

Institutional critiques such as we present in [*Manufacturing Consent: The Political Economy of the Mass Media*] are commonly dismissed by establishment commentators as "conspiracy theories," but this is merely an evasion. We do not use any kind of "conspiracy" hypothesis to explain mass-media performance. In fact, our treatment is much closer to a "free market" analysis, with the results largely an outcome of the working of market forces. Most biased choices in the media arise from the preselection of right-thinking people, internalized preconceptions, and the adaptation of personnel to the constraints of ownership, organization, market, and political power.

In most cases... media leaders do similar things because they see the world through the same lenses, are subject to similar constraints and incentives, and thus feature stories or maintain silence together in tacit collective action and leader-follower behavior.

The mass media are not a solid monolith on all issues. Where the powerful are in disagreement, there will be a certain diversity of tactical judgments on how to attain generally shared aims, reflected in media debate.

Manufacturing Consent, page xii

A panel of media critics organized annually by Carl Jensen, which selects the "ten most censored stories" of the year, gave the first prize for 1987 to a study of these issues by Ben Bagdikian, referring of course not to literal state censorship but to media evasion or distortion of critical issues.

Necessary Illusions, page 358

The basis of the statistics on this page can be found in Ben Bagdikian's *The Media Monopoly* (Beacon Press, 4th edition, 1992). We broadened the scope of the U.S. survey to include all of North America.

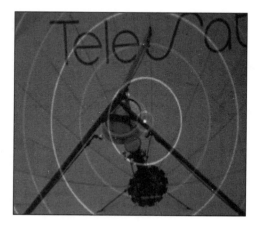

The following was filmed at the University of Washington, in Seattle; KUWR public radio, Laramie, Wyoming; and the auditorium at the University of Wyoming in Laramie. Some parts were re-filmed on the video wall in the Erin Mills shopping center. In the interest of readability, they have been combined.

Chomsky

So what we have in the first place is major corporations which are parts of even bigger conglomerates. Now, like any other corporation, they have a product which they sell to a market. The market is advertisers—that is, other businesses. What keeps the media functioning is not the audience. They make money from their advertisers. And remember, we're talking about the elite media. So they're trying to sell a good product, a product which raises advertising rates. And ask your friends in the advertising industry. That means that they want to adjust their audience to the more elite and affluent audience. That raises advertising rates. So what you have is institutions, corporations, big corporations, that are selling relatively privileged audiences to other businesses.

Well, what point of view would you expect to come out of this? I mean without any further assumptions, what you'd predict is that what comes out is a picture of the world, a perception of the

world, that satisfies the needs and the interests and the perceptions of the sellers, the buyers and the product.

Now there are many other factors that press in the same direction. If people try to enter the system who don't have that point of view they're likely to be excluded somewhere along the way. After all, no institution is going to happily design a mechanism to self-destruct. It's not the way institutions function. So they'll work to exclude or marginalize or eliminate dissenting voices or alternative perspectives and so on because they're dysfunctional, they're dysfunctional to the institution itself.

The influence of advertisers is sometimes far more direct. "Projects unsuitable for corporate sponsorship tend to die on the vine," the London *Economist* (Dec. 5, 1987) observes, noting that "stations have learned to be sympathetic to the most delicate sympathies of corporations." The journal cites the case of public TV station WNET, which "lost its corporate underwriting from Gulf&Western as a result of a documentary called 'Hunger for Profit,' about multinationals buying up huge tracts of land in the third world." These actions "had not been those of a friend," Gulf's chief executive wrote to the station, adding that the documentary was "virulently anti-business, if not anti-American." "Most people believe that WNET would not make the same mistake today," the *Economist* concludes. Nor would others. The warning need only be implicit.

Many other factors induce the media to conform to the requirements of the state-corporate nexus. To confront power is costly and difficult; high standards of evidence and argument are imposed, and critical analysis is naturally not welcomed by those who are in a position to react vigorously and to determine the array of rewards and punishments. Conformity to a "patriotic agenda," in contrast, imposes no such costs. Charges against official enemies barely require substantiation; they are, furthermore, protected from correction, which can be dismissed as apologetics for the criminals or as missing the forest for the trees.

Necessary Illusions, page 8

In 1989, for example, a television special produced by the National Audubon Society was aired without commercials on a cable channel owned by Turner Broadcasting System after eight advertisers pulled out because of pressure from the logging industry. The special, *Ancient Forests: Rage Over Trees*, was deemed too radical by U.S. logging companies. Meanwhile, Domino's Pizza cancelled its advertising on NBC's *Saturday Night Live* because of the show's alleged anti-Christian message.

Unreliable Sources: A Guide to Detecting Bias in News Media, by Martin A. Lee and Norman Solomon (Carol Publishing Group, 1990), page 60

Filter: advertising as the primary income source of the mass-media

Karine Kleinhaus
Do you think that you've escaped the ideological indoctrination of the media and the society that you grew up in?

Chomsky
Do I?

Karine Kleinhaus
Um—hm.

Chomsky
Often not. I mean I—when I look back and think of the things that I haven't done that I should have done, it's—it's very—it's not a pleasant experience.

MIT OFFICE, CAMBRIDGE, MASSACHUSETTS

David Barsamian
So what's the story of young Noam in the schoolyard?

Chomsky
That was a personal thing for me. I don't know why it's of any interest to anyone else. But I do remember it.

David Barsamian
Well you drew certain conclusions from it.

Chomsky
Well, yeah, it had a big influence on me.
I remember when I was about six, I guess, first grade. There was the standard fat kid who everybody made fun of. And I remember in the schoolyard, he was standing right outside the school classroom, and a bunch of kids outside [were] sort of taunting him and so on and one

This Barsamian interview is available on audiotape and in transcript from Alternative Radio. The title is: "The MIT Interviews," February 1990

of the kids actually brought over his older brother, sort of like from third grade, instead of first grade, you know, big kid, and he was going to beat him up or something. And I remember going up to stand next to him feeling somebody ought to help him and I did for a while. And then I got scared and went away and I was very much ashamed of it afterwards, and sort of felt —not going to do that again. That's a feeling that's stuck with me, you should stick with the underdog. And the shame remained—should have stayed there.

"THIRD EAR," BBC-3 (PUBLIC RADIO), LONDON, ENGLAND

Jonathan Steinberg

You were already established, you were a professor at MIT, you'd made a reputation, you had a terrific career ahead of you; you decided to become a political activist. Now, here is a classic case of somebody whom the institution does not seem to have filtered out, I mean you were a good boy up until then, were you? Or you'd always been something of a rebel?

Chomsky

Yeah, pretty much. I had been pretty much outside.

Jonathan Steinberg

You felt isolated. You felt out of sympathy with the prevailing currents of American life, but a lot of people do that. Suddenly, in 1964, you decided: I have to do something about this. What made you do that?

Chomsky

Well, that was a very conscious decision and a very uncomfortable decision because I knew what the consequences would be.

Chomsky first came into prominence as a dissident with the publication of his famous and widely-translated essay "The Responsibility of Intellectuals" in *The New York Review of Books* in the Spring of 1966. A few months later he was a sponsor of the first "Call to Resist Illegitimate Authority," published in *The New York Review of Books* on October 12, which was signed by thousands. This initiative led to the founding of RESIST—a national organization [still alive and resisting, se Resource Guide] focusing on issues of imperialism abroad and repression at home—and figured prominently in the conspiracy trial of Dr. Spock and the other "Boston Five," with Chomsky as an unindicted co-conspirator. On the weekend of October 19-21, 1967, he was a prominent participant in the watershed demonstration that took place at the Pentagon, "a remarkable, unforgettable manifestation of opposition to the war" which "by some estimates involved several hundred people." "The spirit and character of the demonstrations are captured, with marvelous accuracy and perception," by Norman Mailer, his jail cellmate before the day was over, in *The Armies of the Night* (1968), where Chomsky ("by all odds a dedicated teacher," "considered a genius at MIT for his new contributions to linguistics") is insightfully portrayed as "a slim sharp-featured man with an ascetic expression, and an air of gentle but moral integrity." (The first three quotes are from *American Power and the New Mandarins*, page 367; the last three are from page 203 of Norman Mailer's novel ("history as a novel, the novel as history"). No less perceptive is his reference to "the tightly packed conceptual coils of Chomsky's intellections." (See Otero's Introduction to *Language and Politics*.)

The following year "The Responsibility of Intellectuals" was reprinted in Theodore Roszak's *The Dissenting Academy* and soon afterwards in Chomsky's first "non-professional" book, *American Power and the New Mandarins*, a collection of historical and political essays (dedicated "to the brave young men who refuse to serve in a criminal war") which appeared in 1969, arguably the most powerful indictment of the American invasion of Indochina. This book was hailed at the time in *The Nation* as "the first significant work of social and political thought to come out of the Vietnamese catastrophe" and "the first draft of a declaration of intellectual independence." Its immediate success was in part due to his awesome gifts as a debater (both as a writer and as a speaker) and his uncanny ability for surgically dissecting the logical flaws in rival views, not to mention his brilliance. By the end of the decade he had become internationally known and widely admired as an eloquent antiwar spokesman, social critic and activist, sometimes referred to as a hero or a "guru" of the New Left. (By the time the MIT research stoppage of March 4, 1969, took place his presence "was considered so important that he was flown back to MIT each week" from Oxford, where he was giving the Locke Lectures.)

From the Introduction to Volume 3 of
Noam Chomsky: Critical Assessments, by Carlos P. Otero;
on the war in Indochina, see *The Political Economy of Human Rights,
Volume II; The Chomsky Reader*, pages 223-302;
Manufacturing Consent, pages 169-296

Chomsky
The first kind of public, outdoor rally that I spoke to was in October 1965 on the Boston Common. There must have been two hundred or three hundred police—who we were very happy to see I should say, because they were the only thing that kept us from being murdered. The crowd was extremely hostile. It was mostly students who had marched over from the university and they were ready to kill you. And [our] demands were so tame. It was almost embarrassing to say them. You know, we were saying "Stop the bombing of North Vietnam." What about the bombing of South Vietnam which was three times the scale? You couldn't even talk about that.

From "The MIT Interviews," February 1990
Available from Alternative Radio

Chomsky

I was in a very favorable position. I had the kind of work I liked, we had a lively, exciting department, the field was going well, personal life was fine, I was living in a nice place, children growing up. Everything looked perfect. And I knew I was giving it up. At that time, remember, it was not just giving talks. I became involved right away in resistance and I expected to spend years in jail and came very close to it. In fact my wife went back to graduate school in part because we assumed she was going to have to support the children. These were the expectations.

And I recognized that if I returned to these interests, which were the dominant interests of my own youth, life would become very uncomfortable. Because I know in the United States you don't get sent to psychiatric prison and they don't send the death squad after you and so on but there are definite penalties for breaking the rules. So these were real decisions and it simply seemed at that point that it was hopelessly immoral not to.

Those of us who are not under direct attack and who are relatively free to choose a course of action have a responsibility to the victims of American power that we must face with unwavering seriousness. In considering some tactics of protest or resistance, we must ask what its consequences are likely to be for the people of Vietnam or of Guatemala or of Harlem, and what effect it will have on the building of a movement against war and oppression, a movement that will help to create a society in which one can live without fear and without shame. We have to search for ways to persuade vast numbers of Americans to commit themselves to this task, and we must devise ways to convert this commitment into effective action. The goal may seem so remote as to be a fantasy, but for those who are serious, this is the only strategy that can be considered. Persuasion may involve deeds as well as words; it may involve the construction of institutions and social forms, even if only in microcosm, that overcome the competitiveness and the single-minded pursuit of self-interest that proves a mechanism of social control as effective as that of a totalitarian state. But the goal must be to design and construct alternatives to the present ideology and social institutions that are more compelling on intellectual and moral grounds, and that can draw to them masses of Americans who find that these alternatives satisfy their human needs—including the human need to show compassion, to encourage and to assist those who seek to raise themselves from the misery and degradation that our society has helped to impose and now seeks to perpetuate.

American Power and the New Mandarins, pages 397-398

I was on Nixon's enemy list, for example, but it didn't amount to anything...I was up for a five-year jail sentence, which I probably would have had if it hadn't been for the Tet offensive—I was an unindicted co-conspirator. But I wouldn't call that repression, I mean, we were openly violating what's called the law. You can't call that repression. But the point is privileged people are not subject to as much repression. We share the general privilege of society, we share the prerogatives of privilege.

From a talk at McMaster University, Hamilton, Ontario, in 1988

EXCERPT: "THE NEWSREEL" (1968)

Chomsky

I'm Noam Chomsky and I'm on the faculty at MIT and I've been getting more and more heavily involved in anti-war activities for the last few years.

Beginning with writing articles and making speeches and speaking to congressmen and that sort of thing and gradually getting involved more and more directly in resistance activities of various sorts. I've come to the feeling myself that the most effective form of political action that is open to a responsible and concerned citizen at the moment is action that really involves direct resistance, refusal to take part in what I think are war crimes, to raise the domestic cost of American aggression overseas through non-participation, support for those who are refusing to take part. In particular, draft resistance throughout the country.

I think that we can see quite clearly some very, very serious defects and flaws in our society, our level of culture, our institutions. Which are going to have to be corrected by operating outside of the framework that is commonly accepted. I think we're going to have to find new ways of political action.

What justifies an act of civil disobedience is an intolerable evil. After the lesson of Dachau and Auschwitz, no person of conscience can believe that authority must always be obeyed. A line must be drawn somewhere. Beyond that line lies civil disobedience. It may be quite passive.... It may involve symbolic confrontation with the war-making apparatus.... It may go well beyond such symbolic acts...

The limits of civil disobedience must be determined by the extent of the evil that one confronts, and by considerations of tactical efficacy and moral principle. On grounds of principle and tactics, I think that civil disobedience should be entirely nonviolent...

I will not try to describe what everyone knows. To use inadequate words to tell what we have done is an insult to the victims of our violence and our moral cowardice. Yes, civil disobedience is entirely justified in an effort to bring to a close the most disgraceful chapter in American history.

From Chomsky's contribution to an article entitled "Views on disobedience in light of its being increasingly urged by critics of the Vietnam war," in *The New York Times*, November 26, 1967

[I]t ought to be the individual's right to refuse to go along with his community, but the community, not the individual, should specify the consequences. These, in an enlightened society, should vary according to the nature of the insubordination, and according as the insubordination is plausibly rooted in deep philosophical attachments.... The indicated consequence for studied and aggravated civil disobedience seems to me to be obvious: deportation.

From William F. Buckley Jr.'s contribution to the *New York Times* article cited above

[I]nternational law is, in many respects, the instrument of the powerful: it is a creation of states and their representatives. In developing the presently existing body of international law, there was no participation by mass movements of peasants....

[However] there are interesting elements of international law, for example, embedded in the Nuremberg principles and the United Nations Charter, which permit, in fact, I believe, *require* the citizen to act against his own state in ways which the state will falsely regard as criminal. Nevertheless, he's acting legally, because international law also happens to prohibit the threat or use of force in international affairs, except under some very narrow circumstances, of which, for example, the war in Vietnam is not one. This means that in the particular case of the Vietnam war, which interests me most, the American state is acting in a criminal capacity. And the people have the right to stop criminals from committing murder. Just because the criminal happens to call your action illegal when you try to stop him, it doesn't mean it is illegal.

From "Human Nature: Justice versus Power," in *Reflexive Water*, by Fons Elders (Souvenir Press: 1974)

For more on the Nuremberg principles see page 154 of this book
See also: "On the Limits of Civil Disobedience,"
For Reasons of State, pages 285-297

William F. Buckley, Jr.
I rejoice in your disposition to argue the Vietnam question, especially when I recognize what an act of self-control this must involve.

Chomsky
It does—

Buckley
Sure—

Chomsky
—It really does and I think that it's the kind of issue—

Buckley
—And you're doing very well, you're doing very well.

Chomsky
Sometimes I lose my temper. Maybe not tonight.

Buckley
Maybe not tonight, because if you would I'd smash you in the goddamn face.

Chomsky
That's a good reason for not losing my temper—

Buckley
—You say the war is simply an obscenity.
A depraved act by weak and miserable men.

Chomsky
Including all of us. Including myself.

Buckley
Well then—

There may have been a time when American policy in Vietnam was a debatable matter. This time is long past. It is no more debatable than the Italian war in Abyssinia or the Russian suppression of Hungarian freedom. The war is simply an obscenity, a depraved act by weak and miserable men, including all of us, who have allowed it to go on and on with endless fury and destruction—all of us who would have remained silent had stability and order been secured. It is not pleasant to say such words, but candor permits no less.

American Power and the New Mandarins, page 9

For information on ordering "Firing Line" transcripts see Resource Guide.

Chomsky
—Including every—that's the next sentence—

Buckley
—Yeah—

Chomsky
—The same sentence—

Buckley
—Oh, sure, sure, sure. Sure. Because you count everybody in the company of the guilty.

Chomsky
I think that's true in this case—

Buckley
—Uh, ya, but—

Chomsky
—You see, one of the points I was trying—

Buckley
—This is in a sense a theological observation isn't it?—

Chomsky
—No, I don't think so—

Buckley
—Because if someone points out if everyone is guilty of everything then nobody is guilty of anything.

Chomsky
—No, I don't, well, no I don't, I don't believe that. You see, I think, I think the point that I'm trying to make and I think ought to be made is that the real, at least to me, I say this elsewhere in the book [*American Power and the New Mandarins*], the, what seems to me a very, in a sense terrifying aspect of our society, and other societies, is the equanimity and the detachment with which sane, reasonable, sensible people

Anger, outrage, confessions of overwhelming guilt may be good therapy; they can also become a barrier to effective action, which can always be made to seem incommensurable with the enormity of the crime. Nothing is easier than to adopt a new form of self-indulgence, no less debilitating than the old apathy. The danger is substantial. It is hardly a novel insight that confession of guilt can be institutionalized as a technique for evading what must be done. It is even possible to achieve a feeling of satisfaction by contemplating one's evil nature. No less insidious is the cry for "revolution," at a time when not even the germs of new institutions exist, let alone the moral and political consciousness that could lead to a basic modification of social life. If there will be a "revolution" in America today, it will no doubt be a move towards some variety of fascism. We must guard against the kind of revolutionary rhetoric that would have had Karl Marx burn down the British Museum because it was merely a part of a repressive society. It would be criminal to overlook the serious flaws and inadequacies in our institutions, or to fail to ultiize the substantial degree of freedom that most of us enjoy, within the framework of these flawed institutions, to modify them or even replace them by a better social order.

American Power and the New Mandarins, pages 17-18

One who pays some attention to history will not be surprised if those who cry most loudly that we must smash and destroy are later found among the administrators of some new system of repression.

can observe such events. I think that's more terrifying than the occasional Hitler or LeMay or other that crops up. These people would not be able to operate were it not for this apathy and equanimity. And therefore I think that it's in some sense the sane and reasonable and tolerant people who should—who share a very serious burden of guilt that they very easily throw on the shoulders of others who seem more extreme and more violent.

With respect to the responsibility of intellectuals, there are still other, equally disturbing questions. Intellectuals are in a position to expose the lies of governments, to analyze actions according to their causes and motives and often hidden intentions. In the Western world at least, they have the power that comes from political liberty, from access to information and freedom of expression. For a privileged minority, Western democracy provides the leisure, the facilities, and the training to seek the truth lying hidden behind the veil of distortion and misrepresentation, ideology, and class interest through which the events of current history are presented to us. The responsibilities of intellectuals then are much deeper than what [Dwight] Macdonald calls the "responsibility of peoples," given the unique privileges that intellectuals enjoy.... It is the responsibility of intellectuals to speak the truth and to expose lies.

From "The Responsibility of Intellectuals," in *The Chomsky Reader*, page 60 (reprinted from *American Power and the New Mandarins*)

EXCERPT: "PULSE NEWS," CFCF TV,
MONTRÉAL, CANADA (JUNE 10, 1991)

Lynn Desjardins
Twelve million pounds of confetti dropped into
New York City's so-called "Canyon of Heroes."
Americans were officially welcoming the troops
home from the Persian Gulf War.

TICKERTAPE PARADE, NEW YORK CITY

Man on Right
So it worked out really great for us. I mean, it
just goes to show that we're a mighty nation
and we'll be there no matter what comes along;
I mean, it's the strongest country in the world
and you've got to be glad to live there.

Katherine Asals (sound recordist and assistant editor)
So tell me what you feel about the media
coverage of the war?

Man on Left
I guess it was good. It got to be a bit much after
a while, but I guess it was good to know everything. You know, in the case of Vietnam you
didn't really know a lot that was going on, but
here you were pretty much up to the moment
on everything, so I guess it was good to be
informed.

**[I]n retrospect, it is not clear what positive
benefits the Gulf war produced.** Kuwait
has been returned to its previous form of
authoritarian government without significant
reforms and with billions of dollars worth of
damage done to the country. Iraq's economic infrastructure has been ruined and
the Iraqi death count has been estimated as
high as 243,000 as a result of the war. (The
U.S. policy of "bomb now, die later" produced for the Iraqi people epidemics of
cholera, typhoid, and other deadly diseases
and the lack of medicine and medical
equipment to deal with even minor problems. Iraqi children were dying of starvation
and disease, and Bush continued to insist
on an economic boycott of Iraq. p. 420.)
The Kurds and other groups seeking to
overthrow Saddam Hussein were betrayed
by the United States, and Iraq continues to
suffer under Baath Party dictatorship.
Millions of people in the region became
refugees during the war and were forced to
leave their jobs for uncertain futures. The
ecology of the area was ravaged by the war,
which threatened devastation from the oil
well fires that took months to put out, and
the Persian Gulf has been heavily polluted
from oil spills. The Middle East is more
politically unstable than ever, and the Gulf
war failed to solve its regional problems,
creating new divisions and tensions.

The Persian Gulf TV War, by Doug Kellner (Westview Press, 1992), page 1

Chomsky's assessment of *The Persian
Gulf TV War:* "Kellner's meticulous analysis
of the reality and image of the Gulf war provides a picture of our society and our institutions that cannot be ignored by those who
care about their country. It is a powerful and
impressive study, rich in its implications."

See also: Chomsky's "What We Say Goes," in *Collateral Damage,* edited
by Cynthia Peters (South End Press, 1992) pages 49-92,
and *Chronicles of Dissent*, chapters 12,13,14,15

Audiotape and transcript "Reflections on the Gulf War" May 21, 1991,
available from Alternative Radio

Ed Turner (executive VP of CNN)

For the first time, because of technology, we had the ability to be live from many locations around the globe. And because of the format, an all-news network, we can spend whatever time is necessary to bring the viewer the complete context of that day's portion of a story. And by context, I mean the institutional memory that is critical to understand why and how. And that's those who are analysts and do commentary, and those who can explain.

Voice

Slug that last piece, ITN—Israel Post War.

Ed Turner

David Brinkley once said that you step in front of the camera and you get out of news business and into show business. But nonetheless that should not in any way subtract or obscure the need for the basic standards of good journalism.

Producer 1

Hang tight, let me give you a lead for Salinger right now. Okay?—ah, President Bush and Prime Minister Major have, uh, have closed, or have almost rejected the Soviet peace talk—peace efforts. Okay. In Saudi Arabia the door is being left open. Rick Salinger is standing by live in Riyadh with the latest.

Producer 2

—All but closed—

Producer 1

Yeah. All but closed. Right.

Ed Turner

Accuracy, speed, a fair approach, an honesty and integrity within the reporter to try and bring the truth. Whatever the truth may be.

From the beginning of the U.S. deployment, the press was prohibited from having direct access to the troops. Journalists were instead organized by the military into pools that were taken to sites selected by the military itself, and then reporters were allowed only to interview troops with their military "minders" present.... Press and video coverage were also subject to censorship, so that, in effect, the military tightly controlled press coverage of the U.S. military deployment in the Gulf and then the action in the Gulf war.

Reporters without escort who ventured out on their own were detained or told to leave upon arrival at bases and some were even roughed up. During the war, credentials were lifted if reporters broke the rules of the pool system... Reporters were not allowed to forward their material until it had been subjected to "security review," in other words, military censorship.

Such control of press coverage was unprecedented in the history of U.S. warfare. Historically, journalists have been allowed direct access to combat troops and sites, and frontline reporting was distinguished during World War II and Vietnam. The military organized the pool system, however, because they perceived that reporting had been too critical in Vietnam, and they blamed the press for helping erode public support for the war....

Consequently, although there was a pointed debate among the U.S. troops in Saudi Arabia concerning the wisdom of their deployment, the U.S. public was not allowed to hear this debate. Any information that might have raised questions concerning Bush administration policy was considered off limits. Reporters critical of the deployment were not given access to top military brass or allowed to join the pools, while compliant reporters were rewarded with pool assignments and interviews.

The Persian Gulf TV War, by Doug Kellner (Westview Press, 1992), pages 80-83

Media polls have proclaimed, in self-congratulatory fashion, that about 70 percent of the public thought the media did a good job of reporting the war. But if one measures the media by how well they inform the public, a recent study indicates they failed dismally.

The study, conducted by the University of Massachusetts' Center for Studies in Communication, found that the more people watched TV during the Gulf crisis, the less they knew about the underlying issues, and the more likely they were to support the war.

When the research team tested public knowledge of basic facts about the region, U.S. policy and events leading up to the war, they discovered that "the most striking gaps in people's knowledge involved information that might reflect badly upon the Administration's policy"...

While most respondents had difficulty answering questions about the Middle East and U.S. foreign policy, 81 percent of the sample could identify the missile used to shoot down the Iraqi Scuds as the Patriot. That media consumers know facts relating to successful U.S. weapons but not inconsistencies in U.S. foreign policy, the researchers argued, "suggests that the public are not generally ignorant—rather, they are selectively misinformed."

The study concludes that "the Pentagon or the Bush Administration cannot be blamed for only presenting those facts that lend support for their case—it isn't their job, after all, to provide the public with a balanced view. Culpability for this rests clearly on the shoulders of the news media, particularly television, who have a duty to present the public with all the relevant facts."

Extra!, Special Issue/Volume 4, No. 3, May 1991

For a report on the study, conducted by Sut Jhally, Justin Lewis and Michael Morgan, see Resource Guide

Proceeding with the logic of the situation, the first approach to reversing the aggression, namely the UN approach, is sanctions; that could have an effect, but the effect could be slow and over time. On the other hand, the invasion force can't be sustained over time. The bigger it gets, the harder it is to keep there. It's very hard to keep a major military force, an invasion force, in place in the Saudi desert. It's going to be impossible after a couple of months. That means that there are two choices coming up: either you withdraw them or you use them. Withdrawal is politically virtually impossible because of the high moral principles and posturing with which all of this is presented and the tremendous cosmic significance of driving Saddam Hussein out of Kuwait by force with which the whole story is invested. Given that kind of high pinnacle, it's going to be impossible to withdraw. That means the forces will be used, which means we'll have a war. That's the logic of the situation, and it's been pretty clear since early August.

Noam Chomsky on U.S. Gulf Policy, Harvard University, November 19, 1990
(*Open Magazine* Pamphlet Series), page 1

Proponents of a military solution to the Kuwait crisis have asserted repeatedly that there is no proof that sanctions will work. Only war, they say, guarantees Iraq will get out of Kuwait. But there is abundant proof that sanctions can work—and there is considerable evidence they can do so within the next 12 months.

In an extensive analysis of 115 cases beginning with the First World War, we found that economic sanctions helped achieve foreign-policy goals in 34 per cent of the episodes. The odds of success in the Iraqi case are far better, because of the unprecedented co-operation among the sanctioning countries and the comprehensiveness of the embargo.

To test our conclusions more formally, we drew on work by San Ling Lam, an economist at Harvard University, to construct a computer model that analyzes the factors that contribute to successful sanctions.

Since the estimated cost to Iraq—48 per cent of its gross national product—is so far beyond that observed in other cases, the initial results placed the probability of success at nearly 100 per cent. Even when the model was adjusted to account for Saddam Hussein's exceptionally tyrannical control and the estimated cost is, say, halved to 24 per cent of GNP, the probability of success remains above 85 per cent.

In 12 other cases where the model projected an 80 per cent or higher probability of success, sanctions did in fact succeed. On average, in those cases, the potential loss of trade for the target countries was only 36 per cent, and the

average cost to the target was a meager 3.8 per cent of GNP.

By contrast, virtually 100 per cent of Iraq's trade and financial relations are subject to sanctions. The resulting loss of 48 per cent of Iraq's GNP is 20 times the average economic impact in other successful episodes and three times the previous highest cost imposed on any target country.

Critics argue that sanctions are useless against a ruthless dictator who doesn't care what price his people must pay. Yet sanctions have been employed successfully against dictators of all stripes, sometimes convincing them to change policies and sometimes driving them from power....

Successful sanctions against Iraq, a country with nowhere near the resources of the Soviet Union, would provide a far more attractive model for future global co-operation in redressing the misdeeds of smaller nations. But that model is being discarded before being given a real chance. How often is the United States willing to go it alone, and risk military confrontation to face down regional tyrants?

From "Sanctions Will Work—and Soon," by Gary C. Hufbauer and Kimberly A. Elliott, *Globe and Mail*, January 15, 1991, page A15

Gary C. Hufbauer and Kimberly A. Elliott are co-authors, with Jeffrey J. Schott, of *Economic Sanctions Reconsidered* (Institute for International Economics, Washington)

Ed Turner, Executive VP of CNN, is not related to Ted Turner, President and Chairman of the Board of the Turner Broadcasting System, the parent company of CNN

MIT, CAMBRIDGE, MASSACHUSETTS

Chomsky

Now, going to war is a serious business. In a totalitarian society, the dictator just says we're going to war and everybody marches.

EXCERPT: "THE WAR FOR MEN'S MINDS" FROM THE NATIONAL FILM BOARD OF CANADA (NFB–1943)

Narrator (Lorne Greene)

And with this weapon of human brotherhood in our hands we are seeing the war for men's minds not as a battle of truth against lies but as a lasting alliance pledged in faith with all those millions driving forward to create the true new order. The world order of the people first. The people before all.

MIT, CAMBRIDGE, MASSACHUSETTS

Chomsky

In a democratic society, the theory is that if the political leadership is committed to war, they present reasons and they've got a very heavy burden of proof to meet because a war is a very catastrophic affair, as this one proved to be. The role of the media at that point is to allow—is to present the relevant background. For example, the possibilities of peaceful settlement, such as they may be, have to be presented, and then to present—to offer a forum, in fact encourage a forum of debate over this very dread decision to go to war and in this case kill hundreds of thousands of people and leave two countries wrecked and so on. That never happened. There was never, well, you know, when I say "never" I mean ninety-nine point nine percent of the discussion excluded the option of a peaceful settlement.

Usually missing from the news was analysis from a perspective critical of U.S. policy. The media's rule of thumb seemed to be that to support the war was to be objective, while to be anti-war was to carry a bias...

A survey conducted by FAIR of the sources on the ABC, CBS and NBC nightly news found that of 878 on-air sources, only one was a representative of a national peace organization—Bill Monning of Physicians Against Nuclear War. By contrast, seven players from the Super Bowl were brought on to comment on the war.

When anti-war voices were heard, it was very rarely as in-studio guests partaking in substantive discussions. Rather, typical coverage of the peace movement resembled nature footage—outdoors, in the demonstrators' "natural habitat"...

Relying, as network TV did, on random protesters to present a movement's views is to deny that movement its most articulate and knowledgeable spokespeople.

Extra!, Special Issue/Volume 4, No. 3, May 1991

Throughout [the rule of Saddam Hussein] the Iraqi democratic opposition have been in exile... [T]hey're there, and they're perfectly respectable, bankers in London, architects, quite articulate. They have always been excluded from the media. You can understand why. They have always been opposed to U.S. policy. In fact, their positions have always been pretty much those of the peace movement. Prior to August 1990 they were opposed to George Bush's support for Saddam Hussein. They were rebuffed by Washington. They refused to talk to them when they came here to request support for calls for parliamentary democracy in Iraq. They got cut out of the media. From August thorough February, they were opposed to the buildup for war. They didn't want to see their country destroyed. They were calling for a political settlement, and even calling for withdrawal of troops from the region. You could read their reports in the German press, the British press, or in *Z Magazine*. But they were totally blanked out of the American press. I don't know if there was a word about them, in fact. If there was, I couldn't find it.

Chronicles of Dissent, page 338

Transcripts of Chomsky's talks on the "The New World Order," "US Gulf Policy" and "Media Control: The Spectacular Achievements of Propaganda," distributed through the *Open Magazine* Pamphlet Series, have sold over 40,000 copies. An anthology of 13 pamphlets, by Chomsky and others, with an introduction by Howard Zinn, is now in print under the title *Open Fire: An Anthology.* (New Press, 1993) See Resource Guide

EXCERPT: "THE WAR FOR MEN'S MINDS"
(NFB–1943)

Narrator *(Lorne Greene)*
Washington's Office of War Information holds
one of the most vital and constructive tasks of
this war.

Elmer Davis
This is a people's war and to win it the people
ought to know as much about it as they can.
This office will do its best to tell the truth and
nothing but the truth, both at home and abroad.

Narrator *(Lorne Greene)*
First weapon in this world wide strategy of truth
is the great machine of information represented
by the free press, with its powers of molding
public thought and leading public action, with
all its life-lines for the exchange of new ideas
between fighting nations spread across the
earth.

Chomsky

I mean, every time George Bush would appear and say, "There will be no negotiations" there would be a hundred editorials the next day lauding him for going the last mile for diplomacy. If he said you can't reward an aggressor, instead of cracking up in ridicule the way people did in the civilized sectors of the world —like the whole third world—the media said, "a man of fantastic principle," you know, the invader of Panama, the only head of state who stands condemned for aggression in the world. The guy was head of the CIA during the Timor aggression, you know, he says aggression can't be rewarded, the media just applauded.

The reference is to the World Court hearing that condemned the Reagan-Bush administration for "unlawful use of force." They did not use the term "aggression"—not a very precise term in international law.—NC

The U.S. invasion of Panama is a historic event in one respect. In a departure from routine, it was not justified as a response to an imminent Soviet threat....

When the White House decided that its friend Noriega was getting too big for his britches and had to go, the media took their cue and launched a campaign to convert him into the most nefarious demon since Attila the Hun...

Noriega's career fits a standard pattern. Typically, the thugs and gangsters whom the U.S. backs reach a point in their careers when they become too independent and too grasping, outliving their usefulness. Instead of just robbing the poor and safeguarding the business climate, they begin to interfere with Washington's natural allies, the local business elite and oligarchy, or even U.S. interests directly. At that point, Washington begins to vacillate; we hear of human rights violations that were cheerfully ignored in the past, and sometimes the U.S. government acts to remove them...

Why did Americans hate Noriega in 1989, but not in 1985? Why is it necessary to overthrow him now, but not then?...

The reasons for the invasion were not difficult to discern. Manuel Noriega had been working happily with U.S. intelligence since the 1950s... By 1985-6, however, the U.S. was beginning to reassess his role and finally decided to remove him....

One black mark against Noriega was his support of the Contadora peace process for Central America, to which the U.S. was strongly opposed. His commitment to the war in Nicaragua was in question, and, when the Iran-Contra affair broke, his usefulness was at an end. On New Year's Day 1990, administration of the Panama Canal was to pass largely into Panamanian hands, and a few

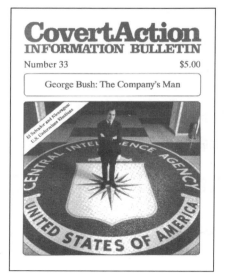

CovertAction
INFORMATION BULLETIN
Number 33 $5.00

George Bush: The Company's Man

years later the rest was to follow, according to the Canal Treaty.... Clearly, traditional U.S. clients had to be restored to power, and there was not much time to spare.

The CODEHUCA (Central American Human Rights Commission) report alleges that "the U.S. Army used highly sophisticated weapons—some for the first time in combat —against unarmed civilian populations"...

F-117A stealth fighters were used in combat for the first time. *Aviation Week and Space Technology* [suggested that] "By demonstrating the F-117A's capability to operate in low-intensity conflicts, as well as its intended mission to attack heavily defended Soviet targets, the operation can be used by the Air Force to justify the huge investment made in stealth technology" to "an increasingly skeptical Congress."

From *Deterring Democracy*, pages 144-166
See also: *Chronicles of Dissent*, chapters 10,11,12

EXCERPT: "THE WAR FOR MEN'S MINDS"
(NFB–1943)

Narrator (Lorne Greene)

The motion picture industry with its worldwide organization of newsreel camera crews—invaluable for bringing into vivid focus the background drama and perspectives of the war. Mobilized too in this all-out struggle for men's minds are the radio networks with all their experience in the swift reporting of great occasion and event. From every strategic center and frontline stronghold their reporters are sending back the lessons of new tactics, new ways of war.

MIT, CAMBRIDGE, MASSACHUSETTS

Chomsky

And the result was it's a media war. I mean there's tremendous fakery all along the line. The UN is finally living up to its mission, you know, "wondrous sea change," *The New York Times* told us. The only wondrous sea change was that for once the United States didn't veto a Security Council resolution against aggression.

People don't want a war. Unless you have to have one. And they would have known that you don't have to have one. Well, the media kept people from knowing that—and that means we went to war very much in the manner of a totalitarian state. Thanks to the media subservience. That's the big story, in my view.

The US is far in the lead since 1970 in vetoing Security Council resolutions and rejecting General Assembly resolutions on all relevant issues. In second place, well behind, is Britain, primarily in connection with its support for the racist regimes of southern Africa. The grim-faced ambassadors casting vetoes had good English accents, while the USSR was regularly voting with the overwhelming majority. The US isolation would, in truth, have been more severe, were it not for the fact that its enormous power kept major issues from the UN agenda. The Soviet invasion of Afghanistan was bitterly and repeatedly censured, but the UN was never willing to take on the US war against Indochina.

The UN session just preceding the "wondrous sea change" (winter 1990) can serve to illustrate. Three Security Council resolutions were vetoed: a condemnation of the US attack on the Nicaraguan Embassy in Panama (US veto, Britain abstained); of the US invasion of Panama (US, UK, France against); of Israeli abuses in the occupied territories (US veto). There were two General Assembly resolutions calling on all states to observe international law—one condemning the US support for the Contra army, the other the illegal embargo against Nicaragua. Each passed with two negative votes: the US and Israel. A resolution opposing acquisition of territory by force passed 151-3 (US, Israel, Dominica). The resolution once again called for a diplomatic settlement of the Arab-Israeli conflict with recognized borders and security guarantees, incorporating the wording of UN Resolution 242, with self-determination for the Palestinians, implicitly calling for a two-state settlement. The US has been barring such a settlement —virtually alone, as the most recent vote indicates— since its January 1976 veto of this proposal, advanced by Syria, Jordan, and Egypt with the backing of the PLO. The US has repeatedly vetoed Security Council resolutions and blocked General Assembly resolutions and other UN initiatives on a whole range of issues, including aggression, annexation, human rights abuses, disarmament, adherence to international law, terrorism, and others.

Deterring Democracy, page 199

For more on the role of the UN, and voting patterns at the UN, see: "UN=US" and "Riding Moynihan's Hobby Horse," in *Letters From Lexington: Reflections on Propaganda*, pages 51-66; *The New World Order*, in the *Open Magazine* Pamphlet Series

[P]erhaps the most outrageous propaganda ploy by the Bush administration and the Kuwaiti government concerned fallacious stories about Iraqi atrocities in Kuwait. In October 1990, a tearful teenage girl testified to the House Human Rights Caucus that she had witnessed Iraqi soldiers remove fifteen babies from incubators and had seen them left to die on the floor of the hospital. The girl's identity was not revealed, supposedly to protect her family from reprisals. This baby-killing story helped mobilize support for U.S. military action ... Bush mentioned the story six times in one month...In a January 6, 1992, Op-Ed piece in *The New York Times*, however, John MacArthur, the publisher of *Harper's* magazine, revealed that the unidentified congressional witness was the daughter of the Kuwaiti ambassador to the United States. The girl had been brought to testify to Congress by the PR firm Hill and Knowlton, who had coached her and helped organize the Congressional Human Rights hearings. In addition, Craig Fuller, Bush's former chief of staff when he was vice-president and a Bush loyalist, was president of Hill and Knowlton and was involved with the PR campaign... Thus it is likely that together the U.S. and Kuwaiti governments developed a propaganda campaign to manipulate the American people into accepting the Gulf war. According to reports, the Kuwaiti account was one of the most expensive PR campaigns in history...it was estimated that the total account was $11 million...

On January 17, 1992, ABC's "20/20" disclosed that a "doctor" who testified that he had "buried fourteen newborn babies that had been taken from their incubators by the soldiers" was also lying. The doctor was a dentist who later admitted that he had never examined the babies and had no way of knowing how they died... (the incubators were found in Kuwaiti hospitals after the war and medical personnel there denied that the Iraqis had killed premature babies)... ABC also disclosed that Hill and Knowlton had commissioned a "focus group" survey, which gathers groups of people together to find out what stirs or angers them. The focus group responded strongly to the Iraqi baby atrocity stories and so Hill and Knowlton featured this in their PR campaigns for the Free Kuwait group...

At the time of the Hill and Knowlton Kuwaiti propaganda campaign, the majority of the public in the United States was against a military intervention in the Middle East and Congress was also tending against the military option. Hill and Knowlton's campaign, however, helped turn things around, mobilizing public opinion in favor of the use of military force against Iraq.

This baby atrocity story was, therefore, a classic propaganda campaign to manufacture consent for the Bush administration policies. It was part of an elaborate web of deception, disinformation and Big Lies to sell the war to the public.

The Persian Gulf TV War, by Doug Kellner (Westview Press, 1992), pages 67-71

Americanism. Who can be against that? Or harmony. Who can be against that? Or, as in the Persian Gulf War, "Support our troops." Who can be against that? Or yellow ribbons. Who can be against that? Anything that's totally vacuous. In fact, what does it mean if somebody asks you, Do you support the people in Iowa? Can you say, Yes, I support them, or No, I don't support them? It doesn't mean anything. That's the point. The point of public relations slogans like 'Support our troops' is that they don't mean anything. They mean as much as whether you support the people in Iowa. Of course, there was an issue. The issue was, Do you support our policy? But you don't want people to think about the issue. That's the whole point of good propaganda. You want to create a slogan that nobody's going to be against, and everybody's going to be for. Nobody knows what it means, because it doesn't mean anything. Its crucial value is that it diverts your attention from a question that *does* mean something: Do you support our policy? That's the one you're not allowed to talk about.

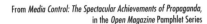

From *Media Control: The Spectacular Achievements of Propaganda*, in the *Open Magazine* Pamphlet Series

Also available on the audiotape, "The Gulf War: Media and Propaganda," March 17, 1991, from Alternative Radio

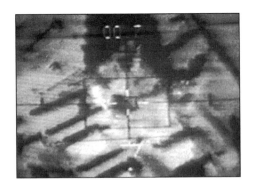

KUWR (PUBLIC RADIO), LARAMIE, WYOMING

Chomsky

Now, remember, I'm not now talking about a small radio station in Laramie. I'm talking about the national, agenda-setting media. If you're on a radio news show in Laramie, chances are very strong that you pick up what was in *The [New York] Times* that morning and you decide that's the news. [*Interviewer Marci Randall Miller nods in agreement*] In fact, if you follow the AP wires you find that in the afternoon they send across tomorrow's front page of *The New York Times*. That's so that everybody knows what the news is. And the perceptions and the perspectives and so on are sort of transmitted down, not to the precise detail, but the general picture is pretty much transmitted elsewhere.

We asked the Montreal *Gazette* if they availed themselves of this service, and, sure enough, they received daily the next day's front page of *The New York Times*. The day we checked, the communiqué began like this:

```
Top of story:-
!Note: S:A:9775:TAF-
Z:U:V:DC31:BC:BC-NYT-FRONTPAGE
BC-NYT-FRONTPAGE<
Here are the stories New York
Times editors are planning for
Friday, Sept. 27, Page 1.  The
N.Y.Times News Service Night
Supervisor is Pat Ryan (212-556-
1927).

TOP
Lead story:
IRAQ-MILITARY (United Nations)
The administration continues dis-
cussions with Saudi leaders about
reinforcing U.S. forces....
```

EXCERPT: "ON THE SPOT" (NFB–1954)

Lloyd Bochner
The foreign news comes here to the foreign news desk. The editor is Bob Hanley. Bob, I suppose you get far more foreign news than you can possibly use in the paper.

Bob Hanley
Yes, we do we get a great deal more than we can accommodate in a day.

Lloyd Bochner
And your job is to weed it out, I suppose.

Bob Hanley
This is the "selection center," as it were. And when I have selected it I pass it across the desk to one or the other of these sub-editors. It comes back to me, and on this chart I design the page—that is, page one and page two.

Lloyd Bochner
Fine, Bob, thank you very much.

MEDIA COURTHOUSE, MEDIA, PENNSYLVANIA

Man
So what do you want to make a film about Media for?

Peter Wintonick
Well—

Man
Such a nice, quiet town.

Peter Wintonick
It's a beautiful town. Well, we're making a film about the mass media so we thought what a good place to come.

Man
You wanted to know where they got the name.

MEDIA BUSINESS AUTHORITY OFFICE

Peter Wintonick
So maybe you could start by introducing yourself.

Bodhan Senkow
Yes, I'm Bodhan Senkow. I'm the Main Street manager and the executive director of the Media Business Authority, and we are in Media, Delaware County, in the southeastern part of Pennsylvania. Media is called "Everybody's Home Town." The motto was developed as a way to promote the community; we're a very high promotion-conscious community. When you walk through Media, you'll be treated very well. And you find that people have taken the idea of being everybody's home town to heart.

We were driving back from Washington, DC, and by chance noticed Media on the map. It was on topic, and on the way. How could we pass it up? We did want to include the voices of some "people on the street" and found several residents with insightful and plainspoken views on the media.—MA

MEDIA TRAIN STATION

Peter Wintonick
The local paper, the *Talk of the Town*—

Woman
The *Town Talk*.

Peter Wintonick
Do you read that?

Woman
Yes, I read the *Town Talk*, yes.

Peter Wintonick
What do you think the difference is between *The Wall Street Journal* and the *Town Talk*?

Woman
Oh—well—I mean the *Town Talk* is completely local news and—it's fun—it's nice to read, it's interesting. You read about your neighbors and see what's going on in the school district and things like that.

TOWN TALK EXECUTIVE OFFICE

Ed Berman (publisher, Town Talk)
We're in business to make bucks just like the big daily newspapers and just like the big radio stations and we do quite well. And rightfully so, because we work very hard at it. I just want to show you a copy of the paper here, the way it is this week. It's plastic-wrapped on all four sides, weatherproof, and hung on everybody's front door. And many, many times you'll find that this paper runs well over a hundred pages a week. This particular edition—you have to remember there are five editions—this happens to be the Central Delaware County edition, which is the edition that covers Media, Pennsylvania.

Ed Berman

What you see here now is the advertising and composition department. Say hello, guys, will ya?

Three employees

Hi, Hi there!

Ed Berman

What we're doing now is we're putting red dots, green dots and yellow dots up on the map wherever there is a store. Now, the red dots are the stores that don't advertise with us at all. The green dots are the ones that advertise with us every week. And the yellow dots are the ones that would run sporadically. Now we have computer print-outs of every one of these stores and what we do is take the print-outs of all the red dots, which are the bad guys, and what our idea is, is to turn these red dots into yellow dots and turn the yellow dots into green dots and eventually make them all green dots so a hundred percent of the stores and a hundred percent of the merchants and service people advertise in our newspaper every week. That way we won't have any more red dots. I guess there'll always be a few red dots but I have high hopes that there will be a lot more green ones than red ones when we're finished.

Mr. Berman also explained that *Town Talk* has an ad-to-news ratio of 65% : 35%, which would make the ad department at *The New York Times* envious. See next page for more on the troubled *Times*.

NEW YORK TIMES BUILDING

Jim Morgan addresses the camera

Jim Morgan

Hi. I'm Jim Morgan. I'm with the corporate relations department of *The New York Times* and I'm here to take you on a tour of *The New York Times*, so—let's begin.

Morgan motions for the crew to follow him as he enters The New York Times *through a set of revolving doors.*
Screen goes BLACK.

While the paper's daily circulation for 1992 was an all-time high of 1,181,500 copies, advertising lineage has fallen about forty percent since 1987. Five years ago, the *Times* ran a hundred and twenty-three million lines of advertising; last year's total was only seventy-seven million lines, though the decline has now slowed. Partly because of a weakened local economy and partly because of special accounting changes and charges, *The New York Times* Company reported a net loss of 44.7 million dollars in 1992.

Today, the company owns five network-affiliated TV stations, thirty-one regional newspapers, the Boston *Globe* [for which it paid one billion one hundred million dollars] an AM and an FM radio station, twenty magazines, two wholesale newspaper distributors, a forest-products division, and an information-services group.

From an article on the *Times* and its publisher, Arthur Sulzberger, Jr., entitled "Opening up the Times," by Ken Auletta, in *The New Yorker*, June 28, 1992

Dungeon sound effects. Echoing, dripping water, clanging metal door etc.

Jim Morgan
So, they're just taking audio in here. Yeah. They're taking audio in here. That's all. Audio. No cameras. No stills. We went over this quite thoroughly, they don't even take a still camera in here.

Mark Achbar
What department are we in?

Jim Morgan
We're in the composing room. This is where the pages are composed. This is the typographical area.

Mark Achbar

What's the ratio of news to advertising?

Jim Morgan

Sixty percent ads. This might seem big but it is average; in fact, below average. Our sixty percent might include on some days maybe twenty pages of classified advertising all to itself where the rest of the newspaper is weighted much heavier news to advertising but the paper in its entirety every day, large or small, is sixty ads, forty news. (*Jim Morgan exits the revolving doors and addresses the camera.*) Well, that completes our tour of *The New York Times* and I hope you found it informative and I hope that you read *The New York Times* every day of your life from now on.

Attentive viewers of the film and readers of this book will note that we did gain access to *The New York Times* as evidenced by the earlier interview with editorial writer Karl E. Meyer, which took place there, and by images of various editorial offices. On our way out after the interview, as we passed by other offices, we stuck our heads in people's doors and asked if we could film. No one had any objections so we wandered the halls with our camera. One member of the editorial board had a set of toy penguin bowling pins and a small vinyl bowling lane in his office. He instructed us not to film them.

We were denied permission to bring along a camera on Jim Morgan's official tour of the paper and therefore could not show the main newsroom or other parts of the plant. Since Mr. Morgan had no objections to an audio recording of his tour, we took what we could get. He didn't mind being filmed *outside* Fortress *NYT*, so we shot an introduction and conclusion to the tour with him. —MA

ERIN MILLS SHOPPING MALL

Chomsky is on the video wall with Marci Randall Miller at KUWR (Public Radio), Laramie, Wyoming, and at the University of Washington in Seattle

Chomsky

Now there are other media too whose basic social role is quite different: it's diversion. There's the real mass media—the kinds that are aimed at, you know, Joe Six Pack—that kind. The purpose of those media is just to dull people's brains.

On a recent "Saturday Night Live," as an obvious plug, one of the actors carried a copy of "The Chomsky Reader" throughout a skit. [*Z Magazine's* Michael] Albert telephoned Chomsky to say, "Hey, you're on television!" and found himself having to explain what "Saturday Night Live" is. So Chomsky doesn't know anything about popular culture. He doesn't watch TV. He doesn't listen to rock & roll. He goes to one movie a year. He has little time for a private life.

From the introduction to "The Rolling Stone Interview with Noam Chomsky," by Charles M. Young, in *Rolling Stone*, May 28, 1992

Chomsky
In fact, for a while, I couldn't get off an airplane in some foreign country without seeing those two smiling faces there, and my heart sinking. It felt like the first scene of *La Dolce Vita* a bit.

Dowell
Noam Chomsky goes to the movies? Fellini movies?

Chomsky
Yeah, I'm not as remote from the popular culture as I sometimes pretend.

Dowell
He didn't let Wintonick and Achbar follow him everywhere, however.

Chomsky
My wife, particularly, laid down an iron law that they were to get nowhere near the house, the children, personal life—anything like that—and I agreed with that. I mean, this is not about a person. It's about ideas and principles. If they want to use a person as a vehicle, okay, but, you know, my personal life and my children and where I live and so on have nothing to do with it.

Dowell
Which helps to explain why Noam Chomsky has not seen *Manufacturing Consent*, and won't.

Chomsky
Partly for uninteresting personal reasons; namely, I just don't like to hear myself and mostly think about the way I should have done it better, and so on. There are, however, some more general reasons. Much as the producers may try to overcome this, and I'm sure they did, there's something inevitable in the nature of the medium that personalizes the issues and gives the impression that some individual—in this case, it happens to be me—is the leader of a mass movement or tying to become one, or something of that kind.

Dowell
Chomsky says he's not any such thing and that movements for social change succeed not because of leaders, but because of largely unknown workers on the front lines. He does understand, however, that people can be reached by a medium that puts a face on ideas that challenge the official story.

Chomsky
There's very little in the way of political organization or other forms of association in which people can participate meaningfully in the public arena. People feel themselves as victims. They're isolated victims of propaganda, and if somehow, somebody comes along and says, you know, the kind of thing that they sort of have a gut feeling about or believed anyway, there's a sign of recognition and excitement and the feeling that maybe I'm not alone.

Dowell
Maybe Chomsky's right. The weekend *Manufacturing Consent* opened in San Francisco, it outgrossed every other movie but *Indecent Proposal*.

Interview with Pat Dowell on "Morning Edition," National Public Radio, USA, May 24, 1993

Presumably, Chomsky was not thinking of the *first* scene of *La Dolce Vita*, in which a statue of Christ, suspended below a helicopter, is flown over the Roman countryside. More likely, he was thinking of...

Scene 3: VIA VENETO. NIGHT.
Via Veneto—a half-mile of smart nightclubs and open-air cafés, airline offices and expensive shops, where an international café society of aristocrats and celebrities, millionaires and pederasts, meet to drink and gossip and escape the boredom of themselves. This is Marcello's beat, here he spends his nights ferreting out the spicy tidbits that will be served up—with photographs—to the sensation-hungry readers of his tabloid magazine. Here the tourists come to gawk, and the photographers prowl like jackals, for this is the center of "La Dolce Vita"—the sweet life.

As Maddalena and Marcello come out of the nightclub, the photographers recognize them and close in.

A VOICE
Hello.

MARCELLO
Hello.

MADDALENA
Ah, you have your friends ready to attack.

CERUSICO
Marcel'—where are you going all dressed up? Miss Maddalena . . .

PAPARAZZO
Maddalena, Maddalena.

They hover around excitedly, shooting pictures.

MADDALENA
No. Please. Let me alone.

CERUSICO
She's back! There she is! Look, she's more photogenic than a movie star.
Maddalena hurries past, annoyed.

MADDALENA
It's the same story every night. Don't they ever get tired?

MARCELLO
Come on, Paparazzo, quit it.

DORIA
Run, run! Where are you going, Marcel'?

PARADISI
How do you expect us to eat? We'll be out of a job.

Maddalena opens the door of her car, a white Cadillac convertible. Marcello slides in beside her. The photographers get pictures of the car, Maddalena, Marcello and Maddalena.

MARCELLO
You should be used to this by now. You're in the limelight.

CERUSICO
Marcel', where are you going? Tell me where you're taking her.

The photographers are still shooting as the white Cadillac speeds away down the Via Veneto.

From Fellini's *La Dolce Vita* (Ballantine, 1961)

UNIVERSITY OF WASHINGTON, SEATTLE

Chomsky

This is an oversimplification, but for the eighty percent or whatever they are, the main thing is to divert them. To get them to watch National Football League. And to worry about "Mother With Child With Six Heads," or whatever you pick up on the supermarket stands and so on. Or look at astrology. Or get involved in fundamentalist stuff or something or other. Just get them away. Get them away from things that matter. And for that it's important to reduce their capacity to think.

EXCERPT: "JOURNALISM" (1940)

Narrator

The sports section is handled in another special department. The sports reporter must be a specialist in his knowledge of sports. He gets his story right at the sporting event and often sends it in to his paper play by play.

The public is not unaware of what is happening, though with the success of the policies of isolation and breakdown of organizational structure, the response is erratic and self-destructive: faith in ridiculous billionaire saviors, myths of past innocence and noble leaders, religious and jingoist fanaticism, conspiracy cults, unfocused skepticism and disillusionment—a mixture that has not had happy consequences in the past.

Year 501: The Conquest Continues, page 64

To make cinematic what would have otherwise been an anecdote told from a lectern, we decided to re-film Chomsky's "Sports Rap", originally shot on videotape, on the huge overhead video screen in Montréal's Olympic Stadium. We were given use of the stadium for two hours on the condition that we would pay for any electricity used. Just turning the lights on in the "Big O" (as it's known to Montréalers) cost $400—a small price to pay for an 89,842,000 cubic foot prop!—MA

Chomsky

Take, say, sports—that's another crucial example of the indoctrination system, in my view. For one thing because it—you know, it offers people something to pay attention to that's of no importance. *(laughter)* That keeps them from worrying about—*(applause)* keeps them from worrying about things that matter to their lives that they might have some idea of doing
something about. And in fact it's striking to see the intelligence that's used by ordinary people in sports. I mean, you listen to radio stations where people call in—they have the most exotic information *(laughter)* and understanding about all kind of arcane issues. And the press undoubtedly does a lot with this.

Un-American whiners who can't hit the curveball. Patsy killjoys. Nerds who had to wait longer than Janis Ian when choosing sides for basketball. Lots of lefties embrace sports just to make like regular guys and gals and battle those stereotypes.

Not Noam Chomsky. Since the spring release of *Manufacturing Consent*, the activist/intellectual has been repeatedly twitted for the unsportsmanlike comments excerpted in that film. Phil Donahue joined NPR [National Public Radio] in asking Chomsky if he wasn't being a little too hard on our national pastimes.... People who know nothing else about Chomsky now say, "He's the guy who hates sports, right?"

Not exactly. Yes, he does think sports is "a way of building up irrational attitudes of submission to authority." But he claims to take in the occasional basketball game (on TV) and not to care "if people want to go out to the ballgame and enjoy themselves." What he finds remarkable, as he said in the movie and in a book excerpt published in *Harper's*, is the level of discourse about everything else, especially politics: "...the very dramatic discrepancy that you find between the knowledge and expertise and competence and cofidence about sports as compared to the diffidence, ignorance and feeling of helplessness and dismay with regard to things that matter to them like politics. What's striking to me is the degree of intellectual effort that goes into it. People have minds, after all, and they want to use them. If there's nothing constructive to use them for, they get involved in who should be playing third base."

He believes that an obsessive interest in sports is systematically encouraged in order to keep Joe Sixpack in his place. Does that mean Joe wouldn't care who's on third if he weren't told to? "People who have meaningful lives, choices to make, and who feel that they can become involved in affecting whether their children have schooling or health care...may be interested in sports, but they're not going to be fanatics. If it begins to take over people's lives and their intellects and emotions and so on, that's a symptom that something's wrong." Trying to wean Mr. Sixpack off sports, however, and turn him on to single-payer insurance is "like saying, 'Let's take beer away 'cause then maybe people will be serious.' If people are getting drunk, the problem lies elsewhere." Besides distracting the public from "things that really matter," however, sports fanaticism breeds its own special viruses. "The macho image, the chauvinism, the very obvious jingoism, all of which can be okay, like you cheer for the home team, but it can become pathological. Like when the Liverpool fans go off and beat up everybody in Italy. Middle-class people with options don't do that. They may cheer for the home team, but then they go home and forget about it."

Chomsky did spend much of his childhood curled up on a couch reading, but he was interested in sports, like any other teenager—even while he was writing about the rise of fascism in the school newspaper. "[For] young Jewish immigrants, first generation, it was considered part of your Americanization to know more about baseball than anyone else." His later suspicions about sports might have something to do with the fact that Philadelphia's A's and Phillies sucked when he was young. "Back in the 1930's, Philadelphia was last in everything—baseball, football, anything you could think of. I've always had a suspicion that boys my age who grew up there have a built-in inferiority complex. The Yankees were always winning the championship. I can remember very vividly the first baseball game I went to when I was about 10 years old, sitting in centerfield right behind Joe DiMaggio and watching the Yankees come from behind in the seventh inning with a seven-run outburst to defeat the A's 10 to 7. Pretty crushing."

Chomsky politely declined Jockbeat's invitation to watch the Yankees crush his adult hometown team, the Red Sox. He hadn't been to a baseball game since 1950. He was therefore surprised to learn that, in that interim, stadiums have installed scoreboards that tell the masses when to cheer and what to say. "You're kidding. I didn't realize things had descended to that level."

From "Out in Leftist Field," Mark Schone's "Jockbeat" column in *The Village Voice*, July 13, 1993

You know, I remember in high school, already I was pretty old. I suddenly asked myself at one point, why do I care if my high school team wins the football game? (laughter) I mean, I don't know anybody on the team, you know. (laughter) I mean, they have nothing to do with me, I mean, why I am cheering for my team? It doesn't mean any—it doesn't make sense. But the point is it does make sense: it's a way of building up irrational attitudes of submission to authority, and group cohesion behind leadership elements, in fact it's training in irrational jingoism. That's also a feature of competitive sports. I think if you look closely at these things, I think, typically, they do have functions, and that's why energy is devoted to supporting them and creating a basis for them and advertisers are willing to pay for them and so on.

People take their sports affiliations very seriously, so the minute we decided to include this section in the film we knew it would become a sore point with some viewers. Our favorite was by Craig MacInnis, a *Toronto Star* movie reviewer:

"...In regard to the social scientist's famed disdain for pro sports, the filmmakers place Chomsky's talking head on a stadium Jumbotron as he holds forth on the evils of salaried gamesmanship.

"The stadium is empty at the time but this only seems smart.

"If you were to let Chomsky talk over the Jumbotron about sports during a sold-out football game, the scrawny little twerp would probably have a hard time getting out of the building alive.

"NFL fans might be unwitting dupes of the industrial-military complex, but some of them still know how to hoist sniffy intellectuals by their tweedy lapels and drop-kick 'em back to MIT."

MacInnis apologized for the tardiness of his review, acknowledging "The fact that this review is being published on a Monday, a relatively soft circulation day compared to say, Friday, Saturday or Sunday, could possibly be taken as evidence of the mainstream media's efforts to further 'marginalize' the theories of maverick social scientist Noam Chomsky."

Could be. The film had opened in Toronto four days before, on the previous Thursday. A Monday review can't do much to help the previous weekend's attendance figures. He had this explanation for his ill-served readers: "My dog, Byng, ate my notes." The story of MacInnis's dog eating his notes took up a third of the article and the headline read: "Bad dog, Byng! Bad, bad dog! Sorry Noam." He claims to have two witnesses, not including the dog, who would not confess but reportedly acted guiltily.

At least MacInnis's review provided us with a serviceable blurb by describing *Manufacturing Consent* as "an intelligent, brilliantly edited and thoroughly rounded documentary."—MA

At the end of this scene we displayed the words "TODAY'S TOPIC: TRAINING IN IRRATIONAL JINGOISM" on the large outdoor sign next to the stadium. This momentarily contravened Québec's archaic language legislation banning English from outdoor signs (the law is still partly in effect). In Canada, provincial governments can suspend the Charter of Rights by invoking a "notwithstanding clause," which says, essentially: notwithstanding your right to freedom of expression (or any other right guaranteed by the Charter), we are going to enforce an unconstitutional law that suspends your freedom of expression (or any other right guaranteed by the Charter).

For a further discussion of freedom of expression, see the section beginning on page 173—MA

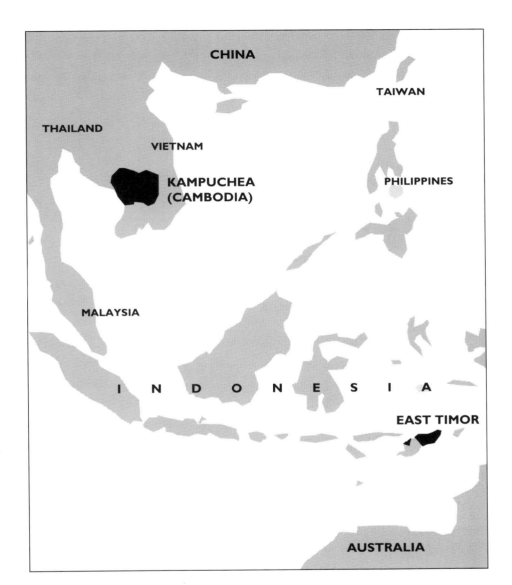

A CASE STUDY

Peter Wintonick

I'd like to ask you a question essentially about the methodology in studying the propaganda model and how would one go about doing that?

Chomsky

Well, there are a number of ways to proceed. One obvious way is to try to find more or less paired examples. History doesn't offer true controlled experiments but it often comes pretty close. So one can find atrocities or abuses of one sort that on the one hand are committed by official enemies and on the other hand are committed by friends and allies or by the favored state itself—by the United States in the U.S. case. And the question is whether the media accept the government framework or whether they use the same agenda, the same set of questions, the same criteria for dealing with the two cases as any honest outside observer would do.

TV PROMO

Filmed on a TV in an electronic-goods store window

Announcer

If you think America's involvement in the war in Southeast Asia is over, think again.

Unidentified Voice

The Khmer Rouge are the most genocidal people on the face of the earth.

Announcer

Peter Jennings reporting, from the killing fields. Thursday.

See: "The Propaganda Model: Some Methodological Considerations," *Necessary Illusions*, Appendix 1, pages 137-180, including a response to Walter LaFeber's critique of the propaganda model which appeared in *The New Republic*, January 9, 1989, described by Chomsky as "one of the very rare attempts to evaluate a propaganda model with actual argument instead of mere invective, and is furthermore the reasoning of an outstanding and independent-minded historian." (pages 148-151)

The interview in MIT's TV studio was the only formal interview we conducted with Chomsky for the film. It also included his earlier discussion of the Gulf War. We contemplated stitching together various discussions and lectures we had already shot about East Timor and Cambodia, but wanted everything to be coherent and well shot with good audio from top to bottom, so we booked two half-hours and started from scratch. —MA

Another, more general critique is "Knowledge, Morality and Hope: Chomsky's Social Thought," in *New Left Review*, 1992—also published in *Noam Chomsky: Critical Assessments*, edited by Carlos P. Otero.

THE AGONY OF CAMBODIA

Since 1975, the Khmer Rouge have sealed off Cambodia from the world and decimated its citizens through starvation and slaughter.

MIT, CAMBRIDGE, MASSACHUSETTS

Chomsky

I mean *the* great act of genocide in the modern period is Pol Pot, 1975 through 1978—that atrocity—I think it would be hard to find any example of a comparable outrage and outpouring of fury and so on and so forth. So that's one atrocity. Well, it just happens that in that case history did set up a controlled experiment.

"OPERATION WELCOME HOME," GULF WAR TICKERTAPE PARADE, NYC

Katherine Asals

Have you ever heard of a place called East Timor?

Man on Right

Can't say that I have.

Man on Left

Where?

Katherine Asals

East Timor?

Man On Left

Nope.

MIT, CAMBRIDGE, MASSACHUSETTS

Chomsky

Well, it happens that right at that time there was another atrocity very similar in character but differing in one respect. We were responsible for it. Not Pol Pot.

Have you ever heard of a place called East Timor?

CBC RADIO (PUBLIC), MONTRÉAL, QUÉBEC

Louise Penney

Hello, I'm Louise Penney and this is "Radio Noon." If you've been listening to the program fairly regularly over the last few months you'll know East Timor has come into the conversation more than once, particularly when we were talking about foreign aid and also the war and a new world order. People wondered why if the UN was serious about a new world order no one was doing anything to help East Timor. The area was invaded by Indonesia in 1975. There are reports of atrocities against the Timorese people. And yet Canada and other nations have consistently voted against UN resolutions to end the occupation. Today, we're going to take a closer look at East Timor. What's happened to it and why the international community is doing nothing to help.

One of the people who has been most active is Elaine Brière, a photo journalist from British Columbia. She's the founder of the East Timor Alert Network and she joins me in the studio now. Hello.

Elaine Brière

Hi.

Louise Penney

One tragedy compounding a tragedy is that a lot of people don't know much about East Timor. Where is it?

Elaine Brière

East Timor is just North of Australia, about four hundred and twenty kilometers, and it's right between the Indian and Pacific oceans. Just south of East Timor is a deep-water sea lane perfect for U.S. submarines to pass through. There's also huge oil reserves there.

Elaine Brière is a co-founder of the East Timor Alert Network, established in 1986, to oppose the Indonesian government's invasion and repression in East Timor. Brière traveled in East Timor in 1974, and, although she was aware of the invasion in 1975, she felt helpless to act until she read Chomsky's essay "Genocide on the Sly," in *Towards a New Cold War.* "I hadn't realized until then that there were other people who cared about what was happening to East Timor and that there were things we could do." She also realized how valuable her pre-invasion photographs of Timor village life could be in illustrating the tragedy of the invasion. After writing to and meeting with Noam Chomsky, she began her activist work.

Brière has addressed the UN Special Committee on Decolonization on three occasions, speaking for the East Timorese people's right to self-determination. She has also written annual reports for the UN Commission on Human Rights. In 1991, after the Dili massacre, the East Timor Alert Network helped activists in the United States set up the East Timor Action Network there.

One of the unique things about East Timor is that it's truly one of the last surviving ancient civilizations in that part of the world.

The Timorese spoke thirty different languages and dialects amongst a group of seven hundred thousand people.

Today, less than five percent of the world's people live like the East Timorese, basically self-reliant. They live really outside of the global economic system.

Small societies like the East Timorese are much more democratic, much more egalitarian, and there's much more sharing of power and wealth. Before the Indonesians invaded, most people lived in small rural villages.

The old people in the village were like the university. They passed on tribal wisdom from generation to generation. Children grew up in a safe, stimulating, nurturing environment.

A year after I left East Timor I was appalled when I heard that Indonesia had invaded. It didn't want a small, independent country setting an example for the region.

MIT, CAMBRIDGE, MASSACHUSETTS

Chomsky

East Timor was a Portuguese colony. Indonesia had no claim to it and in fact stated that they had no claim to it. During the period of colonization there was a good deal of politicization. Different groups developed. A civil war broke out in August '75. It ended up in a victory for Fretilin, which was one of the groupings, described as Populist Catholic in character with some typical leftish rhetoric. Indonesia at once started intervening.

EAST TIMOR, OCTOBER 1975

Interviewer

What's the situation? When did those ships come in?

José Ramos-Horta

They start arriving since Monday. Six, seven boats together, very close to our border. They are not there just for fun, you know. They are preparing a massive operation.

UNIDENTIFIED TIMORESE VILLAGE

Greg Shackleton of Channel 7 in Melbourne, Australia, filed this on-camera report October 15, 1975

Greg Shackleton

Something happened here that moved us very deeply. It was so far outside our experience as Australians that we'll find it very difficult to convey to you, but we'll try.

Sitting on woven mats, under a thatched roof, in a hut with no walls, we were the target of a barrage of questioning from men who know they may die tomorrow and cannot understand why the rest of the world does not care. That's all they want: for the United Nations to care about what is happening here. The emotion here last night was so strong that we, all three of us, felt we should be able to reach out into the warm night air and touch it.

Greg Shackleton at an unnamed village which we will remember forever, in Portuguese Timor.

GREG SHACKLETON
GARY CUNNINGHAM
MALCOM RENNIE
BRIAN PETERS
TONY STEWART

Journalists slain the next day by Indonesian forces

Three men I know say what happened when they killed the Australian journalists in Balibo. Each one talked to me separately at a different time in Dili. Balibo was bombarded first and the people ran away. My friends came back to Balibo from Atambua with Indonesian soldiers. They were civilians but were carrying Indonesian weapons. The soldiers were in charge. The journalists screamed, "Australians, Australians!" An Indonesian leader told others to tie the journalists up, then he told them to use the knife and kill them. The knives are like daggers, on the belt. Afterwards they were burnt. They were killed inside a house with knives and afterwards burned with petrol. I don't know the detail because I did not like to ask questions. I didn't know I would be in Australia or that anyone would ask me, or maybe I could know more. I know only what they told me. I believed them, they seemed sad about this thing. Also I believe it because in Dili we had already experienced this cruel behaviour.

Testimony of "Leong," from Telling: East Timor, Personal Testimonies 1942-1992, page 96

A sixth Australian journalist, Roger East, was killed in Dili on December 8, 1975. "Mr. Siong" was an eyewitness to the execution of many Timorese that day. He was forced by Indonesian soldiers to tie iron pipes to bodies and throw them in the sea:

After we threw in those dead bodies some Chinese Timorese from Colmera came, seventeen or eighteen. I knew all of those people, they were friends and neighbours. All were too frightened to speak, there was no crying, no noise. People came in groups of two or three or four, stood on the wharf and were shot. One group after the other coming and coming, killed and thrown in the sea. Two were couples, one with young children who went with relatives. The other couple were elderly, and the rest were men.

A crowd of people outside the wharf could not see the others shot; they could hear a little, but they did not really know. Sometimes some of the people who were killed had to help us six to tie other people and then after it they were killed. Some are shot and fall into the sea at once, but if they fall on the wharf we have to tie the pipe to them. We are trembling, we are nearly gone mad, but we don't know what to do, just do whatever the Indonesians want.

One killed with those Colmera people was an Australian man. The soldiers push him. He was talking to them saying, "Not Fretilin, Australian." He spoke English. I understood it, sometimes Australians came to the shop were I worked. He wore brown shorts, a cream shirt and sunglasses. I didn't notice if he wore shoes, no. He has short hair turning grey. He looks a strong man. They push him, tell him to face the sea. He refuses to do this. The Indonesians just fire at him. He falls straight into the sea

From Telling: East Timor, Personal Testimonies 1942-1992, page 104

The United Nations Universal Declaration of Human Rights guarantees the right "to seek, receive and impart information and ideas through any media regardless of frontiers."

Yet governments around the world still try to prevent journalists from reporting the news. During the 1991 Gulf War, the U.S. government restricted access of reporters to the battlefront and required prior review of stories they filed. The circumstances were, of course, unusual. Many governments seek to restrict the flow of information when not at war, sometimes to avoid a scandal or public outrage, sometimes to perpetuate their own power. Certain individuals and groups—drug traffickers, political insurgents, corrupt businessmen—have also attempted to restrict the flow of information by attacking or intimidating journalists....

The investigations of the Committee to Protect Journalists (CPJ) attest to this fact. During the first 18 months of the 1990s, at least 54 journalists lost their lives in the line of duty, while more than a thousand others were subjected to a range of attacks, both legal and physical...

Journalists must be prepared to confront well-armed militaries, powerful politicians, or the irate subjects of their exposés. Indeed, the statistics cited above indicate the lengths to which governments and certain of their citizens are prepared to go to prevent others from knowing the truth.

From *Dangerous Assignments: A Study Guide*, page iv, by the Committee to Protect Journalists. The CPJ was established in 1981 to monitor and promote freedom of the press around the world. Walter Cronkite is the honorary chairman. See Resource Guide for ordering information.

BACKGROUND TO THE INVASION

As soon as the Portuguese announced that independence would be granted to the colonies in April, 1974, the tiny elite of Timor (numbering perhaps 3000) formed three political parties (and later a few minor parties): UDT, FRETILIN, and APODETI.... "The UDT leadership predominantly comprised Catholics who were smallholders or administrative officials." (Jolliffe, p. 62). Initially regarded as the most influential of the three parties, "its lack of positive policies, its associations with the 'ancien régime', together with its initial reluctance to support the ultimate goal of full independence, led many of the

party's original followers to swing their support to FRETILIN which by early 1975 was generally considered to have become the largest party..." The reasons for the swing were not only the failures of the UDT but also the successes of FRETILIN.....FRETILIN was a moderate reformist national front, headed by a Catholic seminarian and initially involving largely urban intellectuals...

The third party, APODETI, "apparently attracted little support and has generally been regarded as the smallest of the three political parties to have emerged by May, 1974." It was the only party calling for union with Indonesia.

In January, 1975 the UDT and FRETILIN formed a coalition, which collapsed when the UDT withdrew in May. In August the UDT staged a coup, setting off a bloody conflict that ended a few weeks later in a complete victory of FRETILIN....

What reached the international press was largely the version approved by Indonesia, which "had the monopoly on information from the territory" (Hill, p.12). Foreign visitors later "found that there had been considerably less fighting than had been reported and less people killed" (Hill, p.12)....

The background of the UDT August coup seems to lie primarily in the erosion of support for the UDT during 1975... Just prior to the coup, a high level meeting [between the UDT and Indonesia] had been held... After the Kupang meeting, UDT President Lopes da Cruz said: "We are realists. If we want to be independent we must follow the Indonesian political line. Otherwise it is independence for a week or a month...." In his congressional testimony, Benedict Anderson stated that " my understanding is that the situation which precipitated the civil war in East Timor was a coup by the UDT, which was instigated by Indonesian intelligence," referring to the August coup....

The Australians who were in East Timor have given quite a favorable account of the brief interlude of semi-independence from September to the Indonesian invasion of December 7 [1975. James] Dunn, who led the Australian aid mission in October, wrote on the basis of his visit that:

"The Fretilin administration was surprisingly effective in re-establishing law and order, and in restoring essential services to the main towns. By mid-October, Dili was functioning more or

less normally... The Fretilin administration had many shortcomings, but it clearly enjoyed widespread support from the population, including many hitherto UDT supporters...."

With the victory of FRETILIN in the civil war, Indonesia at once began its armed intervention on the pretext of assisting anti-FRETILIN Timorese, a pretense which, as we will see, is generally accepted in the West, though it has absolutely no basis in fact, so far as we can determine. Indonesian border raids began on September 14... Throughout October and November heavy hand-to-hand fighting took place between Fretilin and Indonesian troops....

These attacks evidently convinced FRETILIN leaders that Indonesia was determined to invade. Appeals for a negotiated settlement by FRETILIN and Portuguese had been rejected by Indonesia, and FRETILIN leaders were coming to believe "that Portugal and Australia, the only third parties showing an interest in the conflict in Timor, could not or would not take steps to deter Indonesia from attaining her objective by military means" (*Dunn Report*, p. 81) In this context, FRETILIN declared the independence of East Timor, which it had been governing for almost three months, on November 28.

A full scale Indonesian invasion was generally expected at this point....Australia relayed to the International Red Cross the information that Indonesian forces had threatened to kill Australians remaining in Dili. "The threats were evidence of a final effort by Indonesia to clear the territory of foreign observers before the invasion began." It was important to ensure that no independent witnesses would be present, including the Red Cross...

On December 6 President Ford and Henry Kissinger visited Jakarta and the following day the Indonesian army carried out the expected full-scale invasion, setting in motion a process described by [a Professor of Anthropology at the University of Michigan who lived mountain people in Timor in 1973-74, Shepard] Forman as "annihilation of simple mountain people" and by others as simply genocide.

The Political Economy of Human Rights, Vol. 1, pages 133-143

East Timor: Nationalism and Colonialism, by Jill Jolliffe (University of Queensland Press, Australia, 1978)

The Timor Story, by Helen Hill (Timor Information Service, Australia, undated)

Chomsky

Ford and Kissinger visited Jakarta, I think it was December 5. We know that they had requested that Indonesia delay the invasion until after they left because it would be too embarrassing. And within hours, I think, after they left the invasion took place, on December 7.

DARKROOM

Elaine Brière

What happened on December 7, 1975, is just one of the great, great evil deeds of history.

Early in the morning bombs began dropping on Dili [the capital city of East Timor]. The number of troops that invaded Dili that day almost outnumbered the entire population of the town.

And for two or three weeks there was just— they just killed people.

When he landed at Hawaii, reporters asked Mr. Ford for comment on the invasion of Timor. He smiled and said: "We'll talk about that later...." [UPI—December 8, 1975] Henry Kissinger, traveling with Ford, had already given his reactions. He "told newsmen in Jakarta that the United States would not recognize the Fretilin-declared republic and 'the United States understands Indonesia's position on the question'." [*Los Angeles Times*, December 7, 1975]

The Political Economy of Human Rights, Vol. 1, page 156

EXCERPT: "BURIED ALIVE" (1989)

Carlos Alfonso (refugee from East Timor)
And when I heard "FIRE" I dived to the ground and felt bodies falling on me—like leaves. There were screams, calls for wife, for mother— it was horrible...

The Department of State desired that the UN prove utterly ineffective in whatever measures it undertook.

This task was given to me, and I carried it forward with no inconsiderable success.
—Daniel Patrick Moynihan

UNITED NATIONS, NEW YORK

José Ramos-Horta (East Timor Representative, UN)
This Council must consider Indonesian aggression against East Timor as the main issue of the discussion. (*Voice under:* The General Assembly in its resolution 3845 and the Security Council have called on the government of Indonesia to withdraw without delay all its forces from the territory. Indonesia's invasion of East Timor was against the United Nations Charter and international law.)

Chomsky (voice over)
When the Indonesians invaded, the UN reacted as it always does, calling for sanctions and condemnation and so on. Various watered-down resolutions were passed but the US was very clearly not going to allow anything to work.

Continuation of Carlos Alphonso's testimony:
I lay on the ground. I had been hit in the hand. The bullet went in and came out the other side. My hand felt as if it were stuck on the ground. I dragged my hand towards me and smeared the blood over my face. I smeared it all over my face and lay there pretending to be dead.

Moynihan also made it clear that he understood the nature of his accomplishment very well. He cites a February 1976 estimate by an Indonesian client in Timor "that some sixty thousand persons had been killed since the outbreak of the civil war" in August — recall that some 2,000 to 3,000 had been killed during the civil war, the remainder since the Indonesian invasion in December—"10 percent of the population, almost the proportion of casualties experienced by the Soviet Union during the Second World War." Thus Moynihan is taking credit for an achievement that he proudly compares to Hitler's in Eastern Europe.

The Chomsky Reader, page 308.
The quotes are from *A Dangerous Place,* by Patrick Moynihan with Suzanne Weaver (Little, Brown 1978)

At the time of Indonesia's invasion of East Timor, José Ramos-Horta was a member of the Fretilin Central Committee. A decision was made by the fledgling government to send representatives overseas—to Western Europe, Africa and the UN—to rally support for Timorese independence. Ramos-Horta was sent as East Timor's representative at the UN, a position he continues to hold.

See: *East Timor Debacle: Indonesian Intervention, Repression, and Western Compliance* by José Ramos-Horta, Introduction by Noam Chomsky (Red Sea Press, 1986)

there were screams, calls for wife, for mother –...

DARKROOM

Elaine Brière

So the Timorese were fleeing into the jungle by the thousands. By late 1977-78 Indonesia set up "receiving centers" for those Timorese who came out of the jungle waving white flags. Those the Indonesians thought were more educated or who were suspected of belonging to Fretilin or other opposition parties were immediately killed. They took women aside and flew them off to Dili in helicopters for use by the Indonesian soldiers. They killed children, and babies. But in those days, their main strategy and their main weapon was starvation.

MIT, CAMBRIDGE, MASSACHUSETTS

Chomsky

By 1978 it was approaching really genocidal levels. The church and other sources estimated about two hundred thousand people killed.

The U.S. backed it all the way. The U.S. provided ninety percent of the arms. Right after the invasion arms shipments were stepped up. When the Indonesians actually began to run out of arms in 1978, the Carter administration moved in and increased arms sales. Other western countries did the same. Canada, England, Holland, everybody who could make a buck was in there trying to make sure they could kill more Timorese.

There is no Western concern for issues of aggression, atrocities, human rights abuses and so on if there's a profit to be made from them. Nothing could show it more clearly than this case.

The government...claims to have suspended military assistance to Indonesia from December 1975 until June 1976. The temporary sanction was "unannounced and unleaked" ([Washington Post writer Lee] Lescaze). It was also a fraud. "We stopped taking new orders. The items that were in the pipeline continued to be delivered to Indonesia," General Howard M. Fish testified before Congress. (*March Hearings*, p. 14). Benedict Anderson testified in the *February 1978 Hearings* that according to a report "confirmed from Department of Defense [Foreign Military Sales] printout" new offers of military equipment were also made during the period of the alleged ban:

If we are curious as to why the Indonesians never felt the force of the U.S. government's "anguish," the answer is quite simple. In flat contradiction to express statements by General Fish, Mr. Oakly and Assistant Secretary of State for East Asian and Pacific Affairs Richard Holbrook, at least four separate offers of military equipment were made to the Indonesian government during the January-June 1976 "administrative suspension." This equipment consisted mainly of supplies and parts for OV-10 Broncos, Vietnam War era planes specially designed for counterinsurgency operations against adversaries without effective anti-aircraft weapons, and wholly useless for defending Indonesia from a foreign enemy. The policy of supplying the Indonesian regime with Broncos, as well as other counterinsurgency-related equipment has continued without substantial change from the Ford through the present Carter administrations.

This violation of their own secret policy was admitted by State Department and Pentagon officials who told the committee, however, that "certainly the Department of State is not deliberately engaged in any deception or violation of the law." They certainly weren't deceiving the Indonesians. In fact, it turns out that the "aid suspension" was so secret that Indonesia was never informed of it.

The Political Economy of Human Rights, Volume 1, pages 144-145

Compared to various societies of the world, Canada and the United States are countries where the state does not use excessive violence against its own population to secure obedience. A large range of action is open to people who aren't outright heroes, and the question for Canadians is whether they feel comfortable being accomplices to mass murder. In the past, the answer has been yes, Canadians do feel comfortable. During the Vietnam War there was a lot of Canadian opposition to the war. There was a lot of rhetorical condemnation. Nevertheless, Canada became the largest per capita military exporter in the world, supplying arms and enriching itself through the destruction of Indo-China. As long as Canadians feel comfortable playing that role, they will continue to play it. If they look at the consequences of that, they'll see that they are playing a role parallel to that of the people we condemn as the "good Germans" under the Nazis. They just sit back quietly and make what profit they can out of the suffering and misery of other people.

From an interview with Richard Titus, *Language and Politics*, page 483

Chomsky

It wasn't that nobody had ever heard of East Timor; crucial to remember that there was plenty of coverage in *The New York Times* and elsewhere before the invasion.

The reason was that there was concern at the time over the breakup of the Portuguese empire and what that would mean. There was a fear that it would lead to independence or Russian influence or whatever. After the Indonesians invaded the coverage dropped. There was some, but it was strictly from the point of view of the State Department and Indonesian generals. It was never a Timorese refugee.

As the atrocities reached their maximum peak in 1978 when it really was becoming genocidal, coverage dropped to zero in the United States and Canada, the two countries I've looked at closely. Literally dropped to zero.

All this was going on at exactly the same time as the great protest of outrage over Cambodia. The level of atrocities was comparable—in relative terms it was probably considerably higher in Timor .

It turns out that right in Cambodia in the preceding years, 1973-1975, there was also a comparable atrocity for which we were responsible.

Few countries have suffered more bitterly than did Cambodia during the 1970s. The "decade of genocide," as the period is termed by the Finnish Inquiry Commission that attempted to assess what had taken place, consisted of three phases—now extending the time scale to the present, which bears a heavy imprint of these terrible years:

Phase I: From 1969 through April 1975, U.S. bombing at a historically unprecedented level and a civil war sustained by the United States left the country in utter ruins. Though Congress legislated an end to the bombing in August 1973, U.S. government participation in the ongoing slaughter continued until the Khmer Rouge victory in April 1975.

Phase II: From April 1975 through 1978 Cambodia was subjected to the murderous rule of the Khmer Rouge (Democratic Kampuchea, DK), overthrown by the Vietnamese invasion of Cambodia in December 1978. [For more detail, see page 105 of this book]

Phase III: Vietnam installed the Heng Samrin regime in power in Cambodia, but the Democratic Kampuchea (DK) coalition, based primarily on the Khmer Rouge, maintained international recognition apart from the Soviet bloc. Reconstructed with the aid of China and the United States on the Thai-Cambodia border and in Thai bases, the Khmer Rouge guerrillas, the only effective DK military force, continue to carry out activities in Cambodia of a sort called "terrorist" when a friendly government is the target.

Manufacturing Consent, pages 260-261 (see also Chapter 6)

The country was ruled by Prince Sihanouk until March 1970, when he was overthrown in a coup supported by the United States. Throughout this period, Sihanouk attempted a difficult balancing act both internally and externally. Within Cambodia, he repressed the left and peasant uprisings and attempted to hold off the right... Externally, he tried to preserve a measure of neutrality against the background of the expanding Indochina war, which, he expect-

ed, would end in a Communist victory.

Sihanouk's neutralist efforts were unappreciated by the United States and its allies.....

Attacks by U.S. and Saigon army forces against border posts and villages in Cambodia intensified from the early 1960s, causing hundreds of casualties a year. Later, Vietnamese peasants and guerrillas fled for refuge to border areas in Cambodia, particularly after the murderous U.S. military operations in South Vietnam in early 1967, giving rise to cynical charges from Washington, echoed in the media, about Communist encroachment into neutral Cambodia....

On March 18, 1969, the notorious "secret bombings" began. One week later, on March 26, the Cambodian government publicly condemned the bombing and strafing of "the Cambodian population living in the border regions... almost daily by U.S. aircraft"... Prince Sihanouk called a press conference on March 28 in which he emphatically denied reports circulating in the United States that he "would not oppose U.S. bombings of communist targets within my frontiers." He then issued an appeal to the international press: "I appeal to you to publicize abroad this very clear stand of Cambodia—that is, I will in any case oppose all bombings on Cambodian territory under whatever pretext."

It will come as no surprise that his appeal went unanswered. Furthermore, this material has been suppressed up to the present time, apart from the dissident literature....

In March 1970, Cambodia was drawn irrevocably into the carnage sweeping Indochina. On March 18, Sihanouk was overthrown in "an upper-class coup, not a revolution," carried out for "interests of domestic and political expediency," and with at least "indirect U.S. support," if not more.... Cambodia was now plunged into civil war, with increasing savagery on both sides.

U.S. bombing continued at a high level after the withdrawal of U.S. forces from Cambodia. By late 1971, an investigating team of the General Accounting Office concluded that U.S. and Saigon army bombing is "a very significant cause of refugees and

Chomsky

The major U.S. attack against Cambodia started with the bombings of the early 1970s. They reached a peak in 1973 and continued up to 1975. They were directed against inner Cambodia. Very little is known about them because the media wanted it to be secret. They knew it was going on they just didn't want to know what was happening. The CIA estimates about six hundred thousand killed during that five-year period which is mostly either U.S. bombing or a U.S.–sponsored war. So that's pretty significant killing. Also the conditions in which it left Cambodia were such that high U.S. officials predicted that about a million people would die in the aftermath just from hunger and disease because of the wreckage of the country.

There's also pretty good evidence from U.S. government sources and scholarly sources that the intense bombardment was a significant force—maybe a critical force—in building up peasant support for the Khmer Rouge, who before that were a pretty marginal element. Well that's just the wrong story.

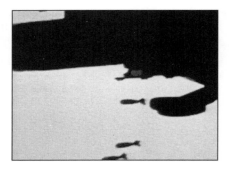

civilian casualties," estimating that almost a third of the seven-million population may be refugees.

Cambodia was being systematically demolished, and the Khmer Rouge, hitherto a marginal element, were becoming a significant force with substantial peasant support in inner Cambodia, increasingly victimized by U.S. terror.

Manufacturing Consent, pages 267-273

Western correspondents evacuated from Phnom Penh after the Khmer Rouge victory were able to obtain a fleeting picture of what had taken place in the countryside. British correspondent John Swain summarizes his impressions as follows:

The United Sates has much to answer for here, not only in terms of human lives and massive material destruction; the rigidity and nastiness of the un-Cambodian-like fellows in black who run this country now, or what's left of it, are as much a product of this wholesale American bombing which has hardened and honed their minds as they are a product of Marx or Mao.... The war damage here [in the countryside], as everywhere else we saw, is total. Not a bridge standing, hardly a house. I am told most villagers have spent the war years living semi-permanently underground in earth bunkers to escape the bombing.... The entire countryside has been churned up by American B-52 bomb craters, whole towns and villages razed. So far I have not seen one intact pagoda. (*Sunday Times* (London), May 11, 1985)

Manufacturing Consent, page 278

Cambodia specialist Milton Osborne concludes that Communist terror [in the late 1970's] was "surely a reaction to the terrible bombing of Communist-held regions" by the U.S. Air Force. Another Cambodia scholar, David Chandler, comments that the bombing turned "thousands of young Cambodians into participants in an anti-American crusade," as it "destroyed a good deal of the fabric of prewar Cambodian society and provided the CPK [Khmer Rouge] with the psychological ingredients of a violent, vengeful, and unrelenting social revolution"....

Manufacturing Consent, page 264

In May, 1993, a UN-sponsored election took place in Cambodia. Since then, a provisional government has formed, with as its co-premiers Hun Sen and Prince Norodom Ranaridhb, son of Prince Sihanouk. But many observers are looking towards Sihanouk, who heads the four-faction Supreme National Council, as the hope for peace in the country. The SNC was a result of the 1991 Paris peace accord brokered by the UN.

There was an incredible 90 percent turnout for the election, despite the fact that the Khmer Rouge refused to contest it but did their best to subvert it.

It's not at all clear that the KR have been defeated. Latest reports indicate that their relations with Thai generals and businessmen are thriving, and they still have plenty of clout. How much is debated.—NC

Chomsky

After 1975, atrocities continued and that became the right story, because now they are being carried out by the bad guys. Well, it was bad enough, in fact current estimates are that— well, you know, they vary. I mean, the CIA claim fifty to a hundred thousand people killed and maybe another million or so who died one way or another. Michael Vickery is the one person who has given a really close detailed analysis. His figure is maybe seven hundred fifty thousand deaths above the normal. Others, like Ben Kiernan, suggest higher figures but so far without a detailed analysis. Anyway, it was terrible, no doubt about it.

Although the atrocities—the real atrocities— were bad enough, they weren't quite good enough for the purposes needed.

Within a few weeks after the Khmer Rouge takeover, *The New York Times* was already accusing them of genocide. At that point maybe a couple of hundred or maybe a few thousand people had been killed. And from then on it was a drum beat, a chorus of genocide.

The big best-seller on Cambodia, on Pol Pot, is called *Murder in a Gentle Land*. Up until April 17, 1975, it was a gentle land of peaceful smiling people and after that some horrible holocaust took place.

Very quickly, a figure of two million killed was hit upon. In fact, what was claimed was the Khmer Rouge boast of having murdered two million people. The facts were very dramatic. In the case of atrocities committed by the official enemy, extraordinary show of outrage, exaggeration, no evidence required, faked photographs were fine, anything goes.

Chomsky says the CIA demographic study is an "estimate of deaths from all causes that is meaningless because of misjudgment of postwar population and politically motivated assessments throughout."

See Manufacturing Consent, note 32, pages 383-384

Phase II of "the decade of genocide" began with the Khmer Rouge takeover in April 1975. Within a few weeks, the Khmer Rouge were accused in the national press of "barbarous cruelty" and "genocidal policies" comparable to the "Soviet extermination of the Kulaks or with the Gulag Archipelago." This was at a time when the death toll was perhaps in the thousands; the half million or more killed during phase I of the genocide never merited such comment, nor were these accompanied by reflection on the consequences of the American war that were anticipated by U.S. officials and relief workers on the scene...or by any recognition of a possible causal link between the horrors of phase II and the American war against the rural society during phase I.

By early 1977, it was alleged that [the Khmer Rouge] had "boasted" of having slaughtered some two million people (Jean Lacouture in the *New York Review*). This figure remained standard even after Lacouture withdrew it a few weeks later, acknowledging that he had misread his source (Ponchaud) and that the actual figure might be in the thousands, but adding that he saw little significance to a difference between thousands killed and a "boast" of two million killed. This position expresses with some clarity the general attitude toward fact during this period and since, as does his further statement that it is hardly important to determine "exactly which person uttered an inhuman phrase"...

Not everyone joined in the chorus. The most striking exceptions were those who had the best access to information from Cambodia, notably, the State Department Cambodia specialists. Their view, based on what evidence was then available (primarily from northwestern Cambodia), was that deaths from all causes might have been in the "tens if not hundreds of thousands," largely from disease, malnutrition, and "brutal, rapid change," not "mass genocide." These tentative conclusions were almost entirely ignored by the media... because they were simply not useful for the purpose at the time.

Manufacturing Consent, pages 280-283

Michael Vickery's *Cambodia: 1975-1982* (South End Press, 1984) is, according to Chomsky, "the major study of the Khmer Rouge period, by one of the few authentic Cambodia scholars, widely and favorably reviewed abroad by mainstream Indochina scholars and others but virtually ignored in the United States, as was the Finnish Inquiry Commission Report."

See also:
- Noam Chomsky's "Decade of Genocide in Review," *Inside Asia* (London, February 1985, reprinted in *The Chomsky Reader*)
- *Manufacturing Consent*, page 382, note 22
- *Murder in a Gentle Land*, by John Barron and Anthony Paul (Reader's Digest Press, 1977)
- "The 'Not-So-Gentle' Land: Some Relevant History," *Manufacturing Consent*, pages 266-270

Chomsky

Also a vast amount of lying. I mean an amount of lying that would have made Stalin cringe, in fact. It was fraudulent. We know that it was fraudulent by looking at the response to comparable atrocities for which the United States was responsible.

Jean Lacouture, who had written a review of François Ponchaud's Cambodia: Year Zero *(Holt, Rinehart and Winston, 1978) in* The New York Review of Books, *wrote this response to a letter from Chomsky:*

Noam Chomsky's corrections have caused me great distress. By pointing out serious errors in citation, he calls into question not only my respect for texts and the truth, but also the cause I was trying to defend. I particularly regret the misleading attributions mentioned above and I should have checked more accurately the figures on victims, figures deriving from sources that are, moreover, questionable. My reading of Ponchaud's book was hasty, emotionally intense, too quick in selecting polemic points. But if I must plead guilty in handling the details of my review, I would plead innocent concerning its fundamental argument.

Faced with an enterprise as monstrous as the new Cambodian government, should we see the main problem as one of deciding exactly which person uttered an inhuman phrase, and whether the regime has murdered thousands or hundreds of wretched people? Is it of crucial historical importance to know whether the victims of Dachau numbered 100,000 or 500,000? Or if Stalin had 1,000 or 10,000 Poles shot at Katyn?

"Cambodia: Corrections," *New York Review of Books,* (May 26, 1977)

Or perhaps, we may add, whether the victims of My Lai numbered in the hundreds, as reported, or tens of thousands, or whether the civilians murdered in Operation SPEEDY EXPRESS numbered 5,000 or 500,000, if a factor of 100 is relatively insignificant? If facts are so unimportant, then why bother to present alleged facts at all?

The Political Economy of Human Rights, Volume II, page 149

When the facts are in, it may turn out that the more extreme condemnations were in fact correct. But even if that turns out to be the case, it will in no way alter the conclusions we have reached on the central question addressed here: how the available facts were selected, modified, or sometimes invented to create a certain image offered to the general population. The answer to this question seems clear, and it is unaffected by whatever may yet be discovered about Cambodia in the future.

The Political Economy of Human Rights, Volume II, page 293

On Cambodia: "Bloodbaths in Indochina: Constructive, Nefarious and Mythical," *The Political Economy of Human Rights*, Volume I, esp. pages 337-354; *Manufacturing Consent*, Chapter 6, The Indochina Wars (II) Laos and Cambodia

Also: "Cambodia" October 1979, an audiotape available from Alternative Radio.

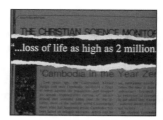

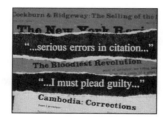

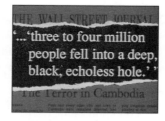

Chomsky
Early seventies Cambodia, Timor, are two very closely paired examples. Well, the media response was quite dramatic.

THE NEW YORK TIMES
INDEX
1975-1979:

"TIMOR"
70 COLUMN INCHES

"CAMBODIA"
1,175 COLUMN INCHES

Several reviewers of *Manufacturing Consent* have accepted these numbers at face value as total column inches of stories for this time period. As indicated, these are column inches of *index listings*, representing far more column inches of actual stories. We did not have the resources to track the thousands of stories, replicate them and measure them.

The index listings were full-size photocopies taped together end to end for all entries under Timor and Cambodia. The National Film Board of Canada's largest soundstage was barely able to contain the fully unraveled Cambodia roll, just over 97 feet long.—MA

A propaganda system will consistently portray people abused in enemy states as worthy victims, whereas those treated with equal or greater severity by its own government or clients will be unworthy. The evidence of worth may be read from the extent and character of attention and indignation.

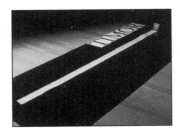

PANEL DISCUSSION, HARVARD UNIVERSITY,
CAMBRIDGE, MASSACHUSETTS

*At an international conference entitled "Anticommunism and the
US: History and Consequences," November 11-13, 1988, sponsored by the Institute of Media Analysis, Inc.*

Karl E. Meyer (*editorial writer,* The New York Times)
Back in 1980 I taught a course at Tufts
University. Well, Chomsky came around to this
class. He made a very powerful case that the
press underplayed the fact that the Indonesian
government annexed this former Portuguese

Communism as the ultimate evil has always
been the specter haunting property owners,
as it threatens the very root of their class
position and superior status. The Soviet,
Chinese, and Cuban revolutions were traumas to Western elites, and the ongoing conflicts and the well-publicized abuses of
Communist states have contributed to elevating opposition to communism to a first
principle of Western ideology and politics.
This ideology helps mobilize the populace
against an enemy, and because the concept
is fuzzy it can be used against anybody
advocating policies that threaten property
interests or support accommodation with

Robert W. McChesney
You elect to term the ideological filter "anti-Communist." Why is this more appropriate
than terming it more broadly the "dominant
ideology," which might permit the filter's
extension to areas that do not lend themselves to anti-Communist interpretation but,
nonetheless, are critical to elite interests?

Edward S. Herman
This is a reasonable suggestion and maybe
we should have done this. Other elements of
the dominant ideology, like the benevolence
of one's own government and the merits of
private enterprise, are referred to at various

Filter: anticommunism as a national religion and control mechanism

colony in 1975. And that if you compare it for
example with Cambodia, where there was an
acreage of things, that this was a Communist
atrocity whereas the other was not a
Communist atrocity. Well, I got quite interested
in this and went to talk to the then deputy
foreign editor of the *Times*.

And I said, "You know we've had very poor
coverage on this," and he said "You know,
you're absolutely right, there are a dozen
atrocities around the world that we don't cover;
this is one, for various reasons." So I took it up.

Communist states and radicalism. It therefore helps fragment the left and labor movements and serves as a political-control mechanism. If the triumph of communism is the
worst imaginable result, the support of fascism abroad is justified as a lesser evil.
Opposition to social democrats who are too
soft on Communists and "play into their
hands" is rationalized in similar terms.

Liberals at home, often accused of being
pro-Communist or insufficiently anti-Communist, are kept continuously on the
defensive in a cultural milieu in which anti-communism is the dominant religion. If they
allow communism, or something that can be
labeled communism, to triumph in the
provinces while they are in office, the political costs are heavy. Most of them have fully
internalized the religion anyway, but they are
all under great pressure to demonstrate
their anti-Communist credentials. This causes them to behave very much like reactionaries.

Manufacturing Consent, page 29

points in the book, but in discussing filters
we wanted to focus on the ideological element that has been the most important as a
control and disciplinary mechanism in the
U.S. political economy.

From an interview in *Monthly Review*, January 1989

Robert W. McChesney is an assistant professor
at the School of Journalism and Mass Communication,
University of Wisconsin-Madison

McGILL UNIVERSITY, MONTRÉAL, QUÉBEC

Arnold Kohen (journalist)

I was working as a reporter and writer for a small alternative radio program in upstate New York and we received audiotapes of interviews with Timorese leaders, and we were quite surprised, given the level of American involvement, that there was not more coverage—indeed, practically any coverage—of the large-scale Indonesian killing in the mainstream American media. We formed a small group of people to try to monitor this situation and see what we could do over time to alert public opinion to what was actually happening in East Timor.

I am originally from New York City—Queens, to be precise. In 1975 I was working with a radio feature program called "Ithaca—Rest of the News," which was a university-based group dedicated to producing documentaries on issues that were overlooked or under-reported by the mainstream news media. Friends in the community introduced me to "Ithaca (New York) Rest of the News," which was an all-volunteer group operating with a minuscule budget. It folded by 1980,

Like many others in the 1970s, I had an interest in Southeast Asia because of America's involvement in Indochina and elsewhere in the region. As it happened, Ithaca, is the site of Cornell University, home of perhaps the best Center for Southeast Asian Studies in the world. A small group of people based in the Cornell community, of which I was one, became interested in the East Timor issue shortly after the Indonesians invaded the territory in 1975.

At first, we produced fact sheets and tried to alert interested groups and individuals around the United States in that way. Then we shifted to a strategy of trying to alert the mainstream media, hopeless as this may have seemed. By 1979 the Ithaca group—made up of students of Southeast Asia, literature, law and other fields of endeavor—had disbanded, but most of us went on to other pursuits and continued working through various institutions to reach American public opinion. We made contacts with *The New York Times, The Washington Post, The Boston Globe* and others. Our goal was to ensure that publications such as these noticed the issue and put out as much accurate information on the situation as possible. Obviously, we did not always succeed but we did create a network of contacts that was ultimately available to East Timor's Catholic Church, refugees, human rights organizations and others. We did this by strict attention to accuracy, professionalism and politeness. There is really no substitute for all of this. And it does pay off.

Arnold Kohen

There was actually one person in the United States who, in my view, would get the Nobel Peace Prize if it meant anything, which, of course, it does not. He was a graduate student at Cornell University, who simply devoted his life to trying to get this issue known. And it was through his efforts that I began to become involved. Now, my name is known, his name is not known, he is the leader, I am the follower. And what it says about intellectual life is that there are a lot of important people who do very serious work and when they build up to a point where someone can help them gain visibility, there are people like me around who are able to help, but that is a supportive role.

From Chomsky's interview with Joop van Tijn on Humanist TV, Holland
(June 10, 1989)

MIT OFFICE, CAMBRIDGE, MASSACHUSETTS

Chomsky

There were literally about half a dozen people who simply dedicated themselves with great commitment to getting this story to break through. They reached a couple of people in Congress. They got to me, for example, and I was able to testify at the UN and write some things and they kept at it, kept at it, kept at it. Whatever is known about the subject mainly comes—essentially comes from their work. There's not much else.

At about that time when I testified at the UN, the *Columbia Journalism Review* suggested that I do an article on the U.S. media and Cambodia. I suggested instead the case of Timor, which was far more important both in what it reveals and for the obvious reason that exposure of the facts might, in any case, help to terminate ongoing atrocities. After some discussion, this request was denied, on the grounds that the Timor story was too obscure to arouse interest... Thus the circle is complete; first, the media suppress a major story, then, a journal devoted to the performance of the media is unwilling to investigate the suppression because it has been so effective.

Toward a New Cold War, page 471, note 3

Despite a personal visit by one of the directors of the film *Manufacturing Consent* to the New York City office of the Columbia *Journalism Review*, and a video copy of the film delivered to that office, their editors refuse to review the film or discuss it. In addition to the obvious relevance of the subject matter, the film played for over six weeks in New York City, was reviewed by *The New York Times*, *The Village Voice*, and *The New York Post*, not to mention every major paper in every major city around the United States where it played (over 225 cities) as well as by the alternative press both local and national. The film has been reviewed in journalism reviews in other countries and by the major press, in every country where it has played. It is being used internally by at least one television network in Canada (Radio Canada, the French language national TV network) to train journalists, and in journalism and communications courses in hundreds of universities.—MA

Chomsky's October 1978 UN statement on East Timor was published in a slightly revised version in *Inquiry*, "East Timor: The Press Cover-up," February 19, 1979, and in *Radical Priorities*, pages 84-94

Karl E. Meyer

I wrote first an editorial called "An Unjust War in East Timor." It had a map and it said exactly what had happened. We then ran a dozen other editorials on it. They were read, they were entered in the congressional record and several congressmen then took up the cause, and then something was done in Congress as a result of this.

MCGILL UNIVERSITY, MONTRÉAL, QUÉBEC

Arnold Kohen

The fact that the editorial page of *The New York Times* on Christmas Eve published that editorial put our work on a very different level. And it gave a great deal of legitimacy to something that we were trying to advance for a long time, and that was the idea and the reality that a major tragedy was unfolding in East Timor.

THE NEW YORK TIMES

Karl E. Meyer

If one takes literally the various theories that Professor Chomsky puts out one would feel that there is a tacit conspiracy between the establishment press and the government in Washington to focus on certain things and ignore certain things. So that if we broke the rules we would instantly get a reaction—a sharp reaction—from the overlords in Washington, [who] would say, "Hey what are you doing, speaking up on East Timor? We're trying to keep that quiet." We didn't hear a thing. What we did hear—and this was quite interesting—is that there was a guy named Arnold Kohen and he became a one-person lobby.

What did Congress do? What happened, according to authoritative international civil servants with whom I spoke at length, was that sufficient American Congressional pressure was generated on Indonesia in 1979-80 so that international humanitarian aid finally reached people who had been starving to death under an Indonesian siege at the rate of thousands a month. This wasn't the only factor in the aid getting there but it was an important one. Still other sources say that were it not for this kind of pressure, kept up over the years, the Indonesian military would have killed far more people from 1979 through the present. Of course, the situation is still terrible in East Timor. But without international pressure, it would have been—and would now be—far worse.

Arnold Kohen

The record is reviewed in volume I of Political Economy of Human Rights. *Congress held important hearings in 1977. The* Times *in fact had a long interview session with James Dunn, the leading Australian government specialist on East Timor, who testified before Congress then. They ran nothing. There were other hearings later; I referred to them in later articles which I think you cite. In the last few years, Congress has done more than run hearings. They curtailed military training (which the Clinton adiminstration is evading) and now some arms.—NC*

The situation is still terrible in East Timor. But without international pressure, it would have been—and would now be—far worse.

Arnold Kohen

Well, you know, I appreciate the nice things that Karl Meyer said about me in his interview but I object to the notion that a one-man lobby was formed or anything like that. I think that if there weren't a large network composed of the American Catholic Bishops Conference, composed of other church groups, composed of human rights groups, composed of simply concerned citizens and others and a network of concern within the news media, I think it would have been impossible to do anything at all at any time and it certainly would have been impossible to sustain things for as long as they have been sustained.

THE NEW YORK TIMES

Karl E. Meyer

Professor Chomsky and a lot of people who engage in this kind of press analysis have one thing in common. Most of them have never worked for a newspaper, many of them know very little about how newspapers work.

When Chomsky came around he had with him a file of all the coverage in *The New York Times*, *The Washington Post* and other papers of East Timor. And he would go to the meticulous degree that if, for example, the London *Times* had a piece on East Timor and then it appeared in *The New York Times* that if a paragraph was cut out he'd compare and he'd say, "Look, this key paragraph, right near the end, which is really what tells the whole story, was left out of *The New York Times* version of the London *Times* thing."

WHAT DID *THE NEW YORK TIMES* CUT OUT OF THE LONDON *TIMES* ARTICLE?

The New York Times published an account written by Gerald Stone, "an Australian television journalist, who is believed to be the first reporter allowed [into East Timor] since the [civil war] began" (4 September 1975). In fact the *Times* story is revised and excerpted from a longer report carried by the *London Times* (2 September 1975). *The New York Times* revisions are instructive.

A major topic of Stone's *London Times*

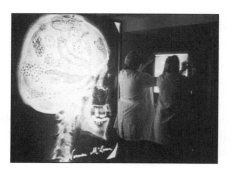

story is his effort to verify reports of large-scale destruction and atrocities, attributed primarily to Fretilin by Indonesian propaganda and news coverage based on it, then and since. These reports, he writes,

> had been filtered through the eyes of frightened and exhausted evacuees or, worse, had come dribbling down from Portuguese, Indonesian, and Australian officials, all of whom had reason to distrust Fretilin.

Here are his major conclusions:

> Our drive through Dili quickly revealed how much distortion and exaggeration surrounds this war. The city has been taking heavy punishment, with many buildings scarred by bullet holes, but all the main ones are standing. A hotel that was reported to have been burnt to the ground was there with its windows shattered, but otherwise intact...

> Undoubtedly there have been some large-scale atrocities on both sides. Whether they were calculated atrocities, authorized by Fretilin or UDT comman-

ders, is another question. Time after time, when I tried to trace a story to its source, I found only someone who had heard it from someone else. Strangely, it is in the interest of all three governments—Portuguese, Indonesian and Australian, to make the situation appear as chaotic and hopeless as possible... *In that light, I am convinced that many of the stories fed to the public in the past two weeks were not simply exaggerations; they were the product of a purposeful campaign to plant lies* (our emphasis).

Stone implicates all three governments in this propaganda campaign.

Of the material just quoted, here is what survives editing in *The New York Times*:

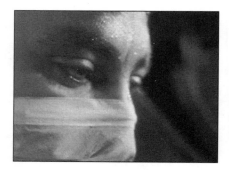

A drive though Dili showed that the city had taken heavy punishment from the fighting. All the main buildings were standing but many were scarred with bullet holes.

Stone's conclusions about the purposeful lies of Indonesian and Western propaganda

Chomsky

There was a story in the London *Times* which was pretty accurate. *The New York Times* revised it radically. They didn't just leave a paragraph out, they revised it and gave it a totally different cast.

It was then picked up by *Newsweek*, giving it *The New York Times* cast. It ended up being a whitewash, whereas the original was an atrocity story.

are totally eliminated, and careful editing has modified his conclusion about the scale of the destruction. What *The New York Times* editors did retain was Stone's description of prisoners on burial detail, the terrible conditions in FRETILIN hospitals (the Portuguese had withdrawn the sole military doctor; there were no other doctors...), "evidence of beating" (this is the sole sub-heading in the article), and other maltreatment of prisoners by FRETILIN.

The process of creating the required history advances yet another step in the *Newsweek* account of Stone's *New York Times* article (International Edition, 15 September, 1975). *Newsweek* writes that "the devastation caused by rival groups fighting for control of Timor is clearly a matter of concern," a comment that is interest-

ing in itself, in view of the lack of concern shown by *Newsweek* for the real bloodbath since the Indonesian invasion. *Newsweek* then turns to "an account of the bloodbath written by Gerald Stone" in the *New York Times*. After quoting the two sentences cited above on the "drive through Dili,"

Newsweek continues:
Stone went on to report seeing bodies lying on the street and many badly injured civilians who had gone without any medical treatment at all. He also revealed that the Marxist Fretilin party had driven the moderate Timorese Democratic Union (UDT) out of the capital and in the process had captured and systematically mistreated many UDT prisoners...Stone's dispatch supported the stories of many of the 4,000 refugees who have already fled Timor.

From this episode we gain some understanding of the machinations of the Free Press. A journalist visits the scene of reported devastation and atrocities by "the Marxist Fretilin party"[see note below] and concludes that the reports are largely false, in fact in large measure propaganda fabrications. After a skillful re-editing job by the *New York Times* that eliminates his major conclusion and modifies others, *Newsweek* concludes that he found the reports were true. Thus the required beliefs are reinforced: "Marxist" terrorists are bent on atrocities, and liberation movements are to be viewed with horror. And the stage is set for general acquiescence when U.S.-backed Indonesian military forces invade to "restore order."

Political Economy of Human Rights, Vol. I, pages 135-137

James S. Dunn, in a report to the Australian Parliament, notes that most of the Fretelin leaders "remained devout practising Catholics"; he refers to the party as "populist Catholic..." He also points out that "from the outset they were at pains to dissociate the party from communist ideology and movements..." a point stressed by all informed observers, relevant here only because of Indonesian claims to the contrary, commonly repeated in the U.S. press.

HARVARD UNIVERSITY PANEL DISCUSSION

Karl E. Meyer

So I said to Chomsky at the time, I said, "Well it may be that you're misinterpreting ignorance, haste, deadline pressure, etc., for some kind of determined effort to suppress an element of the story."

He said, "Well, if it happened once or twice or three times I might agree with you, but if it happens a dozen times, Mr. Meyer, I think there's something else at work."

MIT OFFICE, CAMBRIDGE, MASSACHUSETTS

Chomsky

And it's not a matter of it happening one time two times , five times, a hundred times, it happened all the time.

THE NEW YORK TIMES

Karl E. Meyer

I said, "Professor Chomsky, having been in this business, it happens a dozen times... these are very imperfect institutions."

MIT OFFICE, CAMBRIDGE, MASSACHUSETTS

Chomsky

When it did give coverage it was from the point of view of—it was a whitewash of the United States. Now, you know, that's not an error. That's systematic, consistent behavior—in this case without even any exception.

THE NEW YORK TIMES

Karl E. Meyer

This is a much more subtle process than you get in the kind of sledge-hammer rhetoric of the people that make an A to B equation between what the government does, what people think and what newspapers say, that sometimes what the *Times* does can make enormous difference and other times it has no influence whatsoever.

CBC RADIO (PUBLIC), MONTRÉAL, QUÉBEC

Elaine Brière

So one of the greatest tragedies of our age is still happening in East Timor. The Indonesians have killed up to a third of the population. They're in concentration camps. They conduct large-scale military campaigns against the people who are resisting, campaigns with names like "Operation Eradicate" or "Operation Clean Sweep." Timorese women are subjected to a forced birth-control program. In addition, they're bringing in a constant stream of Indonesian settlers to take over the land. Whenever people are brave enough to take to the streets in demonstrations or show the least sign of resistance, they just massacre them.

It's sort of like if we allow Indonesia to continue to stay in East Timor—the international community—they will simply digest East Timor and turn it into—they're trying to turn it into cash crop.

The importance of media coverage in creating international pressure is clearly illustrated by the massacre of 273 Timorese on November 12, 1991. Approximately 270 people were killed, 160 wounded and many others "disappeared." Among those wounded (by beatings) were two U.S. journalists: Alan Nairn (*New Yorker* magazine) and Amy Goodman (broadcast journalist with WBAI, New York, a progressive, listener-supported radio station). British television journalist Max Stahl smuggled out footage of the massacre giving the atrocity world-wide media coverage. (We would have used some of this footage in *Manufacturing Consent*, but Yorkshire TV refused to make the footage accessible to us for less than $4,000, unlike virtually every other stock-shot source in the world, which allowed us use of footage in exchange for on-screen credit if we would cover duplication costs. A still photographer, Steve Cox, also witnessed the massacre and generously donated the use of his stills, three of which can be seen in the film.—MA)

Although the killing of Timorese does not usually create concern (80 young Timorese men and women were killed three days later, and hundreds disappeared over the next two months), the media coverage of the Dili massacre did create some pressure on Western countries investing in Indonesia to respond. The Canadian government announced a suspension of $30 million in bilateral aid, although existing programs (worth $46 million) continued. Other countries have also cut their aid but the World Bank-led Consultative Group on Indonesia picked up the slack, increasing its aid by $200 million over the previous year.

The media coverage of East Timor at that time also created a surge of interest in East Timor support groups and the East Timor Action Network//U.S. (ETAN/US) was founded as a result.

Sources: Elaine Brière, *Upstream Journal*, March/April 1993, ETAN/US newsletter *Network News, #7,* September 1993

What I saw was a cold-blooded execution and the facts are very simple and very clear. Indonesian soldiers marched up in massed formation and opened fire in unison into a peaceful, defenseless crowd. The next day the national commander of the Indonesian military praised the massacre and said that it was armed forces policy to shoot down defiant Timorese.

I have spent a dozen years covering armies and repressive regimes in places like Central America, Southern Africa and the Middle East, but I have never seen a place where the authorities have succeeded in making so many people so terrified.

When I returned to East Timor in October of this past year, the air of terror was more intense and the repression was greater still. The Indonesian army was sweeping through villages and towns rounding up Timorese who, the army suspected, might be preparing to talk to a UN-sponsored delegation that was due to arrive from the parliament of Portugal. The Indonesians were holding hundreds of meetings across the country, warning that those who spoke to the delegation would be killed.

As the mass broke up people assembled on the street.

By the time it reached the cemetery the crowd had grown quite large. There were perhaps three thousand to five thousand people. Some filed in toward Sebastiao's grave, and many others remained outside, hemmed in on the street by cemetery walls. Then, looking to our right, we saw, coming down the road, a long, slowly marching column of uniformed troops. They were dressed in dark brown, moving in disciplined formation, and they held M-16s before them as they marched. As the column kept advancing, seemingly without end, people gasped and began to shuffle back. I went with Amy Goodman of WBAI/Pacifica radio and stood on the corner between the soldiers and the Timorese. We thought that if the Indonesian force saw that foreigners were there, they would hold back and not attack the crowd.

But as we stood there watching as the soldiers marched into our face, the incon-

Chomsky

I mean this is way beyond just demonstrating the subservience of the media to power. I mean, they have real complicity in genocide in this case. The reason that the atrocities can go on is because nobody knows about them. If anyone knew about them there would be protests and pressures to stop them. So therefore by suppressing the facts, the media are making a major contribution to some of the—probably the worst act of genocide since the Holocaust [relative to population].

ceivable thing began to happen. The soldiers rounded the corner, never breaking stride, raised their rifles and fired in unison into the crowd.

People fell, stunned and shivering, bleeding in the road, and the Indonesian soldiers kept on shooting. I saw the soldiers aiming and shooting people in the back, leaping bodies to hunt down those who were still standing. They executed schoolgirls, young men, old Timorese, the street was wet with blood and the bodies were everywhere.

As the soldiers were doing this they were beating me and Amy; they took our cameras and our tape recorders and grabbed Amy by the hair and punched and kicked her in the face and in the stomach. When I put my body over her, they focused on my head.

They fractured my skull with the butts of their M-16s.

This was, purely and simply, a deliberate mass murder, a massacre of unarmed, defenseless people. There was no provocation, no stones were thrown, the crowd was quiet and shrinking back as the shooting began. There was no confrontation, no hothead who got out of hand. This was not an ambiguous situation that somehow spiraled out of control.

It was quite evident from the way the soldiers behaved that they marched up with orders to commit a massacre. They never issued a warning up and opened fire in unison. This action was not the result of their interaction with the crowd: the Timorese were just standing there or trying to get away.

After the Timorese had been gunned down the army sealed off the area. They turned away religious people who came to administer first aid. They let the Timorese bleed to death on the road.

General Try Sutrisno, the chief of the Indonesian armed forces, said in a speech to graduates of the national defense institute that Timorese like those who gathered outside the cemetery are "people who must be crushed." He said "delinquents like these agitators have to be shot and we will shoot them."

General Sutrisno added on December 9 that as soon as Indonesia's investigation of the massacre is completed "we will wipe out all separatist elements who have tainted the government's dignity."

President Suharto, for his part, responded to the massacre by going out of his way to ridicule the East Timorese. He said that the killings in Dili were a "small thing," and said that when world leaders asked him about it "I showed them a map where East Timor is located, the tiny island called East Timor. That small thing caused everybody to make a fuss. And, he said, "they all laughed."

From Alan Nairn's testimony to the UN Special Committee on Decolonization, July 27, 1992. (Nairn is a writer for New Yorker *magazine)*

The gradual effect of organized and concerted grassroots pressure on U.S. policy on Indonesia can be seen in decisions made by various arms of the government:

Although the U.S. sells fewer arms to Indonesia now than in the 1970s and 1980s, arms sales to Indonesia were over $100 million in 1991. They include high-tech aircraft as well as the M-16 automatic weapons used [in the Dili massacre].

The most recent Congressional Presentation Document estimates that in 1993 the U.S. sold $11 million worth of U.S. weaponry to Jakarta through the Foreign Military Sales (FMS), a government–to–government transaction. Indonesia bought another $32 million in arms commercially.

In late 1992, over objections from the

Bush administration and major corporations such as AT&T, Congress cut off International Military Education and Training (IMET) funds to Indonesia for fiscal year 1992-93. While the program's $2.3 million cost represented only a small portion of total U.S. aid, it was the first time that Congress has taken punitive action against Indonesia on the issue of East Timor....

In late July [1993], the State Department acknowledged that they denied the Jordanian government permission to sell four U.S.-made F5E fighter jets to the Indonesian military. Under the terms of the original sale to Jordan, the State Department had final say on the transfer.... According to a State Department official, a "combination of sensitive issues, including human-rights concerns, made it impossible to approve the transfer."...

Also, in March 1993, the meeting of the UN Human Rights Commission in Geneva passed a resolution condemning Indonesian human rights abuses in East Timor. The Clinton administration co-sponsored the resolution. This is a significant reversal of past U.S. blocking of similar resolutions.

ETAN/US, Network News, #7

Indonesia is Canada's second largest aid recipient. Since 1985, Indonesia has received annual disbursements of $45-$75 million. Canada gives more bilateral aid to Indonesia than the United States does. Japan is number one.

When Indonesia invaded East Timor the Canadian government turned a blind eye. Canada abstained in United Nations votes demanding an immediate withdrawal of Indonesian troops and a mere 6 months after the invasion awarded Indonesia a mixed aid package of $200 million dollars.

The reasons for this bizarre behaviour go back to 1970 when Indonesia was declared "a country of concentration" for Canadian aid and trade. Canada now sells five times as much to Indonesia as it imports. There are over 300 Canadian companies operating in manufacturing, importing, and consulting, including ten companies involved in weapons production.

Canada's military sales to Indonesia since 1975 include ammunition, military vehicles, transport planes and Pratt & Whitney engines for Bell helicopters being assembled in Indonesia.

When the Asia Pacific Foundation, an organization set up to expand trade in the Asian region, argued against using aid as a way to put pressure on Indonesia to improve its record on human rights and observe international law, it failed to mention that its constituency, Canadian business, profits from the Canadian "tied-aid" policy which ensures that Indonesia will buy Canadian goods with its aid dollars, and failed to mention that Indonesia might respond to Canadian pressure in a way that could hurt Canadian business interests in Indonesia (see Issues, Vol.7, No. 1, Winter 1993, published by the Asia Pacific Foundation of Canada).

Elaine Brière, The Indonesia Kit, East Timor Alert Network

In an historic move, the Senate Foreign Relations Committee unanimously approved an amendment linking arms sales to Indonesia to human rights in East Timor. [The measure] requires the president to consult with Congress before approving major weapons deals. It is believed to be the first time arms sales to a U.S. ally have been tied to human rights concerns.... The bill is now in legislative limbo.... Whether enacted this year or not, the amendment has already mobilized and strengthened East Timor's cause in Washington and across the U.S.

Network News, #8, November 1993, pages 1-3

What can young people do about this? Everything. None of these things result from immutable physical laws. They are all results of human decisions in human institutions. The decisions and the institutions can be modified, perhaps extensively, if enough people commit themselves with courage and honesty to the search for justice and freedom.

Radical Priorities, page 277

"IDEAS," CBC (PUBLIC) RADIO, CANADA

David Frum *(Journalist)*

You say that what the media do is to ignore certain kinds of atrocities that are committed by us and our friends and to play up enormously atrocities that are committed by them and our enemies. And you posit that there's a test of integrity and moral honesty which is to have a kind of equality of treatment of corpses.

Chomsky

Equality of principles.

David Frum

I mean that every dead person should be in principle equal to every other dead person.

Chomsky

That's not what I say at all.

David Frum

Well, I'm glad that's not what you say because in fact that's not what you do.

Chomsky

Of course that's not what I do nor would I say it. In fact, I say the opposite. What I say is we should be responsible for our own actions primarily.

David Frum

Because your method is not only to ignore the corpses created by them, but also to ignore the corpses that are created by neither side but which are irrelevant to your ideological agenda.

Chomsky

That's totally untrue.

"Ideas" produces some of the best radio documentaries in the world. Each year, "Ideas" gives over one week of broadcasts to the Massey Lectures, Canada's most prestigious forum on radio. A prominent thinker is given one hour a night for five programs. In 1988, the Massey Lectures were given to Noam Chomsky, but a question–and–answer session with Canadian journalists was also included.

We asked permission to film the recording of the lectures and subsequent discussion, but the producer of the program, Max Allen, then an active member of an organization called "Media People for Social Responsibility," refused to allow our cameras anywhere near CBC's studios. The executive producer of the program, Bernie Lucht, wrote us, "...I'm going to say no to this. I have discussed this with a number of my colleagues and feel the videotaping would be too disruptive of our own recording.... A video crew, over and above those of us directly involved in the production, would upset the intimacy needed to do this work. Finally, our studio area is too small to accommodate the extra people and equipment."

In comparison, BBC, in England, with a studio a quarter the size of CBC's, welcomed us with open arms, as did every tiny community radio station around the world sympathetic to the aims of our film. At the core of Allen's and Lucht's resistance, it seems, was their desire for exclusivity and control.

The round–table discussion with the journalists took place in an auditorium at Ryerson University in Toronto. The discussion was advertised and open to the public. After talking it over with Stuart McLean, dean of journalism at Ryerson, who would chair the panel discussion, we decided to film the public event.

Respecting the producers' concerns not to interfere with the proceedings, we took a sound feed from the control room behind the stage and located our cameras at the back of the theater, up in the projection booth, behind a double layer of glass, and turned the lights off to reduce reflection. Dan Garson, a filmmaker with an 8mm video camera, sat in the audience and set up a mini-tripod on his chair's fold-out desk. We also took a video feed from a remote-controlled surveillance camera mounted on the ceiling of the auditorium. In the end, we had four cameras covering the event. —MA

For information on ordering cassettes and transcripts of "Ideas" programs, see Resource Guide

You're responsible for the predictable consequences of your actions. You're not responsible for the predictable consequences of somebody else's actions.

David Frum

Well, let me give you an example, that one of your own causes that you take very seriously is the cause of the Palestinians, and a Palestinian corpse weighs very heavily on your conscience. And yet a Kurdish corpse does not.

Chomsky

That's not true at all. I've been involved in Kurdish support groups for years. That's absolutely false, I mean just ask the Kurdish—ask the people who are involved in—I mean, you know, they come to me, I sign their petitions and so on and so forth. In fact, if you look at the things we've written, I mean take, say—take a look—I mean, I'm not Amnesty International. I can't do everything. I'm a single human person. But take a look, say, at the book Edward S. Herman and I wrote on this topic. We discussed three kinds of atrocities. What we called "benign bloodbaths", which nobody cares about, constructive bloodbaths, which are the ones we like, and nefarious bloodbaths, which are the ones that the bad guys do. The principle that I think we ought to follow is not the one that you stated. You know, it's a very simple ethical point: You're responsible for the predictable consequences of your actions. You're not responsible for the predictable consequences of somebody else's actions. The most important thing for me and for you is to think about the consequences of your actions. What can you affect.

The ethical value of one's actions depends on their anticipated and predictable consequences. It is very easy to denounce the atrocities of someone else. That has about as much ethical value as denouncing atrocities that took place in the 18th Century. The point is that the useful and significant political actions are those that have consequences for human beings. And those are overwhelmingly the actions which you have some way of influencing and controlling, which means for me, American actions.

From On Power and Ideology, page 51

On the cause of the Palestinians, see: *The Fateful Triangle*; "Rejectionism and Accommodation"

See also:
- *The Chomsky Reader*, pages 371-405 (excerpted from *The Fateful Triangle*)
- *Pirates and Emperors: International Terrorism in the Real World*
- *Towards a New Cold War*
- *Necessary Illusions*
- *Chronicles of Dissent*, chapters 2 and 6; *Language and Politics*, interviews 9, 27 and 36
- Several articles in *Z Magazine*, including October 1993, on the peace accords, and earlier, in *Peace in the Middle East* (1974)

Chomsky

These are the things to keep in mind. These are not just academic exercises. We're not analyzing the media on Mars or in the eighteenth century or something like that. We're dealing with real human beings who are suffering and dying and being tortured and starving because of policies that we are involved in, we as citizens of democratic societies are directly involved in and are responsible for, and what the media are doing is ensuring that we do not act on our responsibilities, and that the interests of power are served, not the needs of the suffering people, and not even the needs of the American people who would be horrified if they realized the blood that's dripping from their hands because of the way they are allowing themselves to be deluded and manipulated by the system.

Simply put, most people are not gangsters. Few people, for example, would steal food from a starving child, even if they happened to be hungry and knew they would not be caught or punished. Someone who did so would be properly regarded as pathological, and, in fact, very few are pathological in this sense. But, in fact, Americans steal food from starving children on a vast scale. In much of Central America, for example, U.S. intervention has led to an increase in agricultural production while nutritional standards decline and millions starve and die, because crop lands have been devoted to export in the interests of agribusiness, not the needs of the domestic population... But since Americans are not gangsters, if they come to understand what they are doing — that they are in fact stealing food from starving children, on a vast scale — they would be appalled and would do something to put an end to this atrocity, as they can. Therefore, they must be protected from an understanding of this aspect of the real world.

From an exchange with Dr. Celia Jakubowicz, printed in *Language and Politics*, page 374

UNION HALL, CAMBRIDGE, ENGLAND

Chomsky

What about the Third World? Well, despite everything, and it's pretty ugly and awful, ah, these struggles are not over. The struggle for freedom and independence never is completely over.

Their courage, in fact, is really remarkable and amazing. I've personally had the privilege—and it is a privilege—of witnessing it a few times in villages in Southeast Asia and Central America and recently in the occupied West Bank, and it is astonishing to see.

MALASPINA COLLEGE, NANAIMO, BRITISH COLUMBIA

Chomsky

And it's always amazing—at least to me it's amazing—I can't understand it, it's also very moving and very inspiring; in fact, it's kind of awe-inspiring. Now they rely very crucially on a very slim margin for survival that's provided by dissidence and turbulence within the imperial societies, and how large that margin is, is for us to determine.

END PART ONE
INTERMISSION

The real victims of the policies I have been describing are millions of suffering, tortured and brutalized people throughout the Third World. Our highly effective ideological institutions protect us from seeing this, except sporadically. If we had the honesty and moral courage, we would not let a day pass without listening to the cries of the victims of our actions, or inaction. We would turn on the radio in the morning and hear the account of a Guatemalan army operation in Quiche province—one supplied and backed by the U.S. and its Israeli client—in which the army entered a town, collected its population in a central town building, took all the men and beheaded them, raped the women and then killed them, and took the children to the nearby river and killed them by bashing their heads against the rocks. A few people escaped and told the story, but not to us. We would turn on the radio in the afternoon and listen to a Portuguese priest in Timor telling how the Indonesian army, enjoying constant and crucial U.S. military and diplomatic support, forced villagers to stab, chop and beat to death people supporting the resistance, including members of their own families. And in the evening we would listen to some of the victims who escaped the latest bombing attack on villages or fleeing civilians in El Salvador—an attack coordinated by U.S. military aircraft operating from their Honduran and Panamanian sanctuaries. We would subject ourselves to the chilling record of terror and torture in our dependencies, compiled by Amnesty International, America's Watch, Survival International, and other respected human rights organizations.

But we successfully insulate ourselves from this grim reality. By doing so, we sink to a level of cowardice and moral depravity that has few counterparts in the modern world, and we also help to fan the flames that will lead to a conflagration that will, very possibly, engulf us as well.

From "The Drift towards Global War," in *Studies in Political Economy,*
vol. 17, summer, 1985

The people of the Third World need our sympathetic understanding and, much more than that, they need our help. We can provide them with a margin of survival by internal disruption in the United States. Whether they can succeed against the kind of brutality we impose on them depends in large part on what happens here. The courage they show is quite amazing... [it] invariably brings to my mind some contemptuous remarks of Rousseau's on Europeans who have abandoned freedom and justice for the peace and repose "they enjoy in their chains." He goes on to say: "When I see multitudes of entirely naked savages scorn European voluptuousness and endure hunger, fire, the sword and death to preserve only their independence, I feel that it does not behoove slaves to reason about freedom." People who think that these are mere words understand very little about the world.

What Uncle Sam Really Wants, pages 100-101

Why wasn't there anything about Israel in the film? We occasionally get this question from audience members who know Chomsky's concern with the Middle East. We do include a section on his solidarity with critics of Israel's Occupation in the context of third world struggles. In fact, we end Part One of the film with it in quite a moving section that sends people out during the intermission to discuss the issues raised by the film.

When it takes five years to make one film, you can't set out to do a current affairs piece. Anything you shoot will be instantly dated because the release of the film is inevitably a year or more away. And with Israel the situation seems to change every week. We simply felt we couldn't do justice to Chomsky's analysis of the Middle East within the time constraints of the film. There is undoubtedly a film to be made with him on this topic, and if there is anyone out there willing to finance such a project, we would be happy to make the film. Also, there are many areas of Chomsky's analysis not covered in the film—notably, Central America. It all points to the need for a series on his diverse areas of interest and concern.

We chose our case studies carefully—following Chomsky's agenda, really. We wrote him at the time we were considering doing the Timor/Cambodia case study and a section on the Gulf War, and he encouraged us. Although the coverage is distorted, it's not like you can't pick up a newspaper practically any day of the week and find out *something* about what's going on in Israel. Not so with East Timor. For many, many people, our film is their introduction to the entire issue and a good deal of activism has been generated as a result of screenings of the film. We also felt we would be remiss to make a film about the media in the 1990s and not have something about the Gulf "War."

To compensate somewhat, included here is a excerpt from *The Fateful Triangle: Israel, the United States and the Palestinians* (1984), followed by a statement of Chomsky's, made just after the 1993 Peace Accord was signed.—MA

These remarks will be critical of Israel's policies: its consistent rejection of any political settlement that accommodates the national rights of the indigenous population; its repression and state terrorism over many years; its propaganda efforts, which have been remarkably successful—much to Israel's detriment, in my view—in the United States. But this presentation may be misleading, in two respects. In the first place, this is not an attempt at a general history; the focus is on what I think is and has been wrong and what should be changed, not on what I think has been right.* Secondly, the focus on Israeli actions and initiatives may obscure the fact that my real concern is the policies that have been pursued by the U.S. government and our responsibility in shaping or tolerating these policies. To a remarkable extent, articulate opinion and attitudes in the U.S.A. have been dominated by people who describe themselves as "supporters of Israel," a term that I will also adopt, though with much reluctance, since I think they should more properly be called "supporters of the moral degeneration and ultimate destruction of Israel," and not Israel alone. Given this ideological climate and the concrete U.S. actions that it has helped to engender, it is natural enough that Israeli policies within the U.S. and in U.S.-Israel relations portends a rather gloomy future, in my view, for reasons that I hope will become clearer as we proceed. If so, a large measure of responsibility lies right here, as in the recent past.

*One of the things that is right is the Hebrew-language press, or, at least, significant segments of it. I have relied extensively on the work of thoughtful and courageous Israeli journalists who have set—and met—quite unusual standards in exposing unpleasant facts about their own government and society. There is nothing comparable elsewhere, in my experience.

From *The Fateful Triangle: Israel, the United States, and the Palestinians,* pages 3-4

I'm often asked why the film doesn't deal with the Middle East, and say I don't know, but I basically agree with the decision, whatever it may have been, because if the Middle East had been included more than peripherally the whole project would be dead in the water, given the power and fanaticism of the commissars. But I'm glad for your clarifications, which make sense, and which I'll try to convey if asked again. —NC

There is a dirty little secret which is worth bearing in mind, and that is that for 20 years, roughly, U.S. rejectionism has blocked any peace process in the Middle East. Anything. Every effort to try to develop a diplomatic settlement has been blocked by U.S. power and intervention.

Now, when I say dirty little secret I mean nobody's allowed to mention it. So the facts are suppressed. They are so deep down the memory hole you can't even dig them up any more. Pretty soon they'll be written out of even scholarly history, probably.

Throughout this whole period there has been a certain area of very broad agreement about the form of a peace settlement. Namely, that it should be based on UN 242 (November 1967), a Security Council resolution which is an agreement among states. It says all states in the region must have the right to live in peace and security. It emphasizes the inadmissibility of acquisition of territory by force and calls for withdrawal of Israeli occupying forces. It was interpreted at the time, including by the United States, as a call for full peace in exchange for full withdrawal.

Now, by the 1970s, the U.S. had changed its position on this, from full withdrawal to partial withdrawal. That is, whatever amount of withdrawal Israel feels like. At that point the United States separated itself from the world— that is, 1971. But the big separation came later in about the mid–1970s when the terms of settlement were changed in the international arena to include UN 242, which was never seriously in question, along with other UN resolutions. Now these other UN resolutions call for the national rights of Palestinians.

So by the mid–1970s, the terms for a diplomatic settlement were a two-stage settlement on the internationally recognized borders with all the wording of 242, with guarantees for the right and security of every state in the region, and so on and so forth. On that, just about everybody was agreed, the Arab States, the PLO, the Russians, the NATO allies, the Third World and so on.

It was blocked by the United States. By blocked, I mean we had to veto it at the Security Council, which threw the Security Council out of the diplomacy in 1976. We had to vote against it every year in the General Assembly. Every

year that there was a vote on it, votes were like 150 to two. The United States and Israel essentially vetoed the General Assembly. We had to block initiatives from other countries, from the Arab countries, from Europe, from the PLO, from everybody, because we simply refused to accept that there should be Palestinian national rights alongside Israeli rights. There was no issue about recognizing Israel's right to live in peace and security. That was essentially settled. Everybody had agreed on that.

So there are basically two questions that have been alive all these years. One is: Is it just the rights of existing states or also the rights of the Palestinians? That is question one. So UN 242 alone or UN 242 plus all other resolutions?

And, secondly, what is meant by withdrawal? Does it mean, as the world understands, and in fact as the U.S. insisted up until 1971, withdrawal to the international borders? Or does it mean such withdrawal as Israel and the United States choose to carry out? Partial withdrawal in their interests.

Since December 1987, a third issue has come up. December 1987, the Intifada started. There was open resistance to Israeli rule. And at that point the U.S. split from the world on a third issue and the question is... What is the status of resistance against military occupation?

Well, there is an international position on this. This is again unmentionable. It has the wrong message, so it is never reported. There is a big UN resolution on this—1986, I think. A major UN resolution on terrorism. Condemns terrorism in all its forms. You know, a big attack on terrorism. It passed 153 to two, [the two being] the United States and Israel. One country, Honduras, abstained, which means it's essentially unanimous, except for the United States and Israel.

Why did the U.S. come out against the resolution on terrorism? Well, there was a paragraph there which was unacceptable. It says that nothing in this resolution infringes on the right of people to resist racist regimes and military occupation. And the U.S. refuses to accept that, just as, say, Nazi Germany would have refused to accept it in 1943. And for roughly the same reasons, if you think about it.

Now, when the Intifada came along, this became a real issue. Here is resistance against a military occupation. Well, the U.S. attitude, the

official U.S. attitude, was stated immediately, that the U.S. regards the resistance to Israeli rule, which could be things like, say, refusing to pay taxes and so on, as "terrorist acts against Israel" and demands that they be terminated. In other words, no form of resistance to this military occupation is permitted. That's the third major issue on which the U.S. departed from the world. And when I say world, notice that there are very few exceptions.

That's the way it stood until the Oslo Agreement, which was just signed. Notice that that agreement accepts U.S. rejectionism totally, 100 percent. The permanent settlement, not the short–term one, but the permanent settlement, the one down the road, is to be based on UN 242 alone, not the other resolutions which call for Palestinian rights, rights as refugees, rights of self-determination and so on.

So the end result is 242 alone, exactly what the U.S. has demanded for 20 years while it has been blocking any peace process.

On the matter of withdrawal, it was made clear and explicit at once that withdrawal will be partial. So the U.S. wins on that one.

On the matter of the Intifada, it wasn't written into the agreement, but the exchange of letters between Arafat and Rabin makes that one explicit. Arafat takes responsibility for ending the Intifada, for ending any form of resistance to Israeli rule, for ending what the United States defines as terrorist acts against Israel, meaning resistance.

With regard to the matter of withdrawal, there is a lot of loose talk but if you look at the details it is a little different. For example, it is commonly said that Israel pledged to withdraw from the Gaza Strip. Well, that is not accurate. If you look at the two contradictory conditions in the agreement, one says withdraw—well, actually, it doesn't even say withdraw, it says "redeploy" in the Gaza Strip. The other one says that Israel will maintain control over the Israeli settlements and any access to them. OK, have a look at the map of the Gaza Strip and take a look at where the settlements are and draw a line around them. There are a lot of different ways of drawing a line. Israel could certainly claim, plausibly, that the line around its settlements, mainly Gush Katif in the south, would include roughly 40 percent of the coastline of the Gaza Strip, which is the only important part. Nobody cares about the desert. It's very narrow, a couple of miles wide and mostly desert, but the coastline is valuable.

Israel could easily claim, whether they will or not we don't know, that their withdrawal leaves out about 40 percent. So they will withdraw from the city of Gaza. So it's kind of like the New York police force withdrawing from Harlem or something. They don't want to be shot at, in other words. But they could keep everything they want.

Now these Gush Katif settlements, especially in the south, they are very important for Israel. They produce a very substantial proportion of their exports, believe it or not. This is a desert, but they use a lot of water. In fact, they steal the water of the Strip, as Israeli commentators point out. They use it for producing almost half of Israel's tomatoes for export and a large part of its flowers, which go to Europe and make a lot of money. There are big tourist hotels down there which have artificial lakes and so on. This is desert, recall. There is no reason to believe that any of that is going to be left. In fact, there are new waterpipes going in right now, to those areas. And the prime minister, Rabin, has made it clear that they are a high priority.

You can't predict the future. Things could change. In effect, what we do will have a big effect on what happens. I'll come to that. But as it stands, the agreement says Israel basically takes what it wants in the Gaza Strip. If you look at the West Bank, the same story is true. If you look at the development plans for the West Bank, look where the roads are, where the settlements are and so on. You see that there has been a long-term plan, in fact it goes back to 1968, to integrate large parts of the West Bank into the Israeli economy while leaving out Palestinian population concentrations. So that's the way the big highways go. So, if you want to get from one Palestinian town to another, you often have to go through Israel, because that's the way the roads go.

What about the third area, Jerusalem? Jerusalem, which was illegally annexed, over Security Council objections, is now legally three times the size of what it was before the '67 war. But that is misleading because when people refer to Jerusalem they are referring to something called Greater Jerusalem. Now, if you look at Greater Jerusalem, and you look at the infra-structure, meaning the waterpipes, the sewage disposal, the roads, the settlements, and everything else, that is a very substantial part of the West Bank. In fact, it includes several hundred thousand Palestinians, who again are off in corners. Well, again, Israel has no intention of withdrawing from Greater Jerusalem.

But basically everybody agrees we don't want responsibility for the population. We want them to administer their own affairs and survive as they may. We want to take what is useful, in particular the water. So Israel takes about five sixths of the water of the West Bank [which represents about a third of the water it uses]. The usable land, the nice suburbs of Tel Aviv and Jerusalem, which happen to be up in the hills around there, the Jordan Valley and so on, that's the way development has been set up. You look at the settlement since the Labor Party started it back in the early 1970s, it has been very heavily hydrologically motivated, as Israeli experts have been pointing out. That is, the settlements have been very much planned in order to make sure that there is control of the water resources, which are very important since this is a semi-arid area.

It's very much back to the status quo. It's back to the situation roughly in the mid–1980s. Not entirely, there are differences; some of those differences include possible opportunities. How those opportunities are met depends in a big way on what happens here.

How could all of this be achieved? I should say that strong supporters of Israel are very clear about this. Thomas Friedman again quite accurately described this in *The New York Times* as "Palestinian surrender." He said Arafat ran up the white flag. But how did it happen? Well, it has a lot to do with the developments in the world system that we've just been talking about. Remember that while the U.S. could block any diplomacy, it couldn't institute its own rejection-ist solution as long as the world was out there.

Well, the world isn't out there any more. The Soviet Union is out of the game. The Third World is out of the game, in part, for two reasons. In part because of the end of non-align-ment, a consequence of the fact that it's a uni-polar world. And secondly, and more important, it's because of this huge catastrophe of capital-ism that swept over most of the world in the 1980s and just ruined the Third World. It is now a disaster area. The idea of some initiative is essentially finished from there.

Now, as for Europe, that's the matter of market control again. Here, a big change took place after the Gulf War. Europe did have independent initiatives. It was calling for political settlements in the terms of the rest of the world. After the Gulf War, it stopped. In fact, the last vote in the General Assembly was December 1990. Up until then, it had been regular. Since then, none. The reason largely is that Europe essentially ceded the Middle East to the United States.

Now, since the New World Order was established in 1945, the U.S. has demanded that the Monroe Doctrine extend to the Middle East, but it hadn't quite got there. Europe finally has accepted that. Europe is still permitted to implement U.S. rejectionist proposals, which in fact is what Norway did in August, but not the independent initiatives that had previously been developed in Europe that had called for a political settlement.

There is another factor, namely the serious decline of the PLO internally—which is a big story but there is no time for that, though it is very important.

U.S. world dominance in many ways is even greater than it was before, that means without parallel in history, even more than 1945 in many ways. There is a lot of danger. But it also means a lot of opportunities. It means for the people of the United States, for us, what we do is much more important even than it has been before, when it was very important. Crucially, the United States has blocked the peace process all along. It has now got what it wants. It's been able to do this because of the quiescence of the American population. There are a lot of openings and all of that could change, so there is a big responsibility for anybody who cares about such things.

From "Keeping the Rabble in Line," recorded in New York City, September 26, 1993, available from Alternative Radio

For more on the Peace Accords, see *Z Magazine*, October 1993

PART TWO

ACTIVATING DISSENT

EXCERPT: "ON THE SPOT" (NFB–1954)

Announcer
On the spot presents:

Fred Davis
In today's assignment we're going to see just what's behind the making of movies. The director and the crew are shooting a documentary film. Let's take a closer look.

Bob, this word "documentary." What would you say is the difference between a documentary film and a— a feature movie?

Bob
Well, there are a good many differences. One would be length. Generally speaking, documentaries are a good deal shorter than feature films. Also, documentaries have something to say in the way of a message. They are *informational* films. Also, another term that's used interchangeably with documentary is the word "actuality"—*actuality* films.

Fred Davis
Bob, is this the thing you hold up in front of the camera before each scene?

Bob
This is a clapper board, yes. This identifies on the visual camera the scene number and the take number, and also, as you heard on the sound track, the editor back at the studio puts the two pieces of film together, matches where the lips and the clapper come together, and there you are: in sync.

There is no one single, all-encompassing definition of the term *documentary*... However, John Grierson's commonly-cited phrase "the creative treatment of actuality" is perhaps the most useful, for at least two reasons. First, it emphasizes the documentary form's concentration on the actual, its basis in real-life events, issues and people. As well, it suggests that far from being transparent windows onto reality, documentaries—like all other forms of filmmaking—are mediated *constructions*, the result of countless decisions made by individuals struggling to produce coherent, thoughtful, and passionate (or so one hopes) *interpretations* of reality.

From *Constructing Reality: Exploring Media Issues in Documentary*, by Arlene Moscovitch (National Film Board of Canada, 1993). (See Resource Guide for more information on the book and the nine hours of films it accompanies)

KUWR (PUBLIC) RADIO, LARAMIE, WYOMING
Seen on the Erin Mills Town Centre video wall

Marci Randall Miller
Before the break you were mentioning the media putting forth the information that the power elite want. I'm not sure if I understand—how *does* the power elite do this, and why do we stand for it? Why does it work so well?

Chomsky
Ok. There are really two questions here. One: is this picture of the media true? And there you have to look at the evidence. I mean, I've given you one example and that shouldn't convince anybody. One has to look at a lot of evidence to see whether this is true. I think anyone who investigates it will find out that the evidence to support it is simply overwhelming, in fact it's probably one of the best supported conclusions in the social sciences. But the other question is: how does it work?

AIRPORT, AMSTERDAM, HOLLAND
Chomsky arrives through electric sliding doors

Patrick Barnard (freelance journalist)
I'm the media guy. What would you like?
I got you an *International Herald Tribune*.

Chomsky
Anything in a Western language. What have you got?

Patrick Barnard
The Financial Times?

Chomsky
Financial Times? Absolutely! (*Barnard laughs*)
That's the only paper that tells the truth.

The business press, for example, often does quite good and accurate reporting, and the rest of the press too, in many cases. The reason is that people in power need to know the facts if they're going to make decisions in their own interests.

From "Noam Chomsky: Media, Knowledge and Objectivity," an interview with David Barsamian, June 16, 1993 (available from Alternative Radio)

To the best of our knowledge, *The Financial Times* has yet to use this endorsement in any advertising campaign. —MA

Peter Wintonick
You got the one where they've been debating back and forth?

Chomsky
NRC Handelsblad.

Peter Wintonick
Han-dels-blad—

GRONIGEN, HOLLAND

In the film, the following sequence is intercut with archival black-and-white footage of boxing matches

Chomsky
Well, this evening's program is scheduled as a debate, which puzzled me all the way through—there are some problems. One problem is that no proposition has been set forth. As I understand debate, people are supposed to advocate something and oppose something. Rather more sensibly, a topic has been proposed for discussion. The topic is the manufacture of consent.

Frits Bolkestein
It's somewhat unusual for a member of the government to debate with a professor in public. It hasn't happened in Holland before. I don't think it's often happened elsewhere.

Moderator
Mr. Bolkestein, the floor is yours.

Bolkestein
Now, we all know that the theory can never be established merely by examples. It can only be established by showing some internal inherent logic. Professor Chomsky has not done so.

The "debate" was sponsored by *NRC Handelsblad*, a "quality, left of center paper" in which Frits Bolkestein had written a full-page attack on Chomsky in the form of a book review. Chomsky's response was published and Bolkestein's rebuttal was printed, as was Chomsky's response to that. When Chomsky was in town for a conference of philosophers–entitled "Knowledge and Language," sponsored by the International Philosophers Project, the newspaper organized a "debate." Whatever it was, it lasted over two hours, with an odd and restricted format including sections "with interruptions" and sections "without interruptions." At times, the participants lost track of their assigned roles and had to be reminded whether they were speaking or interrupting.—MA

A former minister of defence for the Netherlands, Frederick (Frits) Bolkestein had previously been a member of the liberal People's Party for Freedom and Democracy (1978-1982 and 1986-1988) and state secretary for economic affairs (1982-1986).

Before entering politics, he worked for the Shell Group, serving as director of Shell Chemicals in Paris (1973–1976). He has also been vice-chairman of the Atlantic Commission and a member of the Royal Institute of International Affairs.

Moderator

Professor Chomsky.

Chomsky

He's quite right when he says that you can't just pick examples, you have to do them in a rational way. That's why we *compared* examples.

Bolkestein

The truth is that things are not as simple as Professor Chomsky maintains. Another of Professor Chomsky's case studies concerns the treatment that Cambodia has received in the Western press. Here he goes badly off the rails. (*trickle of audience laughter*)

Chomsky

We didn't discuss Cambodia. We compared Cambodia with East Timor. Two very closely paired examples. And we gave approximately three hundred pages of detail covering this in *The Political Economy of Human Rights*, including a reference to every article that we could discover about Cambodia.

Bolkestein

Many Western intellectuals do not like to face the facts and balk at the conclusions that any untutored person would draw.

Chomsky

You know, many people are very irritated by the fact that we exposed the extraordinary deceit over Cambodia and paired it with the simultaneous suppression of the U.S.-supported, ongoing atrocities in Timor. People don't like that. For one thing we were challenging the right to lie in defense of the State, for another thing, we were exposing the apologetics and support for actual, ongoing atrocities. That doesn't make you popular.

Bolkestein

Where did he learn about the atrocities in East Timor or in Central America if not in the same free press which he so derides?

Chomsky

You can find out where I learned about them by looking at my footnotes. I learned about them from human rights reports, from church reports, from refugee studies and extensively from the Australian press. There was nothing from the American press because there was silence.

Bolkestein

Chairman, this is an attempt at intellectual intimidation. These are the ways of the bully. Professor Chomsky uses the oldest debating trick on record. He erects a man of straw and proceeds to hack away at him.

Professor Chomsky calls this the manufacture of consent, I call it the creation of consensus. In Holland we call it *Grondslag*, which means foundation. Professor Chomsky thinks it is deceitful, but it is not. In a representative democracy it means winning people for one's point of view. But I do not think that Professor Chomsky believes in representative democracy, I think he believes in direct democracy. With Rosa Luxemburg, he longs for the creative, spontaneous, self-correcting force of mass action that is the vision of the anarchist. It is also a boy's dream.

Chomsky

Those who believe in democracy and freedom have a serious task ahead of them. What they should be doing, in my view, is dedicating their efforts to helping the despised common people to struggle for their rights and to realize the democratic goals that constantly surface throughout history. They should be serving not

Groningers genieten van debat tussen Bolkestein en Chomsky
'The dreamer' wins debate with 'the cynic'

power and privilege, but rather their victims. Freedom and democracy are by now not merely values to be treasured. They are quite possibly the prerequisite to survival .

Bolkestein

It's a conspiracy theory pure and simple. It is not borne out by the facts. Ah— Mr. Chairman—

Chairman

Yes?

Bolkestein

I have to go to Amsterdam, if you'll excuse me—I'm leaving.

(*applause, laughter*)

Chairman

One thing is sure: that consent has not been manufactured tonight.

ACLU, ROCHESTER, NEW YORK

Chomsky

There's nothing more remote from what I'm discussing or from what we have been discussing than a conspiracy theory. If I give an analysis of, say, the economic system, and I point out that General Motors tries to maximize profit and market share, that's not a conspiracy theory, that's an institutional analysis; it has nothing to do with conspiracies and that's precisely the sense in which we are talking about the media. The phrase conspiracy theory is one of those that's constantly brought up and I think its effect simply is to discourage institutional analysis.

Chomsky
I get a lot of letters. Hundreds. Maybe thousands... These letters are often extremely serious and very thoughtful. I should say that on one topic, finally, I had to write a form letter, saying, "Sorry, I can't respond."

Barsamian
What was that?

Chomsky
Take a guess.

Barsamian
JFK. Conspiracy theories.

Chomsky
That's it. It just got to the point where I couldn't respond any more. Within the bounds of a twenty-four-hour day I couldn't answer the letters. So much to my regret I had to say, sorry, I can't do it.

Barsamian
Does that interest in conspiracy theories tell you something about the political culture?

Chomsky
It tells you something about what's undermining the left. For people who believe in conspiracies, there's one sitting there waiting for them. Here's one for your favorite conspiracy theorist. In case anybody misunderstands, I don't believe this for one moment, but it's the kind of thing that goes around. Just imagine the CIA deciding: How can we undermine and destroy all of these popular movements? Let's send them off on some crazy wild goose chase which is going to involve them in extremely detailed analysis and microanalysis and discussion of things that don't matter. That'll shut them up. That's happening.

Barsamian
It's curious that there are elements of what is called the "left" in this country that have embraced this so fervidly.

Chomsky
In my opinion, that's a phenomenon similar to this feeling of impotence and isolation that you mentioned. If you really feel, Look, it's too hard to deal with real problems, there are a lot of ways to avoid doing so. One of them is to go off on wild goose chases that don't matter. Another is to get involved in academic cults that are very divorced from any reality and that provide a defense against dealing with the world as it actually is. There's plenty of that going on, including in the left.

From David Barsamian's upcoming *Keeping the Rabble in Line*, (Common Courage Press, 1994)

If I point out that General Motors tries to maximize profit and market share, that's not a conspiracy theory, that's an institutional analysis.

MEDIA COURT HOUSE

Peter Wintonick
Do you think somehow that there's a connection between what the government wants us to know and what the media tell us?

Man *(in center)*
It's not communism, but I think to a certain point it is sensitized.

MEDIA SIDEWALK

Man *(on left)*
They don't always tell—I guess, John, they don't always tell the truth the way it goes, huh?

John *(on far right)*
You got that right.

MEDIA TRAIN STATION

Peter Wintonick
Do you think that the information you're getting from this newspaper is biased in any way?

Woman
Oh, yeah.

MEDIA TRAIN STATION

Man
I think by and large it's well done. You get both sides of the stories. You get the liberal side and the conservative side, so to speak.

MEDIA COURT HOUSE

Woman *(on right)*
I don't think you get a very balanced picture because they only have twenty seconds, thirty seconds for a news item and whatever, and they're going to pick out the highlight, and every network is going to cover the same highlight, and that's all you're going to see.

MEDIA TRAIN STATION

Conductor
You get what they want you to hear.

Peter Wintonick
Do you think they're biased in some way—

Conductor
Naaah— Here we go. See you later.

MALASPINA COLLEGE, NANAIMO,
BRITISH COLUMBIA

Chomsky

Is it possible for the lights to get a little brighter
so I can see somebody out there?

UNIVERSITY OF WYOMING, LARAMIE

Frat Man

Yeah—for the last hour and forty-one minutes
you've been *whining* about how the elite and
how the government have been using "thought
control" to keep radicals like yourself out of the
public limelight. Now—uh—you're here. I don't
see any CIA men waiting to drag you off. You
were in the paper, that's where everyone here
heard you were coming from—in the paper—
and I'm sure they're going to publish your
comments in the paper. Now, in a lot of
countries you would have been shot for what
you have done today. So what are you whining
about? This is—we are allowing you to speak
and I don't see any thought control!

Chomsky

First of all, I haven't said one word about my
being kept out of the limelight. The way it
works here is quite different. Now, I don't think
you heard what I was saying, but the way it
works here is that there is a system of shaping,
control, and so on, which gives a certain
perception of the world. I gave one example. I'll
give you sources where you can find thousands
of others. And it has nothing to do with me—it
has to do with marginalizing the public, and
ensuring that they don't get in the way of elites
who are supposed to run things without
interference.

What are you whining about? I don't see any thought control.

"AMERICAN FOCUS," STUDENT RADIO, WASHINGTON, DC

Karine Kleinhaus

In a review of *The Chomsky Reader* it was written that "as he's been forced to the margins he's become strident and rigid" unquote. Do you feel this categorization of your later writings is accurate and that you've been a victim of this sort of process you've been describing?

Chomsky

Well, this business of being forced to—other people will have to judge about the stridency. I don't believe it. But anyway, that's for other people to judge. However, the matter of being forced to the margins is a matter of fact. And the fact is the opposite of what is claimed. Now the fact is that it is much easier to gain access to even the major media now than it was twenty years ago.

In the 1960's, Chomsky was widely respected. His articles on the war appeared in *The New York Review of Books*: Norman Mailer referred to the "tightly packed conceptual coils of Chomsky's intellections": "his name," as Hitchens puts it, "had a kind of cachet." Around the mid-1970's this changed. *The New York Review of Books* quietly dropped him; other liberal magazines followed suit. Perhaps his radicalism no longer appealed to them after the end of the war; perhaps they objected to his views on the Middle East. Cambodia and Faurisson gave the final turn to the screw. Chomsky is now treated with a weird mixture of neglect and abuse. His books are seldom even reviewed—he's not important enough for that, you see—but just about every journal in the country finds space to drop snide misrepresentations of what he's written about Cambodia, the Holocaust, Israel or anything else.

It's this, I think, that's put the bile in his voice. As he's been forced to the margins, he's become strident, rigid. But even if this does account for the change in his manner, it doesn't justify it.

He's taken on too much of the harshness of the world he struggles against. I'd like to see him bring back into his work some of the gentleness, the generosity, of the world he envisions.

I look over what I've written, and I think it's right. But I'm hesitant about it all the same. I don't like the thought that my criticisms might be read with satisfaction by the people who enjoy misrepresenting Chomsky. So perhaps I should say explicitly that I take the trouble to argue with him only because I think he's the most valuable critic of American power we have.

In *American Power and the New Mandarins*, Chomsky's first book of political essays, he gave us his responses to an unusual display in Chicago's Museum of Science and Industry. "What can one say about a country where a museum of science in a great city can feature an exhibit in which people fire machine guns from a helicopter at Vietnamese huts, with a light flashing when a hit is scored? What can one say about a country where such an idea can even be considered? You have to weep for this country."

From his earliest writings to his latest, Chomsky has looked with astonishment at what the powerful do to the powerless. He has never let his sense of outrage become dulled. If his voice has grown hoarse over twenty years, who can blame him? And who can feel superior? No one has given himself more deeply to the struggle against the horrors of our time. His hoarseness is a better thing than our suavity. I think again of Yeats' lines on Swift: "Imitate him if you dare...he/Served human liberty."

"Chomsky Then and Now," by Brian Morton, in *The Nation*, May 7, 1988

In his essay "Pol Pot, Faurisson, and the Process of Derogation," Edward S. Herman notes: "Morton is an editor of *Dissent*, a journal long dominated by Irving Howe and Michael Walzer, social democrats with strong ties to Israel and long hostile to Chomsky. It is perhaps not surprising that Morton found a coarsening in Chomsky by the time of *The Fateful Triangle*, a devastating and extremely well documented attack on U.S. and Israeli policy. It is of interest that Morton was sought out by *The Nation* after it had rejected an invited by sympathetic review of *The Chomsky Reader* by David Finkel." (included, as is Herman's essay, in *Noam Chomsky: Critical Assessments*)

Bill Moyers

You've dealt in such unpopular truths and have been such a lonely figure as a consequence of that, do you ever regret either that you took the stands you took, have written the things you've written, or [do you wish] that we'd listened to you earlier?

Chomsky

I don't. I mean there are particular things which I would do differently because you think about things, you do them differently. But in general I would say I do not regret it, I mean—

Bill Moyers

Do you like being controversial?

Chomsky

No. It's a nuisance.

Bill Moyers

Because this mass medium pays little attention to the views of dissenters—not just Noam Chomsky but most dissenters do not get much of a hearing in this medium.

Chomsky

In fact, it's completely understandable. They wouldn't be performing their societal function if they allowed favored truths to be challenged.

On March 19, 1993, the filmmakers did a workshop at the New School for Social Research in New York. They were introduced by Ingrid Abramovitch, formerly with the Canadian newswire service Canadian Press, now an editor at Success magazine.

Ingrid Abramovitch

Earlier this week I decided to test out one of the filmmakers' principal assertions, that Chomsky—one of the foremost intellectuals currently living in the United States—is virtually ignored by the American media.

I did a Nexis search (Nexis is a media database that stores articles from major newspapers and magazines; Ross Perot was always quoting from Lexis-Nexis during the presidential campaign). It's not comprehensive and can be random.

I typed in "Noam Chomsky" and went through the first thirty entries.

Here's what I found:
- Twenty-one references were from Canadian newspapers.
- Three were British, including one piece from *The Times* on "our continuing fascination with apes." That was about Chomsky's linguistic theories.
- One from the *Jerusalem Post*
- Only five were from the U.S media.
- Two of these were related to Mark and Peter's film.
- One announced a Chomsky book signing in Boston.
- Another was in the Moonie-affiliated paper, *The Washington Times*.
- The last was in *Newsday*: a review of the cyberpunk book (*Showcrash* by Neal Stephenson), whose plot involves the cult prostitutes of Asherach, ancient Sumer, George Steiner, and—somehow—Noam Chomsky.

When Ingrid Abramovitch did her Lexis-Nexis search, *Manufacturing Consent* had been in theatrical release in the United States for only a few months. People in over 300 cities around the world have now seen the film in theaters—over 225 of those cities in the United States; in print, there have been hundreds of reviews and feature articles. (Copies of these can be orded—see Resource Guide, p. 256) Radio and television exposure is difficult to quantify, simply because we lack the resources to monitor everything everywhere, but judging from the scores of interviews requested of the directors and of Chomsky, coverage has been considerable at the local level, and on several occasions has reached national audiences. All of this draws a broad cross-section of people, many of whom had never heard the name Noam Chomsky before, considerably expanding the audience for his analysis.

Consequently, the film may also be in part responsible for a willingness to tolerate Chomsky himself a little closer to the mainstream on TV in North America. In 1993, after the film's release, he appeared on CNBC's "Posner & Donahue" show for two hours, during which several clips from the film were shown and discussed. He was on *Newsworld*, Canada's all-news TV channel, for an hour, opposite CBC's national *Prime Time News* from 9 to 10 p.m. The content of the film was the springboard for much of the discussion. Though *Newsworld*'s audience is small by comparison to that of the main network news, at least for one night Canadians with cable had a choice.

With TV exposure, the buckshot effect is considerable; who knows who'll be watching? As we go to to press, *Manufacturing Consent* has been sold to television in Austria, Australia, Belgium, Canada, England, Finland, Holland, Hungary, Mexico, Norway, Portugal, Spain, Sweden, Switzerland (German and Italian channels) for a total audience in the millions. —MA

PICADILLY CIRCUS, LONDON, ENGLAND

Chomsky (voice over)

Now, notice that that's not true when I cross the border anywhere, so that I've had easy access to media in just about every other country in the world. There's a number of reasons for that. And one reason is I'm primarily talking about the United States and it's much less threatening.

SERPENT'S TAIL, LONDON, ENGLAND
One of Chomsky's U.K. publishers

Martin Woollacott (*writer for* The Guardian, *London*)

Your view there is that the militarization of the American economy essentially has come about because there are not other means of controlling the American population.

Chomsky

In a democratic society—I mean, it may be paradoxical, but the freer the society is, the more it's necessary to resort to devices like induced fear.

The essence of the Chomsky message is that power is evil. The control of the masses by the elite takes different forms in different societies.... Indeed no existing state lacks a power structure, although in a handful there is a degree of genuine popular control.

If high military spending were to be replaced in America by a different kind of investment, about the size and nature of which the whole population debated, then that population would begin to demand a say in decisions across the board—and it is this derogation of power that the American elite cannot bring itself to permit, Chomsky argues.

The masses are controlled in all states by propaganda, says Chomsky, but this is particularly important in democratic societies. Propaganda is provided by a "secular priesthood" of intellectuals, including journalists, who dress the cynical policies of the elite in morally acceptable clothes. Elements of the truth remain, because they are needed for practical reasons and because intellectuals with some moral stature "smuggle" them in. But they have to be sought out and, in effect, decoded.

It is upon this concept that Chomsky's actual technique as an analyst is based. "For

the privileged minority," he has written, "Western democracy provides the leisure, the facilities, and the training to seek the truth lying hidden behind the veil of distortion and misrepresentation, ideology and class interest through which the events of current history are presented to us."

There is undoubtedly something

schematic and arid about the world that Chomsky paints for us. He seems both wholly cynical about the purposes of those in power, and wholly unforgiving. Those who direct American policy—and, by implication, those who direct the policy of any state—are allowed no regrets, no morals, no feelings, and when they change their polices they appear to do so for entirely Machiavellian reasons. Chomsky has little interest in the question of "good in bad"— of how there can be good behaviour in the context of bad policies—and seems to deny the complexity of human affairs by setting up too rigid an antithesis between an inherently amoral elite and an inherently moral mass. His recent work has underlined this because in many ways it represents less a development of his original ideas than a recapitulation of them. Nor do his brief references to alternative ways of organizing human society carry much conviction.

But, when you meet him, Chomsky has a gentle presence, and the aura of a gifted and kindly teacher. His wispy and still boyish looks, in spite of the grey hair and the years, appeal. He is occasionally humorous—something he is not noted for in print—and his love of facts is endearing. He is in the prophetic tradition and you can no more truly argue with him than you could have with Isaiah or Ezekiel. If you oppose you will be gently corrected—if your intentions are deemed to be good—or blasted if they are seen as bad. His inner certainty seems complete.

That indeed remains his great strength and the reason for his value to the rest of us. In an age of equivocation and moral muddle, Chomsky knows what is good and strives to serve it. Whether it is the war in Vietnam, the massacres in Timor, or the Israeli invasion of south Lebanon he has ripped away the curtains to reveal the murderous machinery behind. One does not have to accept his precise formulation of the problem of power or his particular version of Marxist and anarchist ideas to benefit from his rare combination of moral vision and intellectual rigor.

From Martin Woollacott's "Deliver Us From Evil," in *The Guardian,*
January 14, 1989

LONDON, ENGLAND

John Lawton *(producer "Opinions," Channel Four)*
OK, I'll go along with that. Arguably he is the most important intellectual alive today. And if my program can give him five hundred thousand people listening or three quarters of a million people listening, I'll be delighted.

THE BRITISH ACADEMY, LONDON

John Lawton
OK, professor, in your own time.

Chomsky *(to camera in studio)*
Wartime planners understood that actual war aims should not be revealed…*(voice under)* They urged that in public discourse "the interests of other people should be stressed," which "would have better propaganda effect." The Atlantic Charter and Roosevelt's Four Freedoms were suitably vague and idealistic in tone. Only in internal documents, and in the lessons of history, can we discern what we might call the Fifth Freedom: the freedom to rob, exploit, and dominate, and to curb mischief by any feasible means. *(voice over)* A part of the reason why the media in Canada and Belgium and so on are more open is that it just doesn't matter that much what people think. It matters very much what the politically articulate sectors of the population, those narrow minorities, think and do in the United States because of its overwhelming dominance on the world scene. But of course that's also a reason for wanting to work here.

John Lawton
OK. Cut.

Chomsky
That's *con*clude, not *in*clude. Want to go back to the beginning of that paragraph?

What all of this means for much of the Third World, to put it crudely but accurately, is that the primary concern of U.S. foreign policy is to guarantee the freedom to rob and to exploit. Elsewhere, I have referred to this as "the Fifth Freedom," one that was not enunciated by President Franklin Delano Roosevelt when he formulated the famous Four Freedoms.

On Power and Ideology, page 7

The Four Freedoms and the Atlantic Charter illustrate very well the true significance and domestic utility of noble ideals. President Roosevelt announced in January 1941 that the Allies were fighting for freedom of speech, freedom of worship, freedom from want and freedom from fear. The terms of the Atlantic Charter, signed by Roosevelt and Churchill the following August, were no less elevated. These lofty sentiments helped to maintain domestic cohesion during the difficult war years, and were taken seriously by oppressed and suffering people elsewhere, who were soon to be disabused of their illusions.

Turning the Tide, page 45

Opinions is a series of half-hour programs in which a person with something to say is given the opportunity to say it, uninterrupted, on national television.

To ensure exact timing of the program, the producers of *Opinions* obliged Chomsky to use a teleprompter, a machine which, through the use of a one-way mirror, scrolls text for the reader directly in front of the lens. Newsreaders and presidents use this device to allow them to read and appear to be looking straight at the camera/viewer. Apparently, no one had explained this to Chomsky who places trust in media people willing to give him time to express himself (ourselves included). At the end of the recording session, after reading from the teleprompter for an hour and a half, Chomsky, who has scant interest in television technology, finally asked producer John Lawton, "Where was the camera during all of this?" —MA

A part of the reason why the media in Canada and Belgium and so on are more open is that it just doesn't matter that much what people think.

Chomsky *(voice over)*

The United States is ideologically narrower in general than other countries. Furthermore, the structure of the American media is such as to pretty much eliminate critical discussion.

EXCERPT: "THE TEN O'CLOCK NEWS," WGBH, BOSTON, MASSACHUSETTS(1986)

Chris Lydon

Our guests are as far apart on the Contra question as American intellectuals can be—

See full transcript at right

*(sections in **bold** are in the film)*

—John Silber, the President of Boston University, was a member of the Kissinger Commission that diagnosed a security threat in Central America.

Noam Chomsky, the language theorist at MIT, argues in his new book, entitled *Turning The Tide*—that U.S. intervention in Central America is the acute case of our general misuse and misrule of the Third World.

I would like you to begin, President Silber. Address yourself to the waverers, if there are any, in the U.S. Senate. Why would you vote for the Contra money?

Silber
Well, the Senate of the United States has traditionally been in favor of supporting democratic forces as opposed to totalitarian forces. And if they continue that practice they are going to vote against the Sandinistas and they are going to vote in favor of the Contras. On October 15 the Sandinistas passed an edict that suspends the protection against the search of homes without a warrant, that suspends the privacy of mail and allows for the censorship of mail. They suspended the right of free assembly. They have suspended all freedom of the press. They have continued their harassment of their people and suspended virtually all democratic rights. The October 15 decree is much more restrictive and comprehensive than the decree that Hitler passed on February 28, 1933, when he ended the democratic republic of Weimar. Once you see this totalitarian nature of the regime, which was apparent since 1979 in September, and has continued ever since then, it is time for the Senate of the United States to support the Democrats.

Chris Lydon
Noam Chomsky, in a short speech to the U.S. Senate, why would you be agin [sic] the Contra money?

Chomsky
Well, as even the most ardent supporters of the Contras now concede, this is what they

President of Boston University since 1971, John Robert Silber's academic background is in philosophy and law. He is the author of *Straight Shooting: What's Wrong with America and How to Fix It* (1989), and has edited *Works in Continental Philosophy* since 1967. In 1990, Silber ran unsuccessfully as the Democratic gubernatorial candidate for Massachusetts. He has also served as a trustee for the WGBH Educational Foundation since 1971, and has been a member of the Presidential Advisory Board on Radio Broadcasting to Cuba since 1985. He was awarded the Distinguished Public Service award from the National Anti-Defamation League of B'nai B'rith (an organization known to supply Chomsky's detractors with 150-page FBI-style dossiers on him).

call a proxy army which is attacking Nicaragua from foreign bases, is entirely dependent on its masters for directions and support, has never put forth a political program, has created no base of political support within the country, and almost its entire top military command is Somozist officers. Its military achievements so far consist of a long and horrifying series of very well documented torture, mutilation and atrocities, and essentially nothing else. Administration officials are now openly conceding in public that the main function of the Contras is to retard or reverse the rate of social reform in Nicaragua and to try to terminate the openness of that society. The state of siege, for example, which was imposed last fall, and which is very mild, I should say—there is much political opening in Nicaragua, as everyone there up to the American ambassador will tell you—that corresponds roughly to the state of siege which has been in place in El Salvador since early 1980, except in El Salvador it has been associated with a huge massacre of tens of thousands of people. Destruction of the press, so on and so forth. Whereas in Nicaragua it is a reaction to a war that we are carrying out against them with precisely the purpose of trying to retard social reform and to restrict the possibilities of an open and developing society. That is a cruel and savage policy, which we should terminate.

Silber
Are you going to continue that series of plain falsehoods? That's a series of falsehoods the likes of which I've never seen compacted in such a small period of time. The massacres that have occurred in Nicaragua have been the massacres by the Sandinistas of the Miskito Indians. The repression there is massive. It is more serious than anything we have seen in Central America or in any Latin American country to date. It is a genuine dictatorship imposed there. And to describe the leaders of the Contras as being supporters of Somoza is simply fabrication. Robelo, Cruz, Calero, Chamorro are not Somozistas and never have been. And when you take the leadership of the army of the Contras—some of them were members of the National Guard—but then if you are going to object to that, which would be highly unreasonable because that was an army that was not simply followers, or Somozistas, it is important to remember that Modesta Rojas, the vice chairman of the air force of the Sandinistas, was also a member of the National Guard and a very large number of members of the National Guard are the ones who are coordinators of the block committees that imposed the dictatorship by the Sandinistas. This is a series of distortions and fabrications and the effort of the Sandinistas to discredit the Contras by the manufacture of atrocities is now a point that has been very well documented.

Chris Lydon
Noam Chomsky's turn to respond to, among other things, to the original picture of the totalitarian—

Chomsky
—Let's just first start by talking about the facts. I stated again that the military leadership of the Contras is almost entirely drawn from the top, from the Somozist National Guard.

Silber
—Somoza's soldiers—

Chomsky
Forty-six out of forty-eight of the top military commanders according to Edgar Chamorro—this is the top military commander—

Silber
—soldiers are—

Chomsky
Excuse me. Now look, I let you go on. Did I let you?

Silber
You engage in a series of fabrications of truth and it's time that somebody—

Chomsky
May I?

Silber
—had the opportunity of correcting your historical misstatements while you're still around—

Chomsky
Mr. Silber has a very good reason for not wanting me to talk—

Silber
—Mr. Marcos, Mr. Marcos—

Chomsky
—and that is he knows what the truth is and he doesn't want me to —

Silber
—no no no, it's because you have distorted the truth long enough.

Chomsky
May I have a chance to say what—

Silber
—No just let me finish. It is Marcos, Marcos is the very army that helped Aquino into power so when you try to take on the National Guard, as if the National Guard was Somozistas, you misstate the case.

Chris Lydon
—But let him make the case. It's—

Silber
—You also overlook the fact that there are plenty of National Guard members who are supporting the Sandinistas.

Chris Lydon
Mr. Chomsky—

Silber
Now you go ahead and distort the truth again.

Chomsky
Now let me, see, here you're having an action. A good example of totalitarianism, and that is to ensure that the opposition—

Silber
I'm the first one that stopped your monopoly on misinformation.

Chomsky
The idea that I have a monopoly of misinformation of the American press is a little ridiculous.

Silber
No it's not—

Chomsky
Really? I control the American press? Let me repeat. Let's go back to the facts: forty-six out of the forty-eight of top military commanders of the Contras are Somozist officers. You can find that in the Congressional report. You can find that from Edgar Chamorro who is the CIA appointed spokesman. That's exactly what I said and it's exactly true. As to the idea that the Sandinistas have carried out massacres on a par with those that we have been carrying out in Central America, this is really astonishing!
In El Salvador, the number of people massacred since 1978 or since 1979 when we moved in in force is on the order of sixty-thousand. In Guatemala, where we incidentally have been supporting it all the way through with military aid which never terminated and are now supporting it enthusiastically, the number of people massacred is on the order of a hundred thousand.
Mr. Silber referred to the Miskito indians, who were badly treated, I should say, the figures are that approximately sixty or seventy were killed. Whereas in contrast, about five or six thousand people have been killed—and I

don't mean killed, this is not your garden variety killing; this is torture, murder and mutilation, massively documented in great detail—by our forces. Now there are crimes of the Sandinistas, there is no doubt, but they are undetectable in comparison with the crimes that we have supported—

Chris Lydon
I'd like to go back to two central arguments this thing turns on. One is that Sandinista Nicaragua poses a security threat to the United States and to this hemisphere. Secondly, we owe it to the so-called democrats and the democratic notion to help people who are carrying our standard in the region. John Silber, are these equal arguments and do you support them both?

Silber
Well, I don't support the presence of about sixty-five hundred Soviet and Cuban troops in Nicaragua. I don't support the presence of twenty-four armed helicopter gunships supplied by the Soviet Union to Nicaragua, or a hundred and fifty battle tanks or about twelve hundred trucks and three hundred—

Chris Lydon
—But where is the notion that it is a security threat to this country?

Silber
Well, it's not a security threat yet. And neither was Hitler a security threat when he suspended all freedoms of the Germans on February 28, 1933. He wasn't even a security threat that was serious in 1936 when he re-armed the Rhineland. But by the time that the Allies got around to recognizing that he was a threat it cost us tens of millions of lives and it took six years in which to defeat him.

Now, at the present time we can put an end to the Sandinista dictatorship in Central America without using a single American life. All we have to do is help pay for the firemen. There is a fire going on down there. We don't have to put the fire out. But we're asked to pay for the firemen. If we wait, if we decide to do nothing until the Soviets establish a land base there and it develops, as it will develop if we allow it to happen, we will then have to face the fact of a possibility of war. It is not a present threat, it is a vector. If

people don't have sense enough to understand that a small fire in a room is a threat, not because it's a small fire but because small fires have a way of becoming big fires, then we haven't learned anything from history.

Chris Lydon
It's Noam Chomsky's turn on the question of the security threat to the hemisphere and to this country.

Chomsky
Well, to talk of Nicaragua as a security threat is a bit like asking what threat Luxembourg poses to the Soviet Union. Mr. Silber mentioned Hitler and I am old enough to remember Hitler's speeches in which he talked about the threat to Germany posed by Poland from which Germany had to defend itself. And even that's unfair to Hitler to draw that example. It is quite true that Nicaragua is now Soviet-armed and heavily armed. And the reason is that it is being attacked by a superpower which has specifically blocked every other source of supply. For example, up until the May embargo last year twenty percent of Nicaraguan trade was with the Soviet bloc. Prior to that, its arms were coming from everywhere. We then blocked the arms from everywhere else. As we intensified the war, they do exactly what the U.S. government wants them to do; namely, to divert resources

from the social reforms which we really fear, and they turn them towards militarization. The idea that Nicaragua could attack—I might add that the countries of Latin America regard this as hysterical lunacy. Every country, all the

Contadora countries, all the support countries which include all of the relatively democratic countries in Latin America, are pleading with us to call off the war against the country. They understand perfectly well exactly what it's doing. It's forcing them to be a militarized state and it's creating a danger of a wider war in the region. If we want to get the Soviet tanks out of Nicaragua, and there are very few, and the Cuban advisors out, what we should do is very simple and everyone in the government knows it. Call off the war and they will return to what they were doing before we attacked them; namely creating the most effective reforms in the hemisphere, which were widely praised by the World Bank, the Inter-American Development Bank, organizations like OXFAM, which described them as unique in their experience in seventy-six developing countries—

Chris Lydon
We're running out—

Chomsky
—which we have retarded and stopped by this attack.

Chris Lydon
We are running so far overtime that we might just as well keep going. I want you to deal with the question of democracy and our responsibility to aid the cause. You criticized the Sandinistas but do you really want to embrace the Contras as a vehicle of democracy?

Silber
Absolutely. And let's dispense with the myth somehow that these were lovely democrats until we drove them into the hands of the Soviet Union by our opposition. That is a myth. That is a fabrication of history that Mr. Chomsky knows is false. As a matter of fact, when the revolution came to an end in July of 1979 the Sandinistas came to Washington, after having pledged to the Organization of American States that they would hold free elections. They then received $117 million in loans, they received credit from the World Bank through the intercession of the United States. They were very well received and very well treated. And on September of 193—ah, 1979, they already began their process of repression. So the notion that we drove them

into the hands of the Communists is utterly false. It's a fabrication.

Chris Lydon
But the question is: are the Contras a vehicle for democracy?

Silber
The Contras do not have overt support among the Nicaraguan, people at the present time inside Nicaragua, for one obvious reason. Hitler's opponents did not have any obvious support in Germany after Hitler had taken over that country. In a totalitarian state the opposition does not have any effective voice. You don't find that effective voice in the Soviet Union now either. You have isolated groups of refusniks. But in Nicaragua you have a leadership: Robelo, Cruz, Chamorro, Colero—those are major figures, major democratic figures who opposed Somoza, and many of them went to jail and they are literally followed by thousands of people who are opposing the Sandinista dictatorship. To try to write these people off as totalitarian and to come up with that trumped-up nonsense about the atrocities that those people have committed is just a good example of doublethink. This is just a 1984 exercise by Mr. Chomsky for which he has already established a worldwide reputation. It's rubbish.

Chris Lydon
Mr. Chomsky, when you hear this call to come to the rescue of democracy and democratic forces, what do you answer?

Chomsky
I would be delighted if the United States were to reverse its longstanding policies of opposing democratic forces throughout Central America and begin to support those forces.
Now, to return to Nicaragua and to return to the real world, I never described the Sandinistas as perfect democrats or whatever your phrase was. What I did was quote the World Bank, OXFAM, the Jesuit Order and others who recognize that what they were doing was to use the meager resources of that country for the benefit of the poor majority. That's why health standards shot up. That's why literacy shot up. That's why agrarian reform proceeded, the only place in the region. That's why subsistence agri-

culture improved and consumption of food increased and that's why we attacked them. It had nothing to do with democracy.
Now, I also did not say that Cruz and Robelo committed atrocities. In fact, Cruz and Robelo sit in Washington and don't do anything. They are figureheads who we concocted. The people who commit atrocities are the Contra forces led by the National Guard. And of all the figures you mention, one is involved: namely, Colero, who is an ultra-right-wing businessman and represents the extremist, narrow business forces in Nicaragua.
Now, if we had the slightest concern with democracy—which we do not in our foreign affairs and never have—we would turn to countries where we have influence, like El Salvador. Now, in El Salvador they don't call the archbishop bad names; what they do is murder him. They do not censor the press; they wipe the press out. They sent the army in to blow up the church radio station. The editor of the independent newspaper was found in a ditch mutilated and cut to pieces with a machete.

John Silber
Don't you ever —

Chomsky
—May I continue? I did not interrupt you—

John Silber
Don't you ever want to put a time value on anything you say—

Chomsky
Excuse me, that was 19—

John Silber
—Or do you just want to lie systematically on television?

Chomsky
I'm talking about—I'm talking about—I'm talking about 198—

John Silber
—You are a systematic liar—

Chomsky
—Did these things happen or didn't they?

John Silber:
These things did not happen in the context in which you suggest at all.

Chomsky
—Really?

Silber
—And when you suggest that Cruz is simply a figurehead and does nothing, you overlook the fact that Arturo Cruz was the Ambassador of the Sandinistas to the United States.

Chomsky
Yes, and he has always—

Silber
And he was the head banker of the Sandinistas—

Chomsky
Exactly—in the United States

Silber
—until he finally broke with them when he found out that they were utterly totalitarian. **You are a phony, mister, and it's time that the people read you correctly.**

Chomsky
Well, it's clear why you want to divert me from the discussion—

Silber
No, it's not. It's because we get tired of rubbish!

Chomsky
Excuse me. Arturo Cruz, exactly as I said, was in the United States, he was brought to—

Silber
Why was he in the United States?

Chomsky
He was in the United States and he defected in the United States. He was brought back to Nicaragua, as a political figure, because the business-based opposition there had no credible candidate. He did not participate in the elections, as he could have, in part because —

Silber
—he couldn't because he was broke—

Chomsky
May I continue?

Silber
No, because you're lying again.

Chris Lydon
I've got to cut you both off.

Chomsky
I didn't say anything yet.

Silber
The Turbas [pro-Sandinista street militia] were the ones who prevented Cruz from participating in the elections—

Chomsky
That's another fabrication. **But let's continue with—**

Chris Lydon
Except we can't. I'm afraid we're out of time. You've given President Reagan a tough act to follow on Sunday night. **We thank you both, John Silber and Noam Chomsky.**

Chomsky
Yeah, OK.

The fall of [Nicaraguan dictator] Somoza in 1979 aroused fears in Washington that the brutal dictator of El Salvador might be overthrown, leading to loss of U.S. control there as well. The second and still more threatening development was the growth of "popular organizations" in the 1970s: Bible study groups that became self-help groups under Church sponsorship, peasant organizations, unions and the like. There was a fearsome prospect that El Salvador might move towards a meaningful democracy with opportunities for real popular participation in the political process....

The Carter Administration reacted to these threats in El Salvador by backing a coup led by reformist military officers in October 1979, while ensuring that the most reactionary military elements retained a position of dominance....

In February 1980, Archbishop Romero pleaded with President Carter not to provide the junta with military aid, which, he observed, "will surely increase injustice here and sharpen the repression that has been unleashed against the people's organizations fighting to defend their most fundamental human rights"....

But increasing the repression, destroying the people's organizations and preventing independence were the very essence of U.S. policy, so Carter ignored the Archbishop's plea and sent the aid, to "strengthen the army's key role in reforms"....

In March 1980, Archbishop Romero was assassinated. A judicial investigation was initiated, headed by Judge Atilio Ramírez. He accused General Medrano, the death squad organizer and U.S. favorite, and rightwing leader Roberto d'Aubuisson of hiring the assassins, and shortly after fled the country after death threats and an attempt on his life.... Judge Ramírez concludes that "it is undoubtedly the case that from the very beginning, they were involved in a kind of conspiracy to cover up the murder...."

In June, the university was shut down after an army attack that left many killed, including the rector, and facilities looted and destroyed....

Meanwhile, the independent media were eliminated by bombings and terror, another prerequisite for "free elections" to legitimate the client regime. The editor and a journalist [of *La Crónica del Pueblo*] were found with their bodies hacked to pieces with machetes, and [*El*

Independiente] closed after three attempts to assassinate the editor, threats to his family, occupation of the offices by armed forces, and the arrest and torture of staff members. The Church radio station was repeatedly bombed, and shortly after Reagan's election, troops occupied the Archdiocese building, destroying the radio station and ransacking the newspaper offices....

On October 26, 1980, Archbishop Romero's successor, Bishop Rivera y Damas, condemned the armed forces "war of extermination and genocide against a defenseless civilian population"; a few weeks later, Duarte hailed the armed forces for "valiant service alongside the people against subversion" as he was sworn in as civilian president of the junta.

Turning the Tide, pages 102-107

...[D]uring the Salvadorian election [*The New York Times, Time, Newsweek,* and CBS News had not] even mentioned the destruction by physical violence and murder of *La Crónica* and *El Independiente,* or the toll of murdered journalists.

Manufacturing Consent, page 129

GEORGETOWN UNIVERSITY, WASHINGTON, DC

Audience Questioner

The last time you were here you spoke about how when you go overseas you are given access to the mass media, but here that doesn't seem to be the case. Has that changed at all? Have you ever been invited to appear on "Nightline" or "Brinkley"?

Chomsky

Yes, I have a couple of times been invited to speak on "Nightline." I couldn't do it—I had another talk, and something or other, and, to tell you the honest truth, I don't really care very much.

FAIR, the media monitoring group, published a very interesting study of "Nightline." It shows that their conception of the spectrum is ridiculously narrow at least by European or world standards.

Chomsky was once interviewed for "Nightline." A database search in the Sherman Grinberg Film Library (ABC's archive) turned up a thirty-nine-minute interview shot with Chomsky in April, 1988, for their week-long series of special programs, "Nightline in the Holy Land." None of it was aired.

CROSS INDEX: PERSONALITIES:
CHOMSKY, NOAM,
WAR: ARAB / ISRAELI CONFLICT (ABOUT)
DATE = 88/04/08
NOW AT = NY
STORY: ISRAEL SPECIAL / NIGHTLINE IN THE HOLY LAND
LOCATION: CAMBRIDGE, MASS
REPORTER: JORDAN
CAMERA: WORDEN
CONTENT: INTV W/ MASSACHUSETTS INSTITUTE OF TECHNOLOGY (MIT) PROFESSOR NOAM CHOMSKY ABOUT THE CRISIS IN THE ISRAELI OCCUPIED TERRITORIES

VC 1 of 2

• 00:01:31:27

• MS [medium shot] of Chomsky asserting that the U.S. has blocked a peaceful settlement to the Israeli / Arab conflict for the past seventeen years. He delineates examples of U.S. interference in the peace process.

• 00:04:55:25

• He claims the greatest threat to Israeli security is the American Jewish community which is driving Israel to a policy of occupation and military confrontation.

• 00:10:38:08

• He calls the current U.S. efforts for peace in the mideast ill conceived.

• 00:19:17:10

• Chomsky criticizes media coverage of the violent uprisings in the occupied territories because he believes they do not reveal the underlying factors causing the violence.

VC 2 of 2

• 00:00:33:21

• MS of Chomsky discussing the reasons Palestinian youths have continued their uprisings against Israel.

• 00:02:55:21

• Chomsky says the holocaust should serve as a lesson against the subjection of people to horros [sic] and oppression.

• 00:06:38:00

• He contends that Israel's security will improve as it moves toward a political settlement w/the Palestinians.

• 00:15:46:09

• Chomsky asserts that the U.S. has placed barriers against a political settlement.

• 00:16:18:2 Cuts.

The rights to include this footage in *Manufacturing Consent* would have cost $90 per second, with an $1,800 minimum charge. We took a pass.

Since the inception of ABC Network News in 1963, Sherman Grinberg has stored, catalogued and computerized over 70 million feet of film and over 400,000 videocassettes—ABC's entire output of worldwide news coverage. They also represent Pathe News (10 million feet of film) and Paramount News (eight million feet of film). (See Resource Guide)

FAIR (Fairness and Accuracy in Reporting)
studied 865 "Nightline" programs.
Of the 1,530 U.S. guests:

92 percent were white
89 percent were male
80 percent were professionals
government officials or
corporate representatives

There had been little analysis of "Nightline" before this report appeared, despite the fact that it is one of the United States' leading news-information programs. The reason for the choice of guests as a focus was that public affairs shows like "Nightline" often go live, so guests are a crucial element. The study's methodology: analysis of 40 months of transcripts of "Nightline" shows.
(January 1, 1985 to April 30, 1988)

The findings showed that the guests were overwhelmingly white, male and representative of powerful institutions. The worldview the show conveyed was one in which the U.S. was depicted as a society lacking in serious internal turmoil, while the rest of the world was "frighteningly unstable." The issues "Nightline" dealt with were also therefore "closely aligned with the agenda of the U.S. government."

Of course, "Nightline" purports to present as broad a worldview as possible. But it

FAIR's report on "NightLine" left people wondering how other TV news programs might compare to Nightline in diversity and inclusiveness of their guest lists. So FAIR conducted a comparative analysis of the guest lists of ABC's "Nightline" and PBS's "MacNeil/Lehrer NewsHour" for a six-month period in 1989. Despite the fact that "MacNeil/Lehrer" is on public TV, FAIR found that, in most respects, its guest list represented an even narrower segment of the political spectrum than Nightline's.

From the follow-up report, *All the Usual Suspects: MacNeil-Lehrer and Nightline*. Both reports can be ordered from FAIR (See Resource Guide)

Filter: The reliance of the media on information provided by the government, business, and experts funded and approved by these primary sources and agents of power.

undermines this goal by setting up host Ted Koppel as a "diplomat" attempting to find solutions to the problems dealt with on his show.

This worldview—as reflected and promoted by a narrow range of guests—makes "Nightline" a fundamentally conservative political program, serving the interests of those who already wield power.

The study concludes that "Nightline" should be more representative by including "ordinary citizens from all population sectors and roles."

Source: *A Special FAIR Report: Are You on the Nightline Guest List? An Analysis of 40 Months of Nightline Programming*, by William Hoynes and David Croteau (Boston College, 1989) pages 1-4

Chomsky
Let me tell you a personal experience. I happened to be in Madison, Wisconsin, on a listener-supported radio station, a community radio station, a very good one; I was having an interview with the news director [Jeff Hansen, WORT Community Radio]. I've been on that program dozens of times, usually by telephone. And he's very good, he gets to all sorts of people, and he started the interview by playing for me a tape of an interview that he had just had, and had broadcast—with the guy who's some mucky-muck in "Nightline," I think his name is Jeff Greenfield or some such name—does that name mean anything?

ON TV SETS IN A TV STORE

Jeff Greenfield
I'm Jeff Greenfield for "Nightline" in New York.

WORT (COMMUNITY RADIO),
MADISON, WISCONSIN

Jeff Hansen
What about *just* in the selection of guests to analyze things, why is Noam Chomsky never on "Nightline"?

Jeff Greenfield
I—I couldn't begin to tell you.

Jeff Hansen
He's one of the leading intellectuals in the entire world.

JEFF GREENFIELD (1943-)
University of Wisconsin, B.A. (honors), 1968; Yale University, LL.B. (honors), 1967; Legislative aide to Senator Robert Kennedy, Washington, DC, 1967-1968; assistant to Mayor John Lindsay, New York City, 1968-70; Garth Associates, New York City, consultant, 1970-76; writer, political and media critic for CBS and ABC

In his book *The Real Campaign: The Media and the Battle for the White House,* Jeff Greenfield challenges one longstanding assumption: that the media is influential in the outcome of a presidential election. "The thesis of this book," says Greenfield in its pages, "is that television and the media made almost no difference in the outcome of the 1980 presidential campaign." ... in a *New York Times Book Review* piece, Larry Sabato says Greenfield "has a trained eye for appealing anecdotes and revealing illustrations of important concepts. But his style tends to be too breezy, and his writing has been infected with an irritating tendency toward excessive italicization."

Contemporary Authors, New Revision Series,
Volume 24 (1988)

Jeff Greenfield

I have no idea. I mean, I can make some guesses. He may be one of the leading intellectuals who can't talk on television. You know that's a standard that's very important—to us. If you've got a twenty-two minute show, and a guy takes five minutes to warm up—now I don't know whether Chomsky does or not—he's out. One of the reasons why we have, why "Nightline" has the usual suspects is—one of the things you have to do when you book a show is know that the person can make the point within the framework of television. And if people don't like that they should understand that it's about as sensible to book somebody who will take eight minutes to give an answer as it is to book somebody who doesn't speak English. But in the normal give and flow, that's another culture-bound thing. We gotta have English-speaking people. We also need concision.

GEORGETOWN UNIVERSITY, WASHINGTON, DC

Chomsky

So Greenfield or whatever his name is hit the nail on the head. The U.S. media are alone in that it is—you must meet the condition of concision. You gotta say things between two commercials or in six hundred words. And that's a very important fact, because the beauty of concision—you know, saying a couple of sentences between two commercials—the beauty of that is you can only repeat conventional thoughts.

Chomsky was asked to comment on the idea that all commercial media systems, not just those in the United States, compress content:

As for media systems with commercial constraints imposing "concision," that may or may not be true out of the U.S. I'm not sure. It hasn't been true of Britain's commercial TV, which has been considerably more open even than BBC, I'm told (that's my experience too; I think the Opinions *program you filmed the production of was commerical TV). But the point is that outside the U.S., the main radio-TV is generally noncommercial, so the issue you raise doesn't arise. Even commercial radio-TV is often different in format from here. Thus in Italy, at least 15 years ago when I was there, TV had plenty of ads, but they were all at the break between programs. Not like here, where interruptions (especially on radio) are every few minutes. I think the "concision" idea is probably American, and goes beyond the constraint of commercialism. However, one would have to do real research to be sure. I haven't researched it, and am only speaking from personal experience. I might add that here public radio also keeps to these constraints, often. During the Gulf War I was granted a comment on NPR [National Public Radio], but was told that it had to be submitted in advance, and to run exactly 2 1/2 minutes. When it was approved, I was to record it in a studio. My first reading was 2 min. and 36 seconds, and I had to try again, to get within the limit. I've never heard of anything like that elsewhere.—NC*

THIS MODERN WORLD
by TOM TOMORROW

HELLO, AND WELCOME TO *SHORT ATTENTION SPAN NEWS!*

HERES A PICTURE OF THE PRESIDENT!

IT LOOKS LIKE SOMETHING'S HAPPENING IN ANOTHER COUNTRY!

WELL, THAT'S ALL FOR *TODAY!* TUNE IN AGAIN *TOMORROW*-- FOR AS MUCH NEWS AS WE THINK YOU NEED TO KNOW!

TOM TOMORROW © 93

WORT (COMMUNITY RADIO), MADISON, WISCONSIN

Jeff Greenfield

I was reading Chomsky twenty years ago. I think his notion—doesn't he have a—didn't he co-author a new book called *Engineering Consent*, or *The Manufacturing of Consent*? I mean some of that stuff to me looks like it's from Neptune.

NASA IMAGES OF NEPTUNE DIRECT FROM THE VOYAGEUR SPACECRAFT

Announcer

This is the first time the Neptune system has been seen clearly by human eyes. These pictures taken only hours ago by Voyager Two are its latest contribution.

Jeff Greenfield

You know, he's perfectly entitled to say that I'm seeing it through a prism, too, but my view of that—of his notions about the limits of debate in this country—is absolutely wacko.

GEORGETOWN UNIVERSITY, WASHINGTON, DC

Chomsky

Suppose I get up on "Nightline," I'm given whatever it is, two minutes, and I say Ghadaffi is a terrorist and Khomeini is a murderer, the Russians invaded Afghanistan—all this sort of stuff—I don't need any evidence, everybody just nods.

On the other hand, suppose you say something that just isn't regurgitating conventional pieties. Suppose you say something that's the least bit unexpected, or controversial. Suppose you say—
Or suppose you say—

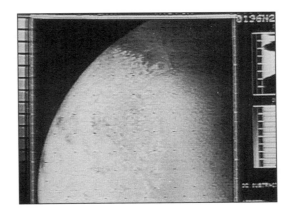

Not only was Jeff Greenfield reading Chomsky, he was on TV with him. When William F. Buckley Jr. interviewed Chomsky on "Firing Line" in 1969, one of the supplementary questioners was a young Jeff Greenfield.

On Ghadaffi and the U.S. bombing of Libya, and the media coverage, see:
- *Culture of Terrorism; Pirates and Emperors; Chronicles of Dissent*, chapter 3
- *Necessary Illusions*, Appendix 5.2
- *Language and Politics*, interview 33
- Also "International Terrorism," February 8, 1987, an audiotape from Alternative Radio

On Khomeini and Iran, and religious fanaticism, see *Language and Politics*, pages 740-741

On the media coverage of the Russian invasion of Afghanistan and the U.S. invasion of Vietnam, *Manufacturing Consent*, chapter 5

"The biggest international terror operations that are known are the ones that are run out of Washington."

A U.S. Army manual on countering the plague [of international terrorism] defines terrorism as "the calculated use of violence or threat of violence to attain goals which are political, religious, or ideological in nature. This is done through intimidation, coercion, or instilling fear"...

LIC [Low Intensity Conflict] is the doctrine to which the United States is officially committed and which has proven its worth in preventing successful independent development in Nicaragua, though it faltered in El Salvador despite its awesome toll. It must be emphasized that LIC... is hardly more than a euphemism for international terrorism, that is, reliance on force that does not reach the level of the war crime of aggression, which falls under the judgment of Nuremberg.

There are many terrorist states in the world, but the United States is unusual in that it is *officially* committed to international terrorism, and on a scale that puts its rivals to shame....

Necessary Illusions, pages 271-273

The basic *fact* is that the United States has organized under its sponsorship and protection a neo-colonial system of client states ruled mainly by terror and serving the interests of a small local and foreign business and military elite. The fundamental *belief,* or ideological pretense, is that the United States is dedicated to furthering the cause of democracy and human rights throughout the world, though it may occasionally err in the pursuit of this objective.

Over the past 25 years at least, not only has official terror been responsible for torture and killing on a vastly greater scale than its retail counterpart, but, furthermore, the balance of terror appears to have shifted to the West and its clients, with the United States setting the pace as sponsor and supplier. The old colonial world was shattered during World War II, and the resultant nationalist-radical upsurge threatened traditional Western hegemony and the economic interests of Western business. To contain this threat the United States has aligned itself with elite and military ele-

ments in the Third World whose function has been to contain the tides of change. This role was played by Diem and Thieu in South Vietnam and is currently served by allies such as Mobutu in Zaire, Pinochet in Chile, and Suharto in Indonesia. Under frequent U.S. sponsorship the neo-fascist National Security State and other forms of authoritarian rule have become the dominant mode of government in the Third World. Heavily armed by the West (mainly the United States) and selected for amenability to foreign domination and zealous anti-Communism, counterrevolutionary regimes have been highly torture- and bloodshed-prone.

Since the installation and support of military juntas, with their sadistic tortures and bloodbaths, are hardly compatible with human rights, democracy and other alleged Western values, the media and intellectuals in the United States and Western Europe have been hard-pressed to rationalize state policy. The primary solution has been massive suppression, averting the eyes from the unpleasant facts concerning the extensive torture and killing, the Diaspora, the major shift to authoritarian government and its systematic character, and the U.S. role in introducing and protecting the leadership of this client fascist empire.

From *The Political Economy of Human Rights,* Volume 1, pages ix, 8, 11

On international terrorism see:

The Real Terror Network: Terrorism in Fact and Propaganda,
by Edward S. Herman (South End, Black Rose Books, 1982)

The "Terrorism" Industry: Structure, Linkages, and Role in Western Ideological Mobilization, by Edward S. Herman and Gerry O'Sullivan
(Pantheon, 1989)

Chomsky's *Culture of Terrorism, Pirates and Emperors , Chronicles of Dissent,* chapter 3; *Language and Politics,* interviews 35 and 38; and "Terrorism Strikes Home: The Mideast, Fundamentalism, Terrorism, and U.S. Foreign Policy," *Z Magazine,* May, 1993

MALASPINA COLLEGE, NANAIMO,
BRITISH COLUMBIA

Just ask yourself, why does any government ever undertake clandestine warfare? Why do they have covert operations? Who are covert operations a secret from?...They're obviously not a secret from the victims, they know all about it. Take the stuff in the Iran/Contra hearings. They weren't a secret from all the mercenary states... The point is that it was a secret from the American population, that's all. Typically, clandestine operations are undertaken when the government is driven underground by its own population. If you can't control the population by force and you can't indoctrinate them, what you do is go underground.... [T]he American population is too dissident, despite all the brainwashing and indoctrination and so on, the less educated, non-elite part of the population just won't go along.

From an interview with David Barsamian, printed in *Language and Politics*, page 735

"What happened in the 1980s is the U.S. government was driven underground."

"Suppose I say the United States is invading South Vietnam— as it was."

Take the Russian invasion of Afghanistan—a simple case. Everybody understands immediately without any specialized knowledge that the Soviet Union invaded Afghanistan. That's exactly what it is. You don't debate it; it's not a deep point that is difficult to understand. It isn't necessary to know the history of Afghanistan to understand the point. Now let's take the American invasion of South Vietnam. The phrase itself is very strange... I doubt if you'll find one case in which that phrase was used in any mainstream journal, or, for the most part, even in journals of the left, while the war was going on. Yet it was just as much an American invasion of South Vietnam as it is a Russian invasion of Afghanistan. By 1962, when nobody was paying any attention, American pilots—not just mercenaries but actual American pilots—were conducting murderous bombing raids against Vietnamese villages. That's an American invasion of South Vietnam. The purpose of that attack was to destroy the social fabric of rural South Vietnam so as to undermine a resistance which the American-imposed client regime had evoked by its repression and was unable to control, though they had already killed perhaps eighty thousand South Vietnamese since blocking the political settlement called for in the 1954 Geneva Accords. So there was a U.S. attack against South Vietnam in the early sixties, not to speak of later years when the United States sent an expeditionary force to occupy the country and destroy the indigenous resistance. But it was never referred to or thought of as an American invasion of South Vietnam.

I don't know much about Russian public opinion, but I imagine if you picked a man off the street, he would be surprised to hear a reference to the Russian invasion of Afghanistan. They're defending Afghanistan against capitalist plots and bandits supported by the CIA and so on. But I don't think he would find it difficult to understand that the United States invaded Vietnam.

The Chomsky Reader, page 34

My view, for what it's worth, is that Kennedy was probably the most dangerous president we've had. (*applause*) There was a really dangerous, macho streak there, which was kind of fanatic. A lot of it is coming out now in the coverage of the Cuban Missile Crisis, which is quite revealing. It looks even worse than it looked before. And an awful lot of this willingness to drive the world to total destruction looks like a matter of protecting your macho image. Now, that kind of stuff is really dangerous. It's much better—the best political leaders are the ones who are lazy and corrupt. It's the ones who are after power—they are the dangerous ones. So the guys who want to watch television and sleep and so on, they are no big problem. I should say the same about corruption. Corruption is a very positive sign of government. You should always be in favor of corruption. If people are interested in enriching themselves or in sex or something like that, then they are not interested in power. And the most dangerous thing is the guys that want power. That's what Kennedy was like, I think. Furthermore, corruption has a way of being exposed for quite simple reasons. When people are corrupt they are usually robbing other rich people. Therefore they are going to block people and when corruption gets exposed it weakens power. And so that's one of the ways you can defend yourself. The same is true of the evangelicals. If we had evangelicals who were really after power, we'd be in trouble. If all they want is gold Cadillacs and sex and so on, no big problem. That's good.

From a talk—entitled "Necessary Illusions," at MIT, May 10, 1989

"The best political leaders are the ones who are lazy and corrupt."

ST. MICHAEL'S COLLEGE,
WINOOSKI, VERMONT

"If the Nuremberg laws were applied, then every post-war American president would have been hanged."

By violation of the Nuremberg laws I mean the same kind of crimes for which people were hanged in Nuremberg. And Nuremberg means Nuremberg and Tokyo. So first of all you've got to think back as to what people were hanged for at Nuremberg and Tokyo. And once you think back, the question doesn't even require a moment's waste of time. For example, one general at the Tokyo trials, which were the worst, General Yamashita, was hanged on the grounds that troops in the Philippines, which were technically under his command (though it was so late in the war that he had no contact with them—it was the very end of the war and there were some troops running around the Philippines who he had no contact with), had carried out atrocities, so he was hanged. Well, try that one out and you've already wiped out everybody.

But getting closer to the sort of core of the Nuremberg-Tokyo tribunals, in Truman's case at the Tokyo tribunal, there was one authentic, independent Asian justice, an Indian, who was also the one person in the court who had any background in international law, and he dissented from the whole judgment, dissented from the whole thing. He wrote a very interesting and important dissent, seven hundred pages—you can find it in the Harvard Law Library, that's where I found it, maybe somewhere else, and it's interesting reading. He goes through the trial record and shows, I think pretty convincingly, it was pretty farcical. He ends up by saying something like this: if there is any crime in the Pacific theater that compares with the crimes of the Nazis, for which they're being hanged at Nuremberg, it was the dropping of the two atom bombs. And he says nothing of that sort can be attributed to the present accused. Well, that's a plausible argument, I think, if you look at the background. Truman proceeded to organize a major counter-insurgency campaign in Greece which killed off about one hundred and sixty thousand people, sixty thousand refugees, another sixty thousand or so people tortured, political system dismantled, right-wing regime. American corporations came in and took it over. I think that's a crime under Nuremberg.

Well, what about Eisenhower? You could argue over whether his overthrow of the government of Guatemala was a crime. There was a CIA-backed army, which went in under U.S. threats and bombing and so on to undermine that capitalist democracy. I think that's a crime. The invasion of Lebanon in 1958, I don't know, you could argue. A lot of people were killed. The overthrow of the government of Iran is another one—though a CIA-backed coup. But Guatemala alone suffices for Eisenhower and there's plenty more.

Kennedy is easy. The invasion of Cuba was outright aggression. Eisenhower planned it, incidentally, so he was involved in a conspiracy to invade another country, which we can add to his score. After the invasion of Cuba, Kennedy launched a huge terrorist campaign against Cuba, which was very serious. No joke. Bombardment of industrial installations with killing of plenty of people, bombing hotels, sinking fishing boats, sabotage. Later, under Nixon, it even went as far as poisoning livestock and so on. Big affair. And then came Vietnam; he invaded Vietnam. He invaded South Vietnam in 1962. He sent the U.S. Air Force to start bombing. Okay. We took care of Kennedy.

Johnson is trivial. The Indochina war alone, forget the invasion of the Dominican Republic, was a major war crime.

Nixon the same. Nixon invaded Cambodia. The Nixon-Kissinger bombing of Cambodia in the early '70's was not all that different from the Khmer Rouge atrocities, in scale somewhat less, but not much less. Same was true in Laos. I could go on case after case with them, that's easy.

Ford was only there for a very short time so he didn't have time for a lot of crimes, but he managed one major one. He supported the Indonesian invasion of East Timor, which was near genocidal. I mean, it makes Saddam Hussein's invasion of Kuwait look like a tea party. That was supported decisively by the United States, both the diplomatic and the necessary military support came primarily from the United States. This was picked up under Carter.

Carter was the least violent of American presidents but he did things which I think would certainly fall under Nuremberg provisions. As the Indonesian atrocities increased to a level of really near genocide, the U.S. aid under Carter increased. It reached a peak in 1978 as the atrocities peaked. So we took care of Carter, even forgetting other things.

Reagan. It's not a question. I mean, the stuff in Central America alone suffices. Support for the Israeli invasion of Lebanon also makes Saddam Hussein look pretty mild in terms of casualties and destruction. That suffices.

Bush. Well, need we talk on? In fact, in the Reagan period there's even an International Court of Justice decision on what they call the "unlawful use of force" for which Reagan and Bush were condemned. I mean, you could argue about some of these people, but I think you could make a pretty strong case if you look at the Nuremberg decisions, Nuremberg and Tokyo, and you ask what people were condemned for. I think American presidents are well within the range.

Also, bear in mind, people ought to be pretty critical about the Nuremberg principles. I don't mean to suggest they're some kind of model of probity or anything. For one thing, they were *ex post facto*. These were determined to be crimes by the victors after they had won. Now, that already raises questions. In the case of the American presidents, they weren't *ex post facto*. Furthermore, you have to ask yourself what was called a "war crime"? How did they decide what was a war crime at Nuremberg and Tokyo? And the answer is pretty simple and not very pleasant. There was a criterion. Kind of like an operational criterion. If the enemy had done it and couldn't show that we had done it, then it was a war crime. So like bombing of urban concentrations was not considered a war crime because we had done more of it than the Germans and the Japanese. So that wasn't a war crime. You want to turn Tokyo into rubble? So much rubble you can't even drop an atom bomb there because nobody will see anything if you do, which is the real reason they didn't bomb Tokyo. That's not a war crime because we did it. Bombing Dresden is not a war crime. We did it. German Admiral Gernetz, when he was brought to trial (he was a submarine commander or something), for sinking merchant vessels or whatever he did. He called as a defense witness American Admiral Nimitz who testified that the U.S. had done pretty much the same thing, so he was off, he didn't get tried. And in fact if you run through the whole record,

and it turns out a war crime is any war crime that you can condemn them for but they can't condemn us for. Well, you know, that raises some questions.

I should say actually, that this, interestingly, is said pretty openly by the people involved and it's regarded as a moral position. The chief prosecutor at Nuremberg was Telford Taylor. You know, a decent man. He wrote a book called *Nuremberg and Vietnam*. And in it he tries to consider whether there are crimes in Vietnam that fall under the Nuremberg's principles. Predictably he says not. But it's interesting to see how he spells out the Nuremberg principles.

They're just the way I said. In fact, I'm taking it from him, but he doesn't regard that as a criticism. He says, well, that's the way we did it, and should have done it that way.

There's an article on this in *The Yale Law Journal* which is reprinted in a book if you're interested—[Chomsky's excellent analysis of war crimes and Vietnam: *The Yale Law Journal*, "Review Symposium: War Crimes, the Rule of Force in International Affairs," Vol. 80, #7, June 1971].

I think one ought to raise many questions about the Nuremberg tribunal, and especially the Tokyo tribunal. The Tokyo tribunal was in many ways farcical. The people condemned at Tokyo had done things for which plenty of people on the other side could be condemned. Furthermore, just as in the case of Saddam Hussein, many of their worst atrocities the U.S. didn't care about. Like some of the worst atrocities of the Japanese were in the late '30's, but the U.S. didn't especially care about that. What the U.S. cared about was that Japan was moving to close off the China market. That was no good. But not the slaughter of a couple of hundred thousand people or whatever they did in Nanking. That's not a big deal.

From a talk at St. Michael's College, Winooski, Vermont (available from Radio Free Maine and Turning The Tide Video—see Resource Guide)

ROWE CONFERENCE CENTER,
ROWE, MASSACHUSETTS

I think it's entirely natural for history to progress from a period when slavery is considered legitimate to a period where it isn't. But I think it would be surprising if history went in the other direction over a long term. It seems to me that, throughout history, it is quite common to find things that were regarded as entirely reasonable, ethical and acceptable in earlier periods regarded with great contempt and disgust in later periods. This is very true of our own traditions. If you read the Bible, say, you find that it is one of the most genocidal texts in our literature. It's God who orders his chosen people to wipe out the Amalakites down to the last man, woman, and child. People wouldn't be enjoined to do that sort of thing today; they wouldn't want to attribute that to their God, today. That's the mark of some sort of moral progress.

From an interview with Richard Beckwith and Matthew Rispoli, printed in *Language and Politics*, page 468

"The Bible is probably the most genocidal book in our total canon."

"Education is a system of imposed ignorance."

Student

My question involves perception and the perpetuation of what you have been talking about. Given the current educational status in the United States, i.e., the *National Geographic* survey that showed that an amazing number of Americans are uneducated about basic facts about geography, etc. I mean, isn't it understandable, not that I'm in agreement with it, but isn't it understandable that many of these perceptions about the ignorant masses just keep on going on and on?

Chomsky

When I was quoting these remarks about the stupid and ignorant masses, I hope you didn't take that to mean that that is what I believe. I was describing the position of elites. And they want the masses to be ignorant and stupid. Now, the fact of the matter is that on significant issues there is no evidence that the ordinary, general population is more stupid and ignorant than the educated elites. In fact I think that there are plenty of important issues in which the opposite is true.

For example, if you went to the Harvard Faculty Club you'd be more likely to get the right answer to, oh, you know, "what's the latitude of the capital of Honduras?" than if you went to the people who sent in money for hurricane relief to the Jesuit Center. On the other hand, if you want to know about understanding of the world, you would get a much better reaction from the people who sent money for hurricane relief into the Jesuit Center because they know what is important. They understand. They may not know the latitude of Tegucigalpa, or even the name of it. But they understand basically what's going on in Central America. And in the Harvard Faculty Club they understand very little about that because they are much too indoctrinated.

I mentioned that the population got out of control during the Vietnam War. Well, there is a test of that. There is a very good test. As I say, this is a very heavily polled society. We know a lot about what people think. By 1969 or 1970, and continuing until today, to the most recent polls that I've seen, an overwhelming majority of the population, say somewhere around seventy percent when asked about the Vietnam War, when given a set of options, they say it was fundamentally wrong and immoral, not a mistake.

Whereas if you go to opinion leaders—what they call opinion leaders—the numbers are much lower. And if you go to articulate intellectuals the number is virtually zero. At the peak of the opposition to the war, they thought it was a mistake.

Well, that shows a much deeper understanding of reality on the part of the ignorant masses than on the part of the educated elites.

Student

But aren't you again referring to a very specific population? I mean a population of college students, activists?

Chomsky

No, no. I'm talking about the whole population of the United States. I'm giving you some figures about the whole population of the United States.

Student

Well, it's not a sentiment that I agree with, but I think that perception—

Chomsky

Fine, well, OK, well now I think we have to ask then "what is the right attitude?" Is the right attitude toward the American invasion of South Vietnam that it was a mistake and we should do it better next time? Or is the right attitude towards an attack on another country where we leave three countries in ruin and kill off several million people and so on, is the right attitude "It's fundamentally wrong and immoral, not a mistake"? Here we might differ. I happen to agree with the overwhelming majority of the American people on that. And I think that the elites can't understand it because it's not in their interest to understand it. Because on issue after issue, you see, if you judge ignorance by ability to answer an SAT test, you get one answer. If you judge ignorance by ability to understand the world, you get a very

SERPENT'S TAIL PUBLISHERS, LONDON,
ENGLAND

Chomsky

There's no more morality in world affairs,
fundamentally, than there was at the time of
Genghis Khan. There are just different factors
to be concerned with—

David Ransom (*an ABC, Australia, television reporter*)
Noam Chomsky, thank you.

GEORGETOWN UNIVERSITY, WASHINGTON, DC

Chomsky

You know, people will quite reasonably expect
to know what you mean. Why did you say that?
I never heard that before. If you said that you
better have a reason, you better have some
evidence, and in fact you better have a lot of
evidence, because that's a pretty startling
comment. You can't give evidence if you're
stuck with concision. That's the genius of this
structural constraint. And in my view, if people
like, say, "Nightline" and "MacNeil/Lehrer" were
smarter, if they were better propagandists, they
would let dissidents on, let them on more, in
fact. The reason is that they would sound like
they're from Neptune.

different answer.

If you're a scientist you'll know that the same is true
with the outer reaches of science. You want to find out
which scientist understands physics. If you give them
a test and ask them how many facts they can remember,
you're going to get the clerks but you're not going to
get the people who understand physics. People who
understand physics understand the way it works. If they
want to bother with the details they'll look them up in
a handbook.

Pretty much the same is true about understanding
the world. Education is a system of imposed ignorance.
It is a system of indoctrination. It is a system which dri-
ves out of you a lot of the capacity to understand
things. And many people who are farther away from
the system of indoctrination, I think, have a far better
perception of many things. That's not a plea for ignorance. I'd like to see people know...where Tegucigalpa
is. That would be very helpful. On the other hand, there
are many perceptions about the world which I think are
better available to those who are freer from the indoctrination system.

From a question-and-answer session after a "Necessary Illusions" talk at the University of
Wyoming in Laramie

There's no more morality in world affairs, fundamentally, than there was at the time of Genghis Khan.

David Ransom, a reporter with ABC Australia, had the good sense to call on Chomsky for commentary and analysis and was open enough to allow us to reveal what is usually a hidden technique of television journalism.

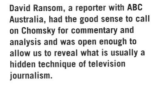

SERPENT'S TAIL PUBLISHERS, LONDON

David Ransom

Okay, can you give us a half a second for a two-shot, that's all. Then we can do anything after that.

Chomsky

That's alright.

David Ransom *(to cameraman)*

Yeah, what about the ah—

Chomsky *(to Mark Achbar)*

Well, I better go up, Mark. I think there's some stuff hanging around there—

David Ransom

Yeah—the idea with this one is it's just a shot where I'm seen talking to you and you're seen listening to me. I'll ask you, though, if you don't speak to me or move your lips so that I can be seen to be asking you a question. The reason for this shot is simply this—

Chomsky

I'm used to it—

David Ransom

—Okay, just don't talk to me and I'll keep going, that's the thing. Ah, the reason for this shot—I'll explain it through because I usually find that's the easiest way to do it—the reason for this shot is I need a shot where you're sitting and seen listening to me while I'm asking you a question. We can use this shot to introduce you, explain who you are, where you fit into the piece I'm doing. But if you don't speak to me, I can also use—Got it? Okay, thanks for your time—Righto!

EXCERPT: "MACNEIL/LEHRER NEWSHOUR," PBS (PUBLIC) USA (SEPTEMBER, 1990)

(Chomsky's air time: 11 mins 52 secs)

Jim Lehrer

Then comes our special conversation on the Middle East crisis. Tonight's is with the activist, writer and professor Noam Chomsky.

Chomsky

Again, there is—has been—an offer on the table which we rejected, an Iraqi offer last April—

Robert MacNeil *(off-camera)*

Okay, I have to ask—

Chomsky

—to eliminate their chemical and other unconventional arsenals if Israel were to simultaneously do the same.

Robert MacNeil

—have to end it there.

Chomsky

We rejected it but I think that should be pursued as well.

Robert MacNeil

Sorry to interrupt you. I have to end it there. That's the end of our time. Professor Chomsky, thank you very much for joining us.

AT&T COMMERICAL

Announcer

AT&T has supported the "MacNeil/Lehrer NewsHour" since 1983, because quality information and quality communication is our idea of a good connection. AT&T: the right choice.

Number of guests in 16 years of Macneil/Lehrer news programs:

more than 10,500

Number of interviews with Noam Chomsky:

1

"AMERICAN FOCUS," STUDENT RADIO, WASHINGTON, DC

Elizabeth Sikorovsky
If there is a narrower range of opinion in the United States, and it is harder to express a variety of different opinions, why do you live in the U.S.?

Chomsky
Well, first of all, it's my country, and, secondly, in many ways, as I said before, it's the freest country in the world—I mean, I think there's more possibilities for change here than in any other country I know.

"IDEAS," CBC PUBLIC RADIO, CANADA

Chomsky
Again, comparatively speaking, it's the country where the State is probably most restricted.

Peter Worthington (editor, *Ottawa Sun*)
But isn't that what you should be looking at comparatively rather—

Chomsky
—Yes, I do—

Peter Worthington
—than in absolute terms—

Chomsky
—Of course—

Peter Worthington
—but you don't give that impression—

Chomsky
Well, maybe I don't give the impression but I certainly *say* it often enough. What I've said over and over again, and I've been saying it all tonight, I've written it a million times, is that the

United States is a very free society. It's also a very rich society. Of course, the United States is a scandal from the point of view of its wealth. I mean, given the natural advantages that the United States has in terms of resources and lack of enemies and so on, the United States should have a level of health and welfare and so on that's an order of magnitude beyond anyone else in the world. We don't. The United States is last among twenty industrialized societies in infant mortality. That's a scandal of American capitalism. And it ends up being a very free society. Which does a lot of rotten things in the world. Okay? There's no contradiction there. I mean, Greece was a free society by the standards of Athens. It was also a vicious society from the point of view of its imperial behavior. There's virtually no correlation—maybe none—between the internal freedom of a society and its external behavior.

Among twenty industrialized countries the U.S ranks 20th in infant mortality rates, with rates higher than East Germany, Ireland, Spain, etc. (*Wall Street Journal*, Oct. 19, 1988)

Necessary Illusions pages 357, note 8

In earlier years, huge propaganda campaigns had been undertaken to overcome deviant ideas among the general public, notably after World War II, when the world was swept by a current of social reform, bitterly fought by the U.S. government at home and abroad. Success in reversing these trends was great in most of the world, including the United States itself, though in Europe and Japan the attack on labor and democracy did not achieve all of its goals and countries adopted a kind of "social contract" that included such depraved ideas as health care, workers' rights, and other departures from the principles for which we serve as a gatekeeper and a model.

In the U.S., the wave was beaten back in part through massive propaganda efforts orchestrated by the Chamber of Commerce and the Advertising Council, which conducted a $100-million campaign to use all media to "sell" the American economic system—as they conceived it—to the American people. The program was officially described as a "major project of educating the American people about the economic facts of life." Corporations "started extensive programs to indoctrinate employees," the leading business journal *Fortune* reported, subjecting their captive audiences to "Courses in Economic Education" and testing them for commitment to the "free enterprise" system—that is, "Americanism." The scale was "staggering," sociologist Daniel Bell (then a Fortune editor) observed, as the business world sought to reverse the democratizing thrust of the Depression years and reestablish the ideological hegemony of the "free enterprise system." A survey conducted by the American Management Association (AMA) found that many corporate leaders regarded "propaganda" and "economic educa-

tion" as synonymous, holding that "We want our people to think right." The AMA reported that Communism, socialism, and particular political parties and unions "are often common targets of such campaigns," which "some employers view...as a sort of 'battle of loyalties' with the unions"—a rather unequal battle, given the resources available, including the corporate media, which offered the services free of charge, then as now.

The results were remarkable, leaving the U.S. off the spectrum of industrial societies on social issues and basic human rights. Health care is one case that finally gained attention, as the highly bureaucratized and inefficient private system began to become too much of a burden to corporations, though the U.S. will remain alone, it seems, in ramming through—again, over popular opposition—a system that is highly regressive (not tax-based) and that attends carefully to the needs of the few huge insurance companies that are to take the central management role, at substantial public cost.

From "The Clinton Vision—The Rationale and Rhetoric of U.S. Foreign Policy: Enlargement, Democracy, and Free Markets," in *Z Magazine*, December 1993

For extensive discussion, Chomsky recommends *Managing Public Opinion: The Corporate Offensive*, by Alex Carey (manuscript, University of New South Wales, 1986). A version of this article also appeared in *Union Strategy and Industrial Change*, edited by S. Frenkel (New South Wales University Press, 1978) and parts of it appeared in *City Lights Review*, # 3 (San Francisco, 1989)

Edward S. Herman and Noam Chomsky dedicated *Manufacturing Consent* to Alex Carey

On the domestic scene in the U.S.:
"The Third World At Home," *Year 501: The Conquest Continues*, pages 275-288; "The Home Front," *Deterring Democracy*, pages 69-88 ; "The Domestic Scene," *On Power and Ideology*, pages 113-135

EXCERPT: "FIRING LINE," 1969

William F. Buckley, Jr.
You start your line of discussion at a moment that is historically useful for you—

Chomsky
That's why I say, you pick the beginning. You pick the beginning—

Buckley
—The grand act of the post-war world—

Chomsky
—Alright—

Buckley
—is that the— communist imperialists, by the use of terrorism, by the use of— by deprivation of freedom, have contributed to the continuing bloodshed and the sad thing about it is not only the bloodshed, but the fact they seem to dispossess you of the power of rational observation.

Chomsky
—May I say something?

Buckley
Certainly.

Chomsky
That's about five percent true, and about—or maybe ten percent true. It certainly is tr—

Buckley
—Why do you give that?—

Chomsky
—May I complete a sentence?

Buckley
Sure.

Chomsky

It's perfectly true that there were areas of the world, in particular Eastern Europe, where Stalinist imperialism very brutally took control and still maintains control, but there are also very vast areas of the world where we were doing the same thing. And there's quite an interplay in the Cold War. You see, the— what you just described is, I believe, a mythology about the Cold War which might have been tenable ten years ago but which is quite inconsistent with contemporary scholarship.

Buckley

Ask a Czech—

Chomsky

Ask a Guatemalan, ask a Dominican, ask a person from the Dominican Republic, ask a person from South Vietnam, you know, ask a Thai, ask—

Buckley

Obviously, if you can't distinguish between the nature of our venture in Guatemala and the nature of Soviet Union's in Prague—

Chomsky

What's the difference?

Buckley

—then we've got a real difficulty.

Chomsky

—explain to me the difference.

(Bell rings)

Buckley

Sorry.

For transcripts and videotapes of "Firing Line" programs, see Resource Guide.

On the Cold War, see "Cold War: Fact and Fancy," *Deterring Democracy*, pages 9-68

On Guatemala, see *Turning the Tide; On Power and Ideology*

On the Dominican Republic, see *The Political Economy of Human Rights, Volume 1*, pages 242-250; *Year 501: The Conquest Continues*, chapters 7, 8; "The Fruits of Victory: The Caribbean," in *Deterring Democracy*, pages 233-235

On Thailand, see *The Political Economy of Human Rights, Volume 1*, pages 218-229

The button in Mr. Buckley's left hand apparently signaled his decision to cut to a commercial or a station break. In the film, his thumb can be observed to be hovering over the button immediately after Chomsky, having been interrupted several times throughout the program, requested sufficient time to complete his sentence. In this instance, Mr. Buckley chose to make his point without allowing Chomsky to complete his, and cut to a break. After the break, he did not respond to Chomsky's challenge.

ERIN MILLS SHOPPING CENTER VIDEO WALL

The screen is blank at first, then, from the Coast Bastion Inn, Nanaimo, British Columbia:

Chomsky

Now, what about making the media more responsive and democratic? Well, there are very narrow limits to that; it's kind of like asking how do we make corporations more democratic. Well, the only way to do that is get rid of them. I mean, if you have concentrated power—I don't want to say that you can do nothing— like the church can show up at the stock- holders meeting and start screaming about not investing in South Africa, and sometimes that has marginal effects. I don't want to say that it has no effects, but you can't really affect the structure of power, because to do that would be a social revolution. And unless you're ready for a social revolution, that is, power is going to be somewhere else, the media are going to have their present structure and they're going to represent their present interests. Now, that's not to say that one shouldn't try to do things, I mean it makes sense to try to push the limits of a system.

Continuation of film clip, left (not shown):
Remember, corporations are the private equivalent of what we call fascism in the political realm. The deci- sion- making structure in a corporation is top down. You give orders and they are executed down below.

If you go to one demonstration and then go home, that's something, but the people in power can live with that. What they can't live with is sustained pressure that keeps building, organizations that keep doing things, people that keep learning lessons from the last time and doing it better the next time.

What Uncle Sam Really Wants, page 98

COMMUNITY ACTIVIST CIRCLE,
NANAIMO, BRITISH COLUMBIA

Young Man

It only takes one or two people that think they
have integrity as journalists to give you some
good press.

Chomsky

Yeah. See that's important and that goes back to
something that came up before. I mean, you
know, things are complex. It's not monolithic.
The mass media themselves are complicated
institutions with internal contradictions. So on
the one hand there's the commitment to
indoctrination and control, but on the other
hand there's the sense of professional integrity.

SARAH MCCLENDON NEWS SERVICE, WASHINGTON, DC

Announcer
She works alone as her own boss, writing newspaper columns and producing radio commentaries for a hodgepodge of small clients across the country. This so-called leather-lunged Texan has been firing questions at chief executives for almost forty years.

Sarah McClendon
And many a young man in this country is being disillusioned totally by his government these days.

Richard Nixon
Well, this is a question which you very properly bring to the attention of the nation.

Ronald Reagan
It's not that we haven't been holding press conferences. I was just waiting for Sarah to come back.

Sarah McClendon
Mr. President, that is very nice of you and I appreciate it. Sir, I want to call your attention to a real problem we've got in this country today.

Announcer
Those unique and often terrifying McClendon questions reflect her desire to dig out information.

Sarah McClendon
I wanted to ask you, and your new man, what he feels the public—(*drowned out by laughter*)

Announcer
With enough know-how and persistence she usually gets her man.

I actually have a high regard for the American media because I think that there is a high level of professional competence in a narrow sense. For example, if some event is taking place somewhere in the world, and I had to choose between the descriptions given by a professional American reporter and reporters from other countries where I know a lot about, I would tend, by and large, to rely on the American reporter. I think there is a high level of professional competence and integrity in a narrow technical sense. That is, I think they are not going to lie. Well, there are some who will, but, by and large, our reporters will, in a sort of technical sense, try to find out what is going on. What goes wrong is the choice of topics, the framework of assumptions, the set of presuppositions within which things are presented, the emphasis, the tone and so on.

From an interview with Joop van Tijn on Humanist TV, Holland, June 10, 1989

Born in 1910, journalist and author Sarah Newcomb McClendon founded Sarah McClendon News Service in Washington in 1946. She wrote *My Eight Presidents* in 1978 and has since covered three more.

In addition to running her own news service, she has contributed to magazines such as *Esquire*, *Penthouse* and *Diplomat*.

McClendon has won many awards, including the Woman of Conscience Award from the National Council of Women in 1983 and the first President's Award for Journalism in Washington from the National Federation of Press Women in 1990. She served with the Women's Army Corps and has been an army advisor to and a member of the defense advisory committee on Women in the Services.

Also see note on page 122 for high praise for the Israeli press.

NATIONAL PRESS CLUB, WASHINGTON, DC

Sarah McClendon

What would you do if you were in a situation where you were trying to be an honest reporter and you were worried sick about your country, and you saw how sick it was and you [were] facing this weak White House and a weak Congress as a reporter. What would you do?

Chomsky

I think there are a lot of reporters who do a very good job. In fact I have a lot of friends in the press who I think do a terrific job. What you—

Sarah McClendon

I know they are, but, I mean, they want to but what would you do—

Chomsky

First of all, you have to understand what the system is. And smart reporters do understand what it is. You have to understand what the pressures are, what the commitments are, what the barriers are, and what the openings are.

Fairness and Accuracy in Reporting (FAIR) organized this press conference for the Washington media to "turn the tables" on media critic Noam Chomsky. Of the 40 or so people who showed up, none was from the mainstream U.S. press, though FAIR invited them all.

SCRUM: AMERICAN CIVIL LIBERTIES UNION, ROCHESTER, NEW YORK

Chomsky

Like, right after the Iran-Contra hearings, a lot of good reporters understood—well things are going to be a little more open for a couple of months—so you could ram through stories that they knew they couldn't even talk about before.

Man

And after Watergate.

Chomsky

And the same after Watergate, and then, you know, it closes up again, and so on.

The question that dominated the Iran-Contra hearings—did Reagan know, or remember, what the policy of his Administration had been?—was hardly a serious one. The pretense to the contrary was simply part of the cover-up operation; and the lack of public interest over revelations that Reagan was engaged in illegal aid to the Contras during a period when—he later informed Congress—he knew nothing about it, betrays a certain realism.

Deterring Democracy, page 74

The crime of Watergate was that the Republican Party had hired a bunch of kind of Keystone Cops to break into the Democratic Party headquarters for reasons which remain obscure to this day. That was the crime. There were some ancillary things.

At exactly the time of the Watergate hearings it was exposed in court cases and through the Freedom of Information Act that the FBI, at that point for 12 or 13 years, had been regularly carrying out burglaries of the Socialist Workers Party, which is a legal political party, for the purpose of disrupting their activities, stealing their membership lists, using the membership lists to intimidate people who joined the party, get them to lose their jobs, etc. That's vastly more serious than Watergate. This isn't a bunch of petty crooks. This is the national political police. It wasn't being done by some loose cannon, it was being done systematically by every administration. It was seriously disrupting a legal political party, whereas Watergate did nothing to the Democratic Party. Did that come up at the Watergate hearings? Not a mention.

What's the difference? The difference is that the Democratic Party represents domestic power, the Socialist Workers Party doesn't. So what the Watergate hearings showed, the great principle that was being defended, was "people with power are going to defend themselves."

Chronicles of Dissent, page 136-137

More on Watergate:
Manufacturing Consent, chapter 6;
"Watergate: Small Potatoes," *Radical Priorities*, pages 175-177

"AMERICAN FOCUS," STUDENT RADIO, WASHINGTON, DC

Chomsky
Most people, I imagine, simply internalize the values. That's the easiest way, and the most successful way; you just internalize the values and then you regard yourself—in a way, correctly—as acting perfectly freely.

You begin to conform, you begin to get the privilege of conformity. You soon come to believe what you're saying because it's useful to believe it, and then you've internalized the system of indoctrination and distortion and deception, and then you're a willing member of the privileged elites that control thought and indoctrination. That happens all the time, all the way to the top. It's a very rare person, almost to the point of non-existence, who can tolerate what's called "cognitive dissonance"— saying one thing and believing another. You start saying certain things because it's necessary to say them and pretty soon you believe them because you just have to.

From an interview with David Barsamian in *Language and Politics,* pages 653-654

ON A TV SET IN A REPAIR SHOP DURING
THE GULF WAR (JANUARY 18, 1990)

Announcer

Alright, let's get to the White House now, where,
I think, veteran correspondent Frank Sesno can
tell us a little bit about self-censorship. That
inertial guidance system is always going on, isn't
it? Is there any formal censorship there?

Frank Sesno *(CNN reporter)*

There's no self-censorship, Reed. If somebody
tells me something I'm going to pass it on—
unless there is a particular and compelling
reason not to. I can't deny that I wouldn't like to
have access to the Oval Office and all the same
maps and charts and graphs that the president is
looking at, but that's not possible, it's not
realistic and it's probably not even desirable.

**Concentration of ownership of the media is high and
increasing.** Furthermore, those who occupy managerial positions in the media, or gain status within them as
commentators, belong to the same privileged elites,
and might be expected to share the perceptions, aspi-
rations, and attitudes of their associates, reflecting their
own class interests as well. Journalists entering the system are unlikely to make their way unless they conform
to these ideological pressures, generally by internaliz-
ing the values; it is not easy to say one thing and
believe another, and those who fail to conform will tend
to be weeded out by familiar mechanisms.

Necessary Illusions, page 8

("Joop Van Tijn in Conversation")

Joop van Tijn *(journalist)*
Hello.

Chomsky
Hi, how are ya?

Joop van Tijn
Fine. Do you want to sit down there, please?
Welcome to Holland. I'll introduce you first in a
few lines:

(to camera, translated from Dutch)

Professor Chomsky, Noam Chomsky, is now
sixty, and he's by and large the most controversial
intellectual of America. It's kind of a platitude,
but that's the way they always label him.

NEWS ITEM: BOOK BURNING

A City TV (Toronto) news report broadcast September 25, 1987

Thalia Assuras *(reporter)*
Chomsky has been called the Einstein of Modern Linguistics. *The New York Times* has said he's arguably the most important intellectual alive today. But his presence here has sparked a protest.

Bui Son *(Free Vietnamese Community of Canada)*
This book has poisoned the world and [it's] all lies in there, and as Vietnamese people, we come here to burn the book.

All Protesters
Vietnam! Vietnam!

Khanh Lekim *(Vietnamese Human Rights Committee)*
He said that in Vietnam there is no violation of human rights, and no crimes in Cambodia. He's wrong.

Bui Son
Chomsky [is] using his profession, he [is] using that to poison the world, and we come here to protest that.

See full transcript at right

Thalia Assuras
Members of the Vietnamese and Cambodian communities were upset over a lecture by a world-renowned scholar at U of T. The seventeen hundred seats at Convocation Hall were sold out for a *Toronto Star* lecture series this afternoon. Speaking today: Noam Chomsky, author of several books. Chomsky has been called the Einstein of Modern Linguistics. *The New York Times* has said he's arguably the most important intellectual alive today. But his presence here has sparked a protest.

Bui Son
This book has poisoned the world and [it's] all lies in there, and as Vietnamese people, we come here to burn the book.

All Protesters
Vietnam! Vietnam!

Thalia Assuras
The book of contention is one co-authored by Chomsky and Edward S. Herman. It's called *After the Cataclysm: Imperial Ideology and Post-War Reconstruction in Indochina* [sic].

Khanh Lekim
He says that nobody was put in prison camp. We have prisoners here. He says that Vietnamese people escaped out of Vietnam because of something else, not because of the Communism. He said that in Vietnam there is no violation of human rights and no crimes in Cambodia. He's wrong.

Bui Son
Chomsky [is] using his profession, he [is] using that to poison the world, and we come here to protest that.

Thalia Assuras
Chomsky says his book in part sought to determine the real extent of the atrocities committed in Cambodia and other countries. It compared figures reported by the media and others.

Chomsky
In the case of Cambodia, the standard picture in the media was that Pol Pot had taken credit for—had boasted, in fact—of having killed two million people in a unified, mass genocide campaign. The analysis of American intelligence at that time is that the numbers who had died were in the tens or hundreds of thousands, not from mass genocide, but from harsh, brutal conditions of labor and overwork and so on and so forth. We said, as far as we can judge, that's probably the most credible assessment.

For a further discussion of Cambodia, see section beginning page 94

"THIRD EAR" BBC-3 (PUBLIC RADIO)
LONDON, ENGLAND

Chomsky

I don't mind the denunciations, frankly. I mind
the lies. I mean, intellectuals are very good at
lying. They're professionals at it. You know,
vilification is a wonderful technique. There's no
way of responding to it. If somebody calls you
an anti-Semite, what can you say? I'm not an
anti-Semite? Or, you know, somebody says
you're a racist, you're a Nazi or something, you
always lose. I mean, the person who throws the
mud always wins because there's no way of
responding to such charges.

For a discussion of other lies and
slander to which Chomsky has been
subjected, see "The Chorus and
Cassandra: What Everyone Knows
About Noam Chomsky," by
Christopher Hitchens, in *Grand Street*,
Autumn 1985 (See Resource Guide)

The person
who throws
the mud
always wins...

GRONINGEN, HOLLAND

Frits Bolkestein (*minister of defense, Holland*)
Professor Chomsky seems to believe that the people he criticizes fall into one of two classes: liars or dupes. Consider what happens when I discuss the case of Robert Faurisson. Let me recall the facts.

Everyone knows Noam Chomsky of the Massachusetts Institute of Technology for his linguistics and his left-wing politics. But the fact that he also maintains important connections with the neo-Nazi movement of our time—that he is, in a certain sense, the most important patron of that movement—is well known only in France. Much like a bigamist who must constantly strain to keep one of his families secret from the other, Chomsky must try to keep his liberal and left-wing American public ignorant of his other, his neo-Nazi following.

Chomsky has said that his contact with the neo-Nazis is strictly limited to a defense of their freedom of speech. He has said that he disagrees with the most important neo-Nazi article of faith, viz. that the Holocaust never happened. But such denials have not prevented him from prolonged and varied political collaboration with the neo-Nazi movement, from agreement with it on other key points, nor—and this has proven essential for the neo-Nazis especially in France—from using his scholarly reputation to promote and publicize the neo-Nazi groups.

From *The Hidden Alliances of Noam Chomsky,* by Werner Cohn
(a 40-page pamphlet distributed by Americans for a Safe Israel, 1988)

If any of you have ever looked at your FBI file and you discover that intelligence agencies in general are extremely incompetent. That's one of the reasons why there are so many intelligence failures. They just never get anything straight, for all kinds of reasons. Part of it is because of the information they get. The information they get comes from ideological fanatics, typically, who always misunderstand things in their own crazy way. If you look at an FBI file, say, about yourself, where you know what the facts are, you'll see that the information has some kind of relation to the facts, you can figure out what they're talking about, but by the time it works its way through the ideological fanaticism of the intelligence agencies, there's always weird distortion.

From *"Noam Chomsky: Questions and Answers with Community Activists, University Common Ministry, Laramie, Wyoming,"* February 10, 1989 (available on cassette and as a transcript from Alternative Radio—see Resource Guide)

HUMANIST TV (PUBLIC), HOLLAND

Joop van Tijn
Let's not go into details because—

Chomsky
—The details happen to be important—

Joop van Tijn
I have only one question on the Faurisson question.

Chomsky
Do the facts matter or don't they matter?

Joop van Tijn
Of course they do.

Chomsky
Well, let me tell you what the facts are, then.

Joop van Tijn
Uh-huh.

BATTERSEA ARTS CENTRE, LONDON, ENGLAND

Angry Man
Right—Faurisson says that the massacre of the Jews in the Holocaust is a historic lie—

Woman in Audience
Can we have the next question please!

Angry Man
NO—

Chomsky
No, this is an important one, it has a lot to do with the topic.

Woman in Audience
Get off—!

KUOW (LISTENER-SUPPORTED RADIO) SEATTLE, WASHINGTON

Ross Reynolds

Your views are extremely controversial, and perhaps one of the things that has been most controversial and that you've been most strongly criticized for was your defense of a French intellectual who was suspended from his university post for contending that there were no Nazi death camps in World War II.

PARIS CAFE

Robert Faurisson

My name is Robert Faurisson. I am sixty. I am a university professor in Lyon, France. Behind me, you may see the courthouse of Paris, the Palais de Justice. In this place I was convicted many times at the beginning of the eighties. I was charged by nine associations, mostly Jewish associations, for inciting hatred, *racial* hatred, for racial defamation, for damage by *falsifying history*.

THE 'PROBLEM OF THE GAS CHAMBERS'

BY ROBERT FAURISSON[1]

(Professor Robert Faurisson wrote the article below in 1978. It was widely circulated in France and was translated and published in the Summer, 1980 issue of The Journal of Historical Review. No one has been able to refute any of the facts presented.)

No one, not even among those individuals who regard the Third Reich with nostalgia, denies the [...] concentration camps under Hitler.

Conclusions after 30 years of research by Revisionist authors:

1. *The Hitler "gas chambers" never existed.*

2. *The "genocide" (or "attempted genocide") of the Jews never took place. In other words: Hitler never gave an order — nor permission — that anyone should be killed because of his race or religion.*

3. *The alleged "gas chambers" and the alleged "genocide" are one and the same lie.*

4. *This lie, which is largely of Zionist origin, has made an enormous political and financial fraud possible, whose principal beneficiary is the state of Israel.*

5. *The principal victims of this fraud are the German people (but not the German rulers) and the entire Palestinian people.*

6. *The enormous power of the official information services has, thus far, had the effect of ensuring the success of the lie and of censoring the freedom of expression of those who have denounced the lie.*

7. *The participants in this lie know that its days are numbered. They distort the purpose and nature of the Revisionist research. They label as "resurgence of Nazism" or as "falsification of history" what is only a thoughtful and justified concern for historical truth.*

GRONINGEN, HOLLAND

Frits Bolkestein

Professor Chomsky and a number of other intellectuals signed a petition in which Faurisson is called a respected professor of literature who merely tried to make his *findings* public.

THE PANTHEON, PARIS, FRANCE

Mark Achbar

Perhaps we can start with just the story of Robert Faurisson and your involvement.

Pierre Guillaume *(Faurisson's publisher)*

More than five hundred people signed. Maybe six hundred. Mostly—uh—*universitaires*—

Serge Thion *(Indochina specialist)*

—Scholars—

Pierre Guillaume

Scholars.

Mark Achbar

What happened to the other four hundred and ninety-nine of them? How come we only hear about Chomsky's signature?

Serge Thion

Well, I think it is because Chomsky is in himself a kind of political power.

HUMANIST TV (PUBLIC), HOLLAND

Chomsky

I signed a petition calling on the tribunal to defend his civil rights. At that point, the French press—which apparently has no conception of freedom of speech—concluded that since I had called for his civil rights I was therefore defending his theses.

The term "findings" is quite neutral. One can say, without contradiction: "He made his findings public and they were judged worthless, irrelevant, falsified..."

From Chomsky's "His Right to Say It," in *The Nation* (February 28, 1981), page 231. See page 189 for several excerpts from this article.

Pierre Guillaume publishes and contributes to *Annales d'Histoire révisionniste* (a journal of revisionist history). He is Faurisson's publisher in France.

Serge Thion, described by Chomsky as "a libertarian socialist scholar with a record of opposition to all forms of totalitarianism," has published, with Guillaume, a collection of papers relating to "The Faurisson Affair." Today, he denies starting the petition, claiming U.S. revisionist Mark Weber, of the California-based Institute for Historical Review, started it.

Voltaire is buried in the Pantheon

The struggle for freedom of speech is an interesting case—and a crucial one, since it lies at the heart of a whole array of freedoms and rights. A central question of the modern era is when, if ever, the state may act to interdict the content of communications.... even those regarded as leading libertarians have adopted restrictive and qualified views on this matter. One critical element is seditious libel, the idea that the state can be criminally assaulted by speech, "the hallmark of closed societies throughout the world," legal historian Harry Kalven observes. A society that tolerates laws against seditious libel is not free, whatever its other virtues. In late-seventeenth-century England, men were castrated, disemboweled, quartered and beheaded for the crime. Throughout the eighteenth century, there was a general consensus that established authority could be maintained only by silencing subversive discussion, and "any threat, whether real or imagined, to the good reputation of the government" must be barred by force (Leonard Levy). "Private men are not judges of their superiors... [for] This wou'd confound all government," one editor wrote. Truth was no defense: truth charges are even more criminal than false ones, because they tend even more to bring authority into disrepute.

Treatment of dissident opinion, incidentally, follows a similar model in our more libertarian era. False and ridiculous charges are no real problem; it is the unconscionable critics who reveal unwanted truths from whom society must be protected.

The doctrine of seditious libel was also upheld in the American colonies. The intolerance of dissent during the revolutionary period is notorious. The leading American libertarian, Thomas Jefferson, agreed that punishment was proper for "a traitor in thought, but not in deed," and authorized internment of political suspects. He and the other founders agreed that "traitorous or disrespectful words" against the authority of the national state or any of its component states was criminal. "During the Revolution," Leonard Levy observes,

Jefferson, like Washington, the Adamses and Paine, believed that there could be no toleration for serious differences of political opinion on the issue of independence, no

acceptable alternative to complete submission to the patriot cause. Everywhere there was unlimited liberty to praise it, none to criticize it.

At the outset of the Revolution, the Continental Congress urged the states to enact legislation to prevent the people from being "deceived and drawn into erroneous opinion." It was not until the Jeffersonians were themselves subjected to repressive measures in the late 1790s that they developed a body of more libertarian thought for self-protection—reversing course, however, when they gained power themselves.

Until World War I, there was only a slender basis for freedom of speech in the United States, and it was not until 1964 that the law of seditious libel was struck down by the Supreme Court. In 1969, the Court finally protected speech apart from "incitement to imminent lawless action." Two centuries after the Revolution, the Court at last adopted the position that had been advocated in 1776 by Jeremy Bentham, who argued that a free government must permit "malcontents" to "communicate their sentiments, concert their plans, and practice every mode of opposition short of actual revolt, before the executive power can be legally justified in disturbing them." The 1969 Supreme Court decision formulated a libertarian standard which, I believe, is unique in the world. In Canada, for example, people are still imprisoned for promulgating "false news," recognized as a crime in 1275 to protect the King.

In Europe, the situation is still more primitive. France is a striking case, because of the dramatic contrast between the self-congratulatory rhetoric and repressive practice so common as to pass unnoticed. England has only limited protection for freedom of speech, and even tolerates such a disgrace as a law of blasphemy. The reaction to the Salman Rushdie affair, most dramatically on the part of self-styled "conservatives," was particularly noteworthy. Rushdie was charged with seditious libel and blasphemy in the courts, but the High Court ruled that the law of blasphemy extended only to Christianity, not to Islam, and that only verbal attack "against Her Majesty or Her Majesty's Government or some other institution of the state" counts as seditious libel. Thus the Court upheld a fundamental doctrine of the Ayatollah Khomeini,

Stalin, Goebbels, and other opponents of freedom, while recognizing that English law protects only domestic power from criticism. Doubtless many would agree with Conor Cruise O'Brien, who, when Minister for Posts and Telegraphs in Ireland, amended the Broadcasting Authority Act to permit the Authority to refuse to broadcast any matter that, in the judgment of the Minister, "would tend to undermine the authority of the state."

We should also bear in mind that the right to freedom of speech in the United States was not established by the First Amendment to the Constitution, but only through dedicated efforts over a long period by the labor movement, the civil rights and anti-war movements of the 1960s and other popular forces. James Madison pointed out that a "parchment barrier" will never suffice to prevent tyranny. Rights are not established by words, but won and sustained by struggle.

It is also worth recalling that victories for freedom of speech are often won in defense of the most depraved and horrendous views. The 1969 Supreme Court decision was in defense of the Ku Klux Klan from prosecution after a meeting with hooded figures, guns, and a burning cross, calling for "burying the nigger" and "sending the Jews back to Israel."

Deterring Democracy, pages 398-401

GRONINGEN, HOLLAND

Frits Bolkestein
Faurisson then published a book in which he
tried to prove that the Nazi gas chambers never
existed.

IN A CAR, PARIS, FRANCE

Robert Faurisson
What we deny is that there *was* an extermina-
tion program, and an extermination actually.
Especially in gas chambers or gas vans.

GRONINGEN, HOLLAND

Frits Bolkestein
The book contains a preface written by
Professor Chomsky in which he calls Faurisson
"a relatively apolitical sort of liberal."

IN A CAR, PARIS, FRANCE

Robert Faurisson
A Communist is a man, a Jew is a man, a Nazi is
a man, I am a man.

Mark Achbar
Are you a Nazi?

Robert Faurisson
I am not a Nazi.

Mark Achbar
How would you describe yourself politically?

Robert Faurisson
Nothing.

BATTERSEA ARTS CENTRE, LONDON, ENGLAND
Angry Man on stage

Angry Man
The preface that you wrote, where—

Chomsky
No—that's not the preface that I wrote, because I never wrote a preface. And you *know* that I never wrote a preface.

Angry Man (*leaving stage*)
Yeah—yeah—Vidal Naquet—

Chomsky
He's referring to a statement of mine on civil liberties which was added to a book in which Faurisson—excuse me—

Angry Man (*shouting*)
You are a linguist—

Chomsky
Yes!—

Angry Man
—and the language you use has meaning!

Chomsky
That's right. And the language I use—

Angry Man
—And when you describe someone as an apolitical liberal or as someone whose views can be dignified by the words, findings or conclusions, that is a judgment and that is a favorable judgment of his views!

Chomsky
On the contrary—

As Chomsky consistently denied acceptance or support of Faurisson's views, any credence to those views given by Chomsky is arguably assignable to those who insisted on misrepresenting Chomsky's position and falsely making him a Faurisson supporter, and who therefore chose to give Faurisson more credibility in order to attack Chomsky. Chomsky also pointed out that Holocaust Revisionist Arthur Butz, who teaches at Northwestern University, received minimal publicity and has had no influence because he has been largely ignored, his civil liberties not attacked, and his crank ideas not made a *cause célèbre* by those who find his views abhorrent.

In an article "The judgment of history," in the *New Statesman*, July 17, 1981, Gitta Serenyi stated that "In April, I suggested that we might confront Arthur Butz, who also argues that the Holocaust was a 'hoax.' Academic opinion was that to do so would only lend 'respectability' to a propagandist whom no one could take seriously. The Faurisson case suggests that this judgment was not wholly correct." Serenyi's reasoning is incomprehensible. Faurisson received great publicity only when "confronted." Butz would presumably get the same benefits if similarly attacked. Faurisson never obtained "respectability" for his findings, but only as a civil liberties victim, again as a consequence of the confrontation.

From "Pol Pot, Faurisson, and the Process of Derogation," by Edward S. Herman, in *Noam Chomsky: Critical Assessment's* edited by Carlos P. Otero (Routledge, 1993)

The "Angry Man" was clutching a copy of "The Hidden Alliances of Noam Chomsky." See page 175

HUMANIST TV (PUBLIC), HOLLAND

Chomsky

May I continue with the facts?

Joop van Tijn

Yes, you can continue with the facts for hours. But, I mean, there a few facts that—yeah, O.K.

Chomsky

Let's get to the so-called preface. I was then asked by the person who organized the petition to write a statement on freedom of speech. Just banal comments about freedom of speech, pointing out the difference between defending a person's right to express his views and defending the views expressed. So I did that. I wrote a rather banal statement called "Some Elementary Remarks on Freedom of Expression" and I told him, "Do what you like with it."

THE PANTHEON, PARIS, FRANCE

Serge Thion

So Pierre produced a book which all the arguments of Faurisson were to be put in front of the court. And we thought it wise to use the text of Noam Chomsky as a kind of warning, a foreword, to say that it was a matter of freedom of expression, freedom of thought, freedom of research.

The book is called *Mémoire en Défense contre ceux qui m'accusent de falsifier l'histoire* (Statement in my defense against those who accuse me of falsifying history).

On the cover of Faurisson's book, *Mémoire en Défense*, Chomsky's statement is called an "avis" (an opinion, a judgment, advice or information, notice, or warning) inside, it's called a "preface."

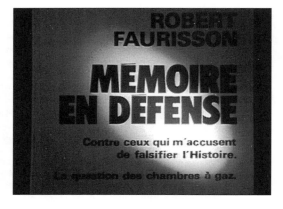

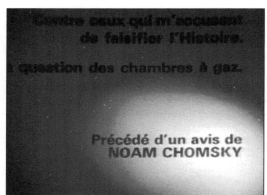

Joop van Tijn

Why did you try at the last moment to get it back from—

Chomsky

—That's the one thing I'm sorry about. That's the one—

Joop van Tijn

—But that's the real, that's the real important thing.

Chomsky

No, it's not.

Joop van Tijn

Of course.

Chomsky

It's not.

Joop van Tijn

Because you—

Chomsky

The fact that I tried to retract it?

Joop van Tijn

Because with that you said that it was wrong of you to do it—

Chomsky

No. I didn't. See, in fact, take a look at what I— I wrote a letter, which was then publicized, in which I said: Look, things have reached a point where the French intellectual community simply is incapable of understanding the issues. At this point it's just going to confuse matters even more if my comments on freedom of speech happen to be attached to this book, which I didn't know existed, so just to clarify things, I better separate them. Now, in

In retrospect, would it have been better not to [try to retract it], maybe. Only in the sense that it would have given less opportunity for people of the [Alan] Dershowitz variety, who are very much committed to preventing free speech on the Arab-Israel issues, and free exchange of ideas. I don't know. You could say on tactical grounds maybe yes, but that's not the way to proceed in my view. You should do what you think is right and not what's going to be tactically useful.

Chronicles of Dissent, page 264

I have defended this principle in far more controversial cases than the present one; for example, at the height of the Vietnam war, with regard to people I believe to be authentic war criminals, or scientists who claim that Blacks are genetically inferior in a country where their history is hardly pleasant and where such views may well contribute to virulent racism, which persists. Whatever one may think of Faurisson, no one accuses him of being the architect of major war crimes, nor does he claim that Jews are genetically inferior, nor does he receive a tiny fraction of the support afforded in these more controversial cases—in which, I might add, my advocacy of principles I continue to hold valid elicited not a peep of protest.

Radical Priorities, page 16

See also "The Treachery of the Intelligentsia: A French Travesty," *Language and Politics*, pages 308-323

The French intellectual community simply is incapable of understanding the issues.

retrospect, I think I probably shouldn't have done that. I should have just said, Fine. Then let it appear. Because it ought to appear. But that's —apart from that, I regard this as not only trivial, but as compared with other positions I've taken on freedom of speech, invisible.

UNIVERSITY OF WASHINGTON, SEATTLE

Chomsky
I do not think that the State ought to have the right to determine historical truth and to punish people who deviate from it. I'm not willing to give the State that right even if they happen to call the—

Male Student
But are you denying that the gas chambers ever existed?

Chomsky
Of course not. But I 'm saying if you believe in freedom of speech, you believe in freedom of speech for views you don't like. I mean Goebbels was in favor of freedom of speech for views he liked. Right? So was Stalin. If you're in favor of freedom of speech, that means you're in favor of freedom of speech precisely for views you despise, otherwise you're not in favor of freedom of speech. There's two positions you can have on freedom of speech, and you can decide which position you want.

I do not think that the State ought to have the right to determine historical truth and to punish people who deviate from it.

BATTERSEA ARTS CENTRE, LONDON, ENGLAND

Chomsky

With regard to my defense of the utterly offensive—the people who express utterly offensive views—I haven't the slightest doubt that every commissar says: You're defending that person's views. No, I'm not. I'm defending his right to express them. The difference is crucial and the difference has been understood outside of fascist circles since the eighteenth century.

UNIVERSITY OF WASHINGTON, SEATTLE

Woman

Is there anything like objectivity, scientific objectivity, reality? As a scientist, why do you stand on this point?

Chomsky

Look, I'm not saying I defend the views. Look, if somebody publishes a scientific article which I disagree with, I do not say the State ought to put him in jail. Right?

Woman

All right! But you don't have to support him right away—

Chomsky

—I don't support him—

Woman

—and say, you know, I support him—

Chomsky

—Oh no—

Woman

—just for the sake of everybody saying whatever they want.

For discussions of freedom of speech, seditious libel (the crime of criticizing government), and censorship, see *Necessary Illusions*, pages 123-133, and "The Courage to Preserve Civil Liberties" and "The Continuing Struggle," *Necessary Illusions*, pages 337-355

Chomsky

Yeah, but—fine. But suppose this guy is taken to court, and charged with falsification. Then, I'm going to defend him even if I disagree with him. And that's what happened—

Woman

But he wasn't taken to court.

Chomsky

Oh, you're wrong.

Woman

But when did you write the support? I mean—

Chomsky

When he was brought to court. And, in fact, the only support that I gave him was to say he has a right to freedom of speech. Period.

EXCERPT: "SPEAKING OUT: CRISIS IN THE MIDDLE EAST"
On TVOntario (public, educational TV) December 12, 1985

Chomsky

There is no doubt in my mind that the example that I gave about this story with the Holocaust did not exist, is very, very typical. How much of the—

Yossi Olmert

I'll give you another example about the Middle East.

Chomsky

How much of the American press believes that Faurisson has anything to say or any press? How much of the press in France—

Olmert

—Since I followed—

TVOntario is the province of Ontario's non-commercial, educational TV network. *Speaking Out* is a live, hour-long current affairs call-in program.

On this 1985 show, Chomsky discussed the crisis in the Middle East with Yossi Olmert, a professor at Tel Aviv University, who went on to become the spokesperson for the Israeli Government Press Office.

Chomsky

—What percentage would you say?

Olmert

I'll tell you.

Chomsky

Is it higher than zero?

Olmert

I tell you.

Chomsky

Is it higher than zero?

Olmert

I tell you, I tell you.

Chomsky

Have you ever seen anything in any newspaper?

Olmert

—You ask me, I try to tell you—

Chomsky

—or any journal saying this man is anything other than a lunatic?

Olmert

Okay. I try to answer. I try to answer. I think that, I just followed the case—

Chomsky

—That's a simple question—

Olmert

—I followed the case five or six years ago and I happened to see that Noam Chomsky was in for strong criticism, even from some of his supporters, for doing something which could be interpreted only in terms of a campaign against Israel.

TVOntario

2180 Yonge Street   Mailing Address:
Toronto, Ontario   Box 200, Station Q
(416) 484-2600   Toronto, Ontario
Telex 06-23547   Canada M4T 2T1

SPEAKING OUT: Telephone Report: 12 December 1985
ISRAEL AND THE MIDDLE EAST
Guests: Professor Josef Olmert- Tel Aviv Univ.; adviser to
        the Israeli government; correspondent to numerous
        international newspapers, radio and tv stations.
        Noam Chomsky- Professor of Linguistics at M.I.T.;
        author, THE FATEFUL TRIANGLE and other books;
        journalist and frequent guest lecturer.

ON-AIR CALLS:
Toronto --------- 3
Burlington ------ 1 (called at 9pm)
               ───
                 4

OFF-AIR CALLS:
Toronto -------- 10
Oshawa --------- 1
LATE:
Toronto -------- 12
Ottawa --------- 1
               ───
                24

PULSEMETER (ATTEMPTS TO GET ON-AIR): 25,809
TALLYPHONE VOTES TOTAL: 5,484
TOTAL NUMBER OF CALLS TO PROGRAM: ---------- (31,321)

Tallyphone Question:
DO PALESTINIANS HAVE A VALID RIGHT
TO SELF-DETERMINATION IN ANY PART OF
THE FORMER TERRITORY OF PALESTINE?
yes --------- 3627
no --------- 1857

note:
With guests like these it is almost impossible to get
phone calls on as well; we were lucky to get four on-air,
and the almost entirely local dialling area origin of the
calls which reached us (on and off-air) indicates how heavy
the attempts to get on-air were. We only gave the on-air
phone number at 9:30:15pm because we wanted to ensure that
enough substance/content had gone out before allowing comments
from callers, and the guests generated so much heat that it took
longer for the LIGHT to get through on a subject of this complex
ity and sensitivity. As it was, we had to dispense with half of
our MAILBAG feature and race through the closing to be able to
finish the show on time. The vote count is a record for this
season (and, if extrapolated to our former show length, for
past seasons as well), and the pulsemeter figure represents
calls attempted in a 25-minute period, another record. There
were some comments from BellTel this morning about our overload
the Central Office.

A Leader in Educational Telecommunications

Chomsky

Going back years, I am absolutely certain I've taken far more extreme positions on people who deny the Holocaust than you have. For example, you go back to my earliest articles and you find that I say that even to enter into the arena of debate on the question of whether the Nazis carried out such atrocities is already to lose one's humanity. So I don't even think you ought to discuss the issue, if you want to know my opinion. But if anybody wants to refute Faurisson there's certainly no difficulty in doing so.

I remember reading an excellent study of Hitler's East European policies a number of years ago in a mood of grim fascination. The author was trying hard to be cool and scholarly and objective, to stifle the only human response to a plan to enslave and destroy millions of subhuman organisms so that the inheritors of the spiritual values of Western civilization would be free to develop a higher form of society in peace. Controlling this elementary human reaction, we enter into a technical debate with the Nazi intelligentsia: Is it technically feasible to dispose of millions of bodies? Must they be ground under foot or returned to their "natural home in the East" so that this great culture can flourish, to the benefit of all mankind? Is it true that the Jews are a cancer eating away at the vitality of the German people? and so on. Without awareness, I found myself drawn into this morass of insane rationality—inventing arguments to counter and demolish the constructions of the Bormanns and the Rosenbergs.

By entering into the arena of argument and counterargument, of technical feasibility and tactics, of footnotes and citations, by accepting the presumption of legitimacy of debate on certain issues, one has already lost one's humanity.

Introduction to *American Power and the New Mandarins*, pages 8-9

In September 1993, Jean-Claude Pressac, a former follower of Faurisson, published *Les Crématoires d'Auschwitz* (The Crematoriums of Auschwitz), which describes in technical detail how the gas chambers and ovens were constructed and operated. Pressac was the first Westerner to be given access to the extensive Auschwitz archives seized by the Soviets in 1945. Pressac explained to *Le Nouvel Observateur* (September 30-October 6, 1993) that he began to have doubts about Faurisson's claims, and that subsequent research convinced him of their falsehood. Over the last decade he has published many technical studies on the subject. The information in the Moscow documents supports his previous research.

Sabrina Mathews

An article in *The New York Times* concerning my involvement in the "Faurisson affair" was headlined "French Storm in a Demitasse." If the intent was to imply that these events do not even merit being called "a tempest in a teapot," I am inclined to agree. Nevertheless, torrents of ink have been spilled in Europe, and some here. Perhaps, given the obfuscatory nature of the coverage, it would be useful for me to state the basic facts as I understand them and to say a few words about the principles that arise....

In the fall of 1979, I was asked by Serge Thion, a libertarian socialist scholar with a record of opposition to all forms of totalitarianism, to sign a petition calling on authorities to ensure Robert Faurisson's "safety and the free exercise of his legal rights."...

The petition aroused considerable protest. In *Nouvel Observateur*, Claude Roy wrote that "the appeal launched by Chomsky" supported Faurisson's views. Roy explained my alleged stand as an attempt to show that the United States is indistinguishable from Nazi Germany. In *Esprit*, Pierre Vidal-Naquet found the petition "scandalous" on the ground that it "presented his 'conclusions' as if they were actually discoveries." Vidal-Naquet misunderstood a sentence in the petition that ran, "Since he began making his findings public, Professor Faurisson has been subject to...." The term "findings" is quite neutral. One can say, without contradiction: "He made his findings public and they were judged worthless, irrelevant, falsified...." The petition implied nothing about the quality of Faurisson's work, which was irrelevant to the issues raised...

Faurisson's conclusions are diametrically opposed to views I hold and have frequently expressed in print (for example, in my book *Peace in the Middle East?*, where I describe the Holocaust as "the most fantastic outburst of collective insanity in human history"). But it is elementary that freedom of expression (including academic freedom) is not to be restricted to views of which one approves, and that it is precisely in the case of views that are almost universally despised and condemned that this right must be most vigorously defended. It is easy enough to defend those who need no defense or to join in unanimous (and often justified) condemnation of a violation of civil rights by some official enemy.

I later learned that my statement was to appear in a book in which Faurisson defends himself against the charges soon to be brought against him in court. While this was not my intention, it was not contrary to my instructions. I received a letter from Jean-Pierre Fay, a well-known anti-Fascist writer and militant, who agreed with my position but urged me to withhold my statement because the climate of opinion in France was such that my defense of Faurisson's right to express his views would be interpreted as support for them. I wrote to him that I accepted his judgment, and requested that my statement not appear, but by then it was too late to stop publication....

Many writers find it scandalous that I should support the right of free expression for Faurisson without carefully analyzing his work, a strange doctrine which, if adopted, would effectively block defense of civil rights for unpopular views. Faurisson does not control the French press or scholarship. There is surely no lack of means or opportunity to refute or condemn his writings. My own views in sharp opposition to his are clearly on record, as I have said. No rational person will condemn a book, however outlandish its conclusions may seem, without at least reading it carefully; in this case, checking the documentation offered, and so on. One of the most bizarre criticisms has been that by refusing to undertake this task, I reveal that I have no interest in six million murdered Jews, a criticism which, if valid, applies to everyone who shares my lack of interest in examining Faurisson's work. One who defends the right of free expression incurs no special responsibility to study or even be acquainted with the views expressed. I have, for example, frequently gone well beyond signing petitions in support of East European dissidents subjected to repression or threats, often knowing little and caring less about their views (which in some cases I find obnoxious, a matter of complete irrelevance that I never mention in this connection). I recall no criticism of this stand.

The latter point merits further comment. I have taken far more controversial stands than this in support of civil liberties and academic freedom. At the height of the Vietnam War, I publicly took the stand that people I regard as authentic war criminals should not be denied the right to teach on political or ideological grounds, and I have always taken the same stand with regard to scientists who "prove" that blacks are genetically inferior, in a country where their history is hardly pleasant, and where such views will be used by racists and neo-Nazis. Whatever one thinks of Faurisson, no one has accused him of being the architect of major war crimes or claiming that Jews are genetically inferior (though it is irrelevant to the civil-liberties issue, he writes of the "heroic insurrection of the Warsaw ghetto" and praises those who "fought courageously against Nazism" in "the right cause"). I even wrote in 1969 that it would be wrong to bar counterinsurgency research in the universities, though it was being used to murder and destroy, a position I am not sure I could defend. What is interesting is that these far more controversial stands never aroused a peep of protest, which shows that the refusal to accept the right of free expression without retaliation, and the horror when others defend this right, is rather selective.

The reaction of the PEN Club in Paris is also interesting. PEN denounces my statements on the ground that they have given publicity to Faurisson's writing at a time when there is a resurgence of anti-Semitism. It is odd that an organization devoted to freedom of expression for authors should be exercised solely because Faurisson's defense against the charges brought against him is publicly heard. Furthermore, if publicity is being accorded to Faurisson, it is because he is being brought to trial (presumably, with the purpose of airing the issues) and because the press has chosen to create a scandal about my defense of civil rights....

As for the resurgence of anti-Semitism to which the PEN Club refers, or of racist atrocities, one may ask if the proper response to publication of material that may be used to enhance racist violence and oppression is to deny civil rights. Or is it, rather, to seek the causes of these vicious developments and work to eliminate them? To a person who upholds the basic ideas professed in the Western democracies, or who is seriously concerned with the real evils that confront us, the answer seems clear.

From "His Right to Say It," by Noam Chomsky in *The Nation* (February 28, 1981), pages 231-234

My day with Faurisson forced me to consider how we come to know what we think we know, what level of evidence we are willing to accept.

What do I know of gas chambers? Growing up Jewish, the knowledge seems practically innate, with so many childhood charitable efforts directed toward "never again" campaigns. But, more recently, what comes to mind is Claude Lanzmann's documentary film *Shoah*, which included the confessions of Nazis as well as the testimony of a man who cleared the bodies from the gas chambers, and the testimony of many other survivors and witnesses of Nazi atrocities; I've read accounts of the Holocaust by respected historians such as Raoul Hilberg, who also appeared in *Shoah*; I've talked to several survivors through the years, among them Sarah Nomberg Prytzyk, who wrote *Auschwitz: True Tales of a Grotesque Land* (University of North Carolina Press, 1985). And now there is Pressac and *his* evidence (see note on page 188).

But if you somehow reject the staggering volume of evidence (do the revisionists hold that the Germans somehow murdered all Jews who would tell the truth and only let Jews who would lie survive?), as Faurisson and other revisionists do, you must find yourself living in a parallel universe. I couldn't for the life of me figure out his project. The scary part was that he's not a moron. He projects at least a semblance of rationality. One presumes the University of Lyon has some kind of admission standards for hiring staff.

By making ever more outrageous statements, he has found a way to solicit the attention he must crave. He's given talks to groups of neo-Nazis (such as the one filmed in the German/Swedish production *The Truth Shall Set You*

Free), for which he gets warm applause. But, to my surprise, I did not sense in Faurisson a gut hatred of Jews. Perhaps I was numb with astonishment at his assertions. If he did possess such sentiments, he certainly contained himself in my presence—and he knew my ethnic heritage, because we discussed it. He just wanted to *convince* me. He continually tried to provoke confrontation so that he could regurgitate his version of history. "I'll make a revisionist of you," he threatened.

Between interviews, on a train in Holland, I talked to Chomsky about the Faurisson phenomenon. He postulated that if you focus laser-like on a sufficiently narrow set of evidence, you can probably convince yourself that gravity doesn't exist either. —MA

[You say you find] it hard to understand what motivates these Holocaust revisionist types, it all seems so outlandish. I don't think it should seem so unusual. After all, there's Holocaust denial right in the mainstream and no one bats an eyelash, because no one has any principled objection to it. The clearest example is the Congress Monthly *article by Edward Alexander, an associate of Werner Cohn's [see page 175], who dismisses Nazi crimes, the Holocaust in particular, as an "exploded fiction." Did anyone care? It's well-known, particularly after Alex Cockburn's article in* The Nation *on August 17, 1992, and the exchange on February 15, 1993. In fact, this is far and away the best-known and most prominent case of Holocaust denial and neo-Nazi apologetics. Have you seen a flicker of interest? What does that tell you?*

Of course, Alexander is referring not to the Jews, but to the Gypsies, who were killed at the same time, in the same manner, for the same reasons, and in about the same proportions. I don't want to imply that the two forms of Holocaust denial are morally on a par; denial of the Nazi crimes against the Gypsies is, plainly, far worse. They are still being mercilessly persecuted, even expelled from Germany to pogroms in Eastern Europe.

A moment's thought about all of this suffices to explain exactly what is going on. —NC

PARIS CAFE

Robert Faurisson
I'm not interested in freedom of speech and all that. I have to win, and that's the question. And I shall win.

Mark Achbar (turns to cameraman)
Cut.

Youths beat historian who denies Holocaust

CLERMONT-FERRAND, FRANCE (REUTER) — A French historian who denies millions of Jews died in the Nazi Holocaust was recovering from surgery yesterday after a savage beating.

Robert Faurisson, 60, suffered a broken jaw and ribs and severe head injuries in the attack by three youths while he was walking his dog in the town of Vichy.

A hospital spokesman in Clermont-Ferrand, the central French city where he was transferred for surgery, said the historian's condition was stable.

"He was conscious but he couldn't speak," said a Vichy fireman who gave Faurisson first aid. "His jaw was smashed. They destroyed his face."

The attack was claimed by a previously unknown group calling itself The Sons of the Memory of the Jews....

"Prof. Faurisson is the first but will not be the last," it said [in a statement]. "Let those who deny the (Holocaust) beware."

Faurisson is a leading member of the revisionist school of history which says there is no evidence that 6 million Jews were gassed to death in Nazi concentration camps during the Second World War.

Montreal *Gazette*, September 19, 1989

It is a poor service to the memory of the victims of the Holocaust to adopt a central doctrine of their murders.

COAST BASTION INN,
NANAIMO, BRITISH COLUMBIA

Woman

I'm just an ordinary mom who just thinks in terms of, I don't want to be some day holding my grandchildren and watching something horrible happen and feel like I didn't do anything. And I mean it's obvious what you're doing. And my question is, on a practical level, where do you see the most practical place to put your energy? I mean, tonight I feel in overwhelm —like, I feel like it's too big, it's too much, to even make a dent in.

Chomsky

The way things change is because lots of people are working all the time. And, you know, they're working in their communities or their workplace or wherever they happen to be, and they're building up the basis for popular movements which are going to make changes. That's the way everything has ever happened in history. You know, whether it was the end of slavery, or whether it was the democratic revolutions, or anything you want, you name it and that's the way it worked. You get a very false picture of this from the history books. In the history books there's a couple of leaders. You know, George Washington, or Martin Luther King, or whatever, and I don't want to say those people are unimportant, like Martin Luther King was certainly important, but *he* was not the civil rights movement. Martin Luther King can appear in the history books because lots of people whose names you will never know, and whose names are all forgotten and who may have been killed, and so on, were working down in the South.

In Albany, Georgia, a small deep-South town where the atmosphere of slavery still lingered, mass demonstrations took place in the winter of 1961 and again in 1962. Of 22,000 black people in Albany, over a thousand went to jail for marching, assembling, to protest segregation and discrimination. Here as in all the demonstrations that would sweep over the South, little black children participated—a new generation was learning to act. The Albany police chief, after one of the mass arrests, was taking the names of prisoners lined up before his desk. He looked up and saw a Negro boy about nine years old. "What's your name?" The boy looked straight at him and said: "Freedom, Freedom."

From *A People's History of the United States*, by Howard Zinn, (Harper and Row, Fitzhenry & Whiteside, 1980) page 446

There are no magic answers, no miraculous methods to overcome the problems we face, just the familiar ones: honest search for understanding, education, organization, action that raises the cost of state violence for its perpetrators or that lays the basis for institutional change—and the kind of commitment that will persist despite the temptations of disillusionment, despite many failures and only limited successes, inspired by the hope of a brighter future.

Turning the Tide, page 253

On schools and their role, see page 157 (education is a system of imposed ignorance)

See also:
- excerpt from "Toward a Humanistic Conception of Education," in *Work, Technology, and Education*, page 48
- "The Functions of the University in a Time of Crisis," *For Reasons of State*, pages 298-315
- "Some Thoughts on Intellectuals and the Schools," *American Power and the New Mandarins*, pages 309-321

SEATTLE TIMES INTERVIEW
WITH PAUL ANDREWS

Chomsky

When you have activists, and people concerned and people devoting themselves and dedicating themselves to social change or issues or whatever, then people like me can appear, and we can appear to be prominent. But that's only because somebody else is doing the work.

HUMANIST TV (PUBLIC), HOLLAND

Chomsky

My work—whether it's giving hundreds of talks a year, or spending twenty hours a week writing letters, or writing books—is not directed to intellectuals and politicians. It's directed to what are called "ordinary people." And what I expect from them is, in fact, exactly what they are. That they should try to understand the world and act in accordance with their decent impulses. And that they should try to improve the world. And many people are willing to do that, but they have to understand—in fact as far as I can see, in these things, I feel that I'm simply helping people develop courses of intellectual self-defense.

The future for the traditional victims looks grim. Grim, but not hopeless. With amazing courage and persistence, the wretched of the earth continue to struggle for their rights. And in the industrial world, with Bolshevism disintegrating and **capitalism long abandoned,** there are prospects for the revival of libertarian socialist and radical democratic ideals that had languished, including popular control of the workplace and investment decisions and, correspondingly, the establishment of more meaningful political democracy as constraints imposed by private power are reduced. These and other emerging possibilities are still remote, but no more so than the possibility of parliamentary democracy and elementary rights of citizenship 250 years ago. No one knows enough to predict what human will can achieve.

We are faced with a kind of Pascal's wager: assume the worst, and it will surely arrive; commit oneself to the struggle for freedom and justice, and its cause may be advanced.

Deterring Democracy, page 64

If by "capitalism" one means anything like free-market capitalism, it rarely existed in the advanced societies for reasons I've discussed often, and less so now. There was a kind of "proprietary capitalism" in England and the U.S. in the 19th century, displaced by a corporate managerial capitalism here primarily in the early 20th century, and by a coordinated state capitalism in Japan and the East Asian NICs [newly industrialized countries]. By the '30s, as Robert Brady pointed out, virtually all capitalist societies were drifting towards some form of fascist-style state capitalism. That took various forms in the postwar world: here, the military Keynesian form, primarily. To call this "capitalism" is highly inaccurate. There has, of course, always been massive state intervention to keep the system viable, expanded in the past 30 years, quite apart from the massive military Keynesian component, which underlies virtually every successful part of the economy. Furthermore, the growth of the TNCs [trans-national corporations] changes the rules of the game considerably, creating vast oligopolies with strategic links to governments and their own quasi-governing institutions. The system has sometimes been called "corporate mercantilism," not unrealistically.—NC

"NON-CORPORATE NEWS" (PUBLIC ACCESS TV), LYNN, MASSACHUSETTS

Ed Robinson

What did you mean by that? What would such a course be?

Chomsky

Well, I don't mean go to school, 'cause you're not going to get it there.

It is tragic that the United States should have become, in Toynbee's words, "the leader of a world-wide anti-revolutionary movement in defense of vested interests." For American intellectuals and for the schools, there is no more vital issue than this indescribable tragedy....

It is perhaps not ridiculous to propose that the schools might direct themselves... to an attempt to offer students some means for defending themselves from the onslaught of the massive government propaganda apparatus, from the natural bias of the mass media, and—to turn specifically to our present topic—from the equally natural tendency of significant segments of the American intellectual community to offer their allegiance, not to truth and justice, but to power and the effective exercise of power....

Traditionally, the role of the intellectual, or at least his self-image, has been that of a dispassionate critic. Insofar as that role has been lost, the relation of the schools to intellectuals should, in fact, be one of self-defense....

In general, the history of imperialism and of imperialist apologia, particularly as seen from the point of view of those at the wrong end of the guns, should be a central part of any civilized curriculum. But there are other aspects to a program of intellectual self-defense that should not be overlooked. In an age of science and technology, it is inevitable that their prestige will be employed as an ideological instrument—specifically, that the social and behavioral sciences will in various ways be made to serve in defense of national policy or as a mask for special interest. It is not merely that intellectuals are strongly tempted, in a society that offers them prestige and affluence, to take what is now called a "pragmatic attitude"..., that is, an attitude that one must "accept," not critically analyze or struggle to change, the existing distribution of power, domestic and international, and the political realities that flow from it... It is not merely that having taken this position (conceivably with some justification, at a particular historical moment), one is strongly tempted to provide it with an ideological justification of a very general sort. Rather, what we must also expect is that political elites will use the terminology of the social and behavioral sciences to protect their actions from critical analysis—the non-specialist does not, after all, presume to tell physicists and engineers how to build an atomic reactor....

The social and behavioral sciences should be seriously studied, not only for their intrinsic interest, but so that the student can be made quite aware of exactly how little they have to say about the problems of man and society that really matter... This can be an important way to protect a student from the propaganda of the future, and to put him in a position to comprehend the true nature of the means that are sure to be used to conceal the real significance of domestic or international policy.

American Power and the New Mandarins, pages 313-318

The social and behavioral sciences should be seriously studied, not only for their intrinsic interest, but so that the student can be made quite aware of exactly how little they have to say about the problems of man and society that really matter.

CITYSCAPE AT DUSK

The camera pans to an apartment building, and zooms in on a man, sitting alone, watching Chomsky on TV

Chomsky

It means you have to develop an independent mind. And work on it. Now, that's extremely hard to do alone. The beauty of our system is: it isolates everybody. Each person is sitting alone in front of the tube. And it's very hard to have ideas or thoughts under those circumstances. You can't fight the world alone, you know. Some people can, but it's pretty rare. The way to do it is through organization. So courses of intellectual self-defense will have to be in the context of political and other organization.

COMMUNITY ACTIVIST CIRCLE, NANAIMO, BRITISH COLUMBIA

Chomsky

And it makes sense, I think, to look at what the institutions are trying to do, and to take that almost as a key. What they're trying to do is what we're trying to combat. If they're trying to keep people isolated and separate and so on, well, we're trying to do the opposite. We're trying to bring them together. So in your local community you want to have sources of alternative action. People with parallel concerns, maybe differently focused, but, at the core, sort of similar values. And a similar interest in helping people learn how to defend themselves against external power, and taking control of their lives, and reaching out to people who need it. That's a common array of concerns. You can learn about your own values, and you can figure out how to defend yourself and so on, in conjunction with others.

There are a vast number of people who are uninformed and heavily propagandized, but fundamentally decent. The propaganda that inundates them is effective when unchallenged, but much of it goes only skin deep. If they can be brought to raise questions and apply their decent instincts and basic intelligence, many people quickly escape the confines of the doctrinal system and are willing to do something to help others who are really suffering and oppressed.

From an interview with *Open Road* (Vancouver, British Columbia), reprinted in *Language and Politics*, page 389

The best way to defend civil liberties is to build a movement for social change with a positive program that has a broad-based appeal, that encourages free and open discussion and offers a wide range of possibilities for work and action. The potential for such a movement surely exists. Whether it will be realized remains an open question. External repression is one serious threat. Factional bickering, dogmatism, fantasies, and manipulative tactics are probably a considerable danger....

In the long run, a movement of the left has no chance of success, and deserves none, unless it develops an understanding of contemporary society and a vision of a future social order that is persuasive to a large majority of the population....

In an advanced industrial society it is, obviously, far from true that the mass of the population have nothing to lose but their chains, and there is no point in pretending otherwise. On the contrary, they have a considerable stake in preserving the existing social order. Correspondingly, the cultural and intellectual level of any serious radical movement will have to be far higher than in the past, as André Gorz, for one, has correctly emphasized. It will not be able to satisfy itself with a litany of forms of oppression and injustice.... It must not succumb to the illusion that a "vanguard party," self-designated as the repository of all truth and virtue, can take state power and miraculously bring about a revolution that will establish decent values and truly democratic structures as the framework for social life.... Furthermore, if a radical movement hopes to be able to combat imperialism, or the kinds of repression, social management and coercion that will be developed by the evolving international economic institutions [such as GATT, IMF, the World Bank, G7], it too will have to be international in its organizational forms as well as in the cultural level it seeks to attain. To construct a movement of this sort will be no mean feat. It may well be true, however, that success in this endeavor is the only alternative to tyranny and disaster....

It is now widely realized that the economist's "externalities" can no longer be consigned to footnotes. No one who gives a moment's thought to the problems of contemporary society can fail to be aware of the social costs of consumption and production, the progressive destruction of the environment, the utter irrationality of the utilization of contemporary technology, the inability of a system based on profit or growth-maximization to deal with needs that can only be expressed collectively, and the enormous bias this system imposes towards maximization of commodities for personal use in place of the general improvement of the quality of life.

Radical Priorities, pages 221-223

The realities are often presented with admirable frankness by the rulers and their ideologists. The London *Financial Times* features a lead article by the economic correspondent of the BBC World Service, James Morgan, under the heading: "The fall of the Soviet bloc has left the IMF and G7 to rule the world and create a new imperial age." We can, at last, approach the fulfillment of Churchill's vision, no longer troubled by the "hungry nations" who "seek more" and thus endanger the tranquility of the rich men who rule by right.

In the current version, "The construction of a new global system is orchestrated by the Group of Seven, the IMF, the World Bank and the General Agreement on Tariffs and Trade (GATT)," in "a system of indirect rule that has involved the integration of leaders of developing countries into the network of the new ruling class"—who, not surprisingly, turn out to be the old ruling class. Local managers can share the wealth, as long as they properly serve the rulers.

Morgan takes note of the "hypocrisy of the rich nations in demanding open markets in the Third World while closing their own." He might have added the World Bank report that the protectionist measures of the industrial countries reduce national income in the South by about twice the amount provided by official aid, largely export-promotion, most of it to the richer sectors of the "developing countries" (less needy, but better consumers). Or the UNCTAD estimate that *non-tariff* barriers (NTBs) of the industrial countries reduce Third World exports by almost 20 percent in affected categories, which include textiles, steel, seafood, animal feed and other agricultural products, with billions of dollars a year in losses. Or the World Bank estimate that 31 percent of the South's manufacturing exports are subject to NTBs as compared with the North's 18 percent. Or the 1992 report of the UN Human Development Program, reviewing the increasing gap between the rich and poor (by now, 83 percent of the world's wealth in the hands of the richest billion, with 1.4 percent for the billion at the bottom of the heap); the doubling of the gap since 1960 is attributed to the policies of the IMF and World Bank, and the fact that 20 of 24 industrial countries are more protectionist today than they were a decade ago, including the US, which celebrated the Reagan revolution by doubling the proportion of imports subject to restrictive measures. "And the upshot of decades of lending for development is that poor countries have lately been transferring more than $21 billion a year into the coffers of the rich," the *Economist* observes, summarizing the gloomy picture.

Year 501: The Conquest Continues, pages 61-62

UNIVERSITY OF WYOMING, LARAMIE

Woman

Are there one or two publications that I as an average person, a biologist, can read to bypass this filter of our press?

Chomsky

Now, if you ask: "What media can I turn to to—get the right answers?" first of all I wouldn't tell you that because I don't think there's an answer. The right answers are what you decide are the right answers. Maybe everything I'm telling you is wrong. Okay? Could perfectly well be, I'm not God. But that's something for you to figure out. I mean, I could tell you what I think happens to be more or less right but there isn't any reason why you should pay any attention to it.

MALASPINA COLLEGE,
NANAIMO, BRITISH COLUMBIA

Woman

What impact do you feel alternative media is currently having or could potentially have? I'm actually a little more interested in its potential. And, just to define my terms, by alternative media I'm referring to media that are or could be citizen-controlled as opposed to state- or corporate-controlled.

Chomsky

You know, that's what kept people together. To the extent that people are able to do something constructive, it's because they have some way of interacting.

It's not a matter of what you read, it's a matter of how you read. You've got to understand—people have to understand that there's a major effort being made to manipulate them. That doesn't mean that the facts aren't there.

From an interview with Paul Andrews of *The Seattle Times*

If you read the media with sufficient cynicism and criticism, and you read it broadly enough, and you understand what's going on, if you understand that there's an intensive effort to make you see things in a particular way, then you can resist.

From an interview with David Barsamian at MIT, February 1990

Chomsky

I mean, I've always felt it would be a very positive thing and it should be pushed as far as it can go. I think it's going to have a very hard time. There's just such a concentration of resources and power that alternative media, while extremely important, are going to have quite a battle.

It's true there are things which are small successes, but it's because people have just been willing to put in incredible effort. Like, say, take *Z Magazine*, I mean, that's a national magazine which literally has a staff of two. And no resources.

Z OFFICE, BOSTON, MASSACHUSETTS

Mark Achbar

So tell us a little about *Z Magazine*, what it is and what makes it different.

Michael Albert *(to Lydia Sargent)*

Go ahead.

Lydia Sargent

Go ahead? Thank you.

Michael Albert

We just wanted to do a magazine that would address all the sides of political life—economics, race, gender, authority, political relations—and we wanted to do it in a way that would incorporate an attention to how to not only understand what's going on but how to make things better, what to aim toward, and to provide at the same time humor, culture, a kind of a magazine that people could relate to and could get a lot out of and could participate in.

Michael Albert and Lydia Sargent founded South End Press in 1978 to fill a need for radical publishing in the United States, dealing with domestic concerns and class, race and gender issues.

Ten years later, Albert and Sargent founded *Z* Magazine. They share editorial and production responsibilities, and, along with Eric Sargent, divide up other tasks (Albert and Sargent live together, and Eric is Lydia's son). Albert points out that *Z* doesn't have a collective structure that could easily serve as a model, but encourages anyone who's interested in publishing to look at the structure of South End Press. *Looking Forward: Participatory Economics for the Twentieth Century,* by Michael Albert and Robin Hahnel (South End Press, 1991), describes in detail the operations and philosophy of a fictional publishing company, called Northstart Press (based on South End).

Z Magazine has 15,000 subscribers and sells a further 8,000 or 9,000 copies retail. *Z Papers* is a quarterly magazine with emphasis on strategy and vision.

Lydia Sargent

And what we wanted to do, which we didn't think was provided by the existing magazines, was to give it a real activist slant, so that it could be very useful to the variety of movements in the country. And we just felt there wasn't a magazine that reflected that, that inspired people and that gave people a sort of a strategy and perhaps even a vision of how things could be better. *Z Magazine* is one of over five thousand alternative publications distributed locally, regionally or nationally throughout North America each year.

Chomsky

South End Press has sort of made it—that is, they're surviving. It's a small collective, again, with no resources, and they put out a lot of books, including quite a lot of good books, but for a South End book to get reviewed is almost impossible.

Look at the *Boston Globe*, for example... Sometimes it's kind of comical. For example, this fall, the National Council of Teachers of English every year gives out what they call an "Orwell Award" for exposure of doublespeak. It was awarded to me for *On Power and Ideology* two years ago. This year it was awarded the book that Edward Herman and I did, *Manufacturing Consent*. Just at the time when that award was given, I think it was November, a *Boston Globe* columnist, a rather left-liberal columnist, incidentally, wrote a column interviewing the guy who is in charge of this award. It was a very upbeat column about what a terrific idea this is to give an award to exposure of doublespeak and she listed some of the people who had gotten it in the past, Ted Koppel, etc. There was a very striking omission: This year's award was not mentioned. It happened to be the first time, I think, that anybody had gotten it for the second time. Furthermore, both of the books in question were books about media. It's not what Ted Koppel does. It was a critique of the media. That's what they are. None of that could be mentioned. South End had a very hard time getting a book review. It's been written up in *Publisher's Weekly*, in fact. I don't have to tell you what it's like. If you don't have access to capital resources, advertisers, the powerful modes of public articulation, your outreach is going to be extremely limited. You can make up for it to some extent with just hard work. There are ways of compensating. Some of these ways are important. For example, dissidents in lots of societies cooperate. I spend an awful lot of time, for example, just xeroxing stuff, copying stuff for friends in other countries who are, in their countries, in roughly the situation I'm in here. They do the same for me. That means that I have access, I don't get a research grant to work on this kind of stuff or time off or whatever, but I do have access to resources that mainstream scholars—or for that matter the CIA—don't have. The CIA or mainstream scholars don't have a very smart and perceptive guy in Israel scanning the Hebrew press for them, picking out the things that are important, doing an interpretation and analysis of them and sending reams of this material to me.

From an interview with David Barsamian at MIT, February 1990

SOUTH END PRESS,
BOSTON, MASSACHUSETTS

Karin Aguilar-San Juan

Editorially and business-wise we make decisions based on a politics that no corporate publisher can really advocate because of their ties to corporate America. We can solicit manuscripts based on what we feel is the relevance for the movement, and we can make our business decisions based on whether we feel people can afford our books, whether we feel that a book might not make that much money but it needs to be out there and maybe there is a thousand people who would buy it, and, and those are criteria that we feel are very precious, in this day of corporate mergers.

Loie Hayes

Likewise, our structure about sharing work and continuing our training process as long as we're at the Press; there are losses there in terms of productivity, but in terms of empowerment all of us are then able to say, "My perspective is different from yours." Then all of our intelligence gets used in making those decisions and not just whoever happens to have done it the longest, whoever happens to have graduated from the "best" schools in order to be the "best" editor, making all the decisions and only using his or her intelligence.

South End Press is a nonprofit, collectively-run book publisher with over 175 titles in print. Since its founding in 1978, it has tried to meet the needs of readers exploring or already committed to, the politics of fundamental social change.

Its goal is to publish books that encourage critical thinking and constructive action on key social and ecological issues in the United States and around the world. It hopes to give expression to a wide diversity of democratic social movements and to provide an alternative to the products of corporate publishing.

Through the Institute for Social and Cultural Change, South End Press works with other political media projects—Z Magazine; Speak Out!, a national speakers' bureau; the Publishers Support Project; and the New Liberation News Service — to increase access to information and critical analysis. Many other progressive organizations in the U.S. and around the world are working toward similar objectives. (see Resource Guide)

David Barsamian

Listener-supported radio in the U.S. has undergone a remarkable growth in the last decade. It's perhaps the fastest growing alternative media. There are many reasons for this; first and foremost it's that it's enormously economical. And it reaches communities that have not been served by community radio before.

And in Boulder, particularly, we see, with someone like Noam Chomsky, who's been there I believe three times in the last six years, he has a tremendous audience, and KGNU is partly responsible for that because we play his tapes on a regular basis, we play his lectures and his interviews, so when he does come to Boulder, and people hear what he has to say, they're able to tune in—it's not something exotic or esoteric that he's talking about, it's material that they're very familiar with. And he's noted this, incidentally—

Chomsky

I mean, if there's a listener-supported radio station it means that people can get daily, every day, a different way of looking at the world—not just what the corporate media want you to see, but a different picture, a different understanding. Not only can you hear it, but you can participate in it. You can add your own thoughts, you know, and you can learn something, and so on. Well, that's the way people become human. That's the way to become human participants in a social and political system.

Why radio? Edward Said calls it *"the oppositional form."* Whereas with television there is the constant drive for the sound bite, with radio, he says, "You have to think in a different way, you have to think consecutively, you have to think with reason rather than with pictures." The fact is that radio is open to intervention.

I have been a radio interventionist, doing combat on the airwaves, since 1978. Alternative Radio, my "organization," is part of a burgeoning movement of community-based, non-commercial stations in alliance with independent producers. I produce and distribute a weekly one-hour public affairs program that is broadcast on more than one hundred stations in the United States and Canada as well as to over seventy countries via shortwave. The technical aspect is not very complicated and the cost is quite modest. The U.S., with all its media problems, has by far the most developed and evolved network of community radio stations in the world.

I began Alternative Radio in late 1986 in a bizarre way. I did something unheard of: I put up on the satellite in one block, three and a half hours of Noam Chomsky, a ninety-minute lecture followed by four 30-minute interviews. It was my first national broadcast. No one told me that most stations usually only have half-hour or one-hour slots. It was the proverbial learning experience. However, the Pacifica network did pick up the programs and listener response was tremendous. AR was on its way.

The satellite system is the electronic umbilical cord linking hundreds of stations. It is run by National Public Radio. But fear not. All they want is your money. I have never heard a peep from them abut the content of any of my programs.

(continued next page)

In France, many local groups have their own radio stations. In a notable case, the progressive cooperative Longo Mai, in Upper Provence, has its own 24-hour-a-day Radio Zinezine, which has become an important community institution that has helped inform and activate many previously isolated farmers. The potential value of noncommercial radio can be perceived in sections of [the U.S.A.] where stations such as Pacifica Radio offer a view of the world, depth of coverage, and scope of discussion and debate that is generally excluded from the major media. Public radio and television, despite having suffered serious damage during the Reagan[/Bush] years, also represent an alternative media channel whose resuscitation and improvement should be of serious concern to those interested in contesting the propaganda system. The steady commercialization of the publicly-owned air waves should be vigorously opposed. In the long run, a democratic political order requires far wider control of and access to the media. Serious discussion of how this can be done, and the incorporation of fundamental media reform into political programs should be high on progressive agendas.

Manufacturing Consent, page 307

Some 400-plus stations have dishes or downlinks, i.e. they are capable of receiving programs. There are some 20 uplinks through which programs are distributed. Working with satellite deadlines is a constant stimulation. It is like having a Damocles sword of tape over your head at all times. The program has to be at the uplink before the scheduled uplink time. Stations record the program off the satellite and air it during a designated time. It is possible to broadcast live off the satellite and that is the case for news and breaking events, hearings, marches, etc. You can find out all about the satellite system and how you as an independent producer can use it by contacting NPR, 2025 M Street, NW, Washington, D.C. 20036. Tel: 202-822-2323.

Of all the electronic media there is no question that radio is the least expensive. And as far as I am concerned it is the most satisfying. There is something very intimate about radio. It doesn't rob or preempt the listener's imagination. And for spoken word, which is what I do, it is the best. An hour is a decent amount of time to cover a subject. Alternative Radio programs focus on the media, U.S. foreign policy, racism, the environment, indigenous rights, NAFTA/ GATT and economic issues and other topics.

Unfortunately, the satellite system is limited to the U.S. That means I have to send tapes via mail to Canada, Australia and elsewhere. Clearly an expensive, inefficient and not as good audio method. I look forward to the day when we'll be globally connected.

How do I support my "operation"? Directly through the sale of printed transcripts and audio cassettes to listeners. I don't charge the stations. It is important that the programs be broadcast so I make it as simple and as painless as possible for the stations. My goal is to disseminate diverse perspectives and views. It does me little good to produce a program and then have it sit on a shelf.

If you are interested in more information and/or would like to establish a community radio station, contact: National Federation of Community Broadcasters, 666 11th Street NW, Washington, D.C. 20001. Tel: 202-393-2355. NFCB is a national service and representation organization for community broadcasters. Audio Craft, a useful how-to book on production techniques written by audio wizard Randy Thom, can be ordered from NFCB.

Outside the U.S. you can contact AMARC, the World Association of Community Broadcasters, 3575 Blvd. St. Laurent, Suite 704, Montréal, Que. H2X 2T7, Canada. Bruce Girard of AMARC has edited *A Passion for Radio*, an informative book about what is happening in community radio in various countries. AMARC has literature available in English, Spanish and French.

If you don't have a good local station and have a shortwave receiver you can hear a number of progressive programs on Radio for Peace International. It operates out of Santa Ana, Costa Rica. For a free schedule and frequency information write to: RPI, P.O. Box 10869, Eugene, OR 97440.

William Barlow of Howard University writes that community radio "has more democratic potential than any other form of mass media operating in the United States." Activists should seriously consider radio as a medium for action and engagement.

Edward Herman in the very first *Z Papers* wrote, "A full fledged democratization of the media can only occur in connection with a thoroughgoing political revolution." That is what we are talking about. The latest merger announcement is Bell Atlantic and TCI. The trend toward greater concentration of power and capital will continue. The amount of literature documenting corporate control and domination of media is staggering. We have done our homework and while that critique is ongoing I believe it is essential for psychological as well as political reasons to project and produce positive alternatives. It is vital that it happen. And radio offers just such an opportunity.

"Alternative Radio—Audio Combat," by David Barsamian
Z Papers, October-December 1993

In *Manufacturing Consent* Herman and Chomsky suggest we look at the programs spelled out for Great Britain in *Bending Reality: The State of the Media, edited by* James Curran, Jake Ecclestone, Giles Oakley, and Alan Richardson (Pluto Press, 1986)

For information on ordering cassettes or transcripts of David Barsamian's interviews, see Resource Guide

"NON-CORPORATE NEWS" (PUBLIC ACCESS), LYNN, MASS

Ed Robinson

Hello. I'm Ed Robinson and this is Non-Corporate News. What is Non-Corporate News and why is it necessary?

(voice over)

I didn't want to just show another film at a library or something. I wanted to make my own statement. I thought it would be more fun to do, and perhaps I'd get other people involved in a project. Besides showing a film, we could make a film or video. The local cable station is hooked up to three communities: Lynn, Swampscott and Salem. So that's thirty thousand people—or thirty thousand homes, I'm not sure —but I'm sure a lot of people will see it and it will be the kind of people who don't go out to see a film. It'll go right into their house so if they're flipping through the channels they might be able to get a completely new idea of the world.

When I write letters to old friends, it usually takes them at least 6 weeks to write back. When I first wrote to Noam Chomsky, after reading his book *Turning the Tide* in 1986, he replied within a week. I'm not sure, exactly, what this says about my friends, Noam Chomsky, or both.

I wrote to him to ask him to recommend other books like his and invited him to speak at the University of Massachusetts. At the time, I thought I was making an unusual request.

His book blew me away, completely changed my view of the world, and propelled me into becoming an activist and joining the Central America Solidarity Association at University of Massachusetts. I started "Non-Corporate News" in 1990 as a way to reach people who, at the end of the day, were too tired to go out and attend a lecture, with the hope of inspiring similar feelings in them.

At first I thought the show would be all original material. I realized this was impossible when, with the help of two high-school students, editing the 30-second introduction to the show took four hours. Before long, 90 per cent of the content came from professionally produced videos rented from the American Friends Service Committee. I became, in the process, a regular copy-right-violating maniac.

The first video of "Non-Corporate News" was, naturally, an interview with Noam Chomsky, parts of which appear in *Manufacturing Consent*. I wrote to Noam after I had edited it, sending a newspaper clipping announcing its upcoming appearance on Warner Cable. He wrote back saying that he had a "special relationship" with Warner Communications (now part of Time-Warner) after they had squelched the distribution of a book of his in 1974 (described further in "A Prefatory Note" in *The Political Economy of Human Rights, Vol. 1*). He urged me to send the information of his appearance on Warner Cable on to Warner Communications.

In the sixties (or maybe early seventies) Abbie Hoffman wrote *Steal This Book*. Now, in the nineties, I think you should *Edit This Video*—and put it on your local public-access station. Or, if you have the time, make your own video and do the same. Public-access video is free, and so is the training on how to use the equipment.

Ed Robinson, November 1993

In a footnote in *Manufacturing Consent*, Herman and Chomsky observe that "The Cable Franchise and Tele-communications Act of 1984 allows cities to require public-access channels, but it permits cable operators to direct these channels to other uses if they are not well utilized. Thus non-use may provide the basis for an elimination of public access." On page 307, they also note: "The rise of cable and satellite communications, while initially captured and dominated by commercial interests, has weakened the power of the network oligopoly and retains a potential for enhanced local-group access. There are already some 3,000 public-access channels in use in the United States, offering 20,000 hours of locally produced programs per week, and there are even national producers and distributors of programs for access channels through satellites (e.g. Deep-Dish Television), as well as hundreds of local suppliers, although all of them must struggle for funding."

Chomsky

So there's kind of networks of co-operation that develop. Like here, for example, is a collection of stuff from a friend of mine in Los Angeles, who does careful monitoring of the whole press in Los Angeles and a lot of the British press, which he reads, and does selections, so I don't have to read the movie reviews and the local gossip and all this kind of stuff, but I get the occasional nugget that sneaks through and that you find if you're carefully and intelligently and critically reviewing a wide range of press. Well, there are a fair number of people who do this and we exchange information.

HARVARD UNIVERSITY,
CAMBRIDGE, MASSACHUSETTS

Edward Herman (co-author with Noam Chomsky of Manufacturing Consent and The Political Economy of Human Rights)

We wrote this two-volume work. We saw one another for a couple of weeks just when we were getting started, but then we wrote two volumes essentially without seeing one another, just by phone, by mail, and exchanging manuscripts. But this takes a lot of communication by mail. My Chomsky file is a couple of feet thick.

My collaborations with Chomsky arose out of shared interests and views, and a perceived synergy in working together—we could meld together our individual ideas and ways of saying things, benefit from mutual editing, and get things done faster and better working collectively. From the beginning we rarely saw one another, but had an active correspondence, exchanging papers and ideas and comments on the passing scene. Sometimes one person had an idea or set of ideas but needed help in elaborating or expanding on it, and the other person liked the basic scheme and wanted to help and participate. There is also the psychological benefit in occasional joint work, knowing that your ideas are appreciated and that you are not alone in your otherwise marginalized thoughts. I can't recall who proposed collective action in individual cases, but it came about very easily and naturally and seemed to serve the demands of efficiency of work as well as giving the psychological boost.

In the case of Manufacturing Consent, at the time we decided to work together on this both of us had fallen behind on planned books on the media (for me) and media-related issues (Chomsky) for Pantheon. In talking over our problems we both hit on the idea of joining forces, allowing us to get out a single book on the media faster and at a higher level than continuing on our own. I already had a plan for a chapter on a theoretical ("propaganda") model, which

Chomsky sympathized and agreed with, and we each had a lot of knowledge about and advanced preparation for writing on specific areas. In fact, we had so much data that eventually we had to contract the scope of the book which we originally envisaged would have substantial chapters on terrorism (comparing, among other things, media treatment of Libya and South Africa as terrorist states) and some domestic issues (coverage of Reaganite economics and environmental policy gutting). We had to cut back quickly as we saw the chapters we initially started to work on ballooning.

We had a division of responsibilities from the beginning that was maintained to the end, with some uncertainty only about who would take responsibility for the concluding chapter. I had the Preface and first four chapters: Chomsky had chapters 5-6, and eventually he took on the first draft writing of chapter 7. The appendices related to the chapters were prepared by the chapter authors. We exchanged outlines from the beginning, but particularly on chapter 1 where we were spelling out a model that we were presumably going to apply from there on. So our discussion and prior agreements on chapter 1 were exceptional. We exchanged manuscripts on the chapters and the most extensive interpenetration of actual composition was greatest in the Preface, chapter 1, and the Conclusions. Otherwise, each author was left to take into account the other's comments on his chapters. In the end, there were very few disagreements about the final outcome. It was a very pleasant and efficient collaboration. We were reassured by one another's careful editing and commentary.

One parenthetical. In a very silly review of *Manufacturing Consent* in *Tikkun*, Carlin Romano went to great pains to explain the allegedly mechanical and artificial quality of the propaganda model as a result of its derivation from Chomsky's linguistic theories. He was not alone in this. The point is absurd in many respects, but one is that I was primarily responsible for the model, and it traces back more clearly to my analysis in *Corporate Control, Corporate Power* than to any other intellectual source.

From a set of answers to questions put to Edward S. Herman by journalist David Peterson (unpublished elsewhere)

I have a Ph.D. in economics from the University of California, Berkeley. As an economist I have done most of my work in the fields of Money and Banking, Financial Institutions, and Corporate Structure and Policy (including monopoly and competition). I taught at the Wharton School of the University of Pennsylvania from 1958 till I took early retirement in 1989. I also taught courses in the Media in the Annenberg School at Penn, continuing teaching a course in Media Bias through 1992.

I wrote many books on financial institutions and financial regulation during my years at Wharton, including a study of bank trust departments and one on conflicts of interest in the savings and loan industry (I found plenty). Perhaps my most important and most generally interesting book in this genre was one called *Corporate Control, Corporate Power*, published by Cambridge University Press in 1981, which dealt with the centralization and evolution of control of the large corporations in the U.S. and the possibilities of reform within the corporate order (which I found unpromising). There was a natural evolution of my writing from financial institutions and power, to the corporate system as a whole, and then to the media.

This was stimulated by my growing interest in foreign policy and attempts as an activist to get my views across and to understand how the media deal with foreign policy issues....

While always interested in foreign policy, it took center stage for me during the Vietnam War era. I published books on the Vietnam War in 1966 and 1971. I got to know Chomsky during the war by our common interests in and shared views on the war and foreign policy, and our first collaborative work occurred during that era (I believe it began with an article in *Ramparts* entitled "Saigon Corruption Crisis: The Search for an Honest Quisling"). [A quisling is a traitor who collaborates with the invaders of his country especially by serving in a puppet government.] We published a short volume on the hot topic of "bloodbaths" in 1973 (it was commonly forecast that we would see one in Vietnam if the United States was to withdraw), which attained some later eminence from the fact that the parent company (Warner) of the publisher of our book (Warner Modular) killed the book and liquidated the subsidiary out of distaste for our work. This episode is described in a preface to

our book *The Washington Connection and Third World Fascism*, an update and expansion of the earlier suppressed volume which South End Press and Black Rose Books published in 1979. After a companion volume to the *Washington Connection*, [entitled] *After the Cataclysm: Postwar Indochina and the Reconstruction of Imperial Ideology*, also published by South End Press and Black Rose Books in 1979, we picked up our collaboration again in 1988 with the publication of *Manufacturing Consent*. We have been talking for some years about a further collaborative effort on the rewriting of the history of the Vietnam War, but I am not sure we will ever do this.

In the 1980s and early 1990s I continued to write on foreign policy, with two books on terrorism, one on "demonstration elections," and several others. I have also written steadily on foreign policy in *Z Magazine* and *Lies of Our Times*.—Edward S Herman

For a list of Edward S. Herman's political writings, see Resource Guide

MIT OFFICE, CAMBRIDGE, MASSACHUSETTS

Chomsky

The end result is that you do have access to resources in a way which I doubt that any national intelligence agency can duplicate, let alone scholarship. So there are ways of compensating for the absence of resources, people can do things.

HUMANIST TV (PUBLIC), HOLLAND

Chomsky

Like, for example, I found out about the arms flow to Iran by reading transcripts of the BBC, and by reading an interview somewhere with an Israeli ambassador in one city and reading something else in the Israeli press. Now, okay, the information is there, but it's there to a fanatic, you know, somebody who wants to spend a substantial part of their time and energy exploring it and comparing today's lies with yesterday's leaks and so on. That's a research job and it just simply doesn't make sense to ask the general population to dedicate themselves to this task on every issue.

From BBC "Panorama," February 1, 1982

Philip Tibenham (BBC reporter)
Khomeini's return and the overthrow of the Shah were, of course, disastrous for Israel. Suddenly there was another Muslim regime denouncing Zionism. What the Israelis desperately wanted was a return to the old relationship in Iran. In October 1980, neighboring Iraq attacked Iran heading for the oilfields of Khuzistan. It was the perfect opportunity for the Israelis to support the Iranian military, the people they'd like to see in power in Iran....

David Kimche (head of Israel's Foreign Office and former deputy director of MOSSAD, Israel's intelligence agency)
They are particularly short of spare parts and mainly American weapons—that's their biggest problem today. In addition to that, they need ammunition, shells, artillery shells and bombs, and things like that. These are their major problems.

Tibenham
So that if Israel wishes to see a strong Iranian army it would be in Israel's interests for America to supply those spare parts?

Kimche
Well, I don't want to reach the obvious conclusion here. I think I made our position plain. We think that the Iranian army should be strong, yes.

Tibenham
So, really, an army take-over is what you're saying?

Kimche
Possibly, yes....

Richard Helms (former head of the CIA and former U.S. Ambassador to Iran)
One doesn't mount coups to change governments or influence events without specific assets in the form of guns, people, groups desirous of helping, people who are prepared to take risk, all of these things, so that this is not a theoretical matter, it's a very practical matter and I wouldn't have any doubt that the United States is trying to find out what assets it can bring to bear.

For further explanation, see *The Fateful Triangle,* pages 458-459, and *The Culture of Terrorism,* page 174

Chomsky

When I say that the information is there, I do not mean that the population has the information. For example, information was there about the U.S. sale of arms to Iran.

Joop van Tijn

Excuse me, you were saying that it was printed, the information.

Chomsky

But let me stress again what I said before. Information can be printed and not be available to people. You see, the information that is printed is available to assiduous researchers who spend a substantial part of their lives and energy to try to put it together and see what it means. For most of the population, information basically is not there. So, for example, when I read in a BBC hour-long program in 1982 that the high-level officials who will later surface in the Iran-Contra hearings are explaining why they are sending arms to Iran, which means American arms, then I can learn it, but the American people did not learn it. When I further read that, in an interview in some city, the Israeli ambassador said: "We are sending"—in 1982—"we are sending arms to Iran in cooperation with the US government at the highest level," then I can put it together, I can put all this material together. I work on it hard enough and I can realize that the United States is, in fact, carrying out a very classic policy. It is following the classic policy that you carry out when you're trying to overthrow some government. To try to overthrow some government, typically you arm its military. Now, if you know something about history, you can see how this fits into a pattern—for example, it is the same pattern that the United States followed in the case of Allende in Chile. Try to overthrow the government, you arm the military. It's the same policy carried out in the case of Sukarno in Indonesia. Trying to overthrow the real confrontation with the government, we continue to arm the military. If you are really an assiduous researcher, you will know that the Pentagon secretary, McNamara, took credit afterwards. He was asked by Congress: "What was the point of sending arms to Indonesia? Did it pay dividends?" He said, "Yes, it paid dividends." You will know that there was a House Committee investigation, which pointed out that the connections that the United States established with the Indonesian military in those years helped to lay the background to the coup.

Joop van Tijn

Excuse me, the question is how do the American people get as informed and capable of putting things together as you are, and as privileged as you are?

Chomsky

Somebody has to do it. Because, see, look what I have just sketched. In order to understand what was going on in the Iran-Contra hearings you have to know things like: What happened in Chile? What happened in Indonesia? What are the classic policies for dealing with a government you are trying to overthrow? What was the Israeli ambassador saying? What were David Kimche and Jacob Nimrodi saying? You have to be able to sort of see all of that and so get at the information—Aha! This fits into exactly the classic pattern. When you have done that, it all falls together. But you cannot expect ordinary people to do that work. So you asked what our book [*Manufacturing Consent*] was about. Well, our book is about helping, not really explaining particular cases but trying to help people understand the way the system distorts the facts so that they can then compensate for the distortion in whatever new cases come along.

From an interview with Joop van Tijn on Humanist TV, Holland, June 10, 1989

HUMANIST TV (PUBLIC), HOLLAND

Chomsky

I'm not given to false modesty. There are things that I can do and I know that I can do them reasonably well, including analysis, and, you know, study, research, I mean, I know how to do that sort of thing and I think I have a reasonable understanding of the way the world works—as much as anyone can. And that turns out to be a very useful resource for people who are doing active organizing, trying to engage themselves in a way which will make it a little bit of a better world. And if you can help in those things, or participate in them, well, that's—you know, that's rewarding.

UNIVERSITY OF WASHINGTON, SEATTLE, WASHINGTON

Woman

I wonder if you can envision a time when people like myself—again, the naive people of this world—can again take pride in the United States, and is that even a healthy wish now? Because it may be this hunger for pride in our country that makes us more easily manipulated by the powers that you talk about.

Chomsky

Ah, I think you first of all have to ask what you mean by your country. Now, if you mean by the country: the government, I don't think you can be proud of it and I don't think you could ever be proud of it (*applause*)—or could be proud of any government—not our government. And you shouldn't be. States are violent institutions. The government of any country, including ours, represents some sort of domestic power structure and it's usually violent. States are violent to the extent that they're powerful, that's roughly

I'm really not interested in persuading people, I don't want to and I try to make this point obvious. What I'd like to do is help people persuade themselves. I tell them what I think, and obviously I hope they'll persuade themselves that that's true, but I'd rather have them persuade themselves of what they think is true. I think there are a lot of analytic perspectives, just straight information, that people are not presented with. The only thing I would like to be able to contribute is that. I think by and large audiences recognize that. I think the reason people come is because that's what they want to hear.

Chronicles of Dissent, page 119

David Barsamian

What are your views on the State? Are you an isolationist? How would you characterize yourself politically?

Chomsky

Reasonably, you're presupposing that there have to be States. But that's a transitory historical phase. The State system is like saying, what kind of feudal system should we have that would be the best one? What form of slavery would be the best kind? There might have been a period in history when it would have been sensible to ask, what's the best form of slavery? The least awful form of slavery? Then you could discuss different forms of slavery and which ones would be best. But there is something wrong with the question because it assumes that some system of coercion and control is necessary. And it isn't... So we're stuck with this State system for a while, at least. This is the way the world was stuck with slavery for a while. But we shouldn't expect it to be permanent. In fact, if it's a permanent condition, it isn't going to last very long because it's a lethal system.

From an interview with David Barsamian, in Language and Politics, page 745

Presupposing that there have to be states is like saying, what kind of feudal system should we have that would be the best one? What form of slavery would be the best kind?

accurate. You look at American history, it's nothing to write home about. You know, why are we here? We're here because, say, some ten million Native Americans were wiped out. That's not very pretty.

Until the 1960s it was still cowboys and Indians. In the 1970s, for the first time really, it became possible even for scholarship to try to deal with the facts as they were. For example, to deal with the fact that the Native American population was far higher than had been claimed, millions higher, maybe as many as ten million higher than had been claimed, and that they had an advanced civilization, and that there was something akin to genocide that took place. Now we went through two hundred years of our history without facing that fact. One of the effects of the 1960s is it's possible to at least begin to come to think about the facts. Well, that's an advance.

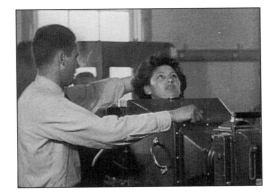

Elizabeth Sikorovsky

Do you think that this activism twenty years
ago has made a difference in how our society
operates now?

Chomsky

It has not changed the institutions and the way
they function. But it has led to very significant
cultural changes. Remember, these movements
of the 60s expanded in the 70s and expanded
further in the 80s and they reached in to other
parts of the society and different issues. These
—a lot of things that seemed outrageous in the
60s are taken for granted today. So for example,
take the feminist movement, for example—
which barely began to exist in the 60s—now it's
part of general consciousness and awareness.
The ecological movements began in the 70s. The
Third World solidarity movements were very
limited in the 60s, it was really Vietnam, and in
the 60s also it was a student movement, as you
say; now it's not. Now it's mainstream America.

**Many American intellectuals seem to be able to
reconcile themselves** to the systematic destruction of
the peasant societies of Indo-China by American technology, just as many of their predecessors found ways
to come to terms with Stalin's purge or Hiroshima and
Nagasaki. This is much less true of the youth of the sixties, to their credit, and I suspect that Vietnam—the
butchery, the deceit, the timid dissent, the contempt-
ible apologetics—will prove to be a formative experience with long-term consequences. On occasion their
revulsion expresses itself as antagonism to technology
and science, or even to rationality. But for the most
part, in my experience at least, it has led to an appreciation of the depth of sustained commitment that will
be necessary if Indo-China is to be saved from oblitera-
tion, and an appreciation of the scale of the cultural and
institutional changes that must be carried out in the
United States if other societies that seek independence
are to be spared a similar fate. Faced with the awesome scale of these tasks, many return to private concerns—a move often mistaken for apathy. It is not the
apathy of the fifties, and a reservoir of sympathy and
potential support remains for those who undertake a
more activist role.

Radical Priorities, page 234

[The] extent [of the hysteria about
political correctness] is truly something to behold, including a stream of
best-sellers with anecdotes, many
concocted, about alleged horrors in
the universities, angry speeches, and
a flood of articles from the news
columns to the sports pages and
journals of opinion....

The phenomenon did not emerge
from nowhere. One crucial component
of the post-affluence class war has
been a far-reaching takeover of the
ideological system by the right, with a
proliferation of right-wing think tanks,
a campaign to extend conservative
control still further over ideologically
significant sectors of the colleges and
universities... and an array of devices
to restrict the framework of discussion
and thought, as much as possible, to
the reactionary end of the already
narrow spectrum....

The next chapter comes as no
surprise to students of cultural
management. After a period of intense
and one-sided ideological struggle, in
which business interests and the right
wing have won a remarkable victory
in the doctrinal and political institutions, what could be more natural
than a propaganda campaign claiming
that it is left-fascists who have taken
the commanding heights and control
the entire culture, imposing their
harsh standards everywhere.

Year 501: The Conquest Continues, pages 53-54

EXCERPT: "A WORLD OF IDEAS,"
PBS (PUBLIC TV), USA (1988)

Bill Moyers

If there is more dissidence now than you can remember, why do you go on to write that people feel isolated?

Chomsky

Because I think much of the general population recognizes that the organized institutions do not reflect their concerns and interests and needs. They do not feel that they participate meaningfully in the political system. They do not feel that the media are telling them the truth or even reflect their concerns. They go outside of the organized institutions to act.

Bill Moyers

We see more and more of our elected leaders and know less and less of what they're doing. (*gesturing toward the camera*) This medium does that.

Chomsky

Very striking. In fact, the presidential elections have been almost removed from the point where the public even takes them seriously as involving a matter of choice.

In a depoliticized society, people are intelligent enough to understand that they are not voting the issues. They are voting for Coca-Cola or Pepsi-Cola. There are no parties even in the limited Western European sense. I don't want to exaggerate the situation in Western Europe, but, in fact, approximately half the population, maybe 45% of the population, that doesn't vote here, its socio-economic constitution is approximately that of those who vote in Europe for one of the reformist labor-based parties: socialist, labor, communist. That is roughly the composition of the group that largely does not vote in the United States. I suppose the reason they don't vote is that they just consider themselves as unrepresented.

From an 1984 interview with Hannu Reime, a Finnish radio journalist, reprinted in *Language and Politics*, page 600

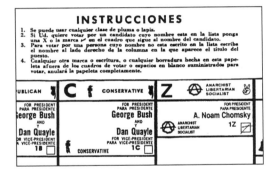

The general population recognizes that the organized institutions do not reflect their concerns and interests and needs.

THE WHITE HOUSE, WASHINGTON, DC

Peter Wintonick is surrounded by a group of boys

Peter Wintonick

So what do you think about what goes on in the White House?

Boy 1

It's kept too private, I think.

Boy 2

They should come out. Yeah. Talk to the people.

Peter Wintonick

Who should talk to the people?

Boy 1 and Boy 2

George Bush.

[I]t is important to bear in mind the extraordinarily narrow spectrum of political discourse and the limited base of political power, a fact that distinguishes the United States from many other industrial democracies. The United States is unique in that there is no organized force committed to even mild and reformist varieties of socialism. The two political parties, which some refer to, not inaccurately, as the two factions of the single "Property Party," are united in their commitment to capitalist ideology and institutions. For most of the period since the Second World War, they have adhered to a "bipartisan foreign policy," which is to say, a one-party State as far as foreign affairs are concerned. The parties differ on occasion with regard to the role of the State, the Democrats generally tending to favor slight increases in State intervention in social and economic affairs, the Republicans tending to favor greater emphasis on private corporate power....

From "The Carter Administration: Myth and Reality,"
in *Radical Priorities*, page 137 (See also pages 138-166)

Chomsky

Well, it means that the political system increasingly functions without public input. It means, to an increasing extent, not only do people not ratify decisions presented to them, but they don't even participate—they don't even take the trouble of ratifying them. They assume that the decisions are going on independently of what they may do in the polling booth.

Moyers

Ratification would be what?

Chomsky

Well, ratification would mean a system in which there are two positions presented to me, the voter. I go into the polling booth and I push one or another button depending on which of those positions I want. That's a very limited form of democracy. Really meaningful democracy would mean that I play a role in forming those decisions, in making, creating those positions, and that would be real democracy. We are very far from that. But we're even departing from the point where there is ratification. When you have stage-managed elections, with the public relations industry determining what words come out of people's mouth, candidates decide what to say on the basis of tests that determine what the effect will be across the population. Somehow people don't see how profoundly contemptuous that is of democracy.

The Reagan era represents a significant advance in capitalist democracy. For eight years, the U.S. government functioned virtually without a chief executive. That is an important fact. It is quite unfair to assign to Ronald Reagan, the person, much responsibility for the policies enacted in his name. Despite the efforts of the educated classes to invest the proceedings with the required dignity, it was hardly a secret that Reagan had only the vaguest conception of the policies of his Administration and, if not properly programmed by his staff, regularly produced statements that would have been an embarrassment, were anyone to have taken them seriously. The question that dominated the Iran-Contra hearings—did Reagan know, or remember, what the policy of his Administration had been?—was hardly a serious one. The pretense to the contrary was simply part of the cover-up operation; and the lack of public interest over revelations that Reagan was engaged in illegal aid to the Contras during a period when—he later informed Congress—he knew nothing about it, betrays a certain realism.

Reagan's duty was to smile, to read from the teleprompter in a pleasant voice, tell a few jokes, and keep the audience properly bemused. His only qualification for the presidency was that he knew how to read the lines written for him by the rich folk, who pay well for the service. Reagan had been doing that for years. He seemed to perform to the satisfaction of the paymasters, and to enjoy the experience. By all accounts, he spent many pleasant days enjoying the pomp and trappings of power and should have a fine time in retirement quarters that his grateful benefactors have prepared for him. It is not really his business if the bosses left mounds of mutilated corpses in death-squad dumping grounds in El Salvador or hundreds of thousands of homeless in the streets. One does not blame an actor for the content of the words that come from his mouth.

Deterring Democracy, pages 73-74

Reporter
The solemn moment is near. But first, the swearing in of Dan Quayle.

Announcer
Please move to your seats.

George Bush *(from his inaugural address)*
For the first time in this century, for the first time in perhaps all history, man does not have to invent a system by which to live. We don't have to talk late into the night about which form of government is better. We don't have to wrest justice from the kings. We only have to summon it from within ourselves. This is a time when the future seems a door you can walk right through, into a room called tomorrow. Great nations of the world are moving toward democracy, through the door to freedom. The people of the world agitate for free expression and free thought, through the door to the moral and intellectual satisfactions that only liberty allows. We know how to secure a more just and prosperous life for man on earth, through free markets, free spree—speech, free elections, and the exercise of free will unhampered by the state. I've spoken of a thousand points of light, of all the community organizations that are spread like stars throughout the nation doing good. To the world too we offer new engagement and a renewed vow. We will stay strong to protect the peace. The offered hand is a reluctant fist. America is never holy herself unless she is engaged in high moral principle. We as a people have such a purpose today. It is: to make kinder the face of the nation and gentler the face of the world.

People talk about a "free market." Sure. You and I are perfectly free to set up an automobile company and compete with General Motors. Nobody's stopping us. That freedom is meaningless. Or let's say you and I are free to open up a newspaper and publish things that the *L.A. Times* isn't publishing. Nobody's going to stop you. It's just that power happens to be organized so that only certain options are available. Within that limited range of options, those in power say, Let's have freedom. That's a very skewed form of freedom. The principle is right. How the freedom works depends on what the social structures are. If the freedoms are such that the only choices that you have objectively are to conform to one or another system of power, there's no freedom.

From an interview with David Barsamian, in *Language and Politics*, page 758

The domestic sources of power remain basically unchanged, whatever the electoral outcome. The major decision-making positions in the executive branch of the government, which increasingly dominates domestic and foreign policy, remain overwhelmingly in the hands of representatives of major corporations and the few law firms that cater primarily to corporate interests, thus representing generalized interests of corporate capitalism as distinct from parochial interests of one or another sector of the private economy. It is hardly surprising, then, that the basic function of the State remains the regulation of domestic and international affairs in the interest of the masters of the private economy, a fact studiously ignored in the press and academic scholarship.

From an interview with Richard Titus, an audio-teleconferencing technician at Athabasca University in Edmonton, Alberta, in *Language and Politics*, pages 477-486

We don't have to talk late into the night about which form of government is better.

George Bush

On "free" markets, "free" enterprise, and Third World "democracy," see *Year 501: The Conquest Continues*, chapters 2,3,4

On "Democracy in the Industrial Societies," see *Deterring Democracy*, chapter 11

UNIVERSITY COMMON MINISTRY,
LARAMIE, WYOMING

Man

Referring back to your earlier comment about
escaping from or doing away with capitalism,
I was wondering what scheme—workable
scheme—you would put in its place?

Chomsky

Me? Well what I would—

Man

What would you suggest to others who might
be in a position to set it up and get it going?

Chomsky

Well, I mean, I think what used to be called
centuries ago "wage slavery" is intolerable.
I mean, I don't think people ought to be forced
to rent themselves in order to survive. I think
that the economic institutions ought to be run
democratically, by their participants, by the
communities in which they exist and so on, and
I think through various forms of free association.

I don't think people ought to be forced to rent themselves in order to survive.

EXCERPT: "THE JAY INTERVIEW," LONDON WEEKEND TELEVISION, ENGLAND (1974)

Peter Jay

Historically, have there been any sustained examples on any substantial scale of societies which approximated to the anarchist ideal?

Chomsky

There are small societies, small in number, that have, I think, done so quite well and there are a few examples of large-scale libertarian revolutions which were largely anarchist in their structure. As to the first, small societies extending over a long period, I myself think the most dramatic example is the Israeli kibbutzim, which, for a long period—it may or may not be true today—really were constructed on anarchist principles, that is, of direct worker control, integration of agriculture, industry, service, personal life, on an egalitarian basis with direct and in fact quite active participation in self-management and were, I should think, extraordinarily successful. A good example of a really large-scale anarchist revolution or largely anarchist revolution, in fact the best example to my knowledge, is the Spanish Revolution in 1936. And in fact you can't tell what would have happened—that anarchist revolution was simply destroyed by force, but during the period in which it was alive I think it was inspiring testimony to the ability of poor working people to organize, manage their affairs extremely successfully, without coercion and control.

Peter Jay

How far does the success of libertarian socialism or anarchism as a way of life really depend on a fundamental change in the nature of man, both in his motivation, his altruism, and also in his knowledge and sophistication?

The kibbutz where we lived, which was about twenty years old, was then very poor. There was very little food, and work was hard. But I liked it very much in many ways. Abstracting it from context, this was a functioning and very successful libertarian community, so I felt. And I felt it would be possible for me to find some mixture of intellectual and physical work.

I came close to returning there to live, as my wife very much wanted to do at the time. I had nothing particularly attractive here. I didn't expect to be able to have an academic career, and was not particularly interested in one. There was no major drive to stay. On the other hand, I did have a lot of interest in the kibbutz and I liked it very much when I was there. But there were things I didn't like too. In particular, the ideological conformity was appalling. I don't know if I could have survived long in that environment because I was strongly opposed to the Leninist ideology, as well as the general conformism, and uneasy—less so than I should have been—about the exclusiveness and the racist institutional setting.

The Chomsky Reader, page 9

"The Jay Interview" is reprinted in *Radical Priorities* under the title "The Relevance of Anarcho-Syndicalism," pages 245-261

On "wage slavery," see "Language and Freedom" in *The Chomsky Reader,* pages 139-155

See also: "Notes on Anarchism," in *For Reasons of State,* pages 370-384; Chomsky/Foucault debate in *Reflexive Water,* pages 169-175; "Noam Chomsky's Anarchism," by Paul Marshall, in *Our Generation,* Volume 22, Nos. 1 and 2, Fall 1990, Spring 1991, pages 1-15

Chomsky

I think it not only depends on it but in fact the whole purpose of libertarian socialism is that it will contribute to it. It will contribute to a spiritual transformation. Precisely that kind of great transformation in the way humans conceive of themselves and their ability to act, to decide, to create, to produce, to inquire. Precisely that spiritual transformation that social thinkers from the left Marxist tradition, from Luxemburg, say, on over through anarcho-syndicalists, have always emphasized. So on the one hand it requires that spiritual transformation, on the other hand its purpose is to create institutions which will contribute to that transformation...

In the original interview, Chomsky went on to say:

...in the nature of work, the nature of creative activity, simply in social bonds among people and through this interaction of creating institutions which permit new aspects of human nature to flourish. And then the building of still further libertarian institutions to which these liberated human beings can contribute: this is the evolution of socialism as I understand it.

An edited transcript of this hour-long interview appears in *Radical Priorities*, pages 245-261

James Peck (editor, The Chomsky Reader)
In an anarchist society, what would the intellectual's role be?

Chomsky
That of intellectual worker. A person whose work happens to be more with the mind than with the hands. Although I would think that in a decent society there ought to be a mixture of the kinds of work that one does. Marx would agree in principle. An anarchist picture of society, or anarchist tendencies in society, offer no privileged role to the organized intelligentsia or to the professional intellectuals. And, in fact, it would tend to blur the distinctions between intellectual and worker, so that workers should take a direct, active role in the mental aspects of whatever work they're doing, its organization and planning, formation of its purposes, and so on. The people whose major professional concern is knowledge and the application of knowledge would have no special opportunity to manage the society, to gain any position of power and prestige by virtue of this special training and talent. And that's not the point of view that the intelligentsia are naturally drawn to.

The Chomsky Reader, "Interview," page 21

On Humboldt's "instinct for freedom" in human nature, see "Language and Freedom," in *The Chomsky Reader,* pages 148-149; "Humboldt" in *Language and Politics,* pages 386, 468, 566, 756.

On the left-Marxist tradition, see "Interview," *The Chomsky Reader,* pages 19-23; *Anarchism,* by Daniel Guérin, introduction by Noam Chomsky (Monthly Review Press, 1970); *Anarcho-Syndicalism* by Rudolph Rocker (Pluto Press, 1989)

As conventional physical, social and economic arrangements fail to meet basic needs, millions of people around the world are searching for better ways of living. The thousands of successful "intentional communities" throughout the world demonstrate that it is possible to create viable alternatives that better address today's social problems.

The Fellowship for Intentional Community helps to provide a sense of connectedness and cooperation among communitarians and their friends by serving as a network to facilitate trust building and information sharing between intentional communities. We also demonstrate applications of cooperative experiences to the larger society through publications, forums, workshops, and other projects. We seek to increase global awareness of the many alternative communities now in existence, and to make referrals for individuals looking for cooperative resources or a home in an intentional community. (See Resource Guide)

Student
What do you think of socialism and communism?

Chomsky
It depends what you mean. Most of these terms have lost any possible meaning, so we have to decide what we mean by them. If we mean by socialism and communism what the terms actually meant, I'm very much in favor of them and so is the overwhelming majority of the American population. That's another thing they don't tell you in civics courses. There are always polls asking people all sorts of questions. One of the amusing poll results has to do with asking people what's in the Constitution. People have very strange ideas about what's in the Constitution. Some of the ideas are quite interesting. For example, there was a poll in 1987 that gave people the following phrase: "From each according to his ability, to each according to his needs" as a principle of social policy. People were asked if that's in the Constitution. About 75% [thought it was].

Now, that's communism. Communism has a principle of social policy that says that social policy ought to be designed so that each person produces according to his ability and each person receives according to need, a basic idea. [The phrase was coined by Marx.] Although nobody says it, [and] you're not allowed to articulate it, the overwhelming majority of the population considers that such an obvious good principle of social policy that they actually believe it's in the Constitution. And if you look at other issues—take, say, welfare measures. That's not socialism and communism; mild social democracy. What does the population think about those?

When people are asked, "Would you prefer social spending to military spending," if you have X amount of dollars and the government's going to use them for military or health, let's say, the proportion in favor of social spending is just enormous, 4 to 1, 7 to 1, depends on how you ask the question. In fact, there's a general drift among the population towards a kind of New Deal-style social democracy or liberalism.

If we mean by socialism and communism things like worker control over production, community control over what happens in the community, democracy, end of wage slavery, ratio-

nal social planning, from each according to his ability, etc., then I think that those are very good things, I think they consummate the ideals that were articulated but never believed, in the political revolutions of the eighteenth century. I think they would be very healthy developments. Notice that we can't discuss these issues in the United States. These are off the agenda. That's very important. This goes back to the first question. If this kind of material were allowed into the educational system, if you're allowed to think and talk about these things and bring out these inarticulate feelings, you are a real threat to established power. Therefore the educational system excludes it.

"Questions and Answers with Freshman Sociology," recorded by David Barsamian at University of Wyoming in Laramie, February 21, 1989.

Bakunin and Kropotkin and others... had in mind a highly organized form of society, but a society that was organized on the basis of organic units, organic communities. And generally they meant by that the workplace and the neighborhood, and from those two basic units there could derive through federal arrangements a highly integrated kind of social organization, which might be national or even international in scope. And the decisions could be made over a substantial range, but by delegates who are always part of the organic community from which they come, to which they return and in which, in fact, they live....

Representative democracy, as in, say, the United States or Great Britain, would be criticized by an anarchist of this school on two grounds. First of all there is a monopoly of power centralized in the State, and secondly—and critically—because representative democracy is limited to the political sphere and in no serious way encroaches on the economic sphere. Anarchists of this tradition have always held that democratic control of one's productive life is at the core of any serious human liberation, or, for that matter, of any significant democratic practice. That is, as long as individuals are compelled to rent themselves on the market to those who are willing to hire them, as long as their role in production is simply that of ancillary tools, then there are striking elements of coercion and oppression that make talk of democracy very limited, if even meaningful.

I think that industrialization and the advance of technology raise possibilities for self-management over a broad scale that simply didn't exist in an earlier period. And that in fact this is precisely the rational mode for an advanced and complex industrial society, one in which workers can very well become masters of their own immediate affairs, that is, in direction and control of the shop, but also can be in a position to make the major substantive decisions concerning the structure of the economy, concerning social institutions, concerning planning regionally and beyond.

Radical Priorities, pages 245-249

[M]any commentators dismiss anarchism as utopian, formless, primitive, or otherwise incompatible with the realities of a complex society. One might, however, argue rather differently: that at every stage of history our concern must be to dismantle those forms of authority and oppression that survive from an era when they might have been justified in terms of the need for security or survival or economic development, but that now contribute to—rather than alleviate—material and cultural deficit. If so, there will be no doctrine of social change fixed for the present and future, nor even, necessarily, a specific and unchanging concept of the goals towards which social change should tend. Surely our understanding of the nature of man or of the range of viable social forms is so rudimentary that any far-reaching doctrine must be treated with great skepticism, just as skepticism is in order when we hear that "human nature" or "the demands of efficiency" or "the complexity of modern life" requires this or that form of oppression and autocratic rule.

Nevertheless, at a particular time there is every reason to develop, insofar as our understanding permits, a specific realization of this definite trend in the historic development of mankind, appropriate to the tasks of the moment.

For Reasons of State, page 371

"AMERICAN FOCUS" STUDENT RADIO, WASHINGTON, DC

Karine Kleinhaus

You've written that in looking at contributions of gifted thinkers one must make sure to understand their contributions but also to eliminate the errors in them. Um, and of your ideas, what would you guess would be discarded and what would be assimilated by future thinkers?

Chomsky

Well, I would assume virtually everything would be discarded. For example, in—here we have to distinguish, I mean the work that I do in my professional area, I mean, if I still believed what I believed ten years ago I'd assume the field is dead. So I assume that when next time you read a student's paper you're going to see something that has to be changed and you continue to make progress. In dealing with social and political issues, in my view, what is at all understood is pretty straightforward. I don't think that—there may be deep and complicated things but, if so, they're not understood. To the extent that we understand society at all, it's pretty straightforward. And I don't think that those simple understandings are likely to undergo much change.

Marxism, in my view, belongs in the history of organized religion. In fact, as a rule of thumb, any concept with a person's name on it belongs to religion, not rational discourse. There aren't any physicists who call themselves Einsteinians. And the same would be true of anybody crazy enough to call themselves Chomskian. In the real world you have individuals who were in the right place at the right time, or maybe they got a good brain wave or something, and they did something interesting. But I never heard of anyone who didn't make mistakes and whose work wasn't quickly improved on by others. That means if you identify yourself as a Marxist or a Freudian or anything else, you're worshipping at someone's shrine.

But as I understand Marx, he constructed a somewhat interesting theory of a rather abstract model of nineteenth-century capitalism. He did good journalism. And he had interesting ideas about history. He probably had about five sentences in his entire body of work about what a postcapitalist society is supposed to look like.

From "Noam Chomsky: Anarchy in the USA," by Charles M. Young, *Rolling Stone*, May 28, 1992, page 47

[A]s Henry Kissinger has accurately commented, in our "age of the expert" the "expert has his constituency—those who have a vested interest in commonly held opinions; elaborating and defining the consensus at a high level has, after all, made him an expert."

Towards a New Cold War, page 91

An expert is someone who articulates the consensus of people with power.

Chomsky

The point is that you have to work. And that's why the propaganda system is so successful. Very few people are going to have the time or the energy or the commitment to carry out the constant battle that's required to get outside of MacNeil/Lehrer or Dan Rather or somebody like that. The easy thing to do, you know—you come home from work, you're tired, you've had a busy day, you're not going to spend the evening carrying on a research project, so you turn on the tube and say it's probably right, or you look at the headlines in the paper and then you watch the sports or something. That's basically the way the system of indoctrination works. Sure the other stuff is there, but you're going to have to work to find it

During an interview for the public-access program "Non-Corporate News," the camera operator and camera set-up are seen. We then cut to the video camera's point of view. Chomsky is seen on a TV monitor, discussing the mental discipline needed to escape the doctrinal confines of MacNeil/ Lehrer or Dan Rather. Our camera slowly pulls back, revealing 39 other TV sets, each tuned to a different station, in a video wall surrounding the TV on which Chomsky is seen. Only Chomsky appears to be speaking in "real time," while the broadcasts on the other TVs appear accelerated. A potent image is created, embodying Chomsky's observation that the task of making sense out of this glut of information and disinformation is a formidable one, and reminding viewers of the need for critical vigilance in any encounter with the media—including *Manufacturing Consent*.

How we did it:

Animator Brian Duchscherer coordinated the technical aspects of the shot. A 35mm single-frame motion-picture camera was set up on a track leading away from the video wall. Shooting one frame at a time, Brian rolled the camera back along the track (by hand) a fraction of an inch. A special computer program provided by David Verrall (National Film Board of Canada) calculated the precise distance the camera was to be moved for each frame given our need for a gradual start-up, then a constant velocity, then a gradual slow-down and stop. Camera assistant Robin Bain kept track of focus. For each frame of film exposed, the 1/2" VHS videotape of Chomsky speaking on the center TV was advanced one frame and then frozen. The film's exposure was one second at F8. An ancient Panasonic industrial 1/2" deck held a remarkably steady image (better than any modern home unit we tried) and kept an accurate frame count. Every third or fourth video frame had to be skipped to compensate for the difference between video, which runs at 30 frames per second, and film, which runs at 24 frames per second. The other 39 TVs—arranged so that the major networks immediately surrounded Chomsky's monitor—were left on. It took about 30 seconds to get set up to expose each frame. The whole 40-second shot, composed of 960 frames, took about two weeks to prepare, and a crew of six people 15 hours to shoot.—MA

Chomsky

Modern industrial civilization has developed within a certain system of convenient myths. The driving force of modern industrial civilization has been individual material gain, which is accepted as legitimate, even praiseworthy, on the grounds that private vices yield public benefits, in the classic formulation. Now, it's long been understood—very well— that a society that is based on this principle will destroy itself in time. It can only persist with whatever suffering and injustice it entails as long as it's possible to pretend that the destructive forces that humans create are limited, that the world is an infinite resource, and that the world is an infinite garbage can.

At this stage of history, *either* one of two things is possible. Either the general population will take control of its own destiny and will concern itself with community interests, guided by values of solidarity, and sympathy, and concern for others, or, alternatively, there will be no destiny for anyone to control.

Predatory capitalism created a complex industrial system and an advanced technology; it permitted a considerable extension of democratic practice and fostered certain liberal values, but within limits that are now being pressed and must be overcome. It is not a fit system for the mid-twentieth century. It is incapable of meeting human needs that can be expressed only in collective terms, and its concept of competitive man who seeks only to maximize wealth and power, who subjects himself to market relationships, to exploitation and external authority, is antihuman and intolerable in the deepest sense. An autocratic state is no acceptable substitute; nor can the militarized state capitalism evolving in the United States or the bureaucratized, centralized welfare state be accepted as the goal of human existence.

From "Language and Freedom," reprinted in *The Chomsky Reader*,
page 153
(see also pages 139-155)

[T]he *Times* business section carries an item on a confidential memo of the World Bank leaked to the *Economist*. [Lawrence Summers, chief economist of the World Bank,] writes: "Just between you and me, shouldn't the World Bank be encouraging *more* migration of dirty industries to the [Third World]?" This makes good sense, Summers explains: for example, a cancer-producing agent will have larger effects "in a country where people survive to get prostate cancer than in a country where under-5 mortality is 200 per thousand." Poor countries are "*under*-polluted," and it is only reasonable to encourage "dirty industries" to move to them....

Quite true. We have the choice of taking them to be a *reductio ad absurdum* argument and thus abandoning the ideology, or accepting the conclusions: on grounds of economic rationality, the rich countries should export pollution to the Third World, which should cut back on its "misguided" efforts to promote economic development and protect the population from disaster. That way, capitalism can overcome the environmental crisis....

Confronted with the memo, Summers said that it was only "intended to provoke debate"—elsewhere, that it was a "sarcastic response" to another World Bank draft.

Year 501: The Conquest Continues, pages 107-108

As long as some specialized class is in a position of authority, it is going to set policy in the special interests that it serves. But the conditions of survival, let alone justice, require rational social planning in the interests of the community as a whole, and by now that means the global community.

GRONINGEN, HOLLAND

Chomsky

The question is whether privileged elites should dominate mass communication, and should use this power as they tell us they must —namely, to impose necessary illusions, to manipulate and deceive the stupid majority, and remove them from the public arena.

The question, in brief, is whether democracy and freedom are values to be preserved, or threats to be avoided.

It should be recognized that capitalism can easily accommodate the idea that individuals are interchangeable tools of production and that the environment should be maintained to be exploited by the masters of the economic and political system. A radical and emancipatory movement is not necessarily anticapitalist. There are many forms of authority and domination apart from those of the capitalist system.

From an interview in *Open Road* (Vancouver, British Columbia), reprinted in *Language and Politics*, page 391

If it is plausible that ideology will in general serve as a mask for self-interest, then it is a natural presumption that intellectuals, in interpreting history or formulating policy, will tend to adopt an elitist position, condemning popular movements and mass participation in decision-making, and emphasizing rather the necessity for supervision by those who possess the knowledge and understanding that is required (so they claim) to manage society and control social change. One major element in the anarchist critique of Marxism a century ago was the prediction that, as Bakunin formulated it:

> According to the theory of Mr. Marx, the people not only must not destroy [the state] but must strengthen it and place it at the complete disposal of their benefactors, guardians, and teachers—the leaders of the Communist party, namely Mr. Marx and his friends, who will proceed to liberate [mankind] in their own way. They will concentrate the reins of government in a strong hand, because the ignorant people require an exceedingly firm guardianship...

Antagonism to mass movements and to social change that escapes the control of privileged elites is also a prominent feature of contemporary liberal ideology.

The Chomsky Reader, pages 83-85

Chomsky

In this possibly terminal phase of human existence, democracy and freedom are more than values to be treasured—they may well be essential to survival. Thank you.

ROWE CONFERENCE CENTER,
ROWE, MASSACHUSETTS

Linda Trichter Metcalf

He's up there thinking for himself. And he's deciphering this tremendously over-weighted body of information which he puts into an order and gives you the feeling that you can do the same thing, that the whole thing is decipherable. And he also gives you the sense that there is a source, there is a center, to the— to a dissenting population, although we feel that there's no center. And I think that is what reactivated in me a desire to get back, get re-acquainted with the political scene after thirty years of alienation from it.

Linda Trichter Metcalf, Ph.D., was one of 60 seminar participants in a three-day discussion with Noam Chomsky at the Rowe Conference Center.

She and her collaborator, Tobin Simon, Ph.D., have also conducted workshops at the Rowe Center on proprioceptive writing. "Proprioception" is a physiological term for kinesthetic sensation—feelings that originate in the body's interior. Nerves called proprioceptors, sending information to the brain, orient the body to its own movement, direction, position and tone.

What some call spirituality, Trichter Metcalf and Simon view as inner intelligence and also find it analogous to proprioception. They teach that, through inner intelligence, we access our thoughts and discriminate among them: in short, know ourselves. (see Resource Guide)

MIT OFFICE, CAMBRIDGE, MASSACHUSETTS

David Barsamian
You do hundreds of interviews and lectures and you're dealing with massacres in East Timor and invasions of Panama, death squads, pretty horrific stuff. What keeps you going? Don't you get burned out on this material?

See continuation of transcript at right

(*section in **bold** is in the film*)

Chomsky
I could talk to you about my personal reactions, but again I don't see why they should interest anyone.

David Barsamian
Is there an inner resource that you call upon when you're feeling despair?

Chomsky
Well, you know, it's mainly a matter of whether you can look yourself in the mirror, I think. If you want to be encouraged, there are ways to be encouraged. Things are much better than they were twenty-five years ago, ten years ago. For example, twenty years ago I wouldn't have been able to go out to Manhattan, Kansas and find people who knew more about whatever-it-was than I did, who were active and involved. When I started giving talks back around 1964, it seemed totally hopeless. A talk would mean getting some neighbor to invite two people over and talk in the living room, or going to a church where there's one drunk guy who's coming in and some other guy who wants to kill you and the organizers. When we organized public meetings back in those days at the University, I remember a meeting at MIT at which we had announced a meeting on Vietnam, Venezuela, etc., in the hope that maybe you could draw in enough people to outnumber the organizers. Also, the hostility was extraordinary. The first public outdoor rally that I spoke to was in October 1965 on the Boston Common, where there was a meeting organized, an international day of protest against the Indochina War, organized by students, like most things. It was really the first major public meeting with a march and rally at the Common. There must have been two hundred to three hundred police, who we were very happy to see, I should say, because they were the only thing that kept us from getting murdered. The crowd was extremely hostile, mostly students who had marched over from the University, they were ready to kill you. The demands were so tame, it was almost embarrassing to say

them: Stop the bombing of North Vietnam, or the bombing of South Vietnam, which was three times the scale, you didn't even talk about that. That went on up through the middle of 1966. You couldn't have an outdoor rally in Boston because you'd get murdered by students and others. Then I felt totally helpless, I couldn't see any point to it all.

David Barsamian
So you are encouraged?

Chomsky
Whether you are encouraged or not is a matter of personality, not of objective fact. In many ways things are a lot better. I think the cultural level of the country is much higher. Outside the educated classes, which are not changed, I think the moral and intellectual level of pubic discourse and public understanding has risen very considerably. I don't doubt that for a moment. And that's encouraging. If you want to be discouraged you can think about the glacial pace of it, the distance that yet has to be travelled before you can make a serious impact on policy. These are questions of mood, not of objective reality. I don't see much point in paying attention to them. Basically you take a kind of Pascal's wager if you don't do anything. Take the environment. If you want to give an objective analysis, you can give a pretty good argument that in a hundred years or two hundred years there's going to be nothing left but cockroaches. No matter what we do. That's quite possible. On the other hand you can try to do something about it, to change things. You've got two choices: Do nothing, in which case you can predict what's going to happen, or do something, in which case maybe you have a chance.

Barsamian
You're committed to doing something.

Chomsky
I try to be.

Available from Alternative Radio as "The MIT Interviews," also printed as "Substitutions for the 'Evil Empire'," in *Chronicles of Dissent*

TRAIN STATION, MEDIA, PENNSYLVANIA

Conductor
Oop. Gotta go. Gotta get these people to town.

Peter Wintonick
OK. Maybe you could say "all aboard" for us.

Conductor
Okay. All aboard!

Peter Wintonick
Bye bye!

Conductor
Bye bye!

(credits begin)

PETER WINTONICK ATTEMPTS TO SLATE A SHOT...

(Sound of electronic slate)

Beep!

(But the light bulb in the slate is not working)

Mark Achbar
No. I didn't see it. Just hit the microphone.

(Peter hits the microphone)

Thud.

GROUP OF PEOPLE OUTSIDE MEDIA COURTHOUSE

Man

Thank you. Bye, Canada. G'bye, Canada.

Woman

Bye!

MIT OFFICE, CAMBRIDGE, MASSACHUSETTS

Ed Robinson

I've gone past the hour you agreed to, thank you very much.

HUMANIST TV (PUBLIC), HOLLAND

Man

In the introduction you said that he's from Harvard.

Chomsky

Oh, I heard that.

Joop van Tijn

Oh yes. Yes, it's true, ya. We'll bleep it.

KUWR (PUBLIC RADIO), LARAMIE, WYOMING

Marci Randall Miller

Sorry about making you answer that in so short a time.

Chomsky

That's OK. It worked. Did we hit it in two minutes or—?

Marci Randall Miller

Well, we did, we did pretty well, actually, that means less sports and that's fine with me.

NATIONAL PRESS CLUB, WASHINGTON, DC

Sarah McClendon
You know, the poor people out there—they don't know what's going on. If the people knew what you said here today there'd be a heck of a change.

Chomsky
There'd be a revolution.

Sarah McClendon
Thank you.

Newsreel Collective New York Times • Pentagon Peoples Republic of Kampuchea Productions du Regard • José Ramos-Horta Gil Scrine • So. Cal. Library for Social Studies United Nations • UPITN

Music
"For What It's Worth"
by Stephen Stills performed by Buffalo Springfield produced by Charles Greene and Brian Stone Courtesy Ten East Music, Springalo & Cotillion (BMI) by arrangement with Warner Special Products © Warner/Chappell Music Inc.
"O Superman" (For Massenet) by Laurie Anderson Performed by Laurie Anderson, Roma Baran, Perry Hoberman Courtesy One Ten Records © 1982 Difficult Music (BM I) by arrangement with Warner Special Products - WEA
"Cross-eyed and Painless" By David Byrne, Brian Eno, Talking Heads performed by Talking Heads published by Index Music/Bleu Disque Co.Inc.(ASCAP) E.G. Music, Ltd. (BMI) Courtesy Sire Records by arrangement with Warner Special Products © Warner/Chappell Music Inc.
"People Get Ready" written by Curtis Mayfield courtesy of Curtom Records, performed by Four the Moment, courtesy JAM Productions Ltd. by arrangement with Warner Special Products © Warner/Chappell Music inc.
"Timor: Songs of the Ema," Centre nationale de la Recherche Scientifique, Musée de L'Homme - Paris "The Music of Cambodia" recordings (1967-68) by Jacques Brunet • With permission of the International Music Council Editors of the UNESCO Collection of Traditional Music Éditeur générale - Alain Daniélou Original Score Composed and Produced by Carl Schultz, Percussion Greg Hohn Sax and WX7 Charlie Robertson Vocalist Carine Karkour
Special Thanks to • ABC News • Alter Ciné American Association of School Administrators Amnesty International • Ass'n for Media Literacy AIVF • Bad Religion • Baseball Diplomacy • Battersea Arts Centre • Black Rose Books • Breatkthrough Films CNN • Campus & Community Radio Assoc. Can. Assoc. of Journalists • Can. Auto Workers Union Can. Paperworkers Union • Mapparium (Boston) Conference on Anti-Communism Conference on Knowledge and Language (Groningen) • Coral Graphics • Development and Peace • East Timor Alert Network • Ecole Internationale • Erin Mills Town Centre • FAIR • Federation of College Broadcasters Fuse Magazine • George Eastman House • Global Village • Harvard U. Trade Union Program

If the universities are to provide the knowledge and skills, as well as the trained manpower needed to sustain an advanced industrial society, a substantial part of the youth will pass through them and they will have to retain a certain degree of freedom and openness....

In a modern industrial society there will be a need for relatively free and open centers of study and thinking which will in turn continually create a challenge to irrationality, autocratic structures, deceit and injustice. A radical or reformist social movement will be able to draw upon these centers for participants as well as ideas, while "radicalizing" them by the opportunities it creates for meaningful social action. No movement for social change can hope to succeed unless it makes the most advanced intellectual and technical achievements its own, and unless it is rooted in those strata of the population that are productive and creative in every domain. It is, in particular, a very important question whether the intelligentsia will see itself as fulfilling a role in social management, or rather as part of the work force. The promise of past revolutions has been betrayed, in part because of the willingness of the intelligentsia to join or serve a new ruling class, a process that can be compared to the willing submission to state and private power in Western state capitalist societies. As a larger component of the productive work in an industrial society comes to involve skilled workers, engineers, scientists and other intellectual workers, new possibilities may develop for the emergence of a mass revolutionary movement that will not be betrayed by the separation of a vanguard intelligentsia from the labor army that it helps to control, either directly or through the ideological instruments it fashions. So one might hope, at least.

Radical Priorities, pages 234-235

"THIRD EAR," BBC-3 (PUBLIC RADIO), LONDON, ENGLAND

Jonathan Steinberg
On that optimistic note, Professor Chomsky, thank you very much indeed.

"AMERICAN FOCUS" STUDENT RADIO, WASHINGTON, DC

(post-interview)

Bill Turnley
So how did it go?

Elizabeth Sikorovsky
Oh, I thought it was sort of—sort of technical sounding. But, you know, there wasn't much of a rhythm.

SCRUM: GEORGETOWN UNIVERSITY, WASHINGTON, DC

Man
Did you ever think of running for president? (laughter)

Chomsky
If I ran for president the first thing I'd do is tell people not to vote for me.

for Media Analysis • Inter Pares • Int'l Jewish Peace Union • Int'l Philospher's Project • Lies of Our Times • Lulu Kaplan's B & B • Media Alliance • Media Foundation • Media Project • Methodist Office UN • MIT Museum • Holocaust Memorial Center • Montréal Machine • Shaw Cable • Nat'l Council of Women • National Press Club • NFB Pacific NRC Handelsblad • NYCLU • Olympic Stadium • Open Road • Pantheon Petrified Films • Project Challenge • PBS • Resist • Seattle Times • Social Justice Committee • Tapol UK • The New York Times • Timiskaming Board of Ed. • University Common Ministry (Wyoming) • United Church • Vidéotron • War Resister's League World Wide Pictures • Yale University Library • Z Magazine

The Filmmakers Gratefully Acknowledge the Support of Werner Abraham Ben Achbar • Marjorie Achbar • Francine Achbar • Jim Adams • Alice the Cat Laurie Anderson • Wendy Anderson • Paul Andrews • Elizabeth Andrews • Kay Armatage David Ashley • Liette Aubin • Peter Ayrton • Jere L. Bacharach • Jon P. Baggaley Ben Bagdikian • Bob Baldock • Max Barber • Patrick Barnard • Erik Barnouw David Barsamian • Gary Bauslaugh • Eric Beauchemin • Sally Bedow • Elaine Bernard Jacques Blanchette • Jason Bogdaneros • Jenny Bolande • Bob Bossin • Robert Boyd Harry Bracken • Elaine Briere • Piet Brinkmann • William F. Buckley Jr. • Harvey Burt Muriel Burt • Christine Burt • Mira Burt-Wintonick • David Byrne • Rob Cates Nim Chimpsky • Marian Christ • Jane Churchill • Bill Clar • Alexander Cockburn Andrew Cockburn • Jeff Cohen • Steve Cohen • Michael Cooke • Sarah Cooper Peter Costa • David Kriegel • Harold Crooks • Robert Cwiklik • Jim Danky • Gloriana Davenport • Bradley Davis • John Demeter • Donald Derosby • Peter Desbarats Bob Di Oreo • John Douglas • Martin Duckworth • Hedy Margolies Elefritz • Peter Elgin Daniel Ellsberg • Judy Epstein • Steve Fischler • Marvin Fischman • Siobhan Flanagan Peter Flemmington • Andrew Forberg • Carol Fripp • Michael Fukushima • Arnie Gelbart Alan Geldart • Liz Gibson • Lynne Giddens • John Givens • Laura Goodman Judy Greene • Fernand Grenier • Ada Griffin • Todd Gustavson • Rudi Haas • Julian Hale Christopher Hitchens • Glenn Hodginns • John Hodgson • Arthur Hynes • Don Irvine Magnus Isaacson • Julian Jacobs • Peter Jennings • Jim Kearns • Doug Kellner Jim Kelman • Mimi Kerman • Merv Kerman • Sumire Kiyose • Tom Klein Beernink Arnold Kohen • Ron Krant • Dr. Nick Laidlaw • Roger Leisner • Lance E. Lindblom Ron Linville • Willie Ludlow • Alison McGillivray • Sue Mach • Sarah McCLendon Medrie MacPhee • Graeme MacQueen • Ron Mann • Don MacWilliams • William Massa Jr. Garth Massey • Peter Matorin • Godwin Mawuru • Curtis Mayfield Todd C. Mayfield • Karl E. Meyer • André Michaud • Nancy Miller • Jean Miquet Rick Moffat • George Mokray • Peter Monet • Jim Moore • Paul Moore • Doug Morris Vincent Mosco • Gail Mott • Bill Moyers • Brian Murphy • Betty Nelson Roberta Newman • Bill O'Leary • Keibo Oiwa • Carlos P. Otero • Jack Panozzo Jay Parini • Cleo Paskal • mark Pavlick • James Peck • Gail Pellett • The People of Media Fred Pernall • Cynthia Peters • Laura Petitto • Marilyn Piety • Pienera • Michael Polanyi Peter Prago • Harvey Quintal • Chengiah Ragavan • José Ramos-Horta • Rod Rankin David Ransom • Marcus Raskin • Ellen Ray • Peter Raymont • Eric Reuland Svend Robinson • Irving Rosenthal • Paul Rosenbaum • Martin Rosenbaum Dimitri Roussopoulos • Ry Ryan • Charles St. Vil • William Schaap • Jay Scheide Roz Schwartz • Lois Segal • Ron Simon • Steven Stills • Brian Stone • Gerald Stone Rick Stow • Tim Strawn • Skinner Mouse • Bob Therriault • Gord Thompson Murray Thomson • Patrick Thibeault • Wendy Tilby • Trisse 'n' Toto • Lisa deMena Travis Lorne Tulk • Werner Volkmer • John Walker • Denise Walsh • Pat Walsh • Jim Wells Sarah Wells • Bernard Welt • Meg Westlund • Nettie Wild • Sr. Julie Williams Peter Williamson • Doug Wilson • Amy Wilson • Tom Wolfe • Mark Wolff Dr. Stanley Yates • Jamie Young • Paul Zilsel • Barrie Zwicker • and Hundreds of Others

SCRUM: MIT, CAMBRIDGE, MASSACHUSETTS

Carol Chomsky
This guy has got to go home, he *really does*.

Man
And people still—people still believe the Boston Celtics [are] the world champion.

Carol Chomsky
Couldn't you—*couldn't* you let him go?

Chomsky
Thanks.

and a GREAT BIG THANKS to:

Noam and Carol Chomsky

ExecutiveProducers (NFB) Colin Neale • Dennis Murphy
Producer (NFB) Adam Symansky
Directors and Producers • Peter Wintonick and Mark Achbar

*Dedicated to Emile De Antonio
and The People of East Timor*

This film is intended to encourage debate
about media and democracy

DE ANTONIO, EMILE (1920–1989)

Just call me "d"

Emile de Antonio, the godfather of political documentary film, was known the world over simply as **"d."** Official mass-media biographies and obituaries tell us that he died on December 15, 1989. *The Boston Globe* called him "a radical beacon" with "unabashedly leftist politics." The newspaper of historical record, *The New York Times*, tells how a 70-year-old anti-establishment filmmaker died of a heart attack in front of his East Village home. That other great arbiter of taste, the film weekly *Variety,* proclaimed, in big type: "Documaker de Antonio dead at 70; attacked the system."

My own memories of de Antonio are somewhat different. I first met the "maitre **d**" several years ago when he came to Toronto for several days to help us finish Ron Mann's **Poetry in Motion.** His lucid ideas about film structure left an impression on me and on that film. He was always willing to help out the younger political filmmakers who regularly beat a path to his office in New York.

De Antonio was a man born to fight. He was the only filmmaker to be put on Richard Nixon's Enemy List. Sometimes he ended up fighting *all* the president's men. Other times he struggled with the personal demons of hard living. If there was ever such a thing as a radical army, de Antonio would certainly have been the progressive general leading media shock troops into a war against oppression. His war was a war for independent and free expression. A war which would overturn conventional and official history by uncovering hidden truths. A war to limit the catastrophic impact of a State gone wild. **d's** strength was that he had a great sense of the historical moment and knew how to love life. He was a great raconteur, an archivist, and an anthropologist, who played with the rich and begged along with the rest of us. In a time when "Great Man" theories are suspect, he was a prime suspect.

Emerging from a privileged background, **d** went to Harvard where he was in the same class (1940) as John F. Kennedy. Self-described as "a Marxist among capitalists," he joined the Young Communist League and the John Reed Society. (He subsequently gave up on Marxist orthodoxy before it was fashionable to do so.) He then served with the U.S. military in WWII and fought the fascists. He read many things while he was enlisted: "Long ago when I was a young man, I read an essay by Sartre on Descartes. It concludes: '

...It is not by chasing after immortality that we will make ourselves eternal; we will not make ourselves absolute by reflecting in our works the desiccated principles which are sufficiently empty and negative to pass from one century to another, but by fighting passionately in our time, by loving it passionately, and by consenting to perish entirely with it.'"

d went on to become a doctoral candidate in English literature, a teacher, an opera translator, an artist's and photographer's representative, a longshoreman and a barge captain. He counted among his friends many of the famous and infamous of New York art circles—John Cage, Robert Frank, Frank Stella, and beyond. He led a chaotic and bohemian life, generally concentrating on alcohol and women. He was married several times. Warhol once made a film in which **d** quickly consumed, in real time, a quart of whisky. He almost died of alcohol poisoning.

Thirty years ago, as he was turning a mid-life 40, he began to make films, thereby demonstrating that there's hope for all of us. As he watched Kennedy's ascent to the podium of power, he turned his radical sights onto cinema and onto the American government. Until then he had always disliked films. He began by compiling and editing found materials into complex collages without using narration, which he found inherently fascist and condescending. He ended up re-defining the documentary.

He wrote: "Documentary. If it isn't political, subversive, it simply isn't. It should be a poor art in a rich industry. It should be an individual, not an industrial product. And poor because it cannot share in the rich escapism which supports starvation and intolerable housing, imperial wars and a drug culture which gnaws in every bin of life....It is our duty to find subjects which are contentious, which are fundamentally political. Don't try to be objective. It's impossible. Find new forms, be aggressive, challenge everything. Don't be afraid to make mistakes. Error is a master....Unless there is room to make mistakes, you have a kind of abstract, technological perfection, which is what most films are about. That is why I intentionally make my films raw and unsweetened, what our friends would call l'art brut." **d** has described his films as: "political theater; to me form is paramount and oppositional. I have always preferred art brut to the smoothness not only of Hollywood films but of 'well-made' films anywhere."

His first film was the very successful **Point of Order** (1963, 97 minutes, B&W). Made with the garbage of 188 hours of old out-takes from CBS television news-

Three people, independent of one another, had the idea of making a film with Noam Chomsky: Emile de Antonio, Peter Wintonick and myself. Fortunately, two of us lived long enough to actually do it. To the one who didn't, and to the people of East Timor, we dedicated our film. —M.A.

reels and the help of distributor Dan Talbot, it is about right-wing Senator Joseph McCarthy's Army hearings in 1954. It was the first postwar documentary without narration and it owed much to John Cage's idea that art can be anything. In 1966 he produced *That's Where the Action Is,* a black and white film about the 1965 New York mayoralty campaign. In *Rush to Judgment* (1967, 110 minutes, B&W), **d** asked the wrong questions surrounding Kennedy's assassination and the resulting Warren Commission report. For his trouble he was harassed by the FBI and various police forces.

The classic *In the Year of the Pig* (1969, 101 minutes, B&W) brought to new levels the art of the collage. It examines, like no other film has since, the origin and nature of U.S. involvement in the Vietnam War. It is a brilliantly arranged argument that was nominated for an Academy Award. Of that "honor" **d** said: "I was invited to wear a black tie and smile. I did not go. I did not win..... Had I won the war might have ended sooner. Documentary occasionally produces sincere criticism. In L.A. the theater was broken into and the screen ruined with tar with the slogan: TRAITOR. The booking was cancelled."

America Is Hard to See (1970, 101 minutes, B&W) concentrates on 1968 and the candidacy of Democratic hopeful Eugene McCarthy. *Millhouse: A White Comedy* (1971, 93 minutes, B&W) picked apart Richard Nixon's career as an illustration of how the democratic process can be media-manipulated. He asked: "Name the films on one hand which ever had a White House so stirred up?....For me being on Nixon's Enemies list was a greater honor than the Academy Award."

Painters Painting (1972, 116 minutes, B&W and color) features the modern artists who were **d**'s friends—(Rauschenberg, Johns, Stella, Warhol, etc.) who made New York the center of the international art world. He was criticized by some for making an apolitical film. He replied: "Is this political? Answer: Life cannot be all politics. I am not Lenin. I love my wife. I read; I also used to drink and swim. I am inconsistent..."

Underground (1976, 88 minutes, colour, made with Haskell Wexler and Mary Lampson) was photographed clandestinely in a safe house with fugitive members of the American revolutionary movement Weather Underground. A widely publicized battle with the FBI took place over the film. The FBI used wiretapping, surveillance and vandalism to gather information about the contacts of the filmmakers. **d**

and company defied grand jury subpoenas to turn over their film. Hollywood rallied to their defense, with people such as Warren Beatty, Sally Field and Jack Nicholson signing a statement deploring the government's actions and defending the right of people to make a film about any subject.

In the King of Prussia (1983, 92 minutes, color, video blown to 35mm) is a re-enactment of the trial of the Plowshares 8, a group of Roman Catholic "radicals" who practiced civil disobedience by attempting to destroy two nuclear missile nosecones.

His last film, *Mr. Hoover and I* (1989), is an autobiographical film culled from de Antonio's life history and from 10,000 pages of FBI documents about him that he received through the Freedom of Information Act. In it **d** strips himself, and the film form, bare.

"In the U.S. we've painted the word 'radical' as somebody unbalanced and willing to sacrifice everybody else for some rather abstract and unusual invisible idea. 'Radical' has a very decent Latin root—it means the 'basis'. A radical solution in not a crazy solution but a root solution, a solution that goes to the heart of the matter. The United States is in need of a radical solution, our economic system is falling apart, our foreign policy is based on threatening the world with extinction. It is clear that virtue is now being measured by money—the richer you are the more virtuous you are. The poor shall suffer by serving the rich. To me that's the most obscene idea that's come along in my country since I've lived there. If I die fighting against these ideas, then it's worth a life, my life at any rate."

My memories, and **d**'s words, never fade. A week after he died I tried to reach his wife Nancy by phone and by some mistake of fate dialed his office number. Uncannily his voice came on the answering machine: "This is Emile de Antonio. I'm not here..." **d** might have left this physical plane and planet, but not for long. He lives on in a rich body of work that he left for the world to ponder and to take as example. He was a great teacher. He has inspired us to question the empty ideals of bourgeois filmmaking and to concentrate on making films which uncompromisingly analyze reality, films which serve the oppressed of the world, while at the same time lifting the self-inflicted oppression which limits the form of our own vision.

—Peter Wintonick

POINT OF ORDER
distributed by:
Zenger Video
10200 Jefferson Boulevard
Culver City, CA USA 90232
tel: (213) 839-2436
or (800) 421-4246

RUSH TO JUDGEMENT
IN THE YEAR OF THE PIG
AMERICA IS HARD TO SEE
MILLHOUSE: A WHITE COMEDY
UNDERGROUND
IN THE KING OF PRUSSIA
distributed by:
MPI Media Group
16101 S. 108th Ave
Orland Park, Il USA 60462
tel: (708) 777-2223
or (800) 323-0442

PAINTERS PAINTING
distributed by:
Mystic Fire Video
P.O. Box 1202
Montauk, NY USA 11954
tel: (800) 727-8433

MR HOOVER AND I does not yet have a distributor.

1967 October 21 As a kid barely out of diapers, Peter Wintonick hears that famous baby doctor Benjamin Spock has been arrested in a protest at the Pentagon in Washington. Writer Norman Mailer and linguist Noam Chomsky share a jail cell after being arrested along with hundreds of others for "refusing to move."

1984 In Toronto, Wintonick meets Mark Achbar at a gathering of volunteers working on Peter Watkin's *The Journey*, a 14.5-hour global film project on nuclear peace and the media.

1985 Apprehensively, Achbar approaches Chomsky for an interview at the University of Toronto after a lecture entitled "The Drift Toward Global War." He finds the man once described in *The New York Times* as "arguably the most important intellectual alive" disarmingly accessible.

1986 Wintonick (unbeknownst to Achbar), after hearing Chomsky speak at Queen's University in Kingston, Ontario, casually proposes a film on Chomsky to a senior bureaucrat at the National Film Board of Canada (NFB). Just as casually, the idea is rejected.

1987 Convinced Chomsky's views are seriously under-represented in the media, Achbar (unbeknownst to Wintonick) works to develop a film with friends in Toronto, but philosophical differences lead to a painful parting of ways.

1987 May 11 In response to a proposal for a film with his political analysis at the core, Chomsky writes, "I was intrigued to hear about your idea of a film project, and naturally pleased that you are considering it and regard it as a useful idea."

1988 Over a bottle of Scotch, Achbar and Wintonick finally recognize their shared goal and pursue the Chomsky film, based in Montréal. They establish their production company, Necessary Illusions (NI), and spend most of the year writing proposals, accumulating letters of support, and applying for grants.

The Canada Council, a federal arts funding agency, awards Achbar $16,000. Wintonick solicits $5,000 from a private investor. TV news boss and movie star Ed Asner comes through with an enthusiastic letter and $250.

1988 August Equipped with two wind-up 16mm Bolex cameras, the filmmakers travel to Long Island, New York, to shoot the book *Manufacturing Consent* hot off the presses. In Japan, Chomsky picks up his $350,000 (US) Kyoto Prize for Basic Science—Japan's most prestigious honor in the field. NI hires a local crew to tag along.

1988 October Equipment upgrade to a government-surplus (motorized) 16mm camera formerly owned by the Royal Canadian Mounted Police. Filming in Toronto and Hamilton as Chomsky records the Massey Lectures, a week-long nightly presentation on the Canadian Broadcasting Corporation's national radio network. (The lectures are later published as *Necessary Illusions: Thought Control in Democratic Societies*, which makes the Canadian paperback best-seller list.)

1989 March At the Genie Awards (Canada's Oscars), the filmmakers meet a white-haired gentleman with a hearing aid, apparently detached from the proceedings. Turns out his hearing is just fine and he's actually listening to a Blue Jays baseball game on his radio. He's philanthropist Dr. Nick Laidlaw, supporter of artists, intellectuals and athletes with subsistence grants from his trust fund. The filmmakers each receive $1,000 per month for a year. Sadly, Dr. Laidlaw does not live to see the film completed.

1989 April Francis Miquet, a former student of Wintonick, joins NI and takes on duties as general manager, line producer, archival researcher, bookkeeper, camera operator and, eventually, associate producer and sound-effects editor.

With desktop publishing, the team lays out a 40-page proposal. Tailoring versions to Canadian and foreign readers, they print 4,000 copies on newsprint. Personalized letters and proposals hit every foundation, corporate charity and rich producer with a fixed address, and every Canadian, U.S. and

European broadcaster. Lucas, Spielberg, CBS, CBC and the Coca-Cola Corporation politely pass on the project. Dutch, Finnish and Norwegian TV eagerly commit to buy the film—C.O.D.

1989 October Out of money. Thousands of feet of unprocessed film lie in cans in Achbar's living room. The filmmakers arrange the cans sympathetically, take fuzzy, terrorist-style polaroids, send them with ransom notes to studio heads at the NFB, and hope someone will liberate the latent images held hostage.

1990 January With the backing of producer Adam Symansky, a co-production deal for technical services is signed with the NFB's Studio C. The film is processed and the images are released unharmed.

1990-91 Deferring half their (already meager) salaries, and fund-raising between shoots, the filmmakers continue sporadic filming in England, France, Holland, Germany, Washington, Seattle, Laramie, Rowe, Rochester, Boston and Nanaimo.

Early 1990s NI contracts Media Network, a non-profit fiscal agent in New York, to channel donations from U.S. sources. In Canada, Vision/TV ("Canada's Faith Network") provides the same service. Vision offers a broadcast license fee, which helps trigger investment from Telefilm (Canada's film and television investment agency). Further contributions come from hundreds of organizations and individuals.

1990-92 A two-and-a half-hour video rough-cut is the best-attended film of the Guelph International Film Festival. A chance conversation with the projectionist reveals that his company has installed "the world's largest permanent point-of-purchase video wall" in a nearby shopping mall.

1991 February Cameras (but not tape recorders) are strictly forbidden on a tour of *The New York Times*. However, an interview is permitted on the premises with editorial writer Karl E. Meyer. The crew sneaks around afterward grabbing shots.

1991-92 While Wintonick continues to edit, dramatic segments are designed and shot. In one sequence, the filmmakers wear medical garb to graphically portray how *The New York Times* surgically removed key sections of a London *Times* article on East Timor before reprinting it. Technicians in the NFB's animation department are puzzled when the filmmakers continue their work in costume long after their cameo cutaways have been filmed.

Illustrative animation is shot and live-action footage already shot is "re-contextualized" or re-filmed on huge video screens in malls, stadiums and other public spaces.

Cutting continues for a year. Assistant editor Katharine Asals and sound editor Francis Miquet continue to unearth and clear archival shots.

Early 1992 The filmmakers realize their material has the potential to sustain both a theatrical feature documentary and, if "re-packaged," a multi-part TV program. They expand the film from its original 75 minutes to 165 minutes and build in an intermission.

1992 June 18 First test print is shown at the Sydney Film Festival in Australia. An audience poll gives *Manufacturing Consent* the highest "loved it" rating of all 47 documentaries in the festival—the first official recognition of many the film will receive in its global tour of more than 50 film festivals.

In *Manufacturing Consent*, Noam Chomsky is interviewed by:

PAUL ANDREWS
The Seattle Times
Seattle, Washington

DAVID BARSAMIAN
Alternative Radio
Boulder, Colorado

WILLIAM F. BUCKLEY, JR.
Firing Line
USA

DAVID FRUM
Washington Post, Saturday Night
Toronto, Ontario

PETER JAY
The Jay Interview
London Weekend Television

RON LINVILLE
TV Dinner
Rochester, New York

ROBERT MACNEIL
MacNeil/Lehrer NewsHour
USA

SARAH McCLENDON
White House Reporter
Washington, DC

MARCI RANDALL MILLER
Student, KUWR Radio
Laramie, Wyoming

BILL MOYERS
A World of Ideas
USA

DAVID RANSOM
ABC
Australia

JONATHAN RÉE
Radical Philosophy magazine
London, England

ROSS REYNOLDS
KUOW Radio
Seattle, Washington

ED ROBINSON
Non-Corporate News
Lynn, Massachusetts

ELIZABETH SIKOROVSKY
KARINE KLEINHAUS
American Focus Student Radio

JONATHAN STEINBERG
Historian, BBC-3 Radio
Cambridge, England

JOOP VAN TIJN
Humanist TV
Holland

PETER WORTHINGTON
(fmr.) Editor, Ottawa Sun
Ottawa, Ontario

MARTIN WOOLLACOTT
The Guardian
London, England

Also appearing:

CARLOS ALFONSO
East Timorese Refugee
Portugal

EDWARD BERMAN
Publisher, Town Talk
Media, Pennsylvania

FRITZ BOLKESTIEN
(fmr.) Minister of Defense
Holland

ELAINE BRIÈRE
East Timor Alert Network
Vancouver, B.C.

GEORGE BUSH
(fmr.) President
United States of America
(Inauguration Address)

NIM CHIMPSKY
Chimpanzee
As seen on TV

ROBERT FAURISSON
Revisionist Author
Paris, France

KELVIN FLOOK
Video Host
Erin Mills Town Center

MICHEL FOUCAULT
Philosopher
Paris, France

JEFF GREENFIELD
Producer, Nightline
New York, New York

PIERRE GUILLAUME
Revisionist Publisher
Paris, France

JEFF HANSEN
Public Radio
Madison, Wisconsin

LOIE HAYES
KARIN AGUILAR-SAN JUAN
South End Press Collective
Boston, Massachusetts

EDWARD S. HERMAN
Wharton School of Finance
University of Pennsylvania

PETER JENNINGS
Executive Editor
World News Tonight, ABC

ARNOLD KOHEN
Journalist
Washington, DC

JOHN LAWTON
Producer, Channel 4
London, England

LINDA TRICHTER METCALF
Workshop Participant, founder,
Rowe, Massachusetts

KARL E. MEYER
Editorial Writer
The New York Times

JIM MORGAN
Corporate Relations
The New York Times

YOSSI OLMERT
Tel Aviv University

JOSE RAMOS-HORTA
East Timor Representative, UN
New York, New York

BODHAN SENKOW
Main Street Manager
Media, Pennsylvania

GREG SHACKLETON
Channel 7
Melbourne, Australia

JOHN SILBER
President, Boston University

SERGE THION
Indochina Specialist
Paris, France

TED TURNER
Executive V.P., CNN
Atlanta, Georgia

LYDIA SARGENT
MICHAEL ALBERT
Editors, Z Magazine
Boston, Massachusetts

TOM WOLFE
Author
New York, New York

Peter Wintonick has worked in film for over two decades.

Manufacturing Consent, Wintonick's first major non-fiction feature, focuses his wide-ranging experience and commitment to social action film on a subject close to him—the media.

His recent work includes four years as the Canadian producer and post-production coordinator for Peter Watkins' fourteen-and-a-half-hour megadocumentary, *The Journey*, about nuclear peace, development and the media. He was associate producer and editor on Nettie Wild's *A Rustling of Leaves: Inside the Philippine Revolution*, about the present political situation in the Philippines (Most Popular Film, Berlin Forum '89; People's Choice, Salute to the Documentary, Canada '89); and was supervising editor on Ron Mann's off-beat *Comic Book Confidential* (Best Documentary, Genie Awards, Canada: Hugo Award, Chicago International Film Festival).

Wintonick produced and directed *The New Cinema*, a video documentary about independent film (Blue Ribbon Award, American Film Festival). He has also edited feature films and, in another lifetime, directed corporate videos and audiovisuals.

He was a witty and frequent contributor to Canada's national film magazine, *Cinema Canada*, analyzing film culture, discovering new trends in young and independent film, and fomenting debate about the future of a national cinema. He has also been a programmer for the Montreal International Festival of New Cinema & Video and has taught university-level film history.

During his career in the commercial film industry, Wintonick worked for and with some of the major movers (and snakes) in the Motion Picture Jungle. After graduating from the film program at Algonquin College in Ottawa, his initiation into the world of film and politics was on the post-production of former Canadian Prime Minister Pierre E. Trudeau's early campaign films. He has aided and abetted the development of many young independent filmmakers, ceaselessly acting as associate producer, editor and consultant on numerous projects.

Since 1975, **Mark Achbar** has applied a wide range of creative abilities and technical skills to over 50 films, videos and books.

Contributing to many aspects of each project he undertakes, Achbar has, in various combinations, directed, produced, written, shot and edited experimental films and videos, social service documentaries, and (even) corporate productions.

Early career efforts integrated administrative positions with camera, sound and post-production on an assortment of dramas and documentaries: *Danger Bay*, a family series for CBC/DISNEY; *Spread Your Wings*, 26 half-hours on youth and creativity for CBC; *Partners in Development*, a PR film for the Canadian International Development Agency; and *When We First Met*, an HBO TV movie.

At Syracuse University, Achbar received a fine arts degree in filmmaking, and endured an internship on *Bill Daily's Hocus Pocus Gang* in Hollywood. He has since worked continually with issue-oriented independent media-makers: as cinematographer on Keith Hlady's *There Is a Rally*, about the huge 1982 peace rally in New York; as videographer and associate producer on Jim Morris' *The Stag Hotel*, on the lives of men in a decaying hotel (Best Documentary, Athens Video Festival); as post-production supervisor on Peter Monet's *East Timor, Betrayed But Not Beaten*, a half-hour documentary featuring Noam Chomsky, about Canada's role in the genocide in East Timor; as videographer, interviewer, researcher, fundraiser, and information systems designer during his three-year support of Peter Watkins' epic peace film, *The Journey*; and as editor, researcher and production coordinator on Robert Del Tredici's *At Work in the Fields of the Bomb*, a photo/text book on H-bombs. The book won the prestigious Olive Branch Award.

In 1986, Achbar received a Gemini nomination for Best Writer on *The Canadian Conspiracy*, a cultural/political satire about Canada taking over the United States. Co-written with director Robert Boyd, the 75-minute program won a Gemini for Best Entertainment Special and was nominated for an International Emmy. *Manufacturing Consent* is Achbar's first feature documentary.

MANUFACTURING CONSENT:
Noam Chomsky and the Media

FILM FESTIVALS

1992
Sydney (Australia)
Festival of Festivals (Toronto)
Independent Feature Project Market
   (New York)
Atlantic (Halifax)
Vancouver
Chicago
Human Rights (Minneapolis)
Denver
Nyon (Switzerland)
Nouveau Cinéma et de la Vidéo (Montréal)
Festival of the Americas
   (Washington and Los Angeles)
São Paulo (Brazil)
Brisbane (Australia)

1993
Palm Springs (California)
Yukon
Berlin (Forum)
Cinéma du Réel (Paris)
Cape Town
Hong Kong
Quinzaine du Cinéma Québecois (Montréal)
Athens (Ohio)
Cinémas du Canada (Paris)
Hong-Kong
EarthPeace (Burlington, Vermont)
Jerusalem
Seattle
Global Visions (Edmonton)
Auckland (New Zealand)
Wellington (NZ)
Auchen (Germany)
Munich
Potsdam (Germany)
American Film and Video (Niles, Illinois)
National Educational Film and Video
   (San Francisco)
Council on Foundations (Washington, D.C.)
Montage '93 (Rochester, New York)
Cambridge (England)
Galway (Ireland)
Daily Mail (Johannesburg)

Charlotte (North Carolina)
Durban (South Africa)
Ghent (Belgium)
Taipei (Taiwan)
Yamagata (Japan,
   the "Olympics" of non-fiction film events)
Blois (France)
Mill Valley (California)
Stockholm
World Community (Courtney, British Columbia)
Thessaloniki (Greece)
Amsterdam (pre-festival)
Sarajevo
International Documentary Association Awards

1994
Bombay
Istanbul
NAT (Copenhagen, Denmark)
Mexico City
and so on .....

AWARDS AND DISTINCTIONS:

Best Political Documentary
1994 Toronto Hot Docs Film Festival

Gold Conch
1994 Bombay International Film Festival

Critics' Award
1994 Bombay International Film Festival

Gold Apple
1993 National Educational Film and Video Festival

Gold Hugo (Best Social/Political Documentary)
1992 Chicago International Film Festival

Gold Sesterce (Grand Prize)
1992 Nyon International Documentary Film Festival

Special Mention, FIPRESCI International Press Jury
1992 Nyon International Documentary Film Festival

Special Mention, Public Jury
1992 Nyon International Documentary Film Festival

**Federal Express Award for Most Popular
Canadian Film**
1992 Vancouver International Film Festival

Special Mention, Unanimous Jury Award
1992 Toronto International Festival of Festivals

Jury Prize for Excellence
1992 Atlantic Film Festival

Public's "Most Loved" Documentary
1992 Sydney International Film Festival

Honorable Mention
1993 American Film and Video Festival

Director's Choice Award
1993 Charlotte Film and Video Festival

Voted **"Best of the Festival"** by public
1993 Edmonton Global Visions Film Festival

TO RENT OR BUY THE 16MM FILM OR VHS VIDEOTAPE OF *MANUFACTURING CONSENT: NOAM CHOMSKY AND THE MEDIA*, PLEASE CONTACT THE APPROPRIATE DISTRIBUTOR

AUSTRIA
Non-Theatrical
Bundesministerium für Unterricht Und Kunst
Plunkergrasse 3-5
A-1150 Wien
tel: (1) 53120-4846 fax: (1) 53120-4848

AUSTRALIA & NEW ZEALAND
Theatrical, Non-theatrical, Home video. Also available: a series of seven, short, "Discussion Starter" videos, drawn from the film, designed for classroom use with this book, complete with study guide.
Gil Scrine Films
24 Empire Street
NSW 2045
tel: (2) 716-6354 fax: (2) 716-8266

CANADA
Theatrical
Libra Films
96 Spadina Avenue
Suite 302
Toronto, ON M5V 2J6
tel: (416) 203-2171 fax: (416) 203-2173

Non-theatrical, Home video, "Discussion Starters"
National Film Board of Canada
P.O. Box 6100
Stn. A
Ville St-Laurent, QC H3C 3H5
tel: 1 800 668-6322 or (514) 283-9000

QUEBEC & CANADA
(French sub-titled version)
Theatrical, Non-theatrical, Home video
Cinéma Libre
4067 St-Laurent Blvd.
Suite 403
Montreal, QC H2W 1Y7
tel: (514) 849-7888 fax: (514) 849-1231

FRANCE (sub-titled)
Theatrical, Non-theatrical, Home video
K-Films
111, rue Saint Maur
75011 Paris
tel: (1) 43 57 65 15 fax: (1) 40 21 91 57

GERMANY (sub-titled)
Theatrical
Freunde der Deutschen Kinemathek
Wolserstraat, 25
1000 Berlin 30
tel: (30) 2 13 60 39 fax: (30) 2 18 42 81

INDIA
Theatrical
Bombay International Film Festival
Ministry of Information and Broadcasting
24 Dr. Gopairao Deshmukh Marg
Bombay-400 026
tel: (22) 3864633 fax: (22) 3860308

Home video
Anand Patwardhan
P.O. Box No 5216
Dadar (E)
Bombay 400 014
tel: (22) 414-3782 fax: (22) 414-2946

JAPAN
Theatrical (sub-titled)
Cinematrix
Kitagawa Bldg., 4th fl
6-42 Kagurazaka
Shinjuku-ku
Tokyo 162
tel: (3) 3266-9704 fax: (3) 3266-9700

Non-theatrical, Home video
(English version)
ADHOC
Nt. Bldg 6
7F 15-8 Nakata 2
Chikusa-KU
Nagoya 464

SPAIN
Theatrical/Non-theatrical/Home video
Sementera
Elkano, 48
08004 Barcelona
tel: (34-3) 303-17-74 fax: (34-3) 329-07-83

SWEDEN
Theatrical/Non-theatrical/Home video
Folkets Bio
St. Nygatan 21 Box 2068
103 12 Stockholm
tel: (8) 4020826 fax: (8) 4020827

UNITED-KINGDOM
Theatrical
ICA Projects
The Mall
London SW1Y 5AH
tel: (71) 930-0493 fax: (71) 873-0051

Non-theatrical, Home video
Connoisseur Video
10A Stephen Mews
London W1P OAX
tel: (71) 957-8957 fax: (71) 957-8968

UNITED-STATES
**Theatrical, Non-theatrical, Home video
& "Discussion Starter" videos (see above)**
Zeitgeist Films
247 Center Street
2nd Floor
New York, NY 10013
tel: (212) 274-1989
to order the home video or additional
copies of this book: 1-800-MANU-CON
fax: (212) 274-1644

Manufacturing Consent has been sold to television in 15 countries so far. Several sub-titled versions now exist on video, however, different countries use different video formats. For further information please contact:

Necessary Illusions
24 Mount Royal West, #1008
Montreal, Quebec
Canada H2T 2S2
tel: (514) 287-7337 fax: (514) 287-7620

RESOURCE GUIDE

POLITICAL BOOKS

BY NOAM CHOMSKY:

American Power and the New Mandarins (New York: Pantheon, 1969)

At War with Asia (New York: Pantheon, 1970)

Problems of Knowledge and Freedom: The Russell Lectures (New York: Pantheon, 1971)

For Reasons of State (New York: Pantheon, 1973)

Peace in the Middle East? Reflections on Justice and Nationhood (New York: Pantheon, 1974)

Language and Responsibility (New York: Pantheon, 1979)

Radical Priorities (Montréal: Black Rose, 1981)

Towards a New Cold War: Essays on the Current Crisis and How We Got There (New York: Pantheon, 1982)

The Fateful Triangle: The United States, Israel and the Palestinians (Boston: South End Press • Montréal: Black Rose Books, 1983)

Turning the Tide: U.S. Intervention in Central America and the Struggle for Peace (Boston: South End Press, 1985 • expanded edition: Montréal: Black Rose Books, 1987)

Pirates and Emperors: International Terrorism and the Real World (New York: Claremont Research and Publications, 1986 • Montréal: Black Rose Books, 1987)

On Power and Ideology: The Managua Lectures (Boston: South End Press • Montréal: Black Rose Books, 1987) Lectures delivered at the Universidad Centroamericana, Managua, in March 1986.

The Chomsky Reader (New York: Pantheon, 1987)

The Culture of Terrorism (Boston: South End Press • Montréal: Black Rose Books, 1988)

Necessary Illusions: Thought Control in Democratic Societies (Boston: South End Press • in Canada, published by Anansi Press distributed by General Publishing, 1989)

Language and Politics (Montréal: Black Rose, 1989)

Terrorizing the Neighborhood: American Foreign Policy in the Post-Cold War Era (Stirling, Scotland: AK Press, 1991)

Deterring Democracy. With a new afterword (New York: Hill and Wang • Scarborough: Harper Collins Canada, 1992)

Chronicles of Dissent (Monroe, ME: Common Courage Press • Vancouver: New Star Books, 1992)

What Uncle Sam Really Wants (Berkeley: Odonian Press, 1992)

Year 501: The Conquest Continues (Boston: South End Press • Montréal: Black Rose Books, 1993)

Rethinking Camelot: JFK, the Vietnam War, and US. Political Culture (Boston: South End Press • Montréal: Black Rose Books, 1993)

Letters From Lexington: Reflections on Propaganda (Monroe, ME: Common Courage Press, 1993)

The Prosperous Few and the Restless Many (Berkeley: Odonian Press, 1993)

Keeping the Rabble in Line (Monroe, ME: Common Courage Press, 1994)

World Orders Old and New (New York: Columbia University Press, 1994)

BY NOAM CHOMSKY AND EDWARD S. HERMAN

Counter-Revolutionary Violence: Bloodbaths in Fact and Propaganda Preface by R. Falk (Andover, MA: Warner Modular Publications, 1973) Module no. 57

The Political Economy of Human Rights (2 volumes) (Boston: South End Press • Montréal: Black Rose Books, 1979)

Manufacturing Consent: The Political Economy of the Mass Media (New York: Pantheon, 1988)

BY EDWARD S. HERMAN:

Corporate Control, Corporate Power
(Cambridge: Cambridge University Press, 1981)

The Real Terror Network: Terrorism in Fact and Propaganda (Boston: South End Press • Montréal: Black Rose Books, 1982)

Demonstration Elections: U.S.-Staged Elections in the Dominican Republic, Vietnam and El Salvador with Frank Brodhead (Boston: South End Press, 1984)

The Rise and Fall of the Bulgarian Connection with Frank Brodhead, (New York: Sheridan Square Publications, 1986)

"Gatekeeper Versus Propaganda Models: A Critical American Perspective," in Peter Golding, Graham Murdock and Philip Schlesinger, eds., **Communicating Politics: Essays in Memory of Philip Elliott** (Leicester: University of Leicester Press, 1986)

"Diversity of News: 'Marginalizing' the Opposition," **Journal of Communications** (Summer 1985)

The "Terrorism Industry": The Experts and Institutions That Shape Our View of Terror with Gerry O'Sullivan (New York: Pantheon, 1989)

"U.S. Mass Media Coverage of the U.S. Withdrawal from UNESCO," one of three chapters in **Hope and Folly: The United States and UNESCO, 1945-1985** with William Preston, Jr. and Herbert Schiller (Minneapolis: University of Minnesota Press, 1989)

Beyond Hypocrisy: Decoding the News in an Age of Propaganda, With a Doublespeak Dictionary for the 1990s (Boston: South End Press • Montréal: Black Rose Books, 1992)

AN INTRODUCTION TO CHOMSKY'S LINGUISTICS WRITINGS

(Compiled and annotated by Carlos P. Otero)

Overviews:
Newmeyer, Frederick, **Grammatical Theory** (Chicago: University of Chicago Press, 1983)

Salkie, Raphael, **The Chomsky Update: Linguistics and Politics** (London: Unwin Hyman, 1990)

Otero, Carlos P., **Chomsky's Revolution: Cognitivism and Anarchism**. Oxford: Blackwell (forthcoming), part III (and references therein)

Textbooks:
Freidin, Robert. **Foundations of Generative Syntax** (Massachusetts: MIT Press, 1992)

Cowper, Elisabeth. **Introduction to Syntactic Theory** (Chicago: The University of Chicago Press, 1992)

Haegeman, Liliane, **Introduction to Government and Binding Theory** (Oxford: Blackwell, 1991)
and references therein

History of Generative Grammar:
Chomsky, Noam, **Generative Grammar: Its Basis, Development and Prospects** (Kyoto: Kyoto University of Foreign Studies, 1987)
Studies in English Linguistics and Literature, Special Issue

Newmeyer, Frederick, **Linguistic Theory in America: The First Quarter-Century of Transformational Generative Grammar** (New York: Academic Press, 1980)
Revised edition, 1986

CHOMSKY'S MOST IMPORTANT LINGUISTIC STUDIES

Early Generative Grammar:
Morphophonemics of Modern Hebrew
(Master's thesis)
(University of Pennsylvania, June 1951)
Published in 1979 by Garland Publications in its series "Outstanding Dissertations." Elaboration of an undergraduate thesis completed in 1949, when he was 20, and revised further in late 1951. The first modern generative (but not yet transformational) grammar, and a crucial step in the path to his first master-work, a new approach to language structure. It was further elaborated in the monumental **The Sound Pattern of English,** which was co-authored with Morris Hall (New York: Harper & Row, 1968)
Paperback edition: (MIT Press, 1991, with a Preface dated August 1990)

The Logical Structure Of Linguistic Theory
Ms, MIT, 1955-56 (close to 1,000 pages; published in part by University of Chicago Press in 1975, in paperback in 1985), technical presentation of the original theory. His first **magnum opus**.

Syntactic Structures
(The Hague: Mouton, 1957)
Little more than an abstract of parts of LSLT, with additional material on algebraic linguistics. This small book placed him overnight at the forefront of the field:
"[Chomsky's] theory proved to be a central strand in the dramatic change in perspective in the history of psychology that thirty years later was to become widely known as the 'cognitive revolution' of the mid-1950s, the starting point of current work in the cognitive sciences. In the late 1950s Chomsky went on to become the founder of algebraic linguistics (a new branch of abstract algebra sometimes referred to as 'mathematical linguistics') 'and by far the best man in the exciting new field,'" in the words of one of the most eminent practitioners, Israeli logician and mathematician Yehoshua Bar-Hillel.

Language and Information: Selected Essays on their Theory and Application
(Reading, MA: Addison-Wesley, 1964)
(Jerusalem: The Jerusalem Academic Press, Ltd., 1964, p.16.)

Aspects of the Theory of Syntax
(The MIT Press, 1965)
A systematic presentation of the "standard theory," the first thorough revision of his original theory.

Studies on Semantics in Generative Grammar
(The Hague: Mouton, 1972)
A non-systematic presentation of the so-called "extended standard theory" (EST).

Essays on Form and Interpretation
(New York: North-Holland, 1977)
The "conditions framework" and other major steps towards the principles-and-parameters theory.

The Principles-and-Parameters Theory: Lectures on Government and Binding
(Dordrecht, Holland: Foris, 1981)
An extensive presentation of a much improved version of generative grammar (His second, and perhaps truly revolutionary, **magnum opus**.)

Barriers
(MIT Press, 1986)
A very small book (95 pages), but a major step towards the current theory.

"A minimalist program for linguistic theory," in **The View from Building 20: Essays in Linguistics in Honor of Sylvain Bromberger** edited by Kenneth Hale & Samuel Jay Keyser. (MIT Press, 1953, 1-52)
A radical revision of the principles-and-parameters theory, now much simpler and deeper (if correct).

SOME SUGGESTED MAGAZINES

(For a more complete listing see the **Alternative Press Index**)

A*C*E, The Association of Clandestine Radio Enthusiasts
P.O. Box 1744
Wilmington, DE, USA 19899
Publishes international reports on pirate and clandestine radio.

The Activist
736 Bathurst Street
Toronto, Ontario, Canada M5S 2R4
The Activist *is Ontario's monthly peace newspaper bringing you the latest news of peace and human rights from around the world, First Nations here at home, peace campaigns, and so much more!*

Adbusters Quarterly: A Magazine of Media and Environmental Strategies
The Media Foundation
1243 W. 7th Avenue
Vancouver, British Columbia, Canada V6H 1B7
(604) 736-9401
Detailed deconstruction of ads and media, counter-advertising strategies. Hip layout.

Afterimage
31 Prince Street
Rochester NY, USA 14607
(716) 442-8676
Theories and happenings in video and other arts.

Alternatives—Perspectives on Society, Technology and Environment
c/o Faculty of Environmental Studies
University of Waterloo
Waterloo, Ontario, Canada N2L 3G1
Canada's environmental quarterly since 1971.

Briarpatch
2138 McIntyre Street
Regina, Saskatchewan, Canada S4P 2R7
The nuclear industry, aboriginal rights, unemployment, progressive social policy, agriculture, and rural issues: 10 times a year.

Bulletin of Concerned Asian Scholars
3239 9th Street
Boulder, CO, USA 80304

Canadian Dimension
707-228 Notre Dame Avenue
Winnipeg, Manitoba, Canada R3B 1N7
Published 8 times a year. An independent journal of the Left commenting on issues of labor, trade, peace movements, politics, US policies, daycare and aboriginal rights.

Counterpunch
1601 Connecticutt Avenue NW
Washington, DC USA 20009
(202) 234-9382
Investigative newsletter edited by Ken Silverstein and Alexander Cockburn.

Covert Action Information Bulletin
1500 Massachusetts Avenue
Room 732
Washington, D.C., USA 20005
Straight information on disinformation.

Drop Out Magazine
992 Valencia Street
San Francisco, CA, USA 94110
"The 100 percent true 'zine for indie media-makers"

Extra!
Fairness and Accuracy In Reporting
130 W. 25th Street
New York City, NY, USA 10001
(212) 633-6700
See listing under organizations: 8 issues per year.

Felix
published by the Standby Program
P.O. Box 184 Prince Street Stn.
New York, NY, USA 10012
(212) 219-0951
Video art and theory, often with political angles

Grand Street
50 Riverside Drive
New York City, NY, USA 10024
Distributed by:
B.DeBoer, Inc
113 E. Center Street
Nutley, N.J., USA 07110

Green Anarchist
P.O. Box H
34 Cowley Road
Oxford, England, UK OX4
Best British left Green periodical.

Ideas and Actions
P.O. Box 40400
San Francisco, CA, USA 94140
Anarcho-syndicalist periodical.

The Independent
625 Broadway, 9th Floor
New York, NY, USA 10012
(212) 473-3400
Published by AIVF, includes articles and listings on independent film and video.

Index on Censorship
39 Islington High St.
London, England, UK N1 9LH
071-278-2313
Underreported, censored; the news behind the news.

In These Times
P.O. Box 1912
Mount Morris, IL, USA 61054
1-800-827-0270 / (312)772-0100
Editorial Offices
2040 N. Milwaukee Ave.
Chicago, IL, USA 60647
Popular socialist periodical

The LPTV Report
P.O. Box 25510
Milwaukee WI, USA 53225
(414) 781-0188
Reports on legal and business issues with some technical information.

Left Business Observer
250 West 85th St.
New York, NY USA 10024
(212) 874-4020

Lies Of Our Times
Institute of Media Analysis
145 W 4th Street
New York City, NY, USA 10012
(212) 254-1061 Fax: (212) 254-9598
For description, see page 56.

Love and Rage
P.O. Box 853
Stuyvesant Station
New York City, NY, USA 10009
(212) 460-8390
Spanish/English revolutionary anarchist paper.

Magicamerica
Videoteca del Sur
P.O. Box 20068
New York, NY, USA 10009
Newsletter on popular video movement in Latin America. In Spanish.

Media Culture Review
100 East 85th St.
New York, NY, USA 10028
(212) 799-4822

Middle East Report
1500 Massachusetts Ave. Ste 119
Washington, DC USA 20005
(202) 223-3677
Excellent source of info and analysis on the region 6 times a year.

NACLA Report on the Americas
475 Riverside Drive
Room 454
New York, NY, USA 10115
(212) 870-3146
Excellent periodical reports on and analyzes Central American and Latin American affairs.

The Nation
72 Fifth Avenue
New York City, NY, USA 10011
(212) 242-8400
Longest established U.S. progressive weekly.

The New Internationalist
55 Rectory Road
Oxford, England, UK OX4 1BW
Reports on world poverty and inequality campaigns for radical change.

Third World Resurgence
P.O. Box 680
Manzanita, OR USA 97130
Terrific source of information about the Third World written by Third Worlders themselves.

Our Generation
C.P. 1258, Succ. Place du Parc
Montréal, Quebec, Canada H2W 2R3
(514) 844-4076
The theory and practice of contemporary anarchism and libertarian socialism.

Open Magazine Pamphlet Series
P.O. Box 2726
Westfield, NJ, USA 07091
(908) 789-9608
Speeches by progressive thinkers in print.

Peace Magazine
736 Bathurst Street
Toronto, Ontario, Canada M5S 2R4
Published 6 times a year. Reports on efforts to find non-violent resolutions of conflicts; examines violence in the media, reform of the UN, militarism, the environment, and disarmament.

Peace News
55 Dawes Street
London, England, UK SE17
The oldest radical pacifist periodical in Britain.

Processed World
41 Sutter Street, Suite 1829
San Francisco, CA, USA 94104
(415) 626-2979
Fax: 626-2685
Cheerfully vicious view of what it's like inside the information industry workworld. Includes great graphics.

The Progressive
409 East Main Street
Madison, WI, USA 53703
(608) 257-4626
Left-leaning liberal periodical.

Propaganda Review
Media Alliance, Building D
Fort Mason Center
San Francisco, CA, USA 94123
Analysis of media manipulations and ideology.

Radical Philosophy
John Fawel
Faculty of Mathematics
Open University
Milton Keynes, England, UK MK7 6AA

Release Print
Film Arts Foundation
346 9th St., 2nd Floor
San Francisco, CA, USA 94103
(415) 552-8760
Published by Film Arts Foundation, essential for West Coast independent producers!

Social Alternatives
Department of Government
University of Queensland
St. Lucia QLD, Australia
Libertarian New Left periodical.

Solidarity
123 Lathom Road
London, England, UK E6
Libertarian New Left periodical.

Third Text
303 Finchley Road
London, England, UK NW3 6DT
Critical articles on culture and media by critics and artists from developing nations, the UK and the US.

This Magazine
16 Skey Lane
Toronto, Ontario, Canada M6J 3S4
A lively left look at Canadian politics and culture, published 8 times a year.

Utne Reader
1624 Harmon Place
Suite 330
Minneapolis, MN, USA 55403
(612) 338-5040
E-mail: editor@utnereader.com
The Reader's Digest of the alternative press.

Video Networks
1111 17th Street
San Francisco, CA, USA 94107
(415) 861-3282
Published by the Bay Area Video Coalition, very helpful listings of festivals, distributors, funders, etc., for independent producers.

Wired
544 Second Street
San Francisco, CA, USA 94107-1427
1-800-SO WIRED
(415) 904-0660 Fax: (415) 904-0669
E-mail: editor@wired.com
The definitive resource for cutting-edge technologies.

Z Magazine
116 St. Botolph St.
Boston, MA, USA 02115
(617) 787-4531
See page 198

MEDIA LITERACY BOOKS

Camera Politica: The Politics and Ideology of Contemporary Hollywood Film Douglas Kellner and Michael Ryan (Bloomington: Indiana University Press, 1988)

CENSORED: The News That Didn't Make the News and Why Project Censored (Chapel Hill, North Carolina: Shelburne Press) *Project Censored selects the top 25 underreported stories of the year. For a free pamphlet listing the top 25 stories, send SASE to:* Project Censored
Sonoma State University
Rohnert Park, California, USA 94928

Critical Theory and Society: A Reader Co-edited by Douglas Kellner and Steve Best (Macmillan and Guilford Press, 1991)

Dangerous Assignments (A Study Guide) The Committee to Protect Journalists
16 East 42nd Street, Third Floor
New York City, NY, USA 10017
(212) 983-5355 Fax:(212) 867-1830

Inventing Reality Michael Parenti (St. Martin's Press, 2nd Edition, 1993)

Manufacturing Consent: The Political Economy of the Mass Media Edward S. Herman and Noam Chomsky (New York: Pantheon Books/Random House, 1988)

Mass Media and Popular Culture Barry Duncan (Toronto: Harcourt Brace Jovanovich, 1988) *Textbook by the president of the Association for Media Literacy.*

The Media Monopoly Ben Bagdikian, (Beacon Press, 4th edition, 1992)

Necessary Illusions Noam Chomsky (Boston: South End Press, 1989)

Networks of Power Dennis Mazzocco (Boston: South End Press, 1994)

The Persian Gulf TV War Douglas Kellner (Boulder: Westview Press, 1992)

Prime-Time Activism: Media Strategies for Organizing Charlotte Ryan (Boston: South End Press, 1991)

Television and the Crisis of Democracy D. Kellner (Boulder: Westview Press, 1990)

Unreliable Sources: A Guide to Detecting Bias in News Media Martin A. Lee and Norman Solomon (New York: Carol Publishing Group, 1990)

PUBLISHING HOUSES

AK Press
P.O. Box 40682
San Francisco, CA 94140-0682
(415) 923-1429

Between the Lines
394 Euclid Avenue, Suite 203
Toronto, Ontario, Canada M6G 2S9
(416) 925-8260

Black Rose Books
C.P.125, Succ. Place du Parc
Montréal, Quebec, Canada H2W 2R3
(514) 844-4076 Fax: (514) 849-1956
U.S.A: 340 Nagel Drive
Cheektowaga, NY, USA 14225
(716) 683-4547
Europe: 99 Wallis Road
London, England, UK E95LN
(081) 986-4854 Fax: (081) 533-5821

Common Courage Press
P.O. Box 702
Monroe, ME, USA 04951
1-800-497-3207

Monthly Review Foundation
122 West 27th Street
New York, NY, USA 10001
(212) 691-2555

The New Catalyst
P.O. Box 189
Gabriola Island, BC, Canada V0R 1X0

New Society Publishers
New Society Educational Foundation
4527 Springfield Avenue
Philadelphia, PA, USA 19143
1-800-333-9093

New Star
2504 York Avenue
Vancouver, BC, Canada V6K 1E3
(604) 738-9429

Odonian Press
P.O. Box 32375
Tucson, AZ USA 85751
(602) 269-4056

Pluto Press
345 Archway Road
London, England, UK N6 5AA
(081) 348-2724

South End Press
116 Saint Botolph Street
Boston, MA, USA 02115
1-800-533-8478

Verso
6 Meard Street
London, England, UK W1V 3HR
(071) 734-0059

Westview Press
5500 Central Avenue
Boulder, Colorado, USA 80301-2877

Zed Books
57 Caledonian Road
London, England, UK N1 9BU
(071) 837-4014

Wire Service

New Liberation News Service
PO Box 325
Kendall Square Branch
Cambridge, MA, USA 021442
(617) 492-8316
NLNS is a radical news service providing stories and graphics to over 200 student and alternative papers across the US every month.

Alternet/Institute for Alternative Journalism
77 Federal Street
San Francisco, CA, USA 94107
(415) 284-1420 fax: (415) 284-1414
Compuserve: 71362.27@compuserve.com
A project of IAJ, Alternet is an alternative news syndication service. See Organizations.

Activism and the Internet

Progressive activism is one of the thousands of topics discussed every day on the Internet, which itself is probably the only functioning anarchy on the planet. There are basically three forms of net communication: public (newsgroups), semi-private (mailing lists) and private (e-mail).

The extent of government surveillance of any of these three levels is unknown, and those who feel their discourse is sensitive might want to investigate the possibilities of PGP encryption, which was invented by a freelance hacker and is, to date, unbreakable. More information on it can be found on the newsgroup alt.security.pgp.

The newsgroup misc.activism.progressive is a repository of announcements, book lists, and similar information pointing the reader to related data on the net and in other media. There are over 4,000 newsgroups currently available in English, so a search of the list for keywords such as "politics" will turn up many others. A list of related mailing lists, is periodically posted to misc.activism.progressive.

Access to the net depends on one's geographical location and occupation. Many university students can get an account on a host machine for the asking. In some areas freenets have been established, providing mail and news access for a small donation, and some local BBSs have begun offering newsgroups and mail. The quality of modem and computer necessary to use the net is not high.

If it seems irritating that you can't just phone a 1-800 number and give them your credit card number, remember that this is because the net isn't a centralized corporation. There is no net headquarters anywhere, no board of directors, no CEO. If you disagree with something, you are free to speak up at any time, but there is no "management" to listen to your complaints.

– Kate McDonnell

Left On Line (LBBS)
18 Millfield St.
Woods Hole, MA 02543
(508) 548-9063
Information highway of the Left. Chomsky, Ehrenreich et al on line. Forums. Libraries. On line university courses with Chomsky and others.

Peacenet
18 DeBoom Street,
San Francisco, CA, USA 94107
(415) 442-0220
Runs great on-line BBS for activists of all types

Some Radio and Audio Sources

Alternative Radio
David Barsamian
2129 Mapleton
Boulder, CO, USA 80304
(303) 444-8788
A weekly, internationally syndicated one-hour radio program. Extensive catalogue of Chomsky lectures and interviews plus many other progressive speakers.

AMARC
World Association of Community Broadcasters
Head office 3575 Blvd. St. Laurent, Suite 704
Montréal, Quebec, Canada H2X 2T7
(514) 982-0351 Fax: (514) 849-7129
AMARC is an international organization serving the community radio movement. It is a network for exchange and solidarity among community broadcasters and its work involves consulting, coordinating and facilitating cooperation and exchange among community radio broadcasters worldwide.

AMARC Latin America
c/o CEPES
818 Avenida Salaberry
Jesus Maria
Lima, Peru
Tel: (51) 14-237-884 Fax: (51) 14-331-744

AMARC Africa
c/o CIERRO
B.P. 358
Ouagadougou
Burkina Faso
Tel: (226) 30-66-86 Fax: (226) 31-28-66

Counterspin
c/o FAIR
130 W. 25th Street
New York, NY, USA 10001
(212) 633-6700
Nationally syndicated weekly radio program

**Feminist International Radio Endeavor
(FIRE)**
c/o WINGS
P.O. Box 33220
Austin, TX, USA 78764-0220
(512) 416-9000

IDEAS
Canadian Broadcasting Corporation
P.O. Box 500
Station A
Toronto, Ontario, Canada M5W 1E6
*Some of the most thoughtful radio programs
in the world. Ask for a schedule & catalogue.*

**National Federation of Community
Broadcasters**
666 11th Street NW
Washington, DC, USA 20001
(202) 393-2355

Pacifica Radio Archive
3729 Cahuenga Boulevard West
North Hollywood, CA, USA 91604
(818) 506-1077

Pacifica Radio National Office
1929 Martin Luther King Jr. Way
Berkeley, CA 94704
(510) 843-0130

People's Video
P.O. Box 99514
Seattle, WA, USA 98199
Michael Parenti audio & video tapes & books.

Radio for Peace International
Apartado 88,
Santa Ana, Costa Rica
(506) 49-1821
*Shortwave radio programming at 0600 and
0030 UTC/15.030 MHz, 13.630 MHz and 7.375
MHz. In Spanish and English*

Radio Free Maine
Roger Leisner
P.O. Box 2705
Augusta, ME USA 04338
(207) 622-6629
*Wide assortment of progressive speakers,
always up to date.*

FILM/VIDEO SOURCES AND SOME OF THEIR
PRODUCTS

ALTERNATIVE VIEWS
P.O. Box 7279
Austin, TX, USA 78713
(512) 918-3386
*Since 1978, Drs. Frank Morrow and Doug
Kellner have produced, hosted, edited, and
distributed more than 380 editions of
Alternative Views, a vehicle for informing the
TV viewing public of news and views not seen
on mainstream media. It provides interviews,
documentaries and news from alternative
sources. It is the longest-running public-access
program in America and is distributed to more
than 55 cable systems, serving 270 cities and
more than 4 million households. In 1989, it
won the coveted George Stoney Award in
Humanistic Communications. Why not bring
Alternative Views to your community?*

**AMERICAN ARCHIVE OF
THE FACTUAL FILM**
The Parks Library, Iowa State University
Ames, Iowa, USA 50011-2140

Journalism 1940, Vocational Guidance Films
Inc. *American Archive of the Factual Film has
hundreds of enlightening movies like this.*

APPALSHOP
306 Madison Street
Whitesburg, KY, USA 41858
(606) 633-0108
*Produces documentaries on history, culture,
and social issues of Appalachia.*

BULLFROG FILMS
Oley, PA, USA 19547
1-800-543-FROG
In Search of the Edge
26 minutes, 1990
Scott Barrie
*Presents the argument that the earth is flat
from a well researched point of view. The film
and accompanying study guide are designed
as an educational tool to help young people
become critical viewers.*

CALIFORNIA NEWSREEL
149 Ninth Street/420
San Francisco, CA, USA 94103
(415) 621-6196

Color Adjustment
87 minutes, 1991
Marlon Riggs
*This exceptional film traces over 40 years of
race relations through the lens of prime time
entertainment. Interviews with black actors,
producers and scholars reveal how deep-seated racial conflict was absorbed into the familiar, non-threatening formats of the prime time
series.*

THE CINEMA GUILD
1697 Broadway
New York City, NY, USA 10019
(212) 246-5522

**Export TV: Anatomy of an Electronic
Invasion**
25 minutes, 1989
Monica Melamid
*Examines TV Marti, a U.S. government broad-
cast service beamed into Cuba by an intricate
satellite and weather balloon linkup in contra-
vention of international law and broadcast
regulations.*

If It Bleeds, It Leads
14 minutes, 1986
John Adkins
Examines local TV spot news coverage of local events involving violence or death, which are frequently used as the lead story on news programs. Raises important questions about sensationalism and the ethical and professional considerations of broadcast journalists.

Making the News Fit
28 minutes, 1986
Beth Sanders
Examines American media coverage of the war in El Salvador and how TV and print journalists cover a war in which the U.S. is deeply involved. Provides viewers with basic background information about the conflict, then analyzes media treatment of major issues such as the 1982 elections and the alleged arms flow from Nicaragua to El Salvador.

COLLISION COURSE VIDEO PRODUCTIONS
P.O. Box 347383
San Francisco, CA, USA 94134-7378
Producer/Distributor of activist video

DEEP DISH TV
339 Lafayette Street
New York, NY, USA 10012
(212) 473-8933
As part of the grassroots community-television movement, Deep Dish TV links community producers, programmers, activists and community members in order to address issues seldom represented in broadcast television. It produces and distributes programs on a range of social issues, often focusing on analysis of the mainstream media. Deep Dish is carried on more than 300 cable systems nationwide. There is no cost to downlink the programs for nonprofit, noncommercial use.

DESPITE TV
178 Whitechapel Road
London, England E1 IBJ
(071) 377-0737
Community producers from London's East End who chronicle urban developments, media misrepresentations, and cultural events.

DIRECT IMPACT
P.O. Box 423
Athens, GA, USA 30603
Makes PSAs for social change.

DIVA-TV
c/o ACT-UP
135 W. 29th Street, No. 10
New York, NY, USA 10001
(212) 564-2437
Video activists documenting the struggle against AIDS, particularly on the political front

DRIFT DISTRIBUTION
219 East 2nd Street SE
New York City, NY, USA 10009
(212) 254-4118
Fax: (212) 254-3154

The Machine that Killed Bad People
120 minutes, 1990
Steve Fagin
Playing with television forms such as the news broadcast, mini-series and the Home Shopping Network, this piece looks at recent events in the Philippines and examines the role of spectacle in the way people learn to see the world.

8mm NEWS COLLECTIVE
c/o Squeaky Wheel
372 Connecticut Street
Buffalo, NY, USA 14213
(716) 884-7172
Producers of "The News Diaries" who utilize an eclectic, confrontational style to challenge the way the news gets reported.

THE EMPOWERMENT PROJECT
3403 Hwy 54 West
Chapel Hill, NC USA 27516
(919) 967-1963

The Panama Deception
90 minutes, 1992
Barbara Trent
The alarming, untold story of the 1989 U.S. invasion of Panama, one of the Bush administration's major foreign policy disasters and public-relations successes. Explains how and why the U.S. media collaborated with the Bush administration to censor information and deceive the American public.

EQUINOX FILMS
200 West 72nd Street
Room 46, 4th Floor
New York City, NY, USA 10023
(212) 799-1515 Fax: (212) 799-1517

The Human Language
Excellent film series features Noam Chomsky and 50 other linguists, plus authors, comedians, Australian aborigines, actors, philosophers, former head hunters in Papua New Guinea, evolutionists, Innu, a cartoonist, a clown, baseball players, dogs and many, many children. These entertaining films "explain" language in a way that intelligent laypeople will understand and enjoy.

FULL FRAME
394 Euclid Avenue
Toronto, Ontario, M6G 2S9
Tel: (416) 925-9338 Fax: 324-8268
Distributes independently produced social and political films and documentaries

FLYING FOCUS VIDEO Collective
2306 N.W. Kearney, No. 231
Portland, OR, USA 97210
(503) 321-5051
Volunteer group that came together to contest Gulf War coverage. Now producing in other areas as well.

GLOBALVISION
1600 Broadway
Suite 700
New York City, NY, USA
(212) 246-0202

Rights and Wrongs
Regular TV program about human rights issues worldwide.

IDERA
200-2673 West Broadway
Vancouver, B.C., CANADA, V6K 2G3
(604) 738-8815
Non-profit distributor, specializes in Latin America & the Caribbean, Asia, Africa (largest collection on Southern Africa in Canada), Film Studies, Women & Development, Peace & Disarmament, International Economics, and Economics and Labour.

LABOR AT THE CROSSROADS
c/o Hunter College, Room 340
695 Park Avenue
New York, NY, USA 10021
(212) 772-4129
"Sweat TV" by workers and students.

LABOR BEAT
37 S. Ashland Avenue
Chicago IL, USA 60607
(312) 226-3330
Public access series on labor issues; shown in 12 cities and counting.

LABOR VIDEO PROJECT
P.O. Box 425584
San Francisco, CA, USA 94142
Produces public-access program on rank-and-file labor issues.

MEDIA COALITION FOR REPRODUCTIVE RIGHTS
c/o Squeaky Wheel/Heather Connor
372 Connecticut Street
Buffalo, NY, USA 14213
(716) 884-7172
Access producers responding to blockades of abortion clinics.

MEDIA NETWORK
39 West 14th Street
Suite 403
New York City, NY, USA
(212) 929-2663
*Media Network is a national (US) membership organization linking independent media producers with audiences who seek alternative points of view on the issues affecting their lives. Helped produce **Manufacturing Consent**.*

MISSION CREEK VIDEO
P.O. Box 411271
San Francisco, CA, USA 94141-1271
*Produces independent documentaries as well as public-access program **Mission Creek Presents**. Offers video classes.*

NATIVE AMERICAN PUBLIC BROAD-CASTING CONSORTIUM
P.O. Box 83111
Lincoln, NE 68501-3111
(402) 472-3522 Fax: (402) 472-1758

Images of Indians
5 parts, 30 minutes each, 1980
Robert Hagopian & Phil Lucas for
KCTS/9, Seattle
Five-part series examines stereotypes drawn by Hollywood movies and the effect these images have on Native Americans' self-image.

NECESSARY ILLUSIONS
24 Mount Royal West #1008
Montréal, Québec, Canada, H2T 2S2
(514) 287-7337 Fax: 287-7620
*Co-produced **Manufacturing Consent**. See profile, objectives on page 15. Always seeking projects to develop and support.*

NEW DAY FILM AND VIDEO
121 West 27 Street
New York City, NY, USA 10001
(212) 645-8548 Fax: 212-645-8652

Current Events 56 minutes, 1991
Ralph Arlyck
This film looks at our society, overwhelmed and numbed by a ceaseless stream of media images, examining how we respond—or don't respond—to the news.

NOT CHANNEL ZERO
P.O. Box 805
Bronx, NY, USA 10466
(212) 966-4510
Documentary forum that shows events in black and Hispanic communities from an Afrocentric perspective.

One For All
c/o Erin O'Meara
3925 N. Downer Avenue
Milwaukee, WI, USA 53211
(414) 963-4833
Viewer-participatory public-access series on community activism.

PBS VIDEO
1320 Braddock Place
Alexandria, VA, USA
1-800-344-3337
Fax: (703) 739-5269

The Agony of Decision: The Media and the Military
90 minutes, 1991
Fred W. Friendly
Focusing on media coverage of the Gulf War, this program is one in a series of roundtable discussions of media issues, hosted by Fred Friendly for PBS. Panelists typically include key players in the formation of U.S. policy. Contact PBS for other programs in this series.

Public Mind
60 minutes per segment, 1989
Alvin Perlmutter & Public Affairs TV
In this excellent four-part documentary, Bill Moyers explores the impact on democracy of a mass culture whose basic information comes from image-making, the media, public opinion polls, public relations and propaganda.

PACIFIC NATIONAL NEWS BUREAU
702 H. Street NW
Washington, DC, USA 20001
(202) 783-1620
News for Pacifica radio stations.

PAPER TIGER TV
339 Lafayette Street
New York City, NY, USA 10012
(212) 420-9045
CBS Tries the NY3
30 minutes, 1988
Paper Tiger TV
*Safya Bukhari-Alston and Brinn Glick discuss the CBS docudrama **Badge of the Assassin**, looking at the Black Panthers, COINTELIPRO and racism on TV. Bukhari-Alston is an activist and Glick is a lawyer for the New York Three.*

Lines in the Sand
28 minutes, 1992
Gulf Crisis TV Project
One in a series of 10 highly-recommended tapes from the Gulf Crisis TV Project that debunk media coverage of the conflict. Images from Iraq and a Middle East history lesson are combined, challenging the lack of information about the Gulf War.

PAPER TIGER TELEVISION/WEST
P.O. Box 411271
San Francisco, CA, USA 94141-1271
(415) 552 PTTV Fax: 695-0916
West Coast Paper Tiger Collective, also produces progressive news program "Finally Got the News".

PEOPLE'S VIDEO
P.O. Box 99514
Seattle, WA, USA 98199
(206) 789-5371
Video (or audio) of Michael Parenti's enlightening political talks.

POV
330 W. 58th Street, Suite 3A
New York, NY, USA 10019
(212) 397-0970
PBS series featuring U.S. indie documentaries.

REPROVISION
P.O. Box 2026
New York, NY, USA 10009
(212) 529-3287
Collective that produces tapes on reproductive rights.

SAWED ON TV
c/o Rob Danielson
2075 S. 13th Street
Milwaukee, WI, USA 53204
(414) 384-7083
Public-access shows available on mining, Native American, environmental and other issues.

SHERMAN GRINBERG FILM LIBRARIES
(212) 765-5170
Fax: (212) 262-1532
For ABC, Pathe News and Paramount News clips.

DAVID SHULMAN
594 Broadway #908
New York, NY, USA 10012
(212) 431-7781

Counterfeit Coverage
27 minutes, 1992
David Shulman and Karen Branan
In the tense days after the Iraqi invasion of Kuwait, stories of Iraqi atrocities—in particular
the removal of 312 babies from life-giving incubators in Kuwaiti hospitals by Iraqi soldiers—helped fuel public pressure on the governments of the West to go to war in the Gulf. That story was almost certainly false: this video investigates how and why it was spread and believed by practically everyone, including the United Nations.

TESTING THE LIMITS COLLECTIVE
31 W. 26th Street, 4th Floor
New York NY, USA 10010
(212) 545-7120
Documents the rising activism regarding AIDS, reproductive rights, and lesbian and gay issues

THIRD WORLD NEWSREEL
335 West 38th Street
5th Floor
New York City, NY, USA 10018
Tel: (212) 947-9277 Fax: (212) 594-6417

Muqaddimah Li-Nihayat Jidal (Introduction to the end of an argument) Speaking for oneself...Speaking for others...
45 minutes, 1990
Elia Suleiman and Jayce Salloum
Combining clips from feature films, documentaries, and news coverage with excerpts of live footage shot in the West Bank and Gaza Strip, this video critiques representation of the Middle East, Arab culture and the Palestinian people by the West.

Panic Is The Enemy
10 minutes, 1986
Third World Newsreel Workshop
This short video examines the press attention showered on Bernhard Goetz after he shot four youths, allegedly in self-defense, in a NYC subway car. Through-on-the street interviews, the video also examines the racist Goetz's form of panic.

THROUGH OUR EYES VIDEO & HISTORY PROJECT
c/o Pam Sporn
3341 Reservoir Oval, No. 6C
Bronx, NY, USA 10467
(212) 542-2700
Bronx teenagers take on the media.

TORRICE PRODUCTIONS
1230 Market Street #123
San Francisco, CA, USA 94103
(415) 826-0128

Peril or Pleasure
29 minutes, 1990
Andrea Torrice
This video explores the ongoing feminist debate about pornography: Can performing in or producing sexually explicit films and magazines be an act of liberation in which women take control of their sexuality? Or is all pornography destructive, objectifying women and playing to men's worst stereotypes? Representatives from both sides are featured, including producers Candida Royalle and Annie Sprinkle and spokeswomen from the Feminist Anti-Censorship Task Force and Women Against Pornography.

UNION PRODUCERS NETWORK (UPNET)
c/o Fred Carroll
UFCW Local 1142
P.O. Box 1750
Santa Monica, CA, USA 90406
(213) 395-9977
Distributes work on labor issues.

VIDÉAZIMUT
An international Coalition for the Right to Communicate
3680 Jeanne-Mance
Montréal, Quebec, Canada H2X 2K5
(514) 982-6660 Fax: (514) 982-6122
This coalition brings together independent producers and nonprofit video collectives from around the world to devise and implement strategies to promote recognition and respect of the right to communicate. They produced a book: **Video the Changing World**, *edited by Nancy Thede and Alain Ambrosi (Montréal: Black Rose). It covers the experience in many countries of associations active with Vidéazimut and Video Tiersmonde.*

V TAPE
183 Bathurst Street Suite 3
Toronto, Ontario, Canada, M5T 2R7
Tel: (416) 863-9879 Fax: (416) 360-0781
Distributor of independently produced films

and videos. Publishes Catalogue of Catalogues, an extensively cross-referenced listing of videotapes and Canadian video distributors. See **East Timor: Betrayed but not Beaten** in East Timor Resource section.

VIDEO DATA BANK
School of the Art Institute of Chicago
37 South Wabash Avenue
Chicago, IL, USA 60603
(312) 899-5172
Fax: (312) 236-0141

Behold the Promised Land
23 minutes, 1991
Ardele Lister
Mixes interviews gathered from Brooklyn, Boston and San Francisco on July 4, 1989, with American "educational" and "promotional" films of the late forties and early fifties to examine the long-term effects of media on a cross-section of Americans.

Everyone's Channel
60 minutes, 1992
David Shulman
Combining archival footage from the early days of cable, rediscovered footage from the 1/2" portapak era, and interviews with access pioneers, this tape provides an illuminating overview of the people, ideas, and technological developments that helped make cable-access TV a reality.

Lying in State
30 minutes, 1989
Norman Cowie
This tape articulates network TV's account of and relationship to the Reagan/Bush years (particularly Reagan's televisual crusade against the government of Nicaragua), appropriating and rebuilding media images and slogans to politicize their meanings.

VIDEO OUT
1102 Homer Street
Vancouver, British Columbia, Canada
V6B 2X6
(604) 688-4336

New Years, Part I and 11
10 minutes, 1987
Valerie Soe

This film explores the conflict of a child caught between her Chinese-American heritage, and the stereotypes and expectations perpetuated by mainstream American film and television images.

'Out' Takes
13 minutes, 1989
John C. Goss
Through the juxtaposition of scenes from two television shows: **Pee Wee's Playhouse** and **Maido Osawage Seshumasu**, a prime-time sitcom from Japan, this video outlines the presence of homophobia and gender roles on broadcast television. Rex Reed's critique of Pee Wee (Paul Reubens) highlights the self-perpetuating closet of Hollywood and the perceived subversive threat of the show's gay subtexts. Reed's opposition to Pee Wee and Reubens's own technique of innuendo and gender-switching both appear equally repressed compared to the explicit frankness of the Japanese series.

THE VIDEO PROJECT
5332 College Avenue
Suite 101
Oakland, CA, USA 94618
1-800-4-PLANET

Nowhere to Hide
28 minutes, 1991
Lon Alpert
At the height of the aerial bombing of Iraq, newsman Lon Alpert, a long-time contributor to NBC News, shot the only footage of the war's impact not censored by either Iraq or the U.S. This tape shows a far different reality than what most Americans saw on the nightly news. Although several networks expressed interest in the footage, all declined to air it, and NBC ended its long affiliation with Alpert, a seven-time Emmy winner.

VIDEO TIERS-MONDE
3680 Jeanne-Mance
Montréal, Quebec, Canada H2X 2K5
(514) 982-6660
Video Tiers-monde provides support to groups in Southern countries using video on an independent basis for informational and educational purposes. With its partner organizations in

Africa and Latin America, VTM mobilizes the resources necessary to support video projects. It designs educational material, recruits and trains facilitators and organizes regional training programs in the South. VTM is actively involved in South-South and South-North networks for exchange and distribution of independent video production.

WALL TO WALL TELEVISION
Elephant House
35 Hawley Crescent
London, England, UK NWI 8NP
(071) 485-7424

The Media Show-Red Hot and Blue
38 minutes, 1990
This edition of an arts and media documentary series charts the making of the International Television AIDS benefit **Red Hot and Blue**. Analyzes the media's role in reaching the masses and the censorship mentality that rules network television.

We Do the Work
1250 Addison St., No. 213A
Berkeley, CA, USA 94702
(510) 549-0775
The only consistent voice of working people on PBS.

WILLIAM GREAVES PRODUCTIONS
230 West 55th Street
26th floor
New York City, NY, USA 10019
1-800-874-8314
Fax: 212-315-0027

Ida B. Wells: A Passion for Justice
53 minutes, 1990
William Greaves and Louise Archambault
Documents the life and times of Ida B. Wells, the African-American journalist, activist, suffragist and anti-lynching crusader of the late 19th and early 20th centuries. An excellent profile of an early pioneer of advocacy journalism.

YALE UNIVERSITY LIBRARY
Manuscripts and Archives
New Haven, CT, USA 06520-7429

Firing Line Video and transcripts available.

An ever-expanding catalogue of videotapes, audiotapes and transcripts of lectures by Noam Chomsky and others can be donated to or ordered from:

Radio Free Maine (audio/video)
Roger Leisner
P.O. Box 2705
Augusta, Maine, USA 04338
(207) 622-6629

Alternative Radio (audio/transcripts)
David Barsamian
2129 Mapleton
Boulder, CO, USA 80304
(303) 444-8788

OF SPECIAL NOTE:

NATIONAL FILM BOARD OF CANADA
P.O. Box 6100
Station A
Montréal, Quebec, Canada H3C 3H5

Tel: (514) 283-9409 Fax: (514) 496-2573
Toll Free 1-800-267-7710 (Canada only)
In the U.S., call the NFB's New York office:
(212) 596-1770

Today, in Canada, only one institution possesses all the resources to produce a rich variety of world-class films from initial script to final print—the National Film Board of Canada—the co-production partner, with Necessary Illusions, of *Manufacturing Consent*.

Founded in 1939 by John Grierson, the NFB has come a long way from its humble beginnings as a two-room operation. Headquartered in Montréal, Québec, since 1956, it has evolved into a sophisticated full-service film arts production complex where 700 staff producers, technicians, administrators and directors join free-lancers to perfect state-of-the-art "live action" media, and develop cutting-edge animation.

Often acting in concert with independent production houses, NFB productions and co-productions range from verité documentaries to experimental theatrical shorts; from TV vignettes to fiction features. Acting as its own educational distributor, the NFB also offers a pan-Canadian distribution and information network for their own and other independently produced Canadian work.

What sets the NFB apart from a modern commercial studio is its mandate. As an agency funded by the Canadian people through their Parliament, the Board's primary responsibility is to make movies that probe the history, politics and social realities of Canada. It also turns its cameras outward, capturing engaging international stories as well.

The resulting oeuvre contains some of the world's finest films. The NFB enjoys an "arm's length" relationship with the Canadian government, giving the NFB complete control over its programs and their content.

Few institutions are as sensitive and responsive to the many perspectives found in society. The NFB's creation of the world's only all-women film-making unit in 1974, for example, stands as an historic initiative. With the aim of achieving social justice and equality, the NFB often gives voice to the dissension and conflicts present in Canada and abroad.

Ultimately, the NFB's role in popular education extends far beyond the classroom, television set, or screen. Community and cultural groups regularly turn to NFB libraries for materials which will engender discussion and debate around topics ranging from disarmament to media literacy to incest survival.

Here are three of their 6,500 titles:

The Constructing Reality package
The package includes nine hours of film and video selections drawn from 34 productions, and a resource book. Sources include complete productions, excerpts, interviews with film-makers and two original productions. The package is not a course on documentary nor a selection of all-time "greats"; rather, it provides an opportunity to consider some critical concepts that an encounter with a passionate, playful or provocative exploration of "real life" can engender. Such concepts include: the relationship between fact and fiction; objectivity; truth; point of view; voice; and the construction of reality.

Distress Signals
An investigation of global television
Dir.: John Walker
54.33 min.
Two thirds of the world have never been to America, but they have seen Dallas. America's number one export isn't steel or lumber. Its's entertainment. Shot in North America, Europe and Africa, Distress Signals probes the frontiers of television's brave new globalised world. From the world's largest TV show market place on the Riviera to a penetrating behind-the-scenes look at CNN, the film explores the forces at work shaping what audiences around the world see on their TV sets.

The World is Watching
Dir.: Peter Raymont
60 mins. and 30 mins versions
The World is Watching vividly answers the question: "Who decides what's news?" by focusing on several journalists working in Nicaragua during the negotiations surrounding the Arias Peace Plan in November 1987. The film-makers won unprecedented access to film inside ABC TV News—following a news crew on the ground in Nicaragua while simultaneously documenting the editorial process in the ABC newsroom in New York City. (Peter Raymont, Harold Crooks, who wrote the film with him, Mr. Jennings, and the legal staff at ABC made it possible for outtakes from this footage to be used in Manufacturing Consent.) Available in the US through:
Icarus Films
200 Park Ave. S.
New York, NY, USA 10003
Tel: (212) 674-3375

ORGANIZATIONS

Alternative Media Information Center (Media Network)
39 W. 14th Street
Suite 403
New York, NY, USA 10011
(212) 929-2663 Fax: 929-2732
Networks to assist social-issue media producers and activists and educators interested in such work. Serves as non-profit sponsor for individuals. (Media Network helped make **Manufacturing Consent** *a reality.)*

Alternative Press Network
Alternative Press Center
P.O. Box 33109,
Baltimore, MD, USA 21218
(301) 243-2471
Lists multitude of social issue publications. Mailing list available on labels for good price.

Alliance for Cultural Democracy
P.O. Box 2478
Champaign, IL, USA 61820
(617) 423-3711
Nationwide organization of community-based arts programs.

Artists Television Access
992 Valencia Street
San Francisco, CA, USA 94110
Exhibits lots of independent media, has cheap editing facilities.

Asian Cinevision
32 E. Broadway
New York, NY, USA 10002
(212) 925-8685
Promotes Asian and Asian-American films and videos. Organizes annual festival.

Association of Independent Video and Filmmakers (AIVF)
625 Broadway
New York, NY, USA 10012
(212) 473-3400
Advocacy and informational group for indies. Publishes **The Independent.**

Bay Area Center for Art & Technology
1095 Market Street, Suite 209
San Francisco, CA, USA 94103
Provides non-profit status (not funding) for California projects. Don t be scared by the name: they're into low-tech, too.

Center for Media and Values
1962 South Shenandoah
Los Angeles, CA, USA 90034
(310) 559-2944 or 202-1936
A nonprofit membership organization that produces resources for teaching critical awareness about media. Also analyzes trends in television, video, film, radio, advertising and print media publishes a magazine.

Center for War, Peace and the News Media New York University
10 Washington Place
New York, NY, USA 10003
(212) 998-7960
Tracks portrayals of Cold War issues, effect of government and corporate policies on media.

Committee of Correspondence
522 Valencia Street
San Francisco, CA, USA 94110
New national left grouping trying to overcome past divisions and build a national left organization.

Committee on Democratic Communications
c/o Law Offices of Peter Franck
90 New Montgomery St., 15th Floor
San Francisco, CA, USA 94105
Project of National Lawyers Guild, produces newsletter on media issues and democracy.

El Salvador Media Project
335 W. 38th Street, 5th Floor
New York, NY, USA 10018
(212) 714-9118 Fax: 594-6417
Works with guerrilla media makers in El Salvador; distributes information in U.S. about Salvadoran politics and war.

Electronic Arts Intermix
536 Broadway, 9th Floor
New York, NY, USA 10012
(212) 966-4605 Fax: 941-6118
Major distributor of art and non-fiction video.

Electronic Frontier Foundation
155 Second Street
Cambridge, MA, USA 02141
(617) 864-0665 Fax: 617-864-0866
E-mail: eff@eff.org
A nonprofit organization founded to educate the public about the democratic potential of computer communications technology. Posts information on legal policy and technical issues and conducts on-line seminars and discussion groups on The WELL, CompuServe and other computer networks.

FAIR (Fairness and Accuracy in Reporting)
130 West 25th Street
New York City, NY, USA 10001
(212) 633-6700 Fax: 212-727-7668
A national media-watch group offering well-documented criticism in an effort to correct bias and imbalance. Through organizing projects, a monthly journal and public speaking, FAIR focuses public awareness on the narrow corporate ownership of the press, the media's allegiance to official agendas and their insensitivity to public interest constituencies. FAIR publishes **EXTRA!** *(listed under Publications).*

Film Arts Foundation
346 9th Street, 2nd Floor
San Francisco, CA, USA 94103
(415) 552-8760
One of the greatest independent film and videomakers group the world has ever known.

GLAAD (Gay&Lesbian Alliance Against Defamation)
150 West 26th Street, Suite 503
New York City, NY, USA 10001
(212) 807-1700
An advocacy group that fights for fair, accurate and inclusive representations of lesbian and gay lives. Publishes an informative bulletin on media representation of lesbian and gay people.

Global Information Network/ Inter Press Service
777 United Nations Plaza
New York, NY, USA 10017
(212) 286-0123 Fax: 818-9249
News wire on issues regarding developing nations. Many of its writers are from those countries.

Independent Media Distributors Alliance
c/o Bob Gale
P.O. Box 2154
St. Paul MN, USA 55102
(612) 298-0117
*Works to improve opportunities for distribu-
tion of work by independents.*

Institute for Alternative Journalism/Alternet
77 Federal Street
San Francisco, CA, USA 94107
(415) 284-1420 fax: (415) 284-1414
Compuserve: 71362.27@compuserve.com
*A nonprofit organization dedicated to
strengthening the alternative press and advocating for diverse and independent media
voices necessary for a healthy democracy.*
Alternet, *a project of IAJ is an alternative
news syndication service. The Institute publishes* **Media Culture Review.** *See
Publications.*

Instituto para America Latina
Apartado 270031,
Lima, 27, Peru
(5114) 617949
*Supports and publishes information about
popular video movement in Latin America.*

Media Alliance
Bldg. D, Ft. Mason Ctr.
San Francisco, CA, USA 94123
Organization of media workers; publishes
MediaFile *newsletter.*

Media Alliance Central America Committee
3891 26th Street
San Francisco, CA, USA 94131
(415) 641-7271
*Monitors Bay Area coverage of Central
America. Has published* **Impress the Press,** *a
media activism & monitoring guide ($3).*

Media Democracy Project
c/o Made in USA Productions
330 W. 42nd St., Suite 1905
New York, NY, USA 10036
(212) 695-3090 Fax: 695-3086
*Works to influence labor coverage in the
media.*

Media Foundation
1243 W. 7th Avenue
Vancouver, B.C., Canada V6H I B7
(604) 736-9401 Fax: (604) 737-6021
*A nonprofit ad agency that provides the cre-
ative resources, technical know-how and mar-
keting expertise to produce inexpensive TV
commercials that address the concerns of
organizations not normally represented by the
mainstream media.*

**National Alliance of Media Arts Centers
(NAMAC)**
1212 Broadway, Suite 816
Oakland, CA, USA
(415) 451-2717 Fax: 834-3741
*Information on arts centers, many of which
have video production and exhibition programs.*

National Alliance of Third World Journalists
P.O. Box 43208
Washington, DC, USA 20010
(202) 462-8197
*Support group fostering expansion of fair
media coverage affecting people of color.*

NAATA
National Asian American
Telecommunications Association
346 9th Street
San Francisco CA, USA 94103
*Organization of Asian American media pro-
ducers.*

**National Coalition of Multicultural Media
Arts**
c/o Community Film Workshop
1130 S. Wabash, Suite 500
Chicago, IL, USA 60605
(312) 427-1245
*Supports efforts of producers and exhibitors
of multicultural video.*

**National Federation of Local
Cable Programmers**
P.O. Box 27290
Washington, DC, USA 20028
(202) 393-2650
*Support, informational, and advocacy group
for access and other cable staff and volun-
teers.*

**National Institute Against Prejudice
and Violence**
31 South Green Street
Baltimore, MD, USA 21201-1562
(410) 328-5170
*A resource and advocacy center that also
monitors the news media to correct bias and
misinformation. Publishes a newsletter.*

Oakland PEN
P.O. Box 70531, Station D
Oakland, CA, USA 94612
(510) 548-3306
*Organizing boycott of network TV for misrep-
resentation of people of color.*

**San Francisco Community
Television Corporation**
1095 Market Street, Suite 704
San Francisco, CA, USA 94103
(415) 621-4224
*Non-profit organization building grassroots
support for public access and plans to eventually manage public access facility in San
Francisco.*

Strategies for Media Literacy
1095 Market Street
San Francisco CA, USA 94103
(415) 621-2911
*Develops curriculum for media literacy in the
schools.*

Union for Democratic Communications
c/o Karen Paulsell
5338 College, #C
Oakland, CA, USA 94618
Phone c/o Kate Caine (312) 327-1221
*US and Canadian network of communication
scholars and activists, fighting for democratization of media.*

**United Church of Christ,
Office of Communications**
700 Prospect Avenue
Cleveland, OH, USA 44115
(216) 736-2222
*Advocacy and informational group dealing
with telecommunications issues.*

Video Data Bank
37 S. Wabash
Chicago IL 60603
(313) 899-5172 and
22 Warren Street
New York NY, USA 10007
(212) 233-3441 Fax: (212) 608-5496
Major distributor of video art, documentaries, theme packages.

The Video Project
5332 College Avenue, Suite 101
Oakland, CA, USA 94618
(510) 655-9050
Non-profit distributor of educational video.

Videoteca del Sur
84 E. 3rd Street, Suite 5A
New York, NY, USA 10003
(212) 477-4684
*Archives and distributor of all sorts of work by indie producers from 19 Latin American countries. Publishes **Magicamerica**.*

Visual Communications
263 S. Los Angeles Street, #307
Los Angeles, CA, USA 90012
(213) 680-4462
Asian Pacific-American arts organization dedicated to multicultural work.

Women Make Movies (Women Make Videos)
225 Lafayette Street
New York, NY, USA 10012
(212) 925-0606
Producer and distributor of tapes by and relating to women.

EAST TIMOR ACTION NETWORK (ETAN/US)
Publication: **Network News**
(Local groups in Ithaca, Los Angeles, Madison, Massachusetts, New Jersey, New York City, Portland, Rhode Island, San Francisco, Seattle, Washington)

White Plains
P.O. Box 1182
White Plains, NY, USA 10602
(914) 428-7299 Fax: (914) 428-7383
E-mail: cscheiner@igc.apc.org

EAST TIMOR ALERT NETWORK (CANADA)
Publication: **ETAN/Canada Newsletter**
(Local groups in Calgary, Guelph, Hamilton, Montréal, Windsor)
Ottawa: P.O. Box 1031, Station B
Ottawa, Ontario, Canada K1P 5R1
Toronto: P.O. Box 562, Station P
Toronto, Ontario, Canada M5S 2T1
Phone/fax: (416) 531-5850
E-mail: etantor@web.apc.org
Vancouver: 104-2120 West 44th Avenue
Vancouver, British Columbia, Canada
V6M 2G2
phone/fax: (604) 264-9973 (604) 739-4947 for up to the day information on East Timor
E-mail: etanvan@web.apc.org

TATA MAI LAU
Publication: Timorese Newsletter
(in English and Timorese)
13 Floor , Apartment B
Lote 38B, Edif. Lei Man
Est. Alm. Marques Esparteiro
Taipa, Macau

TAPOL (The Indonesia Human Rights Campaign)
Publication: TAPOL Bulletin
England: 111 Northwood Road
Thornton Heath
Surrey, England, UK CR7 8HW
(081) 771-2904 Fax: (081) 653-0322
Australia: P.O. Box 121
Clifton Hill
Victoria, Australia 3068

AUSTRALIA-EAST TIMOR ASSOCIATION
P.O. Box 93
Fitzroy
Victoria, Australia 3065

INDONESIAN SOLIDARITY ACTION
P.O. Box 458
Broadway
N.S.W., Australia 2007

EAST TIMOR BOOKS:

Death in Dili
Andrew McMillan (Sydney: Hodder & Stroughton, 1992)

East Timor: A Western-made Tragedy
Mark Aarons and Robert Domm (Sydney: Left Book Club, 1992)

East Timor: Nationalism and Colonialism
Jill Joliffe (University of Queensland Press, 1978)

East Timor: The Struggle Continues
Documents 40 & 50
Available from:
International Working Group for Indigenous Affairs (IWGIA)
Foilstraede 10
DK 1171
Copenhagen, Denmark

Funu: The Unfinished Saga of East Timor
Jose Ramos-Horta (Trenton, NJ: Red Sea Press, Inc., 1987)

Injustice, Persecution, Eviction: A Human Rights Update on Indonesia and East Timor
Available from: Asia Watch
485 5th Avenue
New York City, NY, USA 10017

Indonesia's Forgotten War: The Hidden History of East Timor John Taylor (London: Zed Books, 1991)

**Telling: East Timor, Personal Testimonies
1942-1992** Michele Turner (New South Wales
University Press ltd., 1992)

Available from:
New South Wales University Press
P.O. Box 1
Kensington
N.S.W., Australia 2033
(02) 398-8900 Fax: (02) 398-3408)

Available in North America from:
International Specialized Book Services
Portland, Oregon, USA 97213-3640
(503) 287-3093
Fax: (503) 284-8859

The War Against East Timor
Carmel Budiardjo and Liem Soei Liong
(London: Tapol, 1983)

SOME OF CHOMSKY'S WRITINGS ON EAST TIMOR

"East Timor," **The Chomsky Reader**,

"The Hidden War in East Timor," **Radical
Priorities**, pages 85-94

"Indonesia: Mass Extermination, Investors'
Paradise," **The Washington Connection and
Third World Fascism, The Political Economy
of Human Rights, Volume 1**, pages 205-217

"The United States and East Timor",
Towards a New Cold War, pages 337-370

EAST TIMOR AUDIO/VISUAL

Aggression and Self-Determination
ETAN's 28 minute video about the U.S. role in
East Timor. *Available from ETAN/US.*

Buried Alive
58 minutes
*Film by Gil Scrine features Jose Ramos Horta
and Noam Chomsky. (Several clips in*
Manufacturing Consent *came from* Buried
Alive.)

Available from:
Gil Scrine Films
24 Empire Street
Heberfield
N.S.W., Australia 2045
(02) 716-6354/8266

Cold Blood: The Massacre of East Timor
55 minutes
*British documentary including the November
12, 1991 massacre. Available from ETAN/US.*

Death of a Nation
A 1994 documentary on East Timor by John
Pilger, one of the UK's leading journalists.
Available from:
Central Productions
44-71-637-4602 Fax: 44-71-580-7780

East Timor: Betrayed but Not Beaten
(with Noam Chomsky) 30 minutes
Video by Peter Monet.
Available from:
V-Tape
183 Bathurst Street
Toronto, Ontario, Canada M5T 2R7
*Informative discussion starter on Canada's role
in East Timor.*

East Timor: Turning a Blind Eye
30 minutes.
*Produced by Paper Tiger Television. Focuses
on U.S. policy and the role of the media.
Available from ETAN/US.*

Massacre: The Story of East Timor
*Award-winning audio documentary, produced
by Amy Goodman, who witnessed and was
beaten in the Santa Cruz massacre.*

Expanded, updated, 40-minute version available from:
Pacifica Radio/WBAI
505 8th Avenue
New York City, NY, USA 10018
and ETAN/US.

US and Indonesia: Partners in Genocide
Lecture by Chomsky (May 21, 1982). *Audio
tape available from Alternative Radio.
October, 1994 talk with Jose Ramos Horta
also available.*

Xanana
30 minutes, Australia
*The human side of the imprisoned East Timor
independence leader, through the eyes of
people who have known him. Available from
ETAN/US and ETAN/Vancouver.*

COMPUTER/NETWORKING (E.TIMOR)

Reg. Indonesia and Reg. East Timor are available from:
Web
#104-401 Richmond Street West
Toronto, Ontario, Canada V5V 3A8
(416) 596-0212
E-mail: spider@web.apc.org.

Indonesia and East Timor comprehensive electronic news feeds available from:
Indonesia Publications
7538 Newberry Lane
Lanham-Seabrook, MD, USA 20706
E-mail: apakabar@access.digex.com.

see also: Activism and the Internet, p.244

MISCELLANEOUS (E. TIMOR)

Documents on East Timor
Regular compilation averaging 100 pages of news analysis from around the globe. Available from ETAN/US.
East Timor Photographs
Custom-printed 8 X 10s of Elaine Brière's beautiful black and white photographs of pre-invasion East Timor can be ordered for $35 each from:

ETAN
Suite 104
2120 West 44th Avenue
Vancouver, BC, Canada V6M 2G2
(604) 264-9973

The Indonesia Kit
A study kit by Elaine Brière and Susan Gage (1993). *Available from ETAN/Vancouver.*

Key chains, postcards, T-shirts and buttons available from ETAN/US.

INTENTIONAL COMMUNITIES

Communities Magazine

Rt. 4, Box 169-NC
Louisa, VA, USA 23093
*Community Magazine contains complete, updated listings of intentional communities including some not included in the **Directory of Intentional Communities** (see below). It also covers diverse aspects of cooperative living: leadership, decision-making, economics, conflict resolution, women's issues, new family and relationship styles etc. Quarterly, over 50 pages.*

Directory of Intentional Communities: A Guide to Cooperative Living
Route 4
P.O. Box 169-NC
Louisa, VA, USA 23093
This "bible" of intentional communities, now in it's third edition, lists nearly 500 communities in North America, as well as offering a map locating those communities and a detailed cross-reference chart summarizing their major features. Also listed: 50 communities on other continents and over 250 alternative resources and services. Paperback, approximately 300 pages.

Growing Community
1118-NC Round Butte Dr.,
Ft. Collins, CO, USA 80524
Tel: (303) 490-1550
Growing Community Newsletter connects people with good ideas, services, and inventions, and introduces existing and newly forming intentional communities in the Western states. Practical advice from community veterans about what works and what doesn't. Lists many other resources. Quarterly, 16 pages.

Fellowship for Intentional Community
Center for Communal Studies
8600 University Blvd.
Evansville, IN, USA 47712
(812) 464-1727
The Fellowship for Intentional Community helps to provide a sense of connectedness and cooperation among communitarians and their friends by serving as a network to facilitate trust building and information sharing between intentional communities. They also demonstrate applications of cooperative experiences to the larger society through publications, forums, workshops, and other projects. They also make referrals for individuals looking for cooperative resources or a home in an intentional community.

OTHER

Bill Moyers Transcripts
267 Broadway
New York City, NY, USA 10007
(212) 227-7372
Phone order by Visa, Mastercard or American Express. For research assistance, supply a topic and they'll tell you every related transcript they have from 20 major TV programs.

Complete set of *Manufacturing Consent* reviews and press clippings.
Necessary Illusions, 24 Mount Royal West, #1008, Montréal, Quebec, Canada, H2T 2S2
(514) 287-7337 fax: (514) 287-7620
Please send $40 to cover photocopying and mailing what is now more than a 300-page dossier.

The Proprioceptive Writing Center
565 Congress Street, #201, P.O. Box 8333, Portland, ME, USA 04104 (207) 772-1847
As described on page 223.

Speak Out!
3004 16th Street, Suite 303,
San Francisco CA, USA 94103
(415) 864-4561
A national progressive speakers' bureau serving student and community groups. They list over 100 articulate women and men concerned with a broad range of issues.

FYI

The Hidden Alliances of Noam Chomsky
Werner Cohn (New York City: Americans for a Safe Israel,1988). 114 East 28 Street, New York City, NY, USA 10016

***Mémoire en défense contre ceux qui m'accusent de falsifier l'histoire*—**[A statement in my defense against those who accuse me of falsifying history] Robert Faurisson (Paris: Editions La Vielle Taupe, 1980). P.P. 9805, 75224, Paris Cedex 05.

Revisionist literature
Institute for Historical Review, 1822 1/2 Newport Blvd., Suite 191, Costa Mesa, CA, USA 92627

Copyright Law of the United States:

s 106. Exclusive rights in copyrighted works
Subject to sections 107 through 118, the owner of copyright under this title has the exclusive rights to do and to authorize any of the following:
1) to reproduce the copyrighted work in copies or phonorecords;
2) to prepare derivative works based upon the copyrighted work to the public by sale or other transfer of ownership, or by rental, lease, or lending;
3) to distribute copies or phonorecords of the copyrighted work to the public by sale or other transfer or ownership, or by rental, lease, or lending;
4) in the case of literary, musical, dramatic, and choreographic works, pantomimes, and motion pictures and other audiovisual works, to perform the copyrighted work publicly; and
5) in the case of literary, musical, dramatic, and choreographic works, pantomimes, and pictorial, graphic, or sculptural works, including the individual images of a motion picture or other audiovisual work, to display the copyrighted work publicly.

s 107. Limitations on exclusive rights: Fair use
Notwithstanding the provisions of section 106, the fair use of a copyrighted work, including such use by reproduction on copies or phonorecords or by any other means specified by that section, for purposes such as criticism, comment, news reporting, teaching (including multiple copies for classroom use), scholarship, or research, is not an infringement of copyright. In determining whether the use made of a work in any particular case is a fair use the factors to be considered shall include -
1) the purpose and character of the use, including whether such use is of a commercial nature or is for nonprofit educational purposes;
2) the nature of copyrighted work;
3) the amount and substantiality or the portion used in relation to the copyrighted work as a whole; and
4) the effect of the use upon the potential market for or value of the copyrighted work.

Copyright Law of Canada

In the context of copyright, plagiarism is stealing a work of another person and claiming it as one's own.

"Fair dealing" is the quotation from or reproduction of minor excerpts of a work in which copyright exists for bonafide purposes of private study, research, criticism, review or newspaper summary. The line between fair dealing and infringement is difficult to define. There are no guidelines as to the number of words or passages that can be used without permission from the author. Only the courts can rule whether fair dealing or infringement is involved.

From **Copyright: Questions and Answers,**
Consumer and Corporate Affairs Canada,
Bureau of Corporate Affairs

INDEX

(The index covers only the main body of the book, and not the introduction nor the supplementary material)

©1994...WORDS: CHRISTINE MARLIN/CKCU-FM OTTAWA...PICTURES: TOM TOMORROW...FROM THE COMPANION BOOK TO THE FILM *MANUFACTURING CONSENT* BY MARK ACHBAR AND PETER WINTONICK...

other important titles from

on Anarchism

THE RADICAL PAPERS
Dimitrios Roussopoulos, ed.

An extraordinary collection of essays that pose a real alternative to current views of public affairs. Some of the issues covered are: the limitations of the new ecology movements; "Irangate" and "Contragate"; North American free trade; the origins of male domination; women's role in transforming the urban movement; and a different brand of socialism. These fresh insights are drawn from both history and contemporary social analysis.

The gallery of contributors includes some of the most stimulating social critics of our time: Noam Chomsky, Murray Bookchin, Juan Gómez Casas, Daniel Guérin, Rossella Di Leo, and others.

...attempts to make up the ground the left has lost...The essays...reflect a post-Reagan urgency in left-wing debates.
Kingston Whig-Standard

About the Editor

Dimitrios I. Roussopoulos is an editor, writer and economist. He has written widely on international politics and social change. His most recent publication is *Political Ecology*.

175 pages
Paperback ISBN: 0-920057-86-1 $12.95
Hardcover ISBN: 0-920057-87-X $29.95
Politics/Philosophy/Ecology

FUGITIVE WRITINGS
Peter Kropotkin

George Woodcock, ed.

This collection contains selected essays by Peter Kropotkin who was, unquestionably, the most widely read and respected theorist of anarchism. It is intended to make some of his most representative writings more accessible. The material consists of essays which either have not been previously published or have been out of print since their original publication.

While the entire scope of Kropotkin's political thinking cannot possibly be projected in a single volume, it is hoped that many of his most fundamental conceptions have been exemplified here, for these essays embrace Kropotkin's philosophy at a time when he was struggling to first give them expression. In this context, Kropotkin's very first political essay, "Must We Occupy Ourselves With An Examination of the Ideal of a Future System," written in 1873, which foreshadows most of his later writings, is of value.

About the Editor

George Woodcock — poet, author, essayist and widely known as a literary journalist and historian — has published more than ninety titles. In this volume he has prepared a preface to each essay allowing the reader to enter into the spirit of the time.

240 pages
Paperback ISBN: 1-895431-42-5 $19.99
Hardcover ISBN: 1-895431-43-3 $38.99
Politics/Philosophy

BAKUNIN ON ANARCHISM
Sam Dolgoff, ed.

A new and revised selection of writings, nearly all published for the first time in English, by one of the leading thinkers of anarchism and one of the most important practitioners of social revolution — Michael Bakunin.

A titan among the social philosophers of the age that produced Proudhon, Marx, Blanqui, and Kropotkin, Michael Bakunin was involved in the Dresden uprising in 1848, which led to his imprisonment first in Germany, then in Russia, and his exile in Sibera, from where he escaped to Europe in 1861, and remained until his death in 1876. Bakunin's voluminous writings are brought together in this collection for the general reader and student, having been edited, translated and introduced by Sam Dolgoff.

...with the publication of Sam Dolgoff's lengthy and careful selection the vitality of Bakunin's message is evident once again.
Labour History

[This book] is the most complete — and interestingly varied — anthology I've seen of this neglected writer. It confirms my suspicion that Bakunin is the most underrated of the classical 18th century theoreticians.
Dwight Macdonald

...by far the best available in English. Bakunin's insights into power and authority, tyranny, the conditions of freedom, the new classes of specialists and technocrats, social tyranny, and many other matters of immediate concern are refreshing, original, and often still unsurpassed in clarity and vision. This selection provides access to the thinking of one of the most remarkable figures of modern history. I read it with great pleasure and profit.
Noam Chomsky

453 pages, bibliography
Paperback ISBN: 0-919619-06-1 $18.95
Hardcover ISBN: 0-919619-05-3 $37.95
Politics/Philosophy

BAKUNIN
The Philosophy of Freedom
Brian Morris

Everything about him is colossal...he is full of a primitive exuberance and strength.
Richard Wagner

The life and thought of Michael Bakunin has a contemporary relevance, particularly for his definitions of freedom and his critiques of Marxism and scientism. He was not a conventional intellectual — if anything, he was anti-intellectual — and so never produced a systematic corpus of his ideas in the manner of Marx or Herbert Spencer. But his philosophy is by no means incoherent, and he fully deserves to be recognized as an important and influential political theorist.

This book confirms Bakunin was a holistic thinker. That his anarchism was dominated by a desire to achieve a unity of theory and practice, of fact and value, of thought and action, within the reality of a given historical social order and that he opposed all the dualism which Western culture had bequeathed from mechanistic philosophy and bourgeois political theory — particularly the opposition between individual and society, philosophy and empirical knowledge, nature and humans.

About the Author

Brian Morris holds a doctorate from the London School of Economics and Political Science. He teaches at Goldsmith's College, University of London and has published *Anthropological Studies of Religion* and *Western Conceptions of the Individual*.

159 pages, index
Paperback ISBN: 1-895431-66-2 $18.99
Hardcover ISBN: 1-895431-67-0 $37.99
Political Philosophy/History

WORDS OF A REBEL

Peter Kropotkin

translated, with introduction, by George Woodcock

The first English-language translation of Paroles d'un Révolté

First published in 1885 in Paris, this collection of articles constitutes Kropotkin's first book. Originally titled *Paroles d'un Révolté*, it includes his earliest works from the period 1879 to 1882. In the succeeding years it was translated into Italian, Spanish, Bulgarian, Russian, and Chinese. Long-awaited in English, *Words of a Rebel* is the first complete translation.

A different work from the more familiar books of the older Kropotkin, it is a product of an anarchist agitator and it derives its interest as much from what it reveals about an important transitional phase in the development of anarchism as it does for what it shows us of Kropotkin himself.

Seeing revolution as a popular insurrection, in the broadest terms, Kropotkin believed that public wealth should belong to its producers and consumers and not to the State or the rich.

About the Editor

This volume of Kropotkin's articles was translated from the french by George Woodcock. A celebrated author, Woodcock is also an authority on the life and works of Peter Kropotkin and as a result, *Words of a Rebel* is not just a translation, but a scholarly work as well.

229 pages
Paperback ISBN: 1-895431-04-2 $19.95
Hardcover ISBN: 1-895431-05-0 $38.95
Politics/History

EVOLUTION AND ENVIRONMENT

Peter Kropotkin

George Woodcock, ed.

While at one time Kropotkin's view of our future might have been regarded as a utopian dream, today, as a result of the growing realization that the world's resources of energy and raw materials are finite, that food is our most precious commodity and that most people's working lives are futile and stultifying, the lessons of this book, for both the rich world and the poor, are topical and hopeful.

Evolution and Environment is a collection of seven essays on evolution and environment, written between 1910 and 1915, and never before published — a key text in the evolutionary controversy!

It would not be an exaggeration to describe this book as the crowning achievement of Kropotkin's writing career. In one way or another, it occupied a great deal of his thought, and the very tentativeness of this great book make its perceptions all the more relevant.

255 pages
Paperback ISBN: 0-921689-44-1 $19.99
Hardcover ISBN: 0-921689-45-X $38.99
Philosophy/Environment

BEYOND HYPOCRISY
Decoding the News in an Age of Propaganda
Including A Doublespeak Dictionary for the 1990s
Edward S. Herman

Illustrations by Matt Wuerker

In a highly original volume that includes an extended essay on the Orwellian use of language that characterizes U.S. political culture, cartoons, and a cross-referenced lexicon of *doublespeak* terms with examples of their all too frequent usage, Herman and Wuerker highlight the deception and hypocrisy contained in the U.S. government's favourite buzzwords. This spirited book offers abundant examples of duplicitous terminology, ranging from the crimes of free enterprise celebrated in the boardrooms of Wall Street and the press coverage of elections in El Salvador and Nicaragua, to George Bush's condemnation of Saddam Hussein's invasion of Kuwait — after having just indulged in similarly straightforward aggression in Panama only one year previously.

Rich in irony and relentlessly forthright, Beyond Hypocrisy *is a valuable resource for those interested in avoiding…'an unending series of victories over your own memory.'*
Montreal Mirror

About the Author

Edward S. Herman is Professor of Finance at the Wharton School, University of Pennsylvania. A columnist for *Z Magazine*, he has written a number of books on foreign policy and mass media—*The Real Terror Network*, and with Noam Chomsky, *The Political Economy of Human Rights*, both of which have been published by Black Rose Books.

Matt Wuerker's cartoons have appeared in *Z Magazine*, *The Los Angeles Times*, *The Washington Post*, and *The Progressive*.

239 pages, illustrations, index
Paperback ISBN: 1-895431-48-4 $19.95
Hardcover ISBN: 1-895431-49-2 $38.95
International Politics/Sociology/Communications

COMMON CENTS
Media Portrayal of the Gulf War and Other Events
James Winter

Using eight crucial case studies, ranging from the Gulf War, to Oka, the Ontario NDP budget, and the Montréal Massacre, James Winter shows how media coverage of events consistently casts them in what becomes a 'common-sense' framework.

This 'common-sense' view is the picture we carry around in our heads — a type of conventional wisdom that is inherent in our world view. Given our limited first hand exposure to world events, journalists play a crucial role in formulating our common-sense perspectives, so that today's 'common-sense' view of the world is largely the result of yesterday's mainstream news media coverage.

Winter provides strong evidence of a corporate tilt in the mass media…it is impossible to dismiss [his] arguements.
Vancouver Sun

Like Chomsky, he enjoys contrasting the "common-sense" interpretation with views from alternative sources. As facts and images clash, we end up with a better grasp of the issues at hand.
Montréal Gazette

About the Author

Dr. James Winter holds Bachelor and Master's degrees in journalism, and a Ph.D. in mass communication. He has edited and authored numerous publications dealing with the media and society.

220 pages
Paperback ISBN: 1-895431-24-7 $19.95
Hardcover ISBN: 1-895431-25-5 $38.95
Communications/Current Events/Canadian Studies

THE RAFT OF THE MEDUSA
Five Voices on Colonies, Nations, and Histories
Jocelyne Doray and Julian Samuel, eds.

The five voices, each brilliant and insightful…form a braid of thought that opens out the received ideas that bind colonizer and colonized into a world that oscillates between questions of deracination and re-territorialization. The Medusa tape is a journalistic tour de force. I am delighted there's a book.
Vera Frenkel, video artist

In interviews with five academics and writers — Amin Maalouf, Thierry Hentsch, Sara Suleri, Marlene Nourbese Philip and Ackbar Abbas — history is discussed from a non-European perspective. The interviews examine such issues as Islamic fundamentalism and Occidental modernism, the Partition of India in 1947, the future of Hong Kong, and questions of identity in a postcolonial era.

In addition to the transcript of the video version of *The Raft of the Medusa,* this book also includes an interview with Marwan Hassan by Will Straw, providing a dialogue around the issues raised in the video, and an essay by Charles Acland examining colonial discourse as discussed in *The Raft* and how these themes are expressed in Bram Stokers' *Dracula*.

About the Editors

Jocelyne Doray — editor, video consultant and translator — is currently at work on *L'âge de l'innocence,* a book on child criminals. Julian Samuel is a film and video maker and writer. He has made *Resisting the Pharaohs,* a film about Montréal's arms industry and weapons' sales, and is the author of *Lone Ranger in Pakistan.*

132 pages
Paperback ISBN: 1-895431-76-X $19.99
Hardcover ISBN: 1-895431-77-8 $38.99
International Politics/Cultural Studies

FROM CAMP DAVID TO THE GULF
Negotiations, Language and Propaganda, & War
Adel Safty

A general introduction to the Palestinian-Israeli conflict, that moves on to a detailed examination of Sadat's foreign policy decision-making, concentrating on what took place at Camp David in 1978. As well, Safty examines the role of language, propaganda, and media interpretation of the Palestinian question and, of the war against Iraq.

Naturally, it is controversial, but that is inherent in the subject matter. Safty makes his position clear, and does a careful and responsible job in backing it up. The most interesting part is based on Arabic sources that are not otherwise accessible.
Noam Chomsky, MIT, Cambridge

Safty provides…a well-documented and coherent presentation.
L. Carl Brown, Princeton University

Fascinating study of language and propaganda. Provocative and hard hitting.
Sylvia L'Ecuyer, Radio Canada

Excellent work which challenges established beliefs…beautifully written, a must-read.
Rafe Mair, CKNW Radio

About the Author

Adel Safty, holds a doctorate in political science from the Université de Paris and is currently a political scientist with the University of British Columbia's Faculty of Education. He specializes in Middle East studies and was repeatedly called upon by the CBC as their expert analyst during the Gulf War.

281 pages, index
Paperback ISBN: 1-895431-10-7 $19.95
Hardcover ISBN: 1-895431-11-5 $38.95
International Politics/History

THE ECOLOGY OF THE AUTOMOBILE

Peter Freund and George Martin

More than seventeen million people have been killed on roads since the automobile first appeared. An incalculable number have been seriously hurt. In the future, half the world is likely to be run over in a terminal squabble for oil. We are possessed by a mindless monster which threatens the planet itself.

Considering the widespread impact of the automobile in many contemporary societies, it is surprising how little attention its social and political dimensions receive — even from ecologically oriented thinkers. In this original book, authors Freund and Martin examine the central role that auto production and consumption have played in the 20th century: the overuse and misuse that has caused the major auto markets to be saturated and the costs of auto-centered transport to become prohibitive.

About the Authors

Peter Freund holds a Ph.D. from the New School of Social Research, New York, and teaches at Montclair State, New Jersey. He is co-author of *Health, Illness, and the Social Body* and author of *The Civilized Body*. George Martin holds a Ph.D. from the University of Chicago and also teaches at Montclair State. He is the co-author of *The Welfare Industry* and *Social Welfare in Society*, and the author of *Social Policy in the Welfare State*.

213 pages, index
Paperback ISBN: 1-895431-82-4 $19.99
Hardcover ISBN: 1-895431-83-2 $38.99
Environment/Sociology/Politics

POLITICAL ECOLOGY

Beyond Environmentalism

Dimitrios I. Roussopoulos

As with other social movements for change, the movement for the protection of the environment embraces several schools of thought and action. There is now a strong tendency among ecologists to go beyond engaging in educational efforts, traditional protests, government lobbying, and participating in annual Earth Day activities, and to make a serious commitment to bringing about more fundamental social and political change.

The new direction in thinking which is advanced by Greens (political ecologists) and Green political organizations engaged in electoral action at various levels in liberal democracies can have a far-reaching effect on our lifestyles, our neighbourhoods and cities, and on our politics. Examining various streams of environmentalist and ecological thought, this book presents an overview of the origins and nature of political ecology, as well as a summary of the differences and similarities between political ecology and social ecology.

About the Author

Dimitrios I. Roussopoulos is an editor, writer and economist. He has written widely on international politics, democracy, and social change.

138 pages, index
Paperback ISBN: 1-895431-80-8 $15.99
Hardcover ISBN: 1-895431-81-6 $34.99
Politics/Ecology/Sociology

REMAKING SOCIETY
Murray Bookchin

Drawing materials from history, anthropology, philosophy, and ecology, Bookchin offers an in-depth historical explanation of how the sociecological crisis emerged and why existing political and economic institutions are unwilling and unable to address it.

Remaking Society is a masterpiece, essential to clearing the air of the confusion about the roots of the contemporary social and ecological crises.
Latin American Connection

This straightforward, readable book is a wide-ranging intellectual tour de force. [His] work is motivated by his concerns with ecology, social justice, and anarchism.
Choice

…for those who already have some sympathy for an ecological perspective…[this] is an inspiring primer to Bookchin's theory…a crucial reading for any critical mind.
Montreal Mirror

About the Author

Murray Bookchin has been a pioneering thinker, writer, and activist in the environmental movement for more than thirty years.

222 pages, index
Paperback ISBN: 0-921689-02-0 $18.95
Hardcover ISBN: 0-921689-03-9 $37.95
Ecology/ Philosophy

URBANIZATION WITHOUT CITIES
The Rise and Decline of Citizenship *revised edition*
Murray Bookchin

In this original work, Murray Bookchin introduces provocative ideas about the nature of community, and what it means to be a fully empowered citizen. He believes that the tension that exists between rural and urban society can be a vital source of human creativity, thereby defining a new, richly imaginative politics which can help us recover the power of the individual, restore the positive values and quality of urban life, and reclaim the ideal of the city as a major creative force in our civilization.

To reverse the city's dehumanization, social thinker Bookchin here advocates an agenda for participatory democracy…It is significant.
Publisher's Weekly

Bookchin is the leading ecological thinker of our times. His work ranks alongside Lewis Mumford's monumental works on the culture and history of cities and goes beyond.
City Magazine

…an historical account of the rise and fall of the city-state as the arena of citizen participation…Bookchin gives us a useful history and a call for action.
The New York Times

340 pages
Paperback ISBN: 1-895431-00-X $19.95
Hardcover ISBN: 1-895431-01-8 $38.95
Ecology/Urban Sociology/History

Send for a free catalogue of books
BLACK ROSE BOOKS
C.P. 1258, Succ. Place du Parc
Montréal, Québec
H2W 2R3 Canada

Printed by the workers of
IMPRIMERIE D'ÉDITION MARQUIS LTée
Montmagny, Québec
for
Black Rose Books Ltd.